D1562622

Peasant Classes

PEASANT CLASSES

The Bureaucratization of Property
and Family Relations under
Early Habsburg Absolutism
1511-1636

~ HERMANN REBEL ~

PRINCETON UNIVERSITY PRESS
PRINCETON, NEW JERSEY

Published by Princeton University Press,
41 William Street, Princeton, New Jersey
In the United Kingdom: Princeton University Press,
Guildford, Surrey

Library of Congress Cataloging in Publication Data will be
found on the last printed page of this book

Publication of this book has been aided by the Whitney Darrow Publication
Reserve Fund of Princeton University Press

This book has been composed in Linotron Aldus

Clothbound editions of Princeton University Press Books
are printed on acid-free paper, and binding materials are
chosen for strength and durability

Printed in the United States of America by Princeton
University Press, Princeton, New Jersey

TO THE MEMORY OF
MY FATHER

[The head of the house] is not to withhold wages from his servants without due cause and . . . he is to instruct and direct them, as much as possible, with kind words; he is not to misuse his authority but to recall that he too is a servant and that God and the authorities hold him responsible for everything he does.

*   *   *

[The lady of the house] must not endure nor permit the children or the servants to speak unseemly, libellous, angry and dishonest words . . .

[She must] give her servants, especially the girls, no opportunity to misuse anything, nor to get together with the boys and young men; she must spy on them in the night and visit their sleeping quarters to make sure that none has strayed . . .

—Wolf Helmhard von Hohberg,
Georgica Curiosa Aucta, 1687

He did not want someone he had to call Father suddenly proscribe the entire world he had been permitted by his mother. So the father beat him. Holl put up a struggle. Father beat him, beat him again, and again, until Holl's resistance collapsed, until he gave in, until he became "soft as a diaper."

Two weeks it took The Farmer to accomplish this.

Every morning began in pain. The bed, wet. The shirt, wet. The mute face of the stepmother, whom he had to call Mother from the very first day, hurt him more than the father's brutality. His soul's face had been slapped with similar glances out of his true mother's eyes. With the same sigh they had whipped the damp sheet off the bed; but back there it had only been his mother, whereas here there were girls and day laborers present, laughing at him as soon as he entered the kitchen with his stepmother, her carrying the wet sheet under her arm, and him with his gaze nailed firmly to the floor.

—Franz Innerhofer,
Beautiful Days, 1974

~ CONTENTS ~

~ CONTENTS ~

~ LIST OF MAPS ~

~ FIGURES ~

~ LIST OF TABLES ~

~ PREFACE ~

THIS STUDY begins an inquiry into the social history of Habsburg absolutism as it developed in one of the crownlands of Austria in the period around 1600.

The social complexion of European absolutism in the early modern period continues to present formidable problems for historical interpretation. The earliest absolute states made a contemporaneous appearance with such "modern" phenomena as international capitalist commerce, bureaucratically coordinated military-industrial complexes, and chartered business corporations composed of stockholders and managers; and yet, the lineages between the institutional and social structures of these states and the more recent forms of economic, social, and political life are not as relentlessly continuous as Barrington Moore, Jr. and others have proposed. The upheavals and discontinuities associated with the age of democratic revolution and with the European civil war that followed make implausible those historical explanations that seek direct connections between the conflicts of the early modern period and the ideas and institutions associated with modern liberalism, socialism, and fascism. The task of identifying and interpreting the substance and flow of these older and deeper currents of European national and popular life continues to demand our efforts.

Most prominent among the grand interpretive schemes that have sought to integrate the history of early modern Europe directly into explanations of recent history are those focusing on the economic and institutional aspects of state-building; specifically the recent interpretations developed by Immanuel Wallerstein, D. C. North and Robert Thomas, Perry Anderson, and others have related early modern state institutions to the creation and expansion of a capitalist world economy. Such macro-historical explanations have largely ignored the social-historical dimensions of early modern history. Moreover, these works contain and carry forward, wittingly or not, an older and conservative view of absolutism associated with the work of Otto Brunner, Fritz Hartung, Dietrich Gerhard, and Gerhard Österreich. This view ascribed historical significance to the absolute states according to their variously successful efforts to rationalize and unify particularized feudal societies and thereby prepare them for integration into centralized "modern" states.

What social relations actually existed and how they worked is not a subject for inquiry in these studies. In the older works it is the "ethos" of social life that matters the most: an ethos in transition, moving away from a medieval social spirit based on loyalty and trust toward a modern concern with order, discipline, and obedience. In the more recent discussions about the place of absolute states in the emergent capitalist world economy, the details of social life, particularly of the social life of the majority of the population, the peasantry, have not been considered separately. Rural populations are largely classified by their geographic and political location and are typified as being in various stages of transition from a feudal to a capitalist mode of production relative to their proximity to and involvement with the core areas and institutions of capitalist development. The observation that these "transitions" lasted for two hundred and more years (and, indeed, are not completed even today in several important areas of Europe) and that, in practice, concepts of "transition" leave us uninformed about the actual structures and quality of everyday social life throws doubt on the explanatory value of the dualisms at the basis of both the radical economic and the conservative romantic interpretations of absolutism.

This study focuses on the rural population of Upper Austria during the first half of the seventeenth century with a view to describing and analyzing in detail economic and social relationships at a time of intensive state-building by the house of Habsburg. A further objective is to formulate a hypothesis about rural social life under Habsburg absolutism that will give this period a social historical identity of its own and enable us to establish more complex and meaningful links between the early modern and modern history of this part of the world. There exist, of course, studies of early modern rural societies under

Central European absolutism that avoid grand interpretive schemes. It would be presumptuous to claim a lone pioneering role in this regard. For example, the empirically and conceptually individualistic works by Hermann Wopfner, Werner Stark, Alfred Hoffmann, Otto Büsch, and Eckhart Schremmer have made great contributions to our knowledge of rural social life under German absolutism and I refer to them repeatedly in the pages that follow. The research presented in this study differs from work by these authors in that it focuses on a smaller realm of social and economic intercourse. I am not mainly concerned here with the Austrian state as a whole nor simply with the policies of princes and seigneurs regarding the lower classes; I examine rural individuals and their social relations as members of families, households, and communities. Princes and lords do appear in this account and, at the conclusion, I present an interpretation of the bureaucratic and policing aspects of the Austrian Habsburg state, but even there my primary concern is for a historically significant explanation of the social life of this peasantry.

What first attracted my attention to Upper Austria's rural population in this period was its passionate involvement in the political struggles and civil wars that accompanied the formation of absolute states in Central Europe. From roughly 1500 to 1650, we find Upper Austria's peasants engaged in an almost unbroken series of political and military acts: petitions, gatherings of protest, the occupation and occasional destruction of important buildings in the parish and estate, expulsions of priests, confrontations with estate and state agents, strikes and refusals to render tithes, dues, state taxes, fines, labor services, and obedience, the freeing of prisoners, assassinations, armed gatherings and attacks, and the organization and deployment of peasant armies for full-scale war. No less than thirty-five uprisings occurred in Upper Austria during the sixteenth and seventeenth centuries (compared to a total of twenty-one for the fourteenth, fifteenth, and eighteenth centuries combined); of these, the most significant ones in terms of the number of participants, the degree of organization, and the involvement of royal authorities happened in the years 1511 to 1514, 1525,

1594 to 1597, 1620, 1626 and 1632 to 1636. The history of the Upper Austrian rural people in this period attracts attention not only because they shared in the widespread German peasant rebellions associated with the year 1525 but also because they carried on the struggle before and for well over a century after that date—and because they tied the issues associated with their family life, their social roles, and political status directly to the process of state formation and to the state's developing social awareness.

A second concern of this study is to relate the various individuals and groups that emerge from my analysis to their changing political and economic environments. It is especially their entanglement in the changing state regulations governing property ownership and inheritance, credit and marketing, the exercise of skills and labor, the formation of social and political alliances (both within and without the peasant households), and the power to define social situations, which I seek to investigate and interpret.

Third, I wish to intrepret the ruling ideology of social relationships by which the entire continuum of individuals, families, households, estates, and the state was conceptualized and maintained. In this regard I will pay some attention to the idea of "the whole house." A result of the Greek classical revival of the early modern period, it became the basis of an early modern German and Austrian literature which developed a theory of political economy that focused on the "good economy" of the household. In the specific context of Austrian rural society, the social and political result of this ruling ideology was to redefine the household as a unit in the administration of estate and state. The heads of households became in effect a new class of bureaucrats, nonprofessional and "extension" bureaucrats to be sure, but nevertheless responsible for their "houses" and subject to bureaucratically formulated and dispersed rules and regulations.

Finally, there are consequences of these changes that have a significance beyond the historical time and place with which this study is concerned. Although I can only suggest this larger framework, it is clear that the social and political relations described here laid the foundations for those authoritarian and "patriarchal" traditions that permeated Austrian life for three centuries. The Austrian case is unique but at the same time many of the features of the rural society described here also appeared in other parts of early modern Central Europe and this study has, in that sense, a more universal relevance. Moreover, insofar as the nexus between social forms and state formation contains persistent and unresolved problems even in modern states, this Austrian case study serves to illustrate the consequences of a particular path of development in which capitalist and noncapitalist economic relations and private and bureaucratic political forms coexisted in mutually supportive institutions and relationships—and in which conflicts and flaws within the system were publicly suppressed and ultimately absorbed, with dire results, in the private sphere by individuals and their families.

The primary sources for my analysis were drawn from the centralized Upper Austrian state archives at Linz, from the extensive collection of the Weinberg estate archives, and from the Starhemberg archive at Haag am Hausruck. I have used administrative documents (accounts, case dispositions, administrative correspondence) from Estates and estates* and the Bavarian lien administration documents in the Wagrain estate archive. My most important sources were peasant household inventories covering the period 1609 to 1640 from the estate archives of Frankenburg, Windhag, Schaunberg, Aistersheim, and the Premonstratensian monastery and estate Schlägl. This period and these archives provide the earliest solid bloc of this unique source material.

The detailed analysis of the data provided by the household inventories in the early chapters allows us to develop a description of the peasants' economic and occupational strata in ways not possible until now. In order to offset the static quality of this part of the study and in order to give this social and eco-

---

* Throughout I have capitalized "Estates" when referring to the united political corporations (i.e., *Stände*); "estates" refers to the high nobility's conglomerations of peasant farms, manors, and other rural possessions and incomes.

nomic analysis a historical setting and significance, I turn the second half of this study over to a number of narratives detailing the Habsburg's state extention, during the sixteenth century, into such important aspects of peasant social life as labor and family regulation, property law, and social welfare. These various narratives culminate, in the final chapter, in an account of the reception of the Counter-Reformation. The peasant rebellions that ensued during the decades following the Battle of White Mountain—and my source materials here are primarily the secondary accounts provided by Stieve, Sturmberger, and others as well as the primary sources of the Weinberg and Starhemberg estate archives—disclose how the new police state's invasion of the family and of the peasant community had created a new rural society, patriarchal in appearance and yet thoroughly bureaucratic in its operations and effects.

This research was financed by the Danforth Foundation, the Canada Council, and the University of Iowa. I must especially thank Dr. Alfred Hoffmann, the late Georg Grüll, and Dr. Hans Sturmberger and his staff for introducing me to and making available to me the Austrian archival materials. The accumulated intellectual debt I owe to my teachers both in Toronto and at the University of California at Berkeley and to my colleagues and students in Iowa is beyond itemized accounting, let alone redemption, and I hope they will accept this work, despite its flaws and shortcomings, in partial repayment. Special thanks are due to Jennifer Rebel who, for better and worse, lived with and shared in the making of this book.

Peasant Classes

~ INTRODUCTION ~

Peasant Wars and
Peasant Society

THE COURSE OF UPPER AUSTRIAN RURAL POLITICS, 1511-1636

THE SIXTEENTH-CENTURY REVOLUTIONARY EXPERIENCE of the Austrian peasantry predated the larger German conflict of 1525.[1] In 1511, the subject population of the estates Kammer, Kogl, and Frankenburg arose in protest, refused to pay taxes, and requested that the emperor intervene against the oppressive rule of their lord, the royal lien administrator, Wolfgang von Polheim. When three hundred peasant householders gathered to discuss tyrannicide against Polheim, Emperor Maximilian sent an investigating commission and, in effect, temporarily replaced Polheim's administrators with his own. The latter, during the next three years, carried on interrogations, adjudicated disputes, and upheld many of the peasants' claims. This peasant revolt and the Imperial challenge of a powerful lord's prerogatives over peasant subjects that followed it was a prelude to the final struggle between the Austrian Estates and the Habsburgs over the structure of the Habsburg state. It is also the beginning of those state policies by which the royal bureaucracy interfered directly in the relations between lords and peasant subjects. 1511 marks the beginning of a policy of "peasant protection" (*Bauernschutz*) which, by all modern historical accounts, did not become a part of Habsburg policy until the late seventeenth and eighteenth centuries.

Even before the outbreak of the great peasant war of 1525, then, the Austrian peasantry's status, economic welfare, and social structure began to appear as a significant element in the formation of the absolute state. For the following three hundred years, the rural population became the football with which princes and nobility played the games of state-building and status-maintenance. The Imperial commissars no more brought "peasant protection" to the countryside in the years 1512 to 1514 than they would in the eighteenth century. *Bauernschutz* was a term invented in the later period to put a benevolent and innovative face on bureaucratic activities which had long sought to stabilize, at almost any price, economic and social relations in the countryside and to assert royal authority there. That this policy could as easily turn against the peasantry as support it was already apparent during the early modern peasant revolts.

The Salzburg peasant armies, carrying the revolutionary message and the Twelve Articles of the Swabian peasantry, invaded Upper Austria and drew a number of the Upper Austrian parishes into revolt between March and July of 1525. The first Estate of high nobility (*Herren*) responded by calling for a meeting of the Estates and by fortifying and provisioning several towns in preparation for a siege. The expected confrontation did not materialize chiefly because the peasant parishes, divided into two parties, were not able to form a united militia. The 1525 uprising, for the most part, took the form of quarrels among the peasants over what were the crucial issues and of quarrels between royal authorities and Estates over their proper respective roles in subduing the subject population. The radical party among the peasants tended toward violent disruptions of meetings where they issued such public demands as a rollback in the price of oats (the chief "fuel" of the important transport sector), the abolition of labor services and of the lords' practice of using the peasant farms as feedlots for their own cattle, the establishment of a provincial Commons in place of the existing Estates, and finally, the cessation of the Imperial practice of lien administration (*Pfandherrschaft*), which was rapidly emerging as one of the chief instruments of public finance in the Habsburg state. The moderate party, on the other hand, powerful and dominant in an alliance of rural parishes, contented itself with submitting grievances to the emperor, negotiating with Imperial

4

authorities at meetings in Innsbruck, and demanding political recognition and institutional status for the subject population as a whole. Their attempts at moving on to greater organizational maturity failed, however, and, incapable of establishing basic discipline in their own ranks, the Upper Austrian parish organizations dissolved in the face of a small mercenary force organized by the archduke.

The aftermath of 1525 in Upper Austria shows that the Estates had won that round in their positional struggle with the crown. The suppression of popular dissent was brutal and thorough. Royal mercenary units made a punitive sweep through the province, conducted door-to-door searches and interrogations, and carted the most prominent leaders off to Vienna for subsequent punishment. The Estate authorities, as individual owners of manors and estates, followed up with the collection of fines, extorted protection moneys (*Brandschatzungen*), and military taxes to pay for their half of the costs of the mercenary force that had suppressed the rebellion. Little if any of these moneys ever reached Vienna and the net consequence of the 1525 uprising was that the Estate authorities were more firmly entrenched than before. In the decades that followed, they began to develop bridges to the peasant leadership by "reforming" their parish organizations, by agreeing to abolish completely personal bondage (*Leibeigenschaft*), and by establishing the heritability of tenures; at the same time, by catering at an increasing rate to the fiscal requirements of the royal household, the Estates also maintained a modicum of cooperation with their prince and, indeed, laid the foundations on which the future Austrian state would be built. I have examined these processes of estate management elsewhere; they are too intricate for and not entirely relevant to this study, but nevertheless, in the opening and closing chapters below, I shall attempt to suggest what their most important and unique aspects were and how they dominated the social development of the subject peasantry.

There were a good number of minor uprisings of the peasantry throughout the sixteenth century and these may be explained as conflicts contained by (and not directed against) the changing structures and management practices of estate and state administration. These sporadic and highly localized conflicts came to a head in the years 1594 to 1597 when parishes from all quarters arose in protests against excessive taxation and what were called unreasonable innovations on the part of the estate owners and managers. In this struggle the peasantry put a well-organized and disciplined small army into the field and had to be taken seriously as a political force. The Estates' forces suffered a bloody defeat in November of 1595 and for over a year, until the armistice of January 1597, the peasant armies and councils dominated the public life of rural Upper Austria. Representatives of Estates and peasants negotiated under royal auspices in Prague and on 6 May 1597, Rudolph II issued an Imperial "Interims Resolution" that regulated many of the disputed terms of lord-subject relationships and required each estate owner to draw up a separate agreement, following the resolution's guidelines, with his or her subject population. Negotiations continued until 1598 and were accompanied by brutal military repression under the leadership of the Estates. Invariably, it seems, peasant rebellions had to end with extortion, torture, and gruesome executions.

This settlement of the peasants' protests by Imperial intercession and by a codification of subject duties, which closed the sixteenth century, ushered in a new period in which the pendulum of power swung in the direction of the crown and of those among the nobility who could accept and work within the framework of social and political relationships being established by the crown. The peasant subjects, destined never to become an "Estate," had, at the same time, found a foothold in the laws of the growing absolute state of the eastern Habsburgs; but from a negative point of view one could say that they were both pacified and reduced to individual action in the courts where they were no match for their lords' resources and power. The fundamental trend of the sixteenth century reasserted itself by the early seventeenth century: while the peasantry continued to assert its independence and acquired a reputation for refractoriness, it also learned to accept and act within the narrow bounds of estate management and state politics—and, manipulated in the struggle between lords and prince, its politics re-

mained self-contradictory. Unsure of who their friends and enemies were and divided over their political objectives, the peasant
rebels of the early seventeenth century went to defeat in several
bloody and increasingly insane insurrections.

The succession to the eastern Habsburg crown by the Styrian
archduke Ferdinand in 1619, followed by the allied Estates' defeat at White Mountain, signified a change in the struggle between Estates and crown as well as in the politics of the peasant
subjects. Armed with the military and political resources of the
Catholic League and with the Jesuit-directed Counter-Reformation, Ferdinand II proceeded to assert his overlordship in the
provinces and, with only a few exceptions, the lords of the
Bohemian and Austrian Estates complied. A part of the peasantry, fighting for continuing control of parish and village politics, opposed the prince and the collaborating Estates and sided
with the small Estates faction that tried to continue the resistance through obstructionism and guerrilla actions. In such an
alliance the social and political differences between lords and
peasants were pushed to the background and caused further
internal division. The peasantry of the Hausruck and Mühlviertel, i.e., from the southeastern and northern quarters of
Upper Austria, arose 8,000 strong in 1620 to obstruct and harass
the advance of Maximilian of Bavaria's occupation army into
Upper Austria. The peasants of the Traunviertel, i.e., of the
southwestern quarter of Upper Austria, did not join in this
resistance but rather continued to wage a local struggle with
their authorities against the increasing taxation and fees being
charged against houses and farms. Their resistance ended in
1625 and was absorbed a year later by the great Upper Austrian
uprising that tried to combine the opposition against Bavarian
occupation and Counter-Reformation absolutism with the local
political struggles against the encroachments into village and
household autonomy by lords and their estate managers. Significantly, most of the parishes of the river valleys around Steyr
in the Traunviertel stayed out of the peasant war of 1626.

Two incidents in 1625, both involving the denial by village
leaders and peasant householders of parish posts to Counter-
Reformation priests, set the stage and the mood for the follow-

7

ing year. The Bavarian *Statthalter*, Adam von Herbersdorf, met the second of these resistances at Frankenburg with a show of strength and with memorably staged executions that characterized his rule as brutally repressive and easily made it the object of popular hatred. The broadly based rebellion of 1626 broke out in May of that year and was sparked by a tavern brawl at Lembach in the Mühlviertel in which six Bavarian mercenaries were beaten to death and three Catholic priests murdered in subsequent rioting. Peasant bands captured a number of noble seats north and south of the Danube around Schaunberg, armed themselves and inflicted a major defeat on the *Statthalter's* army, driving him and the Estates into the safety of the citadel at Linz. During the next two months peasant units occupied all the noble and clerical seats and the major towns of Upper Austria with the exception of Linz and Enns; the Danube was closed and only peasant-authorized traffic allowed to pass. The new edition of the Twelve Articles, which the peasant leaders issued as the basis for their negotiations with the Imperial commissars, focused on the expulsion of the Bavarian militia, on the continuation of personal religious self-determination and the reinstatement of Protestant ministers, and on the admission of the peasants to the Estates.

The peasants' negotiations with Imperial commissars, the Estates, the magistracies of the Upper Austrian cities and the Bavarian *Statthalter* Herbersdorf continued throughout the early part of the summer of 1626 and in the end achieved nothing. In August, the peasant militia was defeated by Catholic League army units. After a period of truce in September and October, Herbersdorf's stepson, Gottfried Heinrich von Pappenheim, outflanked the peasant armies of the Hausruck, divided them, and defeated them in a series of rapidly unfolding engagements in November. The usual public dismemberments and executions followed and lasted until July 1628.

The defeat of the massive ~~uprising of 1~~626 revealed that although the royal authorities had the resources, military power, and followers to defeat the peasants' former social and political enemies, the estate owners, this did not mean that anything had changed in the social and political position of the subject

population. The religious and political independence of the peasant parishes was instead greatly diminished; and, in effect, the
Imperial solution to rural conflict in 1597 was reaffirmed.

In the 1630s a different face of peasant politics presented
itself. Already, in the last desperate engagements of 1626, the
complexion of the peasant armies seemed to have changed drastically. Archaeological excavations at Pinsdorf in the Hausruck
near Gmunden have shown that the mass graves at this battle
site contained not the armed fighting men who according to
legend made a last stand here, but the remains of about 400
children, women, and old people who had all been buried without clothes or shrouds. Similarly, the rebellions of 1632 and
1635 had a thoroughly different character from those of 1595-
1597 and 1626—different as these were from each other—in
that the majority of the participants were children, adolescents,
and young men and women who worked as servants and laborers. A few smallholders and self-styled priests provided the
leadership and the revolutionary slogans that carried these partially armed bands through a series of disastrous encounters
with the forces of the Estates and destined the leaders for the
scaffold on the marketplace in Linz. Abandoned by the politically active leadership that had previously dominated the peasant movement, the roving protesting bands of the 1630s fielded
a political program composed of anti-Catholic fanaticism, of
opposition to officially sanctioned marriage, of revolutionary
suicide, religious hallucinations, and millennial faith in the return of the legendary Frederick Barbarossa. Peasant parish leaders meanwhile furnished the men and horses with which the
Estates crushed these rebel preachers and their desperate young
followers.

Although the highly organized and politically significant rebellions of the early and late decades of the sixteenth century
and of the 1620s have rightly occupied the attention of historians
to a far greater degree than the tragic events of the 1630s, the
latter are nevertheless crucial to the story. They not only give
us a better sense of the changes that transformed the lower-
class politics of early modern Austria but also reiterate the point
that there was, in fact, no single peasant movement but there

were movements, different groups and parties among the rural inhabitants, expressing different regional or social interests, forming variable social and political alliances and dissolving them again as they encountered successes and failures.

This is not a book about peasant revolts but about the rural population that produced them, a population crossed by divisions and differences and yet capable of various kinds of united action. What follows is not a sketch of the social and economic background to this long century of peasant rebellions but rather an attempt to analyze the fundamental sources of unity and disunity among the rural inhabitants of Upper Austria's Alpine foothills and river valleys. Here the rebellions form the background to farreaching and enduring changes in the economic, social, and political structures governing the peasants' daily life.

CLASSES AND ORDERS AND THE ANALYSIS OF PEASANT SOCIETIES

One of the first tasks that confronts a historian who wants to write "history from below" is to identify and classify his historical actors. Too often such words as "peasant," "artisan," or "laborer" are used to describe individuals and groups and to ascribe to them ways of thinking and forms of behavior which, upon closer examination, are completely irrelevant to their actual character and circumstances. The history of the peasantries of early modern Germany and Austria which has been, during the past two decades, the focus of a heated debate,[2] is a case in point. Hundreds of pages of research and criticism have been written, positions have been staked out, and such social historical clichés as "early bourgeois revolution," "Systemkonflikt," and "the common man" have been advanced but in all of this little attention has been paid to developing an interpretive framework that is actually suited to the empirically verifiable facts of Central European social life during this period.[3] The result has been a largely polemical debate that is, for the most part, alienated from historical realities.[4] The results of archival research aiming at analyzing specific economic and social groups and their political and social roles, as may be found in the work of David

Sabean, for example,[5] are merely noted in passing and their implications for the continuing debate are largely ignored.[6] Most of the current writings and discussions about the peasantries of early modern Central Europe continue to be based on unsubstantiated generalizations and vague notions concerning economic and social groupings.

A part of the problem lies in the fact that historians are chiefly concerned with the years of peasant protest and rebellion and not with the periods of calm between these cataclysms. Such crisis years do indeed often disclose tensions and conflicts that have built up over a long period and can reveal much about the long-term social history of the lower classes; at the same time, however, a failure to study what "worked" in the decades and years before such an event and what the various participants learned, gained, and lost in the aftermath can only result in a distorted perception of the history of peasant society.

Paradoxically, the conclusion that such an exclusive concentration on peasant rebellions and wars produces is that nothing really changes in the long run for the great mass of people and that, in fact, they have no history. In this sense there seems to be, for example, an underlying consensus about the meaning of the German Peasant Wars of 1525 that transcends the scholarly and ideological differences among its historians. The defeat of the peasants is interpreted in the recent West German literature as a resolution of conflicts between lords and subjects within an essentially stable and accepted social system;[7] in the East German view it reflects the unwillingness and unpreparedness of the peasant class to challenge the existing social relations of production[8]—both sides implicitly seem to agree with Günther Franz's long-held conclusion that the Peasant Wars of the early sixteenth century meant the exclusion of the peasants from participation in the social and political development of Germany for the next three centuries.[9]

To be sure, there remain major differences between Marxist and non-Marxist interpretations of early modern peasant society, nor is there complete agreement within either camp.[10] Moreover, the literature from both sides contains works that explicitly try to deal with the long-term history of the peasantry

and that concern themselves at least with the later peasant rebellions of the sixteenth and seventeenth centuries. But even
the best of these works confine themselves to the terms and
frameworks of the debate that has dealt with the uprisings of
the early sixteenth century. Thus, for example, Helga Schultz
has examined the Upper Austrian peasant war of 1597 in the
classical manner and, following Engels's paradigm, she con-
cludes that in the aftermath of 1525 there was a "refeudalization" of rural life with the peasantry, deprived now of city and
town-based "early bourgeois" support, reduced to regional and
"low" forms of class struggle in which it fought the lords over
the division of the agricultural surplus and in which the larger
political issues and the "social-legal aspects of exploitation"
were reduced to secondary importance.[11] On the non-Marxist
side, Peter Blickle has developed, in a series of monographs and
articles, an interpretation of the long-term meaning of the Peasant Wars of 1525 that at first seems to contradict the notion
that the peasants' defeat eliminated them as significant participants in the political and social development of Central Europe.
In Blickle's view, the "common man" (whom he substitutes for
the notion of "peasantry") came out of the early sixteenth-
century conflicts with an enhanced social and political position
that was guaranteed by territorial and royal law—but he too
concedes that in the final analysis, beginning with the victory
of absolutism in the seventeenth century, the "common man"
was, with the exception of the German Southwest, eliminated
from effective participation in the social and political life of the
emergent absolute states.[12] Among both the Marxists and the
non-Marxists, therefore, there is a remarkable consensus of
opinion about the long-term course and significance of the peasant movements of early modern Europe. The approaches to the
problem differ but the conclusions—that the peasants were locked
into a rigidly feudal social order and did not make lasting history
in this period—remain essentially the same. The reason they
are the same is that despite their theoretical differences, both
camps have a fundamentally similar vision of the economic and
social transformations that changed early modern into modern
society.

The problem of the long-term periodization of peasant social history in the early modern era, which expresses itself in an undue concentration on such cataclysmic upheavals as the German Peasant Wars of 1525, is the result of a reluctance to alter the accepted macro-historical interpretations of the period to fit the actualities of the economic and social groupings found among the population. The divisions of the early modern peasantries into groups of rich, middling, and poor people; into landowners, tenants, cottagers, and lodgers; into innkeepers, millers, farmers, craftsmen, laborers, and servants and other social and economic groupings is familiar to every historian working in this period. However, not only do most historical analyses not concern themselves with precise economic and social descriptions of any of these groups, nor with an analysis of the kinds of social and economic relations that existed within and among them, but, when it comes to drawing up a comprehensive social synthesis, most historians of the period, with some exceptions,[13] turn their backs on the existence of such social differences among the peasantry in favor of simpler and broader social categories that are usually based on macro-economic explanations of social development.[14] Thus, the Marxist interpreters of this period tend to treat the peasantry as a single social class which, from the middle ages until the modern period, existed in an unrelieved period of class oppression under an agriculture-based feudal mode of social production. Social differences within this "peasantry" tended to express themselves in the so-called "lower" forms of the class struggle and therefore did not and could not contribute toward creating a "mature" revolutionary situation in the early modern period.[15] The peasants, no matter what their internal social stratification, were collectively trapped in a feudal society that had not made the "transition" to a capitalist society. Capitalist society would, in any case, emerge not from a rural environment but from an urban industrial setting in the eighteenth and nineteenth centuries; and, although the peasants tried, in part, to ally themselves with urban "progressive" classes and tried, in some regions near and around cities, to destroy feudal society, they became, in the early modern period, the victims of an incomplete and premature attempt at a "bour-

13

geois" revolution.[16] There are Marxist social analysts who have developed more sophisticated frameworks for investigating the problem of social stratification generally and of rural social classes specifically,[17] but their conceptualizations have not yet been applied to the problems of peasant societies in early modern Europe. Instead, preoccupation with a better analysis of the so-called "transition" from feudalism to capitalism threatens to divert the attention of some Marxist historians of the early modern period even further away from detailed social analysis.[18]

A similar view of "transition," but this time from a preindustrial society of orders to an industrial society of classes, has dominated the non-Marxist writings about early modern society and has similarly avoided a detailed analysis and interpretation of the internal social divisions among the rural populations of Germany and Austria. The "society of orders" concept had its origin in the legal status categories of the early modern social system, which was composed of economic, social, administrative, and political corporations called Estates, guilds, chapters, villages, territories, etcetera; in current historical writings it has been the basis of an essentially anti-social science argument that holds that modern categories of social analysis are suited only to modern industrial and urban societies and distort and misrepresent earlier social divisions.[19]

Not only has this point of view deeply influenced the macro-historical interpretation of early modern peasantries we find in the works of Günther Franz, Rainer Wohlfeil, Peter Blickle, and others, but it has also had its most crucial impact on the detailed social analysis of the peasant society; specifically, it has focused the attention of social historians on the peasant household as the smallest unit of social analysis and has diverted analysis away from an examination of individuals and groups of individuals that exist outside of and cut across the lines of social division provided by household, village, and Estate. The sixteenth and seventeenth century administrative conception of the peasant family household, which was summed up in the early modern idea of the "whole house" (das ganze Haus) and which saw the household under the rule of the tenant farmer as the head of the household as the basic economic, social, and

14

political unit of society,[20] has become the basic unit of social division in modern non-Marxist historical literature on peasant social stratification.[21]

We need to look closely at this concept and evaluate its utility for analysis critically. The household and family appear also in the recent Marxist literature on early modern society as integrated units of production and social status.[22] The Russian economic historian A. V. Chayanov has analyzed and expanded this household concept and has shown that it was not just a unit in the class system but that it contained in its internal makeup of individual relationships a continuation of that class system.[23] This conceptualization has not, however, been fully utilized in the Marxist discussions of social class in early modern peasant society and the household continues to be the smallest unit of social analysis.[24]

The net effect both of the Marxists' analysis of an early modern rural society made up of classes and of the non-Marxists' view of an early modern society of orders is that they both accept a social vision of a single peasant stratum that is subdivided into family, household, and village units. Although they use the different kinds of analysis associated with the concepts of classes and orders, they share an essentially identical view of the early modern rural social structure,[25] which they see as being in a state of "transition"—from a feudal to a capitalist mode of social production according to the Marxist analysts and from a society of orders to a society of classes according to the non-Marxists. In both views the dualistic principles of feudalism-capitalism and classes-orders are internally antagonistic and mutually exclusive and, in cases where they are seen to overlap, they are the basis of social "contradiction" and conflict. It is this dualism of concepts and the long-term periodization associated with it that has led to an insufficiently detailed image and a fundamental misinterpretation of the social and political systems of the peasants of early modern Europe.

How this conception of two fundamentally different systems of social stratification leads to a misinterpretation of the nature of early modern and modern societies may be illustrated by the writings of Roland Mousnier, one of the leading recent theorists of classes and orders. For Mousnier, societies of orders have been the prevalent social form in world history and societies of classes, in which "the production of material goods and the creation of wealth are judged the most important social functions and where capitalist production relationships dominate" are historically much rarer. In such class-based societies "the law recognizes only individuals and not social groups."[26] Clearly, the principles of order and class in social organization are mutually exclusive in Mousnier's conception. He admits that there are "intermediate types of social stratification" in societies where the two types are mixed but he sees these only as aspects of, again, systems in transition, in which a society dominated by orders or by classes will eventually emerge. Thus he sees the beginning of a "slow transition from an order-based to a class-based society" in England in the fifteenth century[27] and supports this contention with an unconvincing discussion of the "gentleman" as a new and indeterminate social type who fits both kinds of society. This example suggests that he is not clear about what he means; he would have been able to show the nature of the peculiar English mix of orders and classes far more clearly if he had considered the social behavior of specifically definable traditional aristocratic[28] and peasant groups.[29]

When Mousnier speaks of modern American society, he also sees a society in transition but this time from a society of classes to a society of orders.[30] Again, the empirical work of historians suggests that this view of American society in "transition" from one *kind* of society to another is a false perception. Instead, corporative and order-based institutions have been an intrinsic part of American class society since its earliest days and the real problem of analysis for the social historian is to unravel the continuously shifting and changing relationships between these two bases of the American social system.[31] In a society consisting simultaneously of orders and classes it becomes necessary to investigate not only the way these two bases of social status coexist with a view to finding the "dominant" one[32] but also to discover the way they interact with each other in mutually supportive as well as in contradictory ways. The same considerations apply to the coexistence of feudal and capitalist forms' of social production in a single system. These do not necessarily indicate a society in "transition"; they often together create unique social systems that undergo their own development and historical transformations without being dominated by either one or another kind of stratification system.

Max Weber's conceptualization of social relations offers a path out of these dualistic schemes of historical change. In his sociology of stratification the words "class," "status," and "party" indicate different aspects of a social system of which one or another may be a dominant element but none of which ever exists entirely alone in a society. At the same time, these elements of stratification may shift in relative importance not only in response to macro-historical developments but also to temporary and short-term changes in the production and consumption relationships of a society. Each of them relates to specific spheres of human activity and forms an essential element in a thorough analysis of social stratification and social action:

> Whereas the genuine place of 'classes' is within the economic order, the place of 'status groups' is within the social order, that is, within the sphere of the distribution of 'honor.' From within these spheres, classes and status groups influence one another and they influence the legal order and are in turn influenced by it. But 'parties' live in a house of 'power.' Their action is oriented toward the acquisition of social 'power,' that is to say, toward influencing a communal action no matter what its content may be. . . .
> In any individual case, parties may represent interests determined through 'class situation' or 'status situation' and they may recruit their following respectively from one or the other. But they need be neither purely 'class' nor purely 'status' parties. In most cases they are partly class parties and partly status parties, but sometimes they are neither.[33]

It is with such categories of analysis that the macro-historical dualisms of orders and classes, of "peasants" and "bourgeois," cease to be the focus of historical investigation.

In the Weberian conceptualization of social stratification

17

"classes" may or may not coincide with the legal status groups, or orders, to be found in any given society. The first task of social analysis is to identify the various class characteristics of individuals and groups and to discover the "class situation" in which they find themselves. Such class characteristics form the basis of an objective analysis that goes beyond the concern with the mode of production that is the focus of Marxist analysis. Weber identifies a historical actor's "class situation" by the ownership of properties that may be highly differentiated in kind and quantity, by the disposition of "capital goods of all sorts," of one's own and others' labor, and of transferable monopolies. In the absence of property, the kinds of services rendered to others, the use of services by others, and the nature of these relationships also help determine "class situation."

> But always this is the generic connotation of the concept of class: that the kind of chance in the *market* is the decisive moment which presents a common condition for the individual's fate. 'Class situation' is, in this sense, ultimately 'market situation.'[34]

This kind of analysis is initially directed away from large groupings and focuses attention on the various kinds of individuals and on the social roles they play. It is analysis that aims at understanding what life chances presented themselves to individuals and groups given a dominant and internally differentiated set of "market relationships."

To this fundamentally economic concept of class situation, Ralf Dahrendorf has added another component that draws on the Weberian sociology of dominance. Using the term "imperatively coordinated association," which Max Weber defined as an "association . . . [whose] members are, by virtue of a prevailing order, subject to authority relations," Dahrendorf defines "social class" as "such organized and unorganized collectivities of individuals as share manifest or latent interests arising from and related to the authority structure of imperatively coordinated associations."[35] It is this dual concept of class and class situation that allows us to proceed with an analysis of early modern rural societies that is at once empirically complex and theoretically significant.

The society of orders was also a society of classes. The Austrian Estates and peasants, that is, the orders of authorities and subjects, had collective class characteristics and were themselves internally divided by class. The subject order will be analyzed in this study in great detail with regard to various individuals' and groups' market situations and authority relations. Nor will the household and family disappear in such an analysis. They move even more prominently into the foreground because they represent the society of orders in their formal characteristics and in their actual functioning they are the chief containers for class situations. Our analytical concern is with the movement of individuals into and out of situations defined by the complex interweaving of class and status—and this interweaving took place in the peasant families and households.

Class situation and position in a social order may be used to describe, in their turn, the "status" of individuals and groups. Status can, however, not be objectively analyzed like class or Estate membership but is rather determined by the relative esteem and honor granted to individuals by the communities (however defined) in which they live. Just as "property" is both the prelude to and the outcome of class situations so is the latter the prelude and outcome of status.[36] Early modern peasant societies contained numerous individuals who shared similar legal and economic characteristics and pursued similar occupations and yet managed to acquire entirely different status positions. The early modern period in rural Austria did not simply witness a transitional change by which status, achieved and ascribed through the workings of feudal social production and of legal orders, was replaced by capitalist relations and the criteria of class, but it saw the creation of a distinctive social order in which the legal, economic, social, and political foundations of status changed and produced new status communities among the peasantry. Housecommunities, through the different class and status relations of their members and through their relationships with each other in the estate and village communities, also functioned as the focal points of social status relationships.

Those who had status often also sought power beyond the limitations of their houses and villages and to this end sought to organize political parties. This study focuses briefly on a number of peasant leaders from the 1626 uprising with a view to analyzing their class and status character and identifying their political significance. It will be my contention that the attempt at party formation by these leaders and their allies, while it was in tune with the basic thrust of social development in the Austrian countryside, missed the fundamental realities of power. They did not seek simply to conquer and gain admission to the Estates as it may at first appear. The peasant leaders had understood that the process of what we would now call "societalization"[37] had shifted away from provincial power and toward a bureaucratization of household, estate, and state. What they did not understand was that the legal-rational order of a bureaucratic state need only be internally consistent and rational and that the charismatic authority of those who stand above and outside the bureaucratic structure can override reason and order at will.

~ CHAPTER 1 ~

Settings

IN UPPER AUSTRIA, beginning at the end of the fifteenth century and continuing throughout the period of the *ancien régime*, secular and ecclesiastical magnates pressed their various seigneurial rights and duties and their legal and administrative privileges into economic service while at the same time reinvesting their growing incomes in the acquisition of tenant farms that gave them even greater economic, social, legal, and political authority.[1] The result was that, increasingly and inexorably, personal social and political success went to those who managed best to combine traditional feudal authority with the pursuit of market advantages and profitable enterprises.

LIEN ADMINISTRATION, EMPHYTEUSIS, AND AUTHORITY

Two terms, "feudal capitalism" and *"Wirtschaftsherrschaft,"* have in the past been used to describe the changes that took place in the seigneurial regimes of much of east Central Europe in the early modern period. These terms are to a considerable extent interchangeable and represent the same empirical reality but at the same time they each emphasize particular features of these changes. Werner Stark, in describing the changing seigneurial regimes of Bohemia in the seventeenth and eighteenth centuries, used the term feudal capitalism: "Seigneurial enterprise in that period was internally, in its social structure, feudal, but externally, in its relationship to the market, it was capitalistic."[2] He captured the source of social status tension in this early modern type of agrarian regime to a much greater

21

extent than does the term *Wirtschaftsherrschaft*. This latter term, coined by Alfred Hoffmann in specific reference to what was taking place in Upper Austria in the sixteenth and seventeenth centuries and which translates literally into "economic dominance," attempts to describe specific economic and political characteristics of this east Central European seigneurial system.[3] It was a mixed form of seigneurial domination that combined the rentier relationship between lord and tenants, prevalent in western Central Europe, with the lord's direct involvement, on a large scale, with rural production and marketing, a feature that was associated with the *Gutsherrschaft* of the east Elbian areas.

It is this last feature that is particularly significant for the concept *Wirtschaftsherrschaft*. The objective of the Upper Austrian magnates was not merely to enter the market in a capitalistic manner but also to control as great a portion of it as possible through economic diversification, direct control over significant quantities of goods and over their flow, and the acquisition of exclusive administrative, judicial, and policing functions over specific markets. From both older and recent studies it is increasingly clear that all or some elements of these forms of "feudal capitalism" and "economic dominance" were present throughout east Central Europe besides Upper Austria, and most particularly in neighboring Bavaria, Bohemia, and Inner Austria, but also as far away as Prussia.[4] Throughout the rest of this chapter I shall refer, for reasons that will become clearer in later chapters, to the changes in Upper Austrian estate management as bureaucratic capitalism.

In almost all of the principalities of east Central Europe, including Upper Austria, there was in progress a complex and varied process of seigneurial "modernization" which was in each area shaped by particular historical traditions; by the differing availability of natural resources, labor, and marketing opportunities; and by the modernizing nobilities' varying flexibility and capacity for innovation. As we shall see, these changes in the seigneurial regime produced profound changes in the social organization of the peasants.

The problem of the causes behind the development of Upper

Austrian bureaucratic capitalism is complex and involves in a general way the upswing of the late medieval economy and more particularly the emerging role of the nobility in the administration of the Habsburgs' private properties and public rights and responsibilities. It is not a product of what has been called the "crisis of feudalism."

The Upper Austrian nobility had more than held its own in the struggle for economic survival in the Middle Ages, but with the onset during the late fifteenth century of population growth and of the price revolution which was brought about by, among other things, the increased supply of currency from the nearby silver mines, new economic dangers and opportunities presented themselves to the seigneurial landlords of Upper Austria. The threats offered by the inflationary devaluation of fixed rents and by the increased costs of conspicuous consumption were more than offset by the decreasing costs of labor; by the increase in the economic rent of the soil; by inflationary profit-taking through large-scale investment in land, credit, and commodity markets; and by exploiting the advantages of having economic, social, and political connections that transcended the limits of the local economies. It was less to ward off the economic threats of inflation than to participate in the economic opportunities offered by the period that the Upper Austrian magnates, like their counterparts elsewhere, were induced to expand and "capitalize" their estates.[5] The Upper Austrian and Bavarian magnates were in a particularly favorable position in that they could draw on an expanding labor pool for skilled, diverse, and increasingly cheap labor, an advantage that would distinguish their experience with forced labor and rural industry from developments in Bohemia where labor was scarce. Technological developments combined with improvements in capitalist techniques not only to heighten the productive and commercial capacity of the Upper Austria countryside but also to increase the export of agricultural products and some industrial products at various stages of completion to industrial and mining areas in other parts of Habsburg lands as well as in the German empire and Italy. The rural magnates, both as producers and as recipients of large quantities of grain, meat, and alcoholic beverages, and of such industrial raw materials as flax, were inevitably the initial and greater beneficiaries of these new opportunities in local and foreign trade than the peasantry.[6]

Along with the general upswing in the late medieval economy there were in this period advances in economic theory and praxis in which the Upper Austrian seigneurs shared in several ways. Economically successful members of urban elites strove to enter the ranks of the rural seigneurs and, if successful, brought with them innovative economic concepts and practices.[7] The administrative staffs of the seigneuries were increasingly trained specifically for their job, as is evident in the astonishingly uniform appearance, usefulness, and accuracy of their account books, inventories, and legal contracts. Although it is not certain that the Upper Austrian rural magnates possessed any current theoretical literature on economics,[8] there is evidence that some of them were becoming skilled in the keeping and manipulation of records and accounts themselves. Thus the later seventeenth-century image of the lord scrutinizing his personal account books, which adorns the title page of Christoph Fischer's *Oculus Domini* (1679) and which Stark cites as evidence for the new economic style of the Bohemian feudal capitalist,[9] seems to have had its counterpart in Upper Austria in the first half of the seventeenth century. For example, when we compare the account book for 1635 compiled by the owner of the Upper Austrian estate Weinberg, the Lady Anna Martha von Thürheim, to the more complete and useful and less erratic accounts of her estate managers, we see that it was not up to the professional standards of the period; it is nevertheless a remarkable document in evidence of her careful management that registered even the smallest incomes and expenditures and of her devotion to the spirit if not the letter of good accounting practices.[10]

Partially as a result of the economic revival of the sixteenth century, there developed the beginnings of the particular form of mercantilism associated with the Habsburg absolute state and it too became a strong influence on the emergence of Austrian bureaucratic capitalism. Not only did the Upper Austrian magnates copy the economic and social practices of their prince's mercantilism by treating their estates as miniature mercantile states,[11] but they also had to develop their economic resources if they were to participate prominently and advantageously in the emerging absolute state. The ownership of even several country seats was no longer a sufficient guarantee of status and participation at the highest levels of economic and political affairs, and incomes had to be found to support residences and storage facilities in significant commercial towns and eventually to build and maintain a *palazzo* in Vienna.[12]

There was also contained in the social and economic policies of the early Habsburg state an older practice, namely that of lien administration (*Pfandherrschaft*), and in my estimation it was this more than anything else that gave Upper Austrian estate administration its distinctive form. The Habsburgs began, in the Middle Ages, to pursue a policy of public finance by which they borrowed money from their service nobilities and other urban and professional moneylenders and in return gave to these a portion of their personal properties (*Kammergut*) to administer for a limited period of time and under conditions of emphyteusis; that is, the holder of the lien could use such royal properties as mining rights, rural estates, or tolls, as if they were his own provided he did not use them up or cause them to deteriorate in any way. This practice of lien administration was one of the chief sources of public revenues for the Habsburgs throughout the late medieval and early modern period and was pursued with special vigor (with the exception of the *Salzkammergut*) in the sixteenth and seventeenth centuries. Throughout the duchies it was a means by which the Habsburgs could maintain extensive seigneurial and commercial interests and incomes without becoming involved in the daily administration of these holdings.

It was through *Pfandherrschaft* initially, then through the administration of increasingly greater and "higher" judicial institutions, and finally through the acquisition of tax-collecting functions that the Upper Austrian magnates turned the private, semiprivate, and public properties and incomes of their prince to their own use. At the same time *Pfandherrschaft* did more than simply initiate the greater subsequent involvement of estate management with public rights and revenues; it forced the lien administrator to exercise protective and police functions in the various markets under the particular *Pfandherrschaft*. Finally and perhaps most important, there was the economic, legal, and political education that late medieval and early modern lien administrators received in the course of performing this function. The negotiation process that went into the lien contract, the assessment for the intrinsic value, incomes, and upkeep of the property to be pawned, the periodic renegotiations and the disputes that took place when the time came to redeem the property—all of these required an increasingly sharp and calculating commercial intelligence.[13]

The new bureaucratic capitalist estate administration was a style of thought and praxis that consciously sought to combine in a mutually reinforcing relationship political and police control with economic success. The institutions and practices that served this dual purpose made up the environment of dominance within which (and often against which) the everyday life of the subject peasantry unfolded. They consisted of the following: the accumulated subject peasant holdings owing rents, dues, services, and eventually taxes; the tithe units; and the various regalia including high and low judicial authority, church patronage, collection of tolls, and alcoholic beverage monopolies. In addition, there was a complex of properties consisting of the town and country houses, the woods, and the manorial farms with their houses, outbuildings, and fields that formed the important geographic and economic centers of the estates with which they sustained their growing managerial and laboring personnel and from which their owners coordinated their many interwoven economic, social, legal, political, and cultural activities.

The great estates of early modern Upper Austria emerged from a persistently pursued policy of property purchases by the highest secular and ecclesiastical nobilities beginning about the early fourteenth century.[14] These farmsteads became the chief basis of all of the liquid incomes of the estates and became as well units of political and legal power.[15] The peasant population became the object for experiments in managerial praxis conducted by the lords[16] and the result of these experiments was the formation, by 1600, of a new and uniform class of subject tenants whose economic, social, and political practices were subordinate to and mirrored the bureaucratic capitalism of the estate owners.

Upper Austria's prince, the highest officials of his *Kammergut* and courts, and the members of the Estates exercised authority—and were called "the authorities" (*Obrigkeiten*)—through their property and judicial rights that included privately held jurisdictions over "subjects" (*Untertanen*) who were by law excluded from owning outright properties to which any sort of authority was attached. A measure of the concentrations of authority in early modern Upper Austria is the distribution of this peasant subject population among the various *Obrigkeiten*. Using the tax unit of the period, the "subject hearth" (*Untertanen-Feuerstätte*), as his measure, Georg Grüll has drawn up the following distribution of authority from a 1620/25 register of Upper Austrian authorities:[17]

Royal seigneurial holdings	10,754	Hearths
Prelates	10,337	"
High Nobility (*Herren*)	12,861	"
Low Nobility (*Ritter*)	7,093	"
Royally Privileged Cities	2,609	"
Parish Priests	535	"

This table presents a legally accurate distribution of authority in Upper Austria but it does not show the actual distribution of authority as it was exercised and expressed through the collection of taxes and dues and through the actual management and control of estates. The tax rolls of the early modern period represent this more accurately as follows:[18]

	1527/44		1750	
Royal seigneurial holdings	749	Hearths	1,288	Hearths
Prelates	14,764	"	20,136	"
High Nobility	22,751	"	32,348	"
Low Nobility	1,675	"	3,522	"
Royally Privileged Cities			319	"

The royal practice of yielding its seigneurial holdings under conditions of *Pfandherrschaft* is clearly demonstrated by comparing these tables. Similarly the weaker positions of both the knights' Estate (*Ritter*) and the cities is apparent. The few holdings of the parish priests were administered under the seigneurial authority of members of the first or second Estates. While the highest concentration of authority over the subject population was clearly in the hands of the second Estate as a whole, the substantial number of subject units under ecclesiastical authority cannot be ignored, especially if one takes into account the fact that the greatest single concentration of subject properties was in the hands of the bishop of Passau (2,920 *Feuerstätten* in 1527-1544 and 4,296 in 1750) and that the combined incomes of the two greatest ecclesiastical magnates were twice as great as those of the two most powerful secular lords. These comparisons gave some credence to Franz Christoph Khevenhüller's claim, in 1620, that the Protestant members of the second Estate were motivated to revolt by prospects of being able to appropriate and divide up among themselves the authority of the ecclesiastical magnates. Nevertheless, both the first and second Estates engaged in *Pfandherrschaft* and treated the subjects in the same manner.

The Subject Tenants

The almost castelike separation of land-owning authorities from land-renting subjects was the most fundamental fact of social stratification in the medieval and early modern Upper Austrian countryside. The roots of this social structure, which was composed of those who were legally and hereditarily designated to exercise authority and those who were similarly designated to obey, extended into the early medieval period of Bavarian settlement and into the subsequent unfolding of Upper Austria's seigneurial regime (*Grundherrschaft*). Lordship had preceded the coming of the Bavarian invaders in the period of migration between the fourth and sixth centuries A.D. and there can be no doubt that in its earliest medieval origins the southeast German seigneurial regime was grounded in violently maintained relationships of dominance and submissive dependence. This fundamental dualism as well as the violence that maintained it were preserved through centuries of permutation as successive authorities grafted to it their legal institutions and economic and political purposes.[19]

Each seigneury's subject population was treated, by the early seventeenth century, as a single collective group that was, in its political aspects, equal. The subjects (*Untertanen*) were divided into village groups and administrative departments and were kept informed of innovations and changes in their estate administration's laws and rules through annual meetings (*Taidinge*) which they were by law compelled to attend.[20]

Individually, the subject population was divided into several types of legal status groups. The lowest form of inherited subject status was that of serf in personal bondage (*Leibeigen*). It was a form of servitude that was since late Roman times passed through the female line and enforced by the most brutal forms of punishment. Only slowly did bondsmen achieve the right, for a fee payable to the seigneury, to marry free women and only equally slowly did such dreadful physical punishments as castration and life-long incarceration—meted out for marrying a free woman illegally or for denying one's serf status—come to offend the Christian sensibilities of the Upper Austrian *Obrigkeiten* enough for them to be abolished;[21] it was not until the sixteenth and early seventeenth centuries that personal serfdom disappeared entirely.[22] Increasingly, the majority of the peasantry was personally free—only the subject status itself became increasingly hereditary and in its turn, as we shall see, took on greater degrees of personal unfreedom.

The seigneurial arrangements that involved protective jurisdiction (*Vogtei*), including church patronage, as well as feudal overlordship and service (*Lehenwesen*) and peasant usufruct rights (*bäuerliche Leihe*) to the lord's lands, mills, workshops, and taverns combined to make up each peasant subject's individually unique and mutable legal status under seigneurial authority. By the late sixteenth and early seventeenth centuries there had developed among Upper Austria's seigneurs a new attitude toward the subject peasantry, one that strove to reduce the many differences in legal status among the peasantry as much as possible, if not in fact then at least in effect, and to treat them increasingly as subject "citizens" of the seigneury.[23]

Not all these levelling impulses came from the seigneurial lords nor did they all serve seigneurial purposes. For example, seigneurs had begun, in the fifteenth century, to enter into special protective (*Vogtei*) arrangements with select individuals from among the subject peasantry who then became special clients of their lord and served such particular needs as castle guard duty or the occupation or use of vacant farms. In response to the protests of the other three Estates, Maximilian made the creation of such special status among the subject population illegal in 1502.[24] As I will suggest later in this study, it is likely that the magnates of Upper Austria countered the Imperial attempt at status equalization by continuing this practice in a de facto manner until well into the seventeenth century. Special status derived from the services and from privileges attached to enfeoffed holdings remained an intrinsic part of the legal status structure of the Upper Austrian seigneurial system until 1862[25] but, at the same time, the privileged feudal status of formerly "noble" farms and holdings that had devolved to subject peasant ownership became for practical purposes increasingly meaningless as a source of status by the sixteenth century. Similarly the "free" subject holdings (*freie Eigen*) that had been established to attract settlers in the period of clearing in the fifteenth century had, by the sixteenth century, lost their special tax-exempt status and usufruct rights to the commons and had progressively been burdened with all the dues in kind, labor, and cash that a seigneury's other normally "privileged" holdings had to bear.[26] These latter types of holdings and the fees and services they produced were derived from the earliest medieval forms of dependent cultivation and were at all times the economic mainstay of the Upper Austrian seigneurial system. It was these holdings that became the standard toward which the Upper Austrian bureaucratic capitalists strove in their treatment of the subject peasantry. We are not suggesting that these efforts produced a "second serfdom" in Austria. Subjects were personally free to move, to buy and sell their tenancies (and did so frequently, as we shall see). They were simply subject to uniform police administration and uniform landlord-tenant relations.

In comparison with the relatively straightforward status levelling found in the upgrading of formerly servile peasants and in the devaluation of formerly legally privileged holdings, the authorities' attempts to "level" the political status of their subject population is much more complex and will be the subject for more extensive discussion in later chapters. However, for the present purpose of outlining the strictures of authority within which and against which sixteenth and seventeenth century peasant society developed, two particular problems need to be mentioned. The first is that, as elsewhere in Europe, since the fourteenth-century payments in kind, tithes, and labor services were commuted to cash payments and increasingly acquired the character of rent. Not only did this introduce an equalizing monetary standard but it also made it possible for seigneurs and their estate managers to calculate, manipulate, and rationalize across the board increases in seigneurial dues as the lien contracts, technological change, the inflationary devaluation of rents, and the increasing concentration of their power seemed to necessitate and permit.[27]

Changes in the peasant subjects' ownership of usufruct rights on the seigneury's farms, woods, streams, workshops, mills, smithies, and taverns was the second area of economic levelling of the peasantry within the context of seigneurial authority. By regulating more closely the terms of subject tenantship and by making the process of lease transfer more uniform, Upper Austria's seigneurs used their legal authority to reduce the freedom of disposition held by some of their subject peasantry; at the same time they created new legally defined freedoms of disposition for those peasants who had held their farms for only a life term (Leibgeding) or for even shorter contractually fixed periods of time (Freistift). The system of impartible hereditary tenure which they thereby imposed as uniformly as possible meant a lowering of status not only for those who had formerly held and exercised legally sanctioned rights of free disposition but also for the majority of the peasantry who had already

31

exercised de facto rights of inheritance and free disposition. The legal "upgrading" of such peasant holdings, a process that reached its peak in the period 1550-1575,[28] meant in effect the introduction and, by the end of the sixteenth century, the sharp increase of seigneurial supervision and of fees charged on peasant property transactions. These "levelling" changes in the legal and legally controlled tenant status of the subject population did not, of course, eliminate social status differences among the peasantry but merely redirected them to suit the changing needs of seigneurial organization and authority—with the result that the formerly inferior form of hereditary subject status (*Erbuntertänigkeit*) actually became a prerequisite for achieving a higher economic and social status in the seigneurial regime and the peasant community after the sixteenth century.

The revolution in Austrian estate management of the period lasting from the fourteenth through the seventeenth centuries rested on two foundations that, together, altered the social life of rural Austria in fundamental ways. Members of the first and second Estates bought farmsteads and income-producing properties and expanded the size of their estates drastically. They used their legal authority to change the status of the properties they acquired so that peasant subjects could no longer own them but could only lease them. At the same time, through the growing practice of royal lien administration, they acquired control over the Habsburg *Kammer*'s estates whose peasant subjects were similarly reduced to subject tenants. Just as the royal estates held in lien were necessarily impartible units that were held under conditions of emphyteusis, so the same principles were extended to the individual farmsteads leased by the subject tenants. Peasants in effect held inheritable leases on farms, houses, and other properties owned by their overlords and could use these as if they were their own, provided they could meet the rent and other services required from those properties and provided they did not diminish them in any way. As we shall show, it was the precise applications of these principles of impartibility and emphyteusis that shaped the private family and social life and the public activities of the Austrian peasantry in decisive and far-reaching ways.

32

CONDITIONS OF PEASANT LIFE

There is no single focal point in the Upper Austrian landscape. It is constructed of a bewildering variety of geographic formations and, until recent times, there has been no single concentration of population. It is instead a linear landscape, a thoroughfare between southern Germany and eastern Europe (see maps). The Danube between the episcopal seat at Passau and the influx of the Enns carves her way through the southernmost reaches of the Bohemian and Bavarian forests and divides Upper Austria into distinctly different regions. On the river's north bank there ascend gneiss and granite palisades breached by deep valleys of ash and alder. Airy forests of pine and oak, beechwoods, birch, maple, and mountain elm cover the hills that ascend toward the north to the more melancholy evergreen woodlands surrounding the Moldau. Along the Danube's south bank there is a narrow band of marshy water meadows and wooded ravines where brooks and rivulets flow north to join the deep and narrow main stream. The waters in these tributaries trickled from glaciers and collected in deep Alpine lakes farther to the south. The broad alluvial plain they traverse between the mountains and the river rests on lime deposits that mix with loess topsoil to produce a fertile ground that has made cultivators and husbandmen wealthy since the neolithic age.

If some part or other of what is now Upper Austria has been under cultivation since at least the fourth millennium B.C. and agriculture has been the mainstay of this area's economy ever since, it has never been the only economic pursuit there. The earliest peasants living between the eastern Alps and the Bohemian forest domesticated pigs, cattle, sheep, goats, and horses and cultivated several types of grain, millet, peas, lentils, poppies, and flax. The pile-builders of the Mondseekultur supplemented their diet of fish and waterfowl with bread and with fruit improved by grafting. There were also potters who fashioned the clay they found in the streams in the vicinity of what is now Linz into earthenware. Stonecutters produced implements and weapons in their workshops along the Langensteinerwand south of the present-day city of Steyr; recent exca-

EARLY MODERN UPPER AUSTRIA

Extent of Habsburg Domain

Upper Austria

0   100 Km.

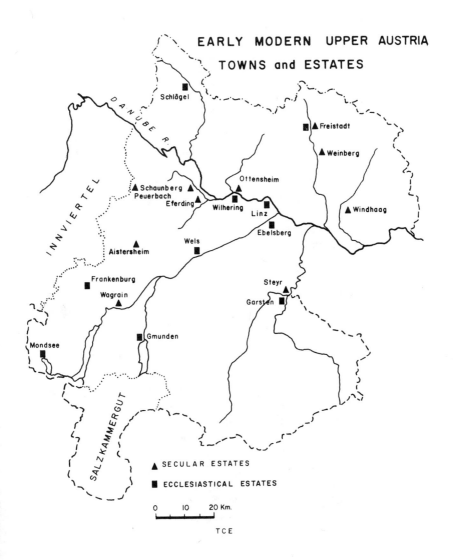

EARLY MODERN UPPER AUSTRIA
TOWNS and ESTATES

DANUBE R.

Schlägel

INNVIERTEL

▲Freistadt

▲Weinberg

Ottensheim
▲Schaunberg
Peuerbach
Eferding
Wilhering
Linz
▲Windhaag

Ebelsberg

Wels

▲
Aistersheim

Frankenburg
Wagrain

Steyr
▲
Garsten

Gmunden

Mondsee

SALZKAMMERGUT

▲ SECULAR ESTATES

■ ECCLESIASTICAL ESTATES

0   10   20 Km.

TCE

vations have shown that some of the raw materials for the stone implements in use in Upper Austria, if not the implements themselves, were imported from northern Europe.[29] This suggestion that even the earliest inhabitants of this area were involved not only in manufacture but also in some form of long-distance trade is confirmed by later developments. Particularly during the Hallstatt period (c. 800 B.C.) the output of the Alpine copper and salt mines from this region was exchanged for products from northern Italy and the Rhine area. These particular trading connections continued to be of primary importance until the early modern period.

By 1600 the Upper Austrian rural economy had achieved a considerable degree of pluralization and far-flung commercial ties. The estate owners had captured control of the markets by mid-sixteenth century but interfered little with the production and marketing activities of the subject population. Legally they were empowered to engage in preemptive buying and, to some extent, they did force their peasants to sell them a portion of their cattle and grain products. It was especially in connection with such grains as hops, which were required for the seigneurial monopolies in brewing and selling beer, that the lords forced their peasants to sell to them exclusively. On the other hand, the Upper Austrian peasantry, beginning in the fifteenth century, became deeply involved in the Central European manufacture and trade in the raw materials and semifinished products of the textile and metal putting-out systems. The peasant population of the Mühlviertel and the Hausruckviertel in western Upper Austria, for example, had established contact with putters-out and textile, hat, and clothing manufacturers in Bavaria while the peasants in the Alpine foothills south of the city Steyr formed an important link in the metal trade between eastern and western Central Europe. Seigneurial influence remained weak in these rural industries until the seventeenth century. Agriculture; salt and metal ore mining; wood product, glass, paper, ceramic, textile, and tool manufacture were the chief sources of wealth for the Upper Austrian peasantry and in all of these pursuits they were, in the sixteenth and seventeenth centuries, relatively free from seigneurial and state interference.

Population growth, peaking first in the fourteenth century and again in the seventeenth, contributed to this economic pluralization; at the same time, it was population growth that increasingly attracted the attention of the authorities to the peasant economy. By 1600 population growth, interacting with economic processes and the development of Austrian bureaucratic capitalist estate management, forced the development of the peasant social system into a new and more controlled framework of status and social competition.

The locations and shapes of Upper Austria's fields tell the story of this medieval and early modern population growth. Along the Danube in the area around Linz and Eferding and stretching down to the Mondsee was the oldest agrarian regime, from before the eleventh century, and it consisted mainly of irregular open fields. Indicative of later settlement and of a more highly developed agricultural technology were the regularly long and adjacent open field strips that fill out the remaining area south of the Danube, which was divided into western and eastern quarters known respectively as Hausruckviertel and Traunviertel.

In the area to the north of the Danube, the greater western part of which was known as Mühlviertel and the lesser as Machland, the clearing process (*Rodung*) of the twelfth and thirteenth centuries left different patterns. Reaching into the wooded hills of the extreme north and surrounding the monastery Schlägl as well as the city of Freistadt were smaller and only partially planned irregular clearings. The later clearings of the thirteenth and early fourteenth centuries that developed more fully the area around Freistadt were major operations financed and supervised by secular and ecclesiastical magnates and stretched in broad adjacent strips from settlements along roads and streams to the edge of the woods. Scattered throughout the four quarters, either to take advantage of mountain terrain or to fill out older areas of settlement, there were isolated farmsteads whose location and field shapes were completely irregular. Three-field crop rotation spread through the entire Upper Austrian area early in the Middle Ages and remained the most prevalent form of exploitation until the nineteenth century. Slash and burn and two-field rotation were of considerable importance well into the seventeenth century but particularly so during the periods of population growth and resettlement of the sixteenth and early seventeenth centuries when the peasant population made sporadic and uncontrolled expansions into the woodlands along the Bohemian frontier.

Although Upper Austria also experienced the population decline of what has become known as the Malthusian Renaissance, the temporary depopulation of the countryside caused no disruptions of the various agrarian regimes that had become established during the high Middle Ages. Upper Austria's peasantry, even though diminished in numbers, continued to put to the plough or use for pasture as much of the available land as possible, if only on an annually variable ad hoc basis. The period of abandoned farmsteads (*Wüstungen*) which lasted from the 1370s to about 1500 seems to have been not only a pause in but also a formative part of the essentially dynamic and increasingly complex relationship between Upper Austria's land and people. It was a period of blurred boundaries, land seizures, and encroachments and when it ended both the nobility and peasantry were more highly stratified than before.[30] In the sixteenth century, Upper Austria's population recommenced a moderately accelerating increase that lasted well into the modern period.

Between the late sixteenth century and the first official Austrian census in 1771, Upper Austria's rural population increased from about 300,000 to nearly 600,000.[31] Behind this increase there lies a complex demographic history of which the general outlines are visible. The baptismal entries in the parish registers of Upper Austria suggest that despite the turmoil and warfare of this period the rural population's increase through births (and, probably, immigration) maintained a persistent upward trend.[32] Because the history of the parish priests in the early seventeenth century was particularly tumultuous, these parish data require corroborating evidence and much further investigation which goes beyond the scope and intent of this study.[33]

The construction of new housing in the territory confirms as well, however, an increase in the population of both cities and countryside for the period in question. For example, the city of Wels experienced a building boom by going from 453 houses in 1576 to 552 in 1626. This last figure dropped sharply to 533 in the period of peasant warfare, 1626 to 1627, and was not reached again until 1880.[34] Similarly, but on a smaller scale, the parish village St. Georgen in the Hausruckviertel went from seven to eleven houses between the mid-fourteenth century and 1558 and to seventeen by 1610. St. Georgen was not ever a particularly noteworthy village and was not a primary target for settlers in this period. If we consider, however, that in 1718 there were only twenty-five and in 1947 thirty houses there, then its period of most intensive growth occurred during the late sixteenth and early seventeenth centuries.[35] The salt-mining area in the south of Upper Austria displayed similar growth during this period. In 1610, for example, a saltworkers' settlement began at the southern tip of the Traunsee with four multifamily dwellings; by 1641 there were twenty-six houses (not all of the apartment type) and by 1646 a total of thirty-two.[36]

A preliminary survey of demographic sources suggests that during the late sixteenth and the early seventeenth centuries Upper Austria's population growth accelerated quite sharply and the territory's resources came under increasing pressure. At the turning of the seventeenth century Upper Austria's population had increased sufficiently to expand beyond the previous boundaries of cleared land under cultivation. Upper Austria's magnates seized and enclosed large portions of traditionally common forest and meadow lands and the peasantry resisted throughout the sixteenth and seventeenth centuries with protracted lawsuits and with violent land seizures of their own.[37] In the Mühlviertel a new wave of clearings pushed back the woods along the southern edge of the Bohemian forest. A fact-finding expedition conducted by the neighboring seigneurial authorities of Weinberg and Freistadt uncovered 133 new (and unauthorized) farmsteads that had been broken out of the forest since 1560.[38] The places of origin of some of these new settlers reveal that migration was an important demographic characteristic of Upper Austria's peasantry in this period. Sixty-three of the homesteaders came from the neighboring woodlands of Upper and Lower Austria, six from Bohemia, four from Upper Austria's metal-manufacturing belt between Kirchdorf and Steyr, four from German areas (the Upper Palatinate, Landshut, and Kassel) and one each from Styria, the Tyrol, Ybbs in Lower Austria, and Switzerland.[39]

The volume of property transactions suggests further that population mobility was not only present at the fringe areas of settlement but was also of some significance in areas of older settlement. For example, of the tenancies of the seigneurial estate Windhag, whose number fluctuated around a total of 400, 141 changed hands more than twice in sales transactions in the period between 1600 and 1650.[40] Between May 1612 and May 1614, sales of tenures (in effect, real estate sales) for Windhag totalled seventy-seven, between April 1617 and April 1618 there were seventy-four such transactions, and between April 1621 and April 1622 there were eighty-two.[41] Other Upper Austrian estates also show such high sales turnover in tenures for this period.[42] The most complete records of such sales available for this period were preserved in the archives of the monastery Garsten and these not only confirm the generally lively condition of the real estate market but also indicate that its greatest activity occurred in the period between the turning of the seventeenth century and the 1620s.[43] Figure 1 illustrates, albeit on the basis of a perhaps too small number of data, the trend characteristics of these transactions during the early seventeenth century. These transactions represent to some degree property turnovers associated with speculation but for the most part they reflect the movement of people within Upper Austria as well as that of migrants into and out of the area.

The reasons for all this movement were varied and intermingled. In the period between the Religious Peace of Augsburg in 1555 and the Peace of Westphalia of 1648, when the principle of "cuius regio, eius religio" engaged the magnates and princes of central Europe in a competitive struggle for parishes and parishioners, there were many who were forced to migrate to follow the changing fortunes of their churches. Others combined religious reasons with economic ones and sought economically as well as confessionally more advantageous loca-

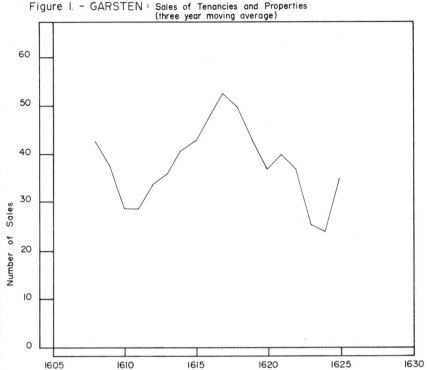

Figure I. - GARSTEN : Sales of Tenancies and Properties
(three year moving average)

tions.[44] In some cases the search for greater "freedom," i.e.,
for a legally defined better personal status, prompted migration
and resettlement by itself.[45] After the peasant war of 1626 the
migration out of Upper Austria reached such proportions that
in the midst of the general population increase some homesteads
were temporarily abandoned.[46] When we place all these in and
outflowing migrants and settlers alongside the commercial and
peasant teamsters, private carriers and messengers, seasonally
itinerant laborers, wandering craftsmen, cattle drovers, horse
traders, gypsies, and "beggars" that populated Upper Austria's
traffic lanes, then the dynamic and mobile character of the population as a whole emerges clearly. Upper Austria's population
at the end of the sixteenth and at the beginning of the seven-

41

teenth centuries was not only increasing but it was also in a state of turbulence and turnover.

The intense pressure of people on the limited absorptive capacity of a mixed agricultural and rural manufacturing economy that we witness in many areas of Europe, including Upper Austria, during the late eighteenth and early nineteenth centuries was still some way off. It seems apparent, however, that by the early seventeenth century the land above the Enns had experienced and was still reacting to its first shock of early modern population growth. Population growth helped change the basic conditions of social life and affected the competition for class and status. It has been suggested by Eckart Schremmer, in a concise posing of the most important questions in this regard, that population increase was involved in a complicated and mutually changing relationship with the exercise of authority through seigneurial agrarian constitutions, with the relative growth of the agricultural, manufacturing, and service sectors of the rural economy and, finally, with changes in the social status structure of the peasantry.[47] In neighboring Bavaria, which is Schremmer's area for study, estate administration responded to this population growth by breaking up its tenant farms into small plots and creating a great class of tenant cottagers who became the labor force in the putting-out industries in textiles that were under the economic and social supervision of the estate owners and their managers. In Upper Austria estate owners responded rather less flexibly and maintained their tenant farms intact and this produced a rather more limited, competitive, and psychologically stressful development of peasant society in the early modern period.

~ CHAPTER 2 ~

The Basic Characteristics
of Rural Households

TRAVELLERS have long been impressed by the stately peasant houses that dapple the landscape throughout the borderlands where Germany, Czechoslovakia, and Austria converge. Even today, the Upper Austrian countryside's most striking features are the single farmsteads from which cleared fields radiate in various asymmetrical patterns. The panoramas that offer themselves around every bend in the road, especially in the foothill regions to the south and in the worn mountain ranges of the north, give a first impression of a tranquil and ancient landscape long in the hands of a dispersed and individualistic civilization of farmers. There are also cottages, inns, and workshops and irregularly shaped clusters of less than a half dozen houses or so and occasionally larger hamlets occur where roads cross, streams merge, where mountain rapids provide hydraulic energy, and where once secular and ecclesiastical lords had their dwellings and sanctuaries; but the most prevalent structure is the solitary farmhouse consisting of a two-storied square or U-shaped structure enclosing a large courtyard open to the sky. With its walls of stone or whitewashed wattle, a roof of red tile or straw, and an arching gateway, the traditional rural house of this region has the appearance and feeling of a stronghold.

If we imagine away the cement "chalet" houses that modern farmers have been building for themselves alongside their older residences as well as the gray stucco "street villages" with which working and middle class families have populated the countryside near larger towns since the 1940s, then we can begin to imagine the landscape as it must have been around 1600. The fields and woods are much the same now as then but arguments have recently developed concerning how much we can deduce about the farm dwellings of the early modern period from those still in existence today. The "old" farmhouses of the present were built for the most part during the eighteenth and nineteenth centuries, it is true, but the chief difference between them and even older structures appears to have been in the substitution of stone for wood and of tile for straw, in the enlarging of older structures and in changes in stylistic details.[1] The locations of the farmsteads have remained unchanged since the late medieval and early modern periods and the building shapes as well as their fundamental architectural features are accurate reflections of what existed during the period under examination here. Moreover, we must recall that the architectural "style leaders" of the sixteenth and seventeenth centuries were the great farmhouses (*Meierhöfe*) from which the farming operations (and such other enterprises as fishpond management, beer-brewing, cattle-feeding, tile manufacture, etc.) associated with the new forms of early modern estate management were conducted. These estate farms, four-square enclosures often measuring over fifty yards a side, became the model for early modern tenant-owners and it is this style that is only now, in the post-1945 period, going out of fashion.[2]

The Upper Austrian farmhouse of the early modern period is central to this study. Isolated from neighboring farms, inward-looking, combining living quarters for one or more households with servants' quarters, baking ovens, threshing floors, well and laundry rooms, stables, haylofts, toolsheds, storage lofts, and cellars for preserves and wines and ciders, workshops and spaces for "industrial" enterprises, the house and courtyard were the focus for the economic, social, and emotional life of this rural population. The only buildings that usually stood outside the farmhouse square were the granary (*Kasten*) and, if the house enterprises were successful and if the need arose, the cottage (*Auszughaus*) to which the stem family elders moved after they had passed the farm and main house to their heir. Who these elders were we shall examine in a moment but a consideration of the question whether their existence "outside"

was an expulsion or a liberation from the main house will have
to wait until later in this study.

THE HOUSECOMMUNITY: INDIVIDUALS, FAMILIES, AND HOUSEHOLDS

Recent work by Professor Michael Mitterauer of Vienna has
given us a clearer picture of the numbers and kinds of individuals
who inhabited the Austrian peasant house around 1600 and of
what their kin and other relationships were.[3] In the absence of
state census materials for this period he resorted to the records
produced by the Counter-Reformation's attempts to keep track
of church attendance per household. From the point of view of
this study his analysis of the soul inventories of the parishes
Berndorf (the *Liber status animarum*, 1649) and Dorfbeuern
(the *Liber animarum parochiae Burensis*, 1648) provide information that is of particular value. The two parishes, located
north of the city of Salzburg in the Salzburg-Upper Austrian
borderlands, reproduce fairly accurately the types of communities from which the data analyzed in the following pages
originate and we shall consider them as Upper Austrian communities. Berndorf parish consisted of a village surrounded by
farm country where single houses or small constellations of
houses predominated. One hundred and eighty-one of the parish's 231 houses were country houses. Dorfbeuern parish on
the other hand consisted almost completely of three villages and
their suburbs. The two parishes were contiguous and their chief
towns only about five kilometers apart, but the family and
household characteristics displayed in the contents of the two
"soulbooks" differ considerably and reflect the economic differences between a predominantly wealthy and agricultural
Berndorf and a relatively poor and industrial Dorfbeuern. This
kind of divergence was common throughout German Austria,
including the Upper Austrian areas to the east of Salzburg.
Looking ahead, we must consider that not only were agricultural
and industrial neighborhoods of Upper Austria intermixed but
that the same intermixture existed within the province's peasant
houses themselves.

The individuals who inhabited the houses could do so as

individuals, as members of a nuclear family or other kin dyad and, finally, as members of a household. Together all of these made up what may be called the "housecommunity." The term is Professor Mitterauer's (Max Weber also used it) and describes most accurately the mixture of relationships that made the inhabitants of the house a unit. The house, its courtyard and outbuildings were the "theater" in which the members of the housecommunity played out their various roles. Other terms such as "co-resident group," "houseful," or "houseyard"[4] might also have been used but none of these captures the physical, social, and emotional character of the Austrian peasant house and what went on in and around it.

The average size of the housecommunity in "rural" Berndorf parish was, at 7.7 individuals, larger than that of the "urban" Dorfbeuern parish with an average of 5.9 individuals. The size of the housecommunity in the two parishes breaks down as follows:

TABLE 2.1
Housecommunity Size

Number of inhabitants per house	Percentage of houses	
	Berndorf (1649)	Dorfbeuern (1648)
1 to 5	30.3%	46.7%
6 to 10	50.2	49.7
11 to 15	15.2	3.6
16 to 20	2.6	—
21 to 25	1.4	—

Clearly the Upper Austrian housecommunities were generally quite large; the housecommunities of rural parishes were simply larger than those in or near villages where, in this case, only two houses out of 167 boasted twelve inhabitants. In Berndorf four houses out of 231 had more than twenty inhabitants.

The occurrence of nuclear families, i.e., of married couples and their unmarried children, as the sole inhabitants of a house was relatively rare in this society, especially in the more rural regions. While 35 percent of the housecommunities of Dorfbeuern consisted of a nuclear family alone, only 13 percent of the Berndorf housecommunities were of this nature. Nuclear families do not seem to have been overly large in either of the parishes. Berndorf's average nuclear family consisted of 5.25 individuals and Dorfbeuern's of 5.35; 81 percent of Berndorf's and 75 percent of Dorfbeuern's nuclear families had four children or less.[5]

While the large nuclear family did not exist and the nuclear family alone did not predominate in the housecommunities of early modern Austria, its basis, namely the married couple, played a most significant role. Ninety-one percent of the housecommunities in Berndorf were headed by a married couple; for Dorfbeuern this figure was 96.4 percent. Only 5.6 percent of the Berndorf housecommunities and 2.4 percent of those of Dorfbeuern were headed by a single male; the figures for housecommunities headed by a single woman were even smaller at 3.5 percent and 1.2 percent respectively. In a later chapter we will consider why the married couple at the head was the single most important unit in the house.

A number of other individuals, both kin and nonkin, made up the housecommunities' remaining populations. Kin were present in the following percentages of housecommunities:

TABLE 2.2
Composition of Housecommunities

| Houses | Percentage | |
	Berndorf	Dorfbeuern
with children	81.4%	82.0%
with stem family elders	29.9	3.0
with other kin	16.5	2.4

As Mitterauer points out, "children" may be a misleading term in this usage for it included people who were well past the age of childhood and even of adolescence but who continued to live in their parental housecommunity. Mitterauer's data also show that few "children" past their late twenties (and virtually none past thirty) remained in their *original* housecommunities. Stem family elders (*Auszügler*) were former heads of the house who had yielded the property and headship to a married couple of the next generation and had moved into an area of the main house or into a separate cottage on the farm designated for this purpose. There they continued to draw on the housecommunities' resources while at the same time building a separate household and living a relatively independent life. Their role in the families and households of the other members of the housecommunities was varied and complicated and will be the subject of further examination below. The fact that the wealthier rural houses of Berndorf could support much greater numbers of stem family elders and other kin is highly suggestive and will also be the subject for further investigation.

Lodgers and servants made up the remaining membership of the rural housecommunities. Fifty-six percent of Berndorf's houses had servants and 38.5 percent had lodgers; of Dorfbeuern's houses only 34.1 percent had servants and 24 percent housed lodgers. It is of some interest to note that in Berndorf the number of houses with more than one lodger (32.9 percent of the total number of houses) far exceeded those with only one (only 5.6 percent of the total number of houses); in Dorfbeuern, where housecommunities were smaller in general, 12.6 percent of all houses had one lodger while 11.4 percent had more than one. The distribution of the servant population followed a similar pattern. There was more room for servants in the single farmstead housecommunities of the rural areas than in the smaller urban and semiurban houses.

Servants and lodgers performed most of the labor connected with farming and rural industries and it was to a housecommunity's advantage to maintain as large a laboring population as it could use and afford. Lodgers could marry and their children played an important role as well. There is an important functional continuum that runs from childhood to servant and

TABLE 2.3
Distribution of Servants

Number of servants per house with servants	Percentage of houses with servants	
	Berndorf	Dorfbeuern
1	43.0%	59.0%
2	32.8	29.5
3	13.3	9.8
4	2.3	1.6
5 or more	8.7	—

lodger status that is as socially significant as the continuum that connects certain childhoods with the headship of the house and, eventually, with the status of stem family elders.

The combinations of family units and individuals that made up the early modern housecommunities of rural Austria could be, within the boundaries of the data presented here, immensely varied. However, rather than explore further the possible variations of individual social types and types of possible relationships within the housecommunity, this study seeks to understand some of the legal, economic, social, and political institutions and impulses that governed the life courses and life chances of the members of the peasant housecommunities. The data from Mitterauer's study of the "soulbooks" provide a sufficient catalog of individuals and of the fundamental family, social, and economic relationships that existed within the housecommunity. To get beyond simply more and more detailed structural taxonomies of "co-resident groups" and beyond the suggestive but finally not really usable "developmental cycle" concept of the family it might be useful to get away from structural and demographic analyses of the family altogether.

In an article directly connected with the study of families in recent history but possessing more general implications, Professor Tamara Hareven has recently explored the individual's transitions into and out of family roles with the aid of a distinction between "individual time, family time, and historical time."[6] For her, individuals have a "life-course" that may be traced and whose successes and failures may yield a number of important insights, not only into the family, but into other issues of social history as well. As attention is focused on the varieties and details of family life and on the interactions between individuals and families, the "family" as a singular object of study begins to lose ground. Such fixed concepts as "family structure" and even the more flexible and dynamic idea of the "family developmental cycle" all appear to be inadequate for coming to grips with the fluid relationships that constitute the "families" one actually finds in the sources. Problems of geographical mobility, temporary residency, and role changes, for example, make the kind of regularity demanded by "phases" in a cycle virtually impossible to trace. To cope with this variety, social historians are inevitably forced into family linkage and reconstitution studies that follow the flow of individuals into and out of families and family roles.[7] But determining the various individuals' kinship relations to families does not yet tell us anything about their legal, economic, occupational, and other role positions in both their families and their housecommunities. It is particularly the problem of the "role" that wreaks havoc with notions of family structure, cycles, and demographic limits on social development.[8] Discussions of a "dominant" family structure or type become obsolete if our focus of inquiry shifts to the nature and the determinants of the several positions individuals may occupy simultaneously in relation to the several other individuals, families, and households that make up the housecommunity.

The direction taken in this study to begin to understand these complicated interrelations takes us away from the census data and demographic information with which Professor Mitterauer has so greatly expanded our knowledge of the housecommunities' populations. While the ultimate interpretive focus of this study will remain on the peasant housecommunity, the analytical focus for the remainder of this chapter and for much of the next several chapters will be the "household." We must recognize that it was individuals and nuclear family units within the housecommunity who formed separate and, occasionally, overlapping households and that it is an analysis of these households within the larger unity that allows us to go far beyond a description of the inhabitants of the house. By household analysis I mean a study of how individuals and nuclear family units as well as housecommunities owned and allocated their resources; the purpose of such study is to arrive at a different description of the housecommunity's material constitution and to open up questions concerning the allocation of property and wealth and of decision-making power within families and housecommunities. It raises, moreover, more general questions concerning the nature of wealth and property in this early modern rural society and how these functioned to channel and determine the quality of human relations.

Such movements of resources within and between families and housecommunities add another dimension to the "life-course" concept and the interaction of the various kinds of "time" that Professor Hareven has introduced into the study of family history. For example, Professor Hareven's life-course concept, which is clearly derived from Erik Erikson's ideas on life-stages and identity-forming crises, seems to be echoed in Peter Berger's discussion of family and individual "life plans," which are an individual's and a family's response to a number of "life careers" available in any given society. This view, explicitly based on George Herbert Mead's ideas about an adaptive and conflict-free identity development, sees the family as "a life-planning workshop" in which individual and family life plans are negotiated and integrated continually to achieve what Professor Berger calls a "grand totalization of all the relevant timetables."[9] The formulation of "life plans" is a crucial aspect of a "life-course" and thinking about individuals and families from this perspective contributes an element of self-idealization and awareness that is not contained in the life-course concept alone. In order to avoid a conflict-free and falsely universalistic view of the family and to do justice to the problems of individual,

51

family, and historical time we ought, however, to modify Berger's use of the "life plan" and ask such questions as the following: "Whose life plans achieved precedence in the family's timetables?" and "In support of whose life plans were the material and spiritual resources of families and housecommunities invested, and what was the result?" It is to these questions that the analysis of household inventories in the following chapters is directed.

By combining information from Professor Mitterauer's inventories of souls with information from inventories of peasants' possessions we can begin to develop some answers to the questions posed at the very outset concerning a social history of the rural population of Austria under developing Habsburg absolutism. Not only was the house the real focus of everyday social life but it was the focus of state ideology and policy as well. Moreover, the relationships among individuals, families and households in the housecommunity take us to one of the central concerns of social history, namely, an understanding of the changing nature and quality of human relationships. This line of thinking leads to a rediscovery of the existential and psychological problems that are always present in any investigation of family and individual life and that remain completely or partially repressed in discussions of "family structures" and their "developmental cycles."[10] For example, Lutz Berkner, in his discussion of the Austrian peasant family's developmental cycle in the eighteenth century, has broached this subject with evidence that suggests that there existed what he calls "psychological strain" between a prospective heir and the parents who owned the tenant farm and house and that this strain increased as the heir reached maturity and wanted to marry. In his view the stem family, the product of an *inter vivos* inheritance agreement whereby the elders in effect "retired" and turned the holding over to the heir who could then marry and begin a nuclear household, functioned to relieve this tension.[11]

The growing strain between tenant and designated heir no doubt existed as a part of the emotional life of an early modern peasant family and of the housecommunity of which it was a part. I shall refer to it again, but must point out at the beginning that Berkner's view of intergenerational tension does not reveal the real sources for nor the other, perhaps more dangerous and even harmful, tensions in the personal and psychological life of the housecommunity. For example, early modern folk tales and anecdotes from rural Central Europe contain a record of infanticides, parental murder-suicides, self-mutilations, rapes, abandonments, and other forms of abusive behavior and they make it abundantly clear that some very serious "strains" other than those between incumbent and heir were tearing at the various members of the peasant housecommunity.[12] Although the social psychology of the Austrian peasantry is not the primary focus of this study, the materials investigated below also require us, as we shall see, to take up this theme of "psychological strain." However, our approach to this problem will be based on a broader investigation into the various positions among members of the peasant housecommunity and, rather than leading to a discussion about the competition between tenants and their heirs, it requires us to focus on the differing and conflicting roles individuals, family, and household units played in the housecommunity.[13] What finally takes us back to the social history of the Habsburg state is the discovery that these emotional strains in the family were not simply a "natural" or "universal" aspect of all family life but that they resulted from historical changes in the power relationships between the authorities and their prince and reflected the new norms and role expectations imposed on the inner life of the housecommunity by the state apparatus.

The Household Inventories

Just as the Upper Austrian estate owners held the Habsburgs' estates in lien under conditions of impartibility and emphyteusis, so their peasant tenants held their farms under the same conditions. Household inventories were an essential part of such conditions of tenure. The landlords used them to enforce their control over their properties and to ensure that the incumbent tenants did not let their properties go to waste. When an inventory was taken at the death of a tenant or his wife and the total liens against the couple were greater than the total assets of the farm, a landlord usually declared that tenant bankrupt (*crida*) and could remove the surviving members of the family from the holding. Inventories were primarily, then, legal instruments with which the landowners asserted their control over their properties; as we shall see, these conditions of tenure enforced by the inventories introduced serious limits on the social and economic status possibilities of individual members of the subject population. The inventories, however, served the members of the tenant class as well by defining and maintaining the economic and social status differences that separated them from the nontenants.

Many of the administrative documents preserved in the estate archives of Upper Austria demonstrate clearly that peasant life there during the early modern period was, as elsewhere, a life of conflict and competition, pride and envy. When, in the sixteenth century, Upper Austrian estate administrations compelled their subjects to accept a more uniform legal status as hereditary tenants and subjects and created more highly developed judicial and bureaucratic institutions on their estates, they did so in part to pacify their peasantry and to divert potentially or actually violent conflicts into supervised arbitration and legal channels. The most serious of all the critical events that could spark conflict among the subject population was the death of a tenant and the subsequent disposition of his farm and goods among the heirs. It was therefore also in part to ease the tensions associated with death and disputed inheritance that the recording of detailed household inventories emerged as an important weapon in the bureaucratic arsenal of Upper Austria's seigneurial estates in the second half of the sixteenth century.

Inventories after the death of a householder were an essential part of administering such other family institutions as marriage and stem family arrangements. Marriage contracts, for example, most often stipulated that in the event of either spouse's death, the estate would be equally divided between the surviving spouse on the one hand and the children (or other designated heirs) on the other. To carry out this kind of division, an inventory of the estate became necessary. Inheritance that was associated with stem families required inventories of the "retired" parents' goods after one or another of them died. Inventories were an essential element in determining and recording the financial responsibility of godparents and guardians. They were an opportunity to record the liens outstanding against the household as well as the moneys owing to the household. They were, finally, the means by which the estate managers and their representatives determined the size of the transfer fines on the estate of the deceased to which the lord, both as owner of the tenancy and as legal political overlord, was entitled. Any single one of these reasons was sufficient for an inventory-taking. For example, if we examine the records of the estate Frankenburg in the period 1609-1624 it is apparent that no transfer fines were collected and yet no fewer than 181 inventories were drawn up in that period.[14] Their purpose was to enforce the lord's control over his leases and to assist in the execution of marriage contracts and inheritance dispositions. After 1624 there is a gap in the Frankenburg inventories but when these resume in 1630 we find that the collection of transfer fines (*Freigeld*) had been added to the inventories' several purposes.[15] The inventories were a many-sided bureaucratic tool that undoubtedly contributed toward a pacification and regulation of peasant family and social life in the early modern period; they were also the obvious means of surveillance of the peasant householders' affairs and of determining the continuing viability of a tenant family's incumbency.

A clue concerning the political significance of inventories is contained in the peasants' protests in the 1594-1597 Upper Austrian rebellion regarding when transfer fines were to be collected and what items should be listed for such taxation. The implicit point of contention was that the household inventory was admittedly a necessary administrative tool but it also meant a complete and undesirable disclosure of an individual householder's personal and communal activities as producer, consumer, employer, creditor, and debtor. From the point of view of estate management we can understand the necessity of such surveillance. Austrian estate managers practiced, by the end of the sixteenth century, a form of estate mercantilism that required increased accountability and predictability. By linking the inventories with taxation and fair property division in inheritance, their actual policing function was obscured. The regularizing of peasant inheritance practices and the elimination of family quarrels over property were essential functions of the inventories but even those "ordering" functions ultimately benefited the estates' owners and managers more than they did the peasant families. The passion and violence that traditionally accompanied quarrels over the exchange of property and money were, in the eyes of estate management, wasteful.

This study is based on information obtained from household inventories but it is not a recent original idea to investigate household inventories to gain insight into the everyday lives of a "historical" peasantry. In sixteenth- and seventeenth-century Austria, such penetration was the reason for the inventories' existence in the first place.

Included here (see the Appendix to this chapter) is an inventory drawn up for the estate magistracy of Frankenburg in 1613.[16] It is worth examining for two reasons. First, it displays the typical formulary praxis for inventory-taking that had developed in Upper Austria by this period. The parties involved in the transaction, both on part of the estate administration and on behalf of the family and representatives of the deceased, the various kinds of property and their value, the liens against the household as well as the loans still outstanding, and its actual disposition, all appear clearly and prominently and may be taken in at a glance. The majority of the inventories I examined conformed to this model despite the fact that they came from different estates and were drawn up by a wide variety of individual officials; such uniformity attests to the high degree of professionalization of the managers and administrative assistants of the estates. Preserved for easy retrieval and perusal in large leather-bound volumes, the inventories were clearly not merely intended to record data and contracts for the regulation of peasant property settlements but also to assess the changing capacity of and activities on the tenant farms. For example, when the estate authorities determined that the valuation of a property was too high, as was the case with the example I present here, this judgment was based on past evaluations recorded in past inventories.[17] The precise extent to which the various administrations used the inventories for purposes of historical evaluation is impossible to determine. On occasion I turned pages in a volume of inventories from which fell the pounce that had dried the ink over three and a half centuries ago—an occurrence that suggests that not all inventories were used for later reference.

Most significant, from the point of view of this study, is that in the example presented here the farmstead continues in the same family's hands. Had the assets of the deceased's estate not been more than the liens against it then the estate manager of Frankenburg could have invoked the principle of emphyteusis, declared the family's tenure void, ordered them off the farm, and sold it to a new tenant. The relative difference between assets and debits is small and this results in a very small sum that is eventually divided, in the contract that concluded most inventories, among those heirs who do not inherit the tenancy as a whole. It was clearly to the advantage of the chief heir, in this case the widower, to balance a fairly high amount of debts against an estate's value. How such calculations of tenure, indebtedness, and inheritance worked and what they meant for the social and economic relationships in peasant households will be analyzed in later chapters at some length.

This particular inventory also represents a type of household that is of particular interest to this study. Unlike the use made of peasant household inventories by other researchers,[18] my purpose is to describe, on the basis of 867 inventories, several economic, occupational, and social groups among the Upper Austrian peasantry.[19] The inventory I have chosen for closer examination here allows me to demonstrate particularly well how I determined, by examining household goods and properties, the membership of an individual in one or another of these groupings.

Reading through the inventory that was recorded after Barbara Khaislinger's death one can follow the tour taken by the officials responsible for the inventory-taking. Before the tour began, everyone involved in the transaction was recorded, beginning with the deceased and surviving spouses, the bailiff in charge, the assistants in the inventorying—most of whom were the bailiff's trustees but at least one of whom represented the family of the deceased—and finally the heirs and their godparents who acted as their representatives. Some of the officials as well as the widower can be identified by the form of address as men of respect in the community and, later in this study, I shall recall this feature of the inventories. The tenancy was then identified and a value placed on it. It is difficult to say why the value placed on it by the bailiff at the time of the inventory-taking was reduced by the higher estate authority but this might have been done to increase the pressure on this particular family. The real estate that went with the two tenancies named in this inventory was not described in detail as part of the inventory-taking. Since the property was permanently impartible such a description was not essential to inheritance proceedings. We can, however, on the basis of the value of the real estate attempt to make an estimate on the size of these holdings. Since a middling Upper Austrian farm was worth, during the early seventeenth century, between 300fl to 500fl and consisted of about fifty acres of arable meadows and woods,[20] then the holdings in this sample inventory must have consisted of between 125 to 175 acres. This was a substantial amount of land for a peasant of this period and suggests that farming was an important part of this household's economy. If this household's real properties show it to have been a farming operation, and, according to its value a large one at that, then other properties such as inns, mills, and smithies, and their respective values in turn provide occupational categories as well and give some measure of the household's financial commitment to a particular occupation. The value of the real (or "fixed") property is one of several subtotals that appears in the inventory. By treating this and the several other subtotals as well as the total values of the inventories comparatively, with some statistical techniques we can draw outlines of the economic character and behavior of various groupings among the peasantry.

For purposes of analysis I do not distinguish between the sexes among the tenant householders. The inventory would have been the same had the male tenant died. The tenancy and all its attachments were held as communal property by a married couple and for purposes of social status analysis there is no difference between men and women in the tenant class. There were considerable distinctions between the sexes among the nontenants and I have kept the sexes apart in that part of my analysis.

After the preliminary identifications and the valuation of the tenancy were made, the actual tour of the property began in the stables, worked its way through the implement shed, the granary, and, in this case, the room set aside for the preparation of flax. The corridors and bedrooms of the farm building's living quarters completed the tour and the final accounting took place at the kitchen table, no doubt accompanied by those staples of Upper Austrian peasant hospitality: smoked bacon, bread, and pear cider.

If the real property gave a rough indication of the major occupational focus of the household, then the list of movables, considered in detail, allows the researcher to construct a more detailed image of the occupational structure of each household. My decision concerning the economic and occupational character of each household was in many ways a difficult one but it had to be made for the sake of classifying the peasant households in occupational groupings. In the case of this household, the agricultural base of the household's economy is confirmed by the livestock and grain holdings among the movables. When a householder's inventory consisted just of farmland, livestock, and agricultural produce, I classified his or her occupational status as that of "farmer." In this particular case, however, the movables contain two further elements that are of considerable significance for defining this householder in occupational terms. In the first place, the presence of yarn and flax in various stages of processing and the several spinning wheels together suggest that this household's economy had expanded and diversified its economic base in order to participate in Upper Austria's widespread putting-out textile industry. When this form of production—which might, instead of textiles, also include such activities as shingle, pail, or spoon manufacture—was added to a substantial agricultural base, then I defined the household as that of a "diversified farmer."[21] Secondly, the relatively expensive horse and carting equipment in this inventory are evidence that this household was also involved in the transport sector of the rural economy. This was a further important diversification, one that not only involved some considerable capital outlay on part of the householder but one that also linked the household more directly to the distribution and marketing of agricultural and, possibly, industrial products. This transport function, in every case in which I encountered it, was supported by a strong agricultural basis as well as some sort of industrial diversification, and in each case where it appeared I classified that household's chief occupational function as that of teamster. In some rare cases some or all of these three functions were evident in the inventories of individuals who were, however, designated in the inventory itself as millers or as innkeepers; in those cases, as in others where the occupation of the householder was explicitly stated somewhere, I kept the classification that appears in the document. There were a number of inventories that did not specifically identify the economic function of the household nor did they contain enough information to allow me to make a plausible identification of the occupation of the householder; these do not appear in the occupation group tables that appear in the analyses below.

The lists of creditors and debtors that occupy such a prominent place in the inventories are a rich source of information about the economic as well as the social life of the Austrian peasantry. The names of the debtors and creditors as well as their locations are useful for linking kin and fictive kin relationships with credit relationships and in establishing both the business radius of individual members of the Upper Austrian peasantry[22] as well as a statistically verifiable "market region" or *Wirtschaftsraum*[23] of that peasantry as a whole. Such investigations go beyond this study and I will take them up again elsewhere. For the purpose in hand, I confine myself to using the total debts and credits in the inventories as measures of credit activity and, in correlation to the total values of fixed and movable properties, as a part of the economic profile of the various groupings among the peasantry. Working with several Upper Austrian inventories from the sixteenth century, Georg Grüll has concluded that, because several of these showed a debt that added up to more than 50 percent of their total assets, economic conditions for the peasantry as a whole were not favorable.[24] In this study I take up this theme and demonstrate that the function of debt in the peasant economy was somewhat more complex than this and that indebtedness was in most cases something other than a measure of poverty; it was rather an essential and unavoidable ingredient of economic and social success.

The variables by which I measure the ingredients of a household's or of a group of households' wealth are thus the subtotals that appear in the inventories, that is, the total value of the inventoried household, the value of the fixed goods (farms, buildings), the total value of the movables (livestock, implements, crops in storage, household goods), the moneys owed to the household, the debts against it, and the tax levied on the lot. For each household I entered these data along with the following on a computer card: the seigneurial estate under whose authority the household belonged, the year in which it was drawn up, the chief occupation to which the household was geared, the legal status (if any) of the farmstead and whether or not the household was "bankrupt" (if the debits equalled or exceeded the assets). On the basis of statistical calculations I am able to discuss several significant aspects of the appearance and use of wealth among the Upper Austrian peasantry as a whole and present economic profiles of specific economic, occupational, and family groups. In the various tables that describe these groups I use, aside from means and standard deviations, Pearson correlation coefficients. These latter appear in a correlation matrix and measure the existence of statistically significant relationships and of their direct or inverse character. The inferences I draw from these correlations focus on comparing the relationships of the ingredients of wealth and the characteristic economic activities among the various subgroups of the peasant population. It is these coefficients that help to describe the dynamics of rural economic and household life.

My choice of estate archives for inventory sources was governed by several considerations. In the first place, the estates Schaunberg, Aistersheim, Frankenburg, Windhag, and Schlägl contained the earliest large blocks of inventories from the early modern period. I looked at inventories from other estate archives as well but these were too scattered and fragmented for my purposes. Moreover, the five estates in question are representative of the new large bureaucratic capitalist enterprise under the ownership and management of members of the first and second Estates. Their peasant populations represent therefore the predominant social types in this rural population. Finally, the geographic locations of these particular estates (see map) cover the chief areas of peasant rebellions around 1600.

In summary, the Imperial bureaucracy had imposed at the end of the sixteenth century a *modus vivendi* between the Austrian estate owners and their subject peasantry that had ambiguous results: by regulating such transactions as inventory-taking it hastened that process by which the estate owners and their managers sought to bring the subject population's economic and social intercourse under the control of their estates' laws; on the other hand, it also to some extent tried to limit and gain control over the authorities' grasp on their subjects' personal affairs. The Resolution of 1597 that ended the uprising of 1595 specified, for example, that certain personal belongings such as clothing and certain of the household's equipment, in particular wagons and horses and field implements, were not to be inventoried—but from even a cursory examination of the inventories it is clear that this rule was not obeyed. It is difficult to judge with any precision the degree of independence the subject population maintained even against those rules and institutions that the estates were empowered to create and with which they tried to increase their subjects' dependence on their bureaucracies and courts. It is not inconceivable, for example, that the Upper Austrian peasantry could, on the basis of its simple and traditional means of recording purchases, sales, and payments with tally sticks,[25] maintain and enforce a complex network of credit transactions entirely without the benefit of the household inventories or the credit documents that had to be purchased from and were enforced by estate officials and courts. Morover, the actual effectiveness of the estates' laws and courts in protecting their subjects against transgressions by outsiders was severely limited and the peasant communities often had to continue to protect themselves quite apart from their estates' magistracies. Most significant with regard to the question of the relative dependence of peasant life on seigneurial institutions and bureaucratic documents is that the spread, before the decade of the 1620s, of a putting-out system of rural production in textiles, metal, and wood products in Upper Austria took place largely without the direct support or interference of seigneurial authority. This study uses household inventories to show, for example, that some of the most significant innovations in the peasantry's economic and social behavior were rooted in these independently financed and relatively unregulated rural industries. On the other hand, however, an analysis of the inventories will also show that the most successful and powerful members of the subject population were those who understood how best to exploit their simultaneous dependence on and independence from the institutions of their overlords. For these householders the inventories became instruments for social and economic advancement.

PROPERTY

The 300,000 or so peasant subjects who populated Upper Austria at the turn of the seventeenth century have appeared in the historical literature on this period as a single group. There is some value and appropriateness in this, for they were increasingly treated as "subjects," a single legal and political group, and much of their historical experience can be grasped only if we consider them in this way. At the same time, however, the overall character of this subject peasantry changed as it changed internally, as the various groupings in the peasant social system came apart and together again in new ways, and as some tensions among the vertical and horizontal strata were eased and new points of strain and pressure developed. In the following analysis, we will be concerned with these changes within the Upper

Austrian peasantry's social system and particularly with show-
ing how certain changes in the economic and occupational status
systems combined with the changes in legal status we have
already noted.

The subject peasantry of Upper Austria was poor by the standards of the time. Compared to the 4,188fl and 4,266fl that make
up the total inventory value of the two wealthiest peasant households in the inventory population under study, the complete
assets of a well-to-do burgher in a middling country market
town could total over 20,000fl[26] and there is the record of a
country squire who increased his assets from almost 30,000fl
in 1601 to over 97,000fl in 1618.[27] The fact that the two poorest
inventoried "households" in my sample, those of two servant
girls, were worth no more than 2fl and 7fl, gives some perspective on the range of abundance and poverty in this rural
society.

High and low economic status is a relative matter and there
were obviously those among the Upper Austrian peasantry who
were, compared to their fellow countrymen, wealthy and whose
wealth gave them high social status. Wealth conferred status
because it allowed those who had it to do things that those who
did not have it could not do; in my analysis I shall focus not
only on the relative levels of wealth and on the relative proportions of the ingredients of wealth at the various economic
levels, but I shall also discuss how wealth was increased, spent,
and used, for it is often this active element in wealth that confers
or withholds social status.

A description of the wealth of the entire inventory population
appears in Table 2.4. These figures demonstrate the peasants'
collective economic strength. For example, in the early seventeenth century there were approximately 40,000 official tax units
or "hearths" (*Feuerstätten*) in the entire province[28] and if this
number is multiplied by the average valuation of real property
per inventory household then we can project an estimate of
about 10,650,000fl for all peasant holdings in the province. If
we add to this a similarly estimated 4,821,000fl of movables,

TABLE 2.4

Inventory Breakdown. Total Population (867 CASES)

	Total Assets	Real Property	Movables	Loans	Debts	Freigeld
Sum	405,686	230,858	104,502	67,889	191,442	19,327
Mean	467	266	120	78	220	22
S.D.	473	257	138	198	290	31
Correlation Matrix						
Total Assets						
Real Property	.86					
Movables	.84	.73				
Loans	.66	.25	.36			
Debts	.50	.62	.42			
Freigeld	.65	.56	.57	.42	.42	

NOTE: Blank spaces in the correlation matrix signify an absence of significant correlations. All amounts in guilders.

then the total value of the Upper Austrian peasantry's properties would approximate 15,500,000fl. This is an extremely conservative estimate for not only were there more taxable households than the official number but obviously not all the individual "households" inventoried here represented a "tax unit" in the way in which this was understood by the term *Feuerstätte*. In other words, the total wealth of the entire subject population was probably much greater. Nevertheless, it is clear from even my projected total that the wealth in the hands of the peasant sector was sizable.

Wealth was above all measured in terms of real estate: tenant land and farmsteads. Even though real property was worth more than twice as much as movables, I think it is noteworthy that movable wealth was as great as these figures indicate. The most important ingredients of this movable wealth were holdings in livestock, foodstuffs, tools, and expensive personal belongings, including cash holdings and such major items as bedding and, in some cases, clothing (this despite the fact that according to the 1597 Imperial guidelines no such personal items were to be inventoried). The peasant sector of the Upper Austrian economy obviously did not suffer from a scarcity of commodities.

CREDIT

The fact that almost one-third of peasant property was in the form of commodities suggests lively marketing activity and the credit activities that appear in the inventories support this impression. Clearly, there were more debtors than creditors here. Debts exceeded loans two and one-half times and out of an inventory population of 867, 341 households were not active in any way at all as creditors while only 16 households were free of debt. This seems to verify the contention of Georg Grüll and others that the peasant of this period was crushed by indebtedness.[29] Credit relationships need not be interpreted in such a gloomy fashion, however. Instead, the sheer volume of credit transactions displayed in Table 2.4 indicates the existence of an extremely active credit market and of an obviously viable credit system. One of the major problems of a preindustrial agricultural economy is the establishment of some form of credit system that not only satisfies the capital requirements of agricultural and industrial production and marketing but also inspires confidence and widespread usage. Such a viable system clearly existed in seventeenth-century Upper Austria. Instead of merely observing that these peasants were deeply in debt, we must also examine what possibilities of economic and social action opened up for them as a result of their obviously extensive and functioning credit market. When we consider the proportion of debts in relation to assets and incomes it becomes clear that these peasants were not on the whole overly adventurous in their credit activity. Both movable and real properties as well as outstanding loans could be called on as collateral to cover debts and clearly most of the peasants in this population remained well within those margins of fiscal responsibility. In fact, their total outstanding debt amounted to less than the total value of their real estate holdings and real estate was the single most important form of collateral. In the correlation matrix in Table 2.4, the strongest correlation between outstanding debts and the other constituent elements of wealth is that between real property and debts. This suggests that the more real property a householder acquired the more prone he was to go into debt. On the other hand, it also suggests that the acquisition of more (or more valuable) property involved great indebtedness. These propositions are not mutually exclusive and probably both applied.

When Upper Austria's peasants played the role of creditors they displayed different behavior. For one thing, the strongest correlation in Table 2.4 between the extension of some form of credit and the other economic characteristics of the households is that with the total value of the households. The greater the total assets of a household became, the greater became the tendency of that householder to extend credit of some kind. The fact that there is no correlation between loans and debts suggests that those who were predominantly creditors were different from those who were primarily debtors. The breakdown of the inventory population into subgroups will reveal the debtor and creditor groups as well as those that combined both functions in their economic behavior.

A further noteworthy feature of the use of wealth among Upper Austria's peasantry is that the ownership of fixed and movable properties was closely related. The two tended to increase and decrease in a direct relationship which suggests that the acquisition by members of the subject peasantry of farmsteads alone, to the exclusion of some form of agricultural or craft or industrial activity, was not common. Although the real estate market was, as we saw, extremely active around 1600, speculation in real estate alone was clearly not a significant source of wealth among this peasantry.

The amount of taxes levied against each household is quite low. By law the transfer fine (*Freigeld*) should have averaged 10 percent of the sum of the total inventory values but instead it is only 4.8 percent. In some cases no transfer tax was collected and in most cases less than the standard 10 percent was actually levied; only rarely does more than 10 percent appear. Later in this study we will discuss the unequal distribution of the taxation of wealth as one measure of the social status of the economic and occupational groups in the inventory population.

WEALTH AND OCCUPATIONS

If we take the total inventory as a measure of the economic status level of each household, then the households can be divided into the following economic groups:

Group	Value Range (in guilders)	No. Cases
1	0-99	146
2	100-199	119
3	200-499	291
4	500-999	235
5	1,000-1,999	64
6	2,000-	12
	Total	867

The inventories of the lower groups were represented in considerable number and showed great diversity and I have compensated for this by introducing a gradient of valuation into the economic groupings.

In Table 2.4 the mean total value of 467fl was matched by three inventories in my sample but none of the values for the other economic characteristics of these three inventories corresponded to the averages in Table 2.4. As was perhaps to be expected, there is no "average" household in this population. The fact that the median total inventory value was, at 363fl, well below the mean value, suggests that the curve for the inventory population is skewed toward the lower status groups. When we compare the characteristics of the individual economic subgroups (Tables 3.1-3.6) with those of the total inventory population the relationships between means and medians change drastically and there the mean values for the total inventory value of each subgroup were virtually identical with the median values. Moreover, the standard deviations in these later tables indicate a much tighter clustering of the households around the mean, indicating more normal distributions for the subgroups than for the population as a whole. Not only does this measure verify my choice of value range for the economic status groupings but it will also serve, in later tables, as a measure of the degree of economic homogeneity of specific occupation groups.

The occupational groupings that emerge from this inventory population appear in Table 2.5 where they are cross-tabulated with the six economic groups. Several occupation groups are clearly more significant than others, either because they appear in considerable numbers or because of their particular distribution in the economic groups. With the help of this table it is possible to gain an overview of the occupational sources of wealth in the rural population. While the agrarian foundations of the economic and social structure appear prominently, it is equally clear that a large proportion of the population was engaged in some craft or industrial activity—and that some of these groups were economically better off than, say, farmers. If we count farmers, diversified farmers, cotters, vintners, and fishermen as agriculturalists and diversified farmers; teamsters, weavers, smiths, innkeepers, cobblers, turners, milliners, potters, wheelwrights, tailors, carpenters, tanners, sawmillers, cloth dyers, coopers, clockmakers, rake-makers, and pail-makers as involved in a rural industry, we obtain a ratio of 3:2 in the size difference between the former and the latter group. If we add to this the further consideration that the male and female lodger and servant population often also practiced a craft, then this part of the population contributes an additional even though unspecifiable number to the latter figure in the ratio. It is impossible to arrive at a precise figure from the inventories; however, we can say that skills and diverse opportunities for economic action other than farming existed to a considerable extent in this rural society and, while it appears that the majority of the tenant population was directly and primarily involved in agriculture, a good number of the members of the Upper Austrian peasantry were engaged in craft or industrial diversification.

An initial overview of the household inventories discloses a peasant society that was highly pluralistic. There was a wide

TABLE 2.5
Occupational and Economic Status Cross-Tabulations

Rank	Occupation	Economic Status Groups						Total	Percentage of Overall Total
		1	2	3	4	5	6		
1	Farmer (% in economic group)	1 (1)	35 (29)	172 (59)	77 (33)	2 (3)	—	287	33.1
2	Diversified Farmer	—	—	14 (5)	85 (39)	16 (28)	—	115	13.3
3	Male Lodger	54 (37)	27 (23)	16 (6)	3 (1)	—	—	100	11.5
4	Teamster	—	—	—	23 (10)	24 (38)	5 (42)	52	6.0
5	Auszügler (stem family elder)	12 (8)	9 (8)	17 (6)	8 (3)	4 (6)	1 (8)	51	5.9
6	Weaver	8 (6)	7 (6)	21 (7)	3 (1)	3 (5)	—	42	4.8
7	Female Lodger	27 (19)	3 (3)	—	—	—	—	30	3.5
8	Male Servant	9 (6)	7 (6)	1	—	—	—	17	2.0
9	Female Servant	9 (6)	3 (2)	—	—	—	—	12	1.4

		1	2	3	4	5	6		
10	Cotter	9 (6)	2 (2)	1	—	—	—	12	1.4
11	Smith	—	2 (2)	6 (2)	3 (1)	—	—	11	1.3
12	Miller	—	2 (2)	5 (2)	—	2 (1)	2 (3)	11	1.3
13	Innkeeper	—	1 (1)	—	—	5 (8)	4 (33)	10	1.2
14	Cobbler	3 (2)	4 (3)	2 (1)	—	—	—	9	1.0
15	Turner	1 (1)	2 (2)	1	3 (1)	—	—	7	.8
16	Milliner	2 (1)	2 (2)	1	1	—	—	6	.7
17	Baker	1 (1)	1 (1)	3 (1)	1	—	—	6	.7
18	Vintner	—	—	1	4 (2)	—	1 (8)	6	.7
19	Potter	1 (1)	3 (3)	—	1	—	—	5	.6
20	Wheelwright	1 (1)	—	3 (1)	—	—	—	4	.5
21	Tailor	—	—	4 (1)	—	—	—	4	.5

Table 2.5 (cont.)

Rank Occupation	Economic Status Groups						Total	Percentage of Overall Total
	1	2	3	4	5	6		
22 Fisherman	—	1 (1)	3 (1)	—	—	—	4	.5
23 Brewer	—	—	— (1)	1	2 (3)	—	3	.3
24 Lumberman	—	—	1	2 (1)	—	—	3	.3
25 Carpenter	2 (1)	—	1	—	—	—	3	.3
26 Butcher	1 (1)	—	1	—	—	—	2	.2
27 Bailiff (Richter)	—	—	—	2 (1)	—	—	2*	.2

* Note: There were several additional occupations of two or fewer numbers in the inventories, including cloth dyer, tanner, rake and pailmaker, clocksmith et al.

range of economic stratification and, as the occupational distribution suggests, this existed within housecommunities and even
households. Similarly, the wide range of occupations and their
wide distribution across economic groups reinforces the impression of diversity. It is this internal pluralism of the households
and its meaning for class and role divisions in families that
forms a chief focus of the following analysis. The "house," i.e.,
the tenant farmstead, was clearly the focus of this rural population's activities. Nothing shows this more clearly than the
level of credit development revealed by the inventories; "credit,"
as I will show below, did not merely involve borrowing and
lending activities but also expressed a wide range of family and
social activities and is an excellent source for analyzing the social
life of this rural society.

~ APPENDIX TO CHAPTER 2 ~

INVENTORY

FOLLOWING the death of Barbara, the honorable Hanns Khaislinger at Huettern's blessed wife, their common fixed and movable goods were inventoried by Thomas Mestro, bailiff of the earldom of Frankenburg and by the honorable Michael Staindl at Endtringel, Balthauser Seiringer at Cog, Wolfen Ertl at Zwispallen, and Matheusen Hueber at Oberthamperg as follows:

Heirs

Hanns Khaislinger, widower
Children: Wolf, Christof, Margaretha, Salomee and Sibilla. Their godparents are Balthauser Wezl at Wezl, Wolf Timpl at Verweng.

Fixed Property

Buildings and fields composing the Jankl and Weber Farms at Huettern were valued at 1,500fl by the assessors on behalf of the estate magistracy. But because the authorities felt that this estimate was too high by 200fl, there remain

1,300fl

Movable Property			
First a horse with harness	17fl		
four oxen	80fl		
2 steers	24fl		
7 cows	72fl		
2 calves	9fl		
8 pigs	14fl		
13 chickens		5sh	6&
All the wagons and carting equipment together	20fl		
3 iron harrows and 3 ploughs	5fl		

Wheat 1/4		4sh	
15 *metzen* (measures) rye	22fl	4sh	
4 *metzen* lentil and barley mixture	4fl	4sh	
16 *metzen* oats	10fl		
3 bags and 3 sheets of canvas	2fl		
fine yarn 14 *stren* (measure)		6sh	
yarn of medium quality 23 *stren*		5sh	26&
50 pounds of processed flax	5fl		
partially processed flax 26 pounds	1fl	2sh	12&
unprocessed flax 12 pounds		2sh	12&
4 chests	3fl		
3 spinning wheels and one spool rack		5sh	
4 axes and one handsaw	1fl	2sh	
scythes and sharpening tools	1fl		
4 madeup beds and accessories	20fl		
one grindstone	1fl		
granary equipment	1fl		
vats and barrels	2fl		
several drills and woodworking knives		6sh	
pitch		6sh	
kitchen utensils	3fl		
Total of movable property	327fl	4sh	26&

Loans

First Leinhart Hueber on Hueb	87fl		
from this principal sum one year's interest	4fl	2sh	24&

Sebastian Schmidt at Ott- nang	14fl
Harstumben at Lenzing	14fl
Herr Aichmair at Veggla- prugg	5fl

(etc., etc., a total of 11 debtors)

Total loans   164fl   2sh   24&

Debts

First owing to Christoffen at Obschachen	200fl
to Tobias Hochrainer	300fl

(etc., etc., a total of 25 creditors; 5 in the high debt range, 12 in the medium—20fl to 100fl—range, and 8 in the low debt range)

Total debts   1,466fl   2sh

There remains of the
property   325fl

According to the marriage contract prepared by the estate magistracy and brought forth here, half, i.e. 162fl, belongs to the father and the other half to the children. The father is to keep the half awarded to him without further division for the rest of his life.

Contract

The father shall take over the property and the debts and owe the children the 162fl. However, because, according to the marriage contract, the father is to retain possession of the property and also because the children are still to some extent small and without education and because he has to raise them on the farm and supply them with all necessities, the godparents have granted the father a 42fl reduction. This amount shall rest interest free until Candlemas next year and thereafter the proper interest shall be paid.

Enacted May 22 Anno 1613

~ CHAPTER 3 ~

Economic Groups

THE POOR

THE LOWEST ECONOMIC GROUP appears in Table 3.1. Seventy-three of these 146 householders did not own real property of any kind. The other 50 percent usually owned the lease on a small house and garden; some very few owned outright a small piece of independent land (*lediges Grundstück*). The "true" average value of real estate in this economic group was therefore 39fl and this corresponds much more closely to an average market valuation of a small property than the 19fl that actually appears in Table 3.1. These real estate values indicate that the property owners in this group tended to be the very small holders and cottagers who were a significant part of the work force of the Upper Austrian countryside. From Georg Grüll's previously cited study of late clearings in the woods of the Mühlviertel, where fifty-seven new homesteads were valued at up to 40fl and only twenty were more, we can guess that these properties were generally also in old marginal or newly cleared locations.[1] Over 53 percent of the properties in Table 3.1 were in the wooded hills of the Mühlviertel under the monastery Schlägl.

The occupational composition of this group, as was revealed by Table 2.5, tells a lot about it and makes some of its economic characteristics more understandable. The most numerously represented occupation consisted of male and female lodgers (*In-leute*). These were individuals who rented their quarters and

TABLE 3.1

Inventory Breakdown. Economic Group 1 (146 cases)

	Total Assets	Real Property	Movables	Loans	Debts	Freigeld
Sum	7,901	2,879	2,385	2,647	3,657	497
Mean	54	19	16	18	25	3
S.D.	25	24	11	23	21	3
Correlation Matrix						
Total Assets						
Real Property	.52					
Movables	.30					
Loans	.37	−.48	−.18*			
Debts	.47	.47	.18*			
Freigeld	.63	.34		.30	.30	

NOTE: All amounts in guilders in this and subsequent tables.
* Signifies a low significance (.05) level in this and subsequent tables.

worked as day-laborers either for their landlord or for other employers in the village or its surroundings.[2] There was also a considerable number of *Auszügler*, i.e., of stem family elders who lived with their heirs' families, as well as of male and female servants, cottagers, and weavers and individuals who represented less common craft occupations.

None of this group's properties, incomes, and expenditures involved substantial sums. Everything was on a small scale, in some cases pathetically so. The 16fl average for movables, for example, seems extremely small when we consider that it took between four to six measures of rye at a total noninflationary cost of about 3fl to provide bread for one person for a year or that a peasant from the middling groups would spend between 10fl and 20fl on a single bed or that a fair to middling pair of oxen cost over 30fl. Even though this group's commodity holdings were very low, its debts, which were in most cases consumption debts, were high. However, the ratio between extended credit ("loans") and debts is low at 1:1.4. This low ratio is similar to that of high economic status groups, but occurs with the latter for different reasons.

The amounts owed to members of this lowest status group were only rarely the result of actual loans, but tended to be unpaid wages owed by employers for daily or, in the case of servants, yearly labor. In some cases these arrears were sums owed by putters-out for piecework. In some cases, the money owed to members of this group consisted of inheritance properties still being managed by a sibling or godparent.

The correlation in Table 3.1 between total wealth and real estate holding indicates that the highest economic status in this group went to those who possessed some kind of real estate. This is further supported by the fact that as a member of this group owned more valuable real estate, the moneys owed him or her in fees or wages or inheritance declined. This inverse correlation between credits and real properties suggests that those who owned real property were self-employed or, if they worked for others, in a better position to demand payment of their fees and wages. In addition, owners of real property were more prone to go into debt. The absence of a correlation between loans and debts indicates further that those who had relatively large amounts owed to them were not in a position to contract debts themselves. This means, paradoxically, that at this lowest level of society the ability to go into debt signified higher social status than a large amount of uncollected "loans" that were a sign of great economic and social weakness. The sons and daughters of even relatively wealthy families who did not inherit the family farm or business could often end up in this lowest economic group. If they came from a wealthier family, they often inherited a piece of land or a large sum of money that was administered for a time by a sibling or a godparent. If the family's affairs were orderly and well-managed and these individuals retained some clout in their families, these lands and moneys rapidly became a part of their estates. But if individuals in this group were personally not well-connected, then their debtors and guardians were less prepared to pay them. The humble men and women of this economic stratum were at most times victims or at least potential victims both of the market and of those in positions of higher status and social authority. The *Freigeld* the estate owners levied from the poor was well above the average at 6 percent. I shall discuss the sexual and occupational divisions of this group below and there the meaning of the economic indicators I have described will emerge even more clearly and more poignantly.

TABLE 3.2
Inventory Breakdown. Economic Group 2 (119 cases)

	Total Assets	Real Property	Movables	Loans	Debts	Freigeld
Sum	16,734	8,449	3,689	4,377	8,978	873
Mean	140	71	31	36	75	7
S.D.	28	51	27	47	58	5
Correlation Matrix						
Total Assets						
Real Property	.34					
Movables						
Loans		−.75	−.27			
Debts	.29	.38		−.31		
Freigeld						

The second lowest economic group contained a much larger proportion of property owners (Table 3.2). Only 26 out of 119 inventories showed no real property at all. Almost 30 percent of the households in this group were those of small farmers and a further 23 percent were those of male lodgers (see Table 2.5). Female lodgers were a rarity here, making up only 3 percent of this group's population. Stem family elders, weavers, and male servants existed in proportions of 8, 6, and 6 percent respectively. Female servants were also rare here at 3 percent. The remaining significant occupations in this group included cobblers, potters, and a few cottagers.

The ratio between real and movable property found for all

the inventories already appears in this grouping at 2.3:1. The
ratio of debts to extended credit is at 2:1 still relatively small
but it should be noted that some important distinctions appear
here. While debts were fairly evenly distributed, relatively fewer
members of this group appear to have acted as creditors. High
economic status in this group correlated most significantly with
ownership of real property and a tendency to go into debt. There
were some notable exceptions to this. The second highest inventory in this group, for example, was that of a male lodger
from the monastery Schlägle who died in 1627. He had no real
property but his movables included 17fl in cash, 262 pounds of
wool, and hatmaker's tools. His largest debt was 50fl owed to
the estate manager (possibly a fine but also possibly some kind
of capital debt—the wool was valued at 65fl). He also had a
number of smaller consumption debts, including debts owed to
a cobbler and a tailor.[3] Another well-placed male lodger without
real property in this group, whose most important assets consisted of 165fl of outstanding loans, showed signs of some labor
diversification (scythes, spinning wheels) and also appeared as
a major debtor.[4]

The credit correlations that appear for this group in Table 3.2
are intricate but they can be explained in the following way:
the inverse relationship between real property and the sums
owed to members of this group suggests that those who owned
land were less prone to extend credit than those who did not.
Extended credit among these people still signified to a great
extent wage labor or piecework that had not yet been paid for
and from this correlation coefficient we might suppose that
owners of real property were less prone to hire themselves out
but worked their small holdings instead. Even the most highly
placed among them show relatively small amounts of extended
credit. They are, however, greater debtors as both the correlation between the total size of the inventory and debts and the
inverse correlation between debtor and creditor status demonstrate.

The members of this economic group made a living at a near-
poverty level but they had some resources and skills and managed them in diverse ways. As with those in the lowest economic
stratum these people too were potential victims of crises in the

market for two main reasons. The landless, whose incomes
stemmed from what usually amounted to a combination of agricultural labor, performance of craft skills, and industrial piecework, could not be sure of their wages at any time, but particularly at times of crisis. Those who engaged in some kind of
sustenance agriculture were generally burdened with enormous
consumption debts that were called in during times of crisis by
creditors who were often trying to pay off their own creditors.
Clearly, the individuals thus called on in this economic group
were not creditors themselves who could in turn pass their
economic emergencies on to an even lower body of debtors.

MIDDLING PEASANTS

Group three described in Table 3.3 was predominantly a group
of farmers (59 percent) who engaged in livestock and grain
farming both for their own consumption as well as for the
market. Only 20 households out of a total of 291 owned no real

TABLE 3.3
Inventory Breakdown. Economic Group 3 (291 cases)

	Total Assets	Real Property	Movables	Loans	Debts	Freigeld
Sum	100,205	61,539	25,934	12,378	61,918	4,801
Mean	344	211	89	42	212	16
S.D.	83	96	46	79	258	14
Correlation Matrix						
Total Assets						
Real Property	.60					
Movables	.53	.24				
Loans		−.66	−.27			
Debts	.17	.27	.13*	−.24		
Freigeld	.30	.20	.13*			

property at all in this group. Of the top third of this group only one householder owned no real property and that was an *Auszügler* from the estate Frankenburg who was extremely active as creditor.[5] Next to weavers at 7 percent, the *Auszügler* appeared in some force at 6 percent. Even some male lodgers (but no female ones) were in this group, comprising 6 percent of it. Diversified farmers, i.e., those who were both farmers and linked as producers or processors to Upper Austria's rural industries, appear to have been a minority in this group at 5 percent. Significantly, they form the core of the next higher economic group.

The ratio between real and movable property in Table 3.3 conforms to the average in Table 2.4 of 2.4:1 and both elements of a household's overall wealth were evenly distributed among this group's population. The ratio between sums owed to members of this group and debts they incurred takes a leap in favor of the latter. Debts were five times greater than extended credit. This group depended on credit for economic survival and was only in a limited way able to extend credit to others. High economic status in this group was firmly established on the basis of both real and movable properties that in turn correlated with each other. The correlations also show that higher economic status and in particular increased holdings in real property were accompanied by the increased use of credit or, stated in another way, by increased dependence on credit. A survey of the inventories shows that debts ranged from high capital debts to smaller consumption debts. This is to be expected from a group that has generally committed itself to narrowly defined agricultural specialization and produced rye and cattle for the market.

There are several interesting inverse correlations in Table 3.3. The greater the values of real and movable properties in a household the smaller were the sums owed to those households. These inverse correlations between real property and loans and to a lesser degree between movable properties and loans are further supported by the inverse correlation between debts and loans.

83

This suggests that householders at this economic level who were
borrowing heavily were not the same as those who were able
to extend credit. Those who had invested in the means of agricultural production did not have the moneys for loans nor
could they wait too long for payments since they needed cash
incomes to meet their own obligations. At the lower levels of
this economic group, individuals were still working for wages
and these appear as well in the loans column. Also, among the
poor and propertyless in this group there appear in the loans
column inheritance settlements that had not yet been paid to
them and this contributes further to their apparent "creditor"
status. As a whole, this economic status group, particularly its
farming members, was potentially both a beneficiary as well as
a victim of the market. The encouragement to take advantage
of rising prices in cattle and grains was there but along with it
went indebtedness and increased dependency on a very limited
line of products. The danger of even a temporary collapse of
the market in these products threatened these householders with
financial ruin. When I discuss the rebellion of 1626 in chapter
8 below, this group will play a significant role.

TABLE 3.4
Inventory Breakdown. Economic Group 4, (235 CASES)

	Total Assets	Real Property	Movables	Loans	Debts	Freigeld
Sum	158,116	98,446	41,597	17,173	76,144	7,614
Mean	672	418	177	73	324	32
S.D.	134	139	81	114	223	29
Correlation Matrix						
Total Assets						
Real Property	.58					
Movables	.37					
Loans		−.51	−.24			
Debts	.26	.51		−.22		
Freigeld	.36	.29			.37	

One of the groups that formed the core of economic group four (Table 3.4) had overcome these difficulties by diversification. Diversified farming households, which made up 36 percent of this group, were not, however, in such a clear majority so that their group characteristics could become the characteristics of this economic group as a whole. Undiversified and yet economically successful farmers were also present here in some force at 33 percent. The result is that the economic qualities of this economic group as a whole are in most respects the same as those of the previous one. Although the scale of operations is greater and the participation of this group in the market is more complex, similar property and credit conditions determined economic behavior.

Only two households in this group owned no real estate. They were both *Auszügler* who had achieved this relatively high economic status through moneylending operations.[6] Nearly everyone else owned farms or homesteads of substantial value, which, taken altogether, balance the movables in the astonishingly standard ratio of 2.4:1. The distributions for both types of property are normal and represent the internal consistency of the data. This group as a whole was still a debtor group, although with a ratio of 1:4.4 between loans and debts, the trend is beginning to reverse from the peak reached in the previous group. While in the previous group, real estate holdings did not quite balance the moneys owed by the group as a whole, in this group total real property exceeded total debts by a substantial margin. This margin was not, however, so substantial that these debts could be covered by the group's movable property and credit assets—i.e., by potential and actual liquid assets—alone. In this society such economic strength was reserved for the highest economic groups. In other words, a market failure could still threaten this group with bankruptcy and subsequent loss of tenancy under the terms of emphyteutic tenure.

The correlations among the components of these households' economies appear similar to those of group three. The nexus among increased real and movable properties, indebtedness, and high economic position already observed in the previous eco-

nomic group appears here also with some variations in the correlations of Table 3.4. The absence of any correlation between
real and movable properties in this group, for example, significantly indicates a parting of the ways between those who relied
primarily on land and farming and those who were involved in
an industrial commodity market and were not completely dependent on farming. Although no longer absolutely essential
for high economic position, real property remained the primary
source of wealth, however, and this is further supported by the
stronger correlation (than in group three) between real property
and indebtedness. Those with larger farmsteads in this group
felt freer to borrow, had greater wage arrears and/or administered properties for godchildren and others. The inverse correlation between property holdings and loans suggests that,
although this group was in a better position to extend credit
and probably had to do so to be active in the market, the reinvestment rate in land, capital goods, and marketable commodities was very high. The wealthier members of this group lent
little of their profit out to others but rather used it themselves.
The high correlation between real estate and indebtedness indicates that those whose enterprises were primarily agricultural
and whose debts could be backed by land and buildings were
either more prone to seek credit or that those who extended
credit preferred to deal with such property owners. In either
case, it is my impression that debts in this economic group were
primarily capital debts, which suggests that along with heavy
reinvestment went considerable risk-taking in order to compete
in Upper Austria's rural markets. Agriculturists who appear
near the top in this group had to commit themselves to better
stables, granaries, more seed and young stock, seasonably variable labor, and so forth, and they therefore shared the substance
of the diversified farmers' capital requirements as well as the
risks of possible overextension already noted for group three.
Diversification and the further development of a teamster function—10 percent of the members of this group were teamsters—
were the results of carefully adjusted economies and provided,
as we shall see, the bridges to even higher economic position.

The Wealthy

Economic groups five and six display the kinds of rewards possible for the more or less calculated risks incurred by the two middle groupings of this peasant population: a valuable accumulation of properties and commodities as well as an advantageous participation in the agricultural and industrial commodity and credit markets.

TABLE 3.5
Inventory Breakdown. Economic Group 5 (64 cases)

	Total Assets	Real Property	Movables	Loans	Debts	Freigeld
Sum	88,355	45,083	22,765	19,641	31,198	4,261
Mean	1,380	704	355	306	487	66
S.D.	300	294	194	359	461	55
Correlation Matrix						
Total Assets						
Real Property	.34*					
Movables	.30*					
Loans	.44	−.48				
Debts	.37	.59				
Freigeld			.24	.24		

Everyone in group five (Table 3.5) owned real estate and these holdings were evenly distributed. The slight proportional increase of movables to real property (1:1.9), which is even more pronounced in the next economic group, indicates higher production as well as higher consumption levels for these householders. It also suggests that the amounts of land and the size of the farmstead were actually less important than with the middling peasants. Here income was obviously not automatically committed to reinvestment in one's own business but rather toward more luxurious consumption as well as to the businesses of others. This group extended over 300fl credit on the average, an amount that indicates that members of this group not only sold their produce on credit but were also active as outright moneylenders. The ratio between loans and debts is 1:1.6, which further suggests that, even though the average size of debt is considerable, the same fiscal compulsions that limited the creditor status and increased the indebtedness of groups three and four are not present here. This was obviously the most advantageous result of higher economic status: a greater freedom to manipulate assets, incomes, and expenditures. It is remarkable, for example, that here both real and movable properties correlated with high economic status in an only minor way while high economic status was accompanied by increased activity in the credit market as both creditor and debtor.

The inverse correlation between real property and creditor status further refines our perception of credit relationships at this level of society. If incomes were heavily invested in real estate holdings, a good source of further credit and further economic growth for a household, then this restricted the householder's capacity as creditor. Two distinct possibilities for further economic progress presented themselves at this point in a household's history. If the householder decided to invest in land and further commit himself to agriculture, then this severely curtailed his ability to participate in the market for short-term gains without becoming a debtor himself—something he was able to do, of course, on the basis of his increased real estate holdings. If the householder decided to commit his incomes to investments in sales on credit and outright loans, then he could not become involved in the real estate market to as great an extent. Following both courses was possible for only a limited number of individuals. Although members of this economic group were financially more secure, both courses of action involved risks of bad investment and possible overextension and failures could occur in times of market crisis. The occupational core of this group was composed of teamsters (38 percent) and diversified farmers (25 percent). Most teamsters incorporated proto-industrial diversification into their economic activities and together these groups exhibited very similar characteristics.

TABLE 3.6
Inventory Breakdown. Economic Group 6 (12 cases)

	Total Assets	Real Property	Movables	Loans	Debts	Freigeld
Sum	34,375	14,408	8,132	11,673	9,547	1,285
Mean	2,864	1,200	677	972	795	107
S.D.	828	405	319	778	890	66
Correlation Matrix*						
Total Assets						
Real Property						
Movables	.64	.57				
Loans	.67					
Debts						
Freigeld						

* At significance level .001, there were no significant relationships. If we relax this to .05, then there are only the relationships that appear on this graph.

The twelve individuals who make up group six (Table 3.6) illustrate the collective economic characteristics of members of the highest economic stratum in Upper Austrian peasant society. The value of the combined assets of their households alone was greater by 10,000fl than the combined assets of the 265 households that made up groups one and two. The people in this group, five teamsters, four innkeepers, one miller, one vintner, and one *Auszügler* (a former miller),[7] represented occupations that were not necessarily dependent on a large accumulation of land or of real estate and this is reflected in the proportion of movable to fixed property (1:1.8).[8] Movables for this group included large holdings in livestock, investment in raw materials, draft animals, and carting equipment, the dishes and bedding associated with public houses, and clearly included essential capital goods as well as those consumer goods one would associate with high economic status. The fact that real property did not correlate with such high status but that movables did further strengthens this observation. The information contained in Table 4.11 below suggests that this was particularly true of innkeepers who constituted, without question, the highest economic and, as we shall show, one of the highest social status groups among the peasants of seventeenth-century Upper Austria.

Of all the economic groups in this society, this is the only one in which loans exceed indebtedness (at a ratio of 1.2:1). Moreover, the highest correlation for this group occurs between the total wealth of householders and their loans. As one might expect, the wealthiest were also the most significant creditors. Members of this group could invest heavily in a number of rural enterprises with a good chance of success. The scale of their investment becomes clear, for example, if we consider that the average size of extended credit of this group was three times that of group five. At the same time the absence of correlations shows that debts were not adjusted to any of the assets. It is precisely the absence and low significance level of correlations among the ingredients of wealth that is probably the most significant feature of this group's economic behavior. The abandonment by the wealthy of that careful disposition of assets and incomes that we witnessed in particular with groups three and four and, to a lesser degree, with group five, may be explained by their substantial economic power. However, that this freewheeling economic style was not without its dangers is suggested by the fact that two of these householders, both teamsters, turned out to be "bankrupt" when the final balance was drawn and were placed in danger of losing their tenancies. The remainder were well within the limits of fiscal responsibility. If we delete the two overextended households from this group, the average debt owed by the remaining householders drops from 795fl to 462fl, which is even somewhat lower than the average debt of the previous economic group.

The individuals in this and some from the previous economic group were wealthy and powerful because they coordinated production and provided the credit links between producers, traders, and consumers. They controlled small portions of the markets in commodities and credit and they were employers as well.

They held their wealth and power, however, only as especially successful members of a dependent and socially and economically limited subject population. It was in part this contradictory set of status qualities that made them political leaders of the peasants in the sixteenth and seventeenth centuries—and that, as we shall see, also accounts for the character of their political leadership.

SUMMARY

By dividing the inventory population into different economic groups and analyzing the basic material characteristics of these strata, a complex picture emerges. As might be expected, there was a continuum running from poor to wealthy with a concentration of persons in the middle ranks. The curve describing this continuum is, however, relatively flat and skewed considerably toward the lower end of the economic scale; the extremes of wealth and poverty in this rural population were as great as was the distance between the wealthy and everyone else. Particularly significant and perhaps more unexpected was the finding that the relative magnitudes of the components of wealth and the interrelationships among them varied considerably from group to group. There was not only economic stratification but also a variation in economic behavior. The poor, middling, and wealthy members of this rural population were differentiated not only by their "property" but also by the ways they used their property.

The fundamental discontinuity that appears among the uses of wealth between the various economic groups suggests that by altering the use of their resources members of this rural population might have improved their position—or, conversely, suffered reverses. These economic strata were not necessarily populated by the same people year after year nor were their boundaries insurmountable. Moreover, members of these groups were not all members of the same class. They faced and dealt with different market situations and achieved, or were forced into, different kinds of economic and social relations. To disentangle the characteristics of class relations in this society from economic position requires an even more detailed examination of the various kinds of "market positions" possible in this society. This is best done by an examination of occupational differences and the economic characteristics and options that accompanied these.

~ CHAPTER 4 ~

Rural Industry and Occupational Groups

THE ADDITION of an industrial sector to traditional agricultural enterprises has for some time been appreciated by historians as a powerful and, for the most part, benign influence on the social development of rural lower classes in the *ancien régime*. Rudolf Braun's classic investigations into the history of the textile putting-out system in the Zürich Oberland advanced the idea that the reception of rural industries among the peasantry was essentially creative, that within the context of the traditionally narrow margins of wealth and subsistence it offered a new range of possibilities for rural life.[1] Children who could not inherit the family farm or workshop no longer had to leave the area but could find work that was at once close to and yet relatively independent from their families; young country men and women could unfold and express their personalities in less restricted family and familial relationships as well as in increasingly diverse forms of consumption; the diversification of tastes had its profoundest effects on—and was in turn affected by—cultural growth in the countryside, which expressed itself in the religions and fashions of country people. The impact of early industrialization on rural society in the Zürich Oberland took place, however, in a distinctly different economic and social setting from that in Upper Austria. There it was a culture of small holders and cottagers who took on these new activities, and a child could get away from the parental home and set up his or her own shop and become truly independent. In Upper Austria, on the other hand, where the proliferation of cottages and small holdings was severely restricted, the rural textile industry unfolded within the confines of tenant households and families and the chances for social independence for the young were greatly reduced: the overall social and economic impact of rural indus- trialization in such a setting was, as we shall see, drastically different from that shown by Braun.[2]

On the previous pages some of the economic advantages of a person's involvement in Upper Austria's emerging rural in- dustries were apparent. The upper ranks of the low, middle, and high economic groups among the peasantry tended to be populated by those who were employed in or had invested money in some form of rural industry or in the marketing associated with industry. The potential dangers for Upper Austrian rural society from this new wealth were twofold. In the first place, implicit in the new system was an increased economic vulner- ability of all rural lower classes. At the lowest levels such vul- nerability persisted and even increased as the consumption debts of rural workers increased and as they increasingly worked for deferred wages; at the same time, the wealthier property-own- ing groups were tempted into increasingly greater and riskier investments and credit transactions. On the whole, accompa- nying the economic freedom that came with the addition of rural industry to agricultural production, there came the peas- antry's more intense orientation toward and dependence on well-functioning markets in credit, labor, and commodities of all kinds. As a corollary of the new wealth and the new economic freedom there appears an increased dependence of the peasantry on the authorities that controlled the markets and the com- mercial routes as well as an increased vulnerability to shifts in the economic power struggles among the authorities. The sec- ond potential danger to the rural social system, one that has been observed by Braun and others, was that of the emergence of new social conflicts between representatives of the new and the traditional forms of production and economic status.[3] In the following pages I want to explore for the case of Upper Austria to what extent occupational groups represented a form of vertical stratification that cut across economic lines and to what extent

the new and old occupations were in turn subject to the economic
and political aspects of the market.

LABOR: LODGERS AND SERVANTS

The economically more advantaged male and female "indwell-
ers" (*Inleute*), or lodgers (Tables 4.1 and 4.2), were more numerous than the servant class (Tables 4.3 and 4.4) in the inventory population because they often had something to inventory
where the latter had nothing. Even though members of the
lodger group derived their name from their housing status and
pursued a great variety of occupational specializations and were
therefore not, by modern definition, an "occupational" group,
it is nevertheless important to bring them together here as a
single occupational group for it is as such that they appeared
in the rural labor market. They constituted an extremely flexible
labor force and for individual members of this group, flexibility
and diversification in skills and technology rather than specialization seem to have been the most desirable characteristics.
This is shown by the collections of tools and materials found
in their inventories. Combinations of two or more types of
agricultural implements, metal-working tools, some textile-
working tools and materials, and the axes, saws, and augers
necessary for various kinds of woodwork were usually found
among the movables of male lodgers. Female lodgers tended to
be more intensely involved in the textile putting-out networks
and their movables consisted of combinations of spools, spinning
wheels, seamstress and milliner materials, as well as some agricultural tools. In a very few cases such signs of occupational
flexibility were completely absent and in such cases it is likely
that the lodgers performed simpler labor services and depended
on the tools their employers might furnish. From the generally
lower economic status of these latter types we can conclude that
their lack of personal equipment brought with it a lowering of
income. The high correlation coefficient in Table 4.1 between
economic status and movables indicates that this was especially
true for male lodgers.

TABLE 4.1
Inventory Breakdown. Male Lodgers (100 cases)

	Total Assets	Real Property	Movables	Loans	Debts	Freigeld
Sum	12,355	3,673	2,476	6,083	4,839	755
Mean	123	36	24	60	48	7
S.D.	119	59	25	82	54	8
Correlation Matrix						
Total Assets						
Real Property	.62					
Movables	.55					
Loans	.80					
Debts	.70	.47	.49	.49		
Freigeld	.61	.46	.34	.45	.40	

NOTE: All amounts in guilders in this and subsequent tables.

TABLE 4.2
Inventory Breakdown. Female Lodgers (30 cases)

	Total Assets	Real Property	Movables	Loans	Debts	Freigeld
Sum	1,514	275	429	807	553	101
Mean	50	9	14	26	18	3
S.D.	39	18	10	31	16	4
Correlation Matrix						
Total Assets						
Real Property	.69					
Movables						
Loans	.81		−.31*			
Debts	.55			.48*		
Freigeld	.80	.62			.45*	

* Signifies a low significance (.05) level in this and subsequent tables.

There were a number of differences between the sexes among the better-off laboring groups in this society and these are worth going into. Most significant, first of all, is the fact that among rural working classes differences in sex were reflected in significant differences in economic and occupational status. This was not the case with the tenant members of the Upper Austrian peasantry where property and status were jointly held in the conjugal community and the household inventory tended to represent a family holding regardless of whether it was the male or female head of the household who had died. A second feature of the sexual division of the labor force as recorded by the inventories was that men outnumbered women by a considerable proportion. Although I cannot here investigate the demographic reasons for this, it appears that women tended to leave home less frequently to go out to live as lodgers and work on their own, which suggests in turn that there was a relatively large "hidden" labor force consisting mainly of women who were simply a part of their father's or of another relative's household and whose personal possessions were not sufficient to warrant an inventory on the occasion of their death. Clearly, the mixed agricultural and industrial opportunities for work attracted male labor to a far greater extent than female labor and men were better paid. At these lower levels in society in particular, women were a separate and depressed status group. Male lodgers tended to own more real property than women and were able, for this reason, to participate on more favorable terms as debtors in the credit market. This is further verified by comparisons of the ratios in Tables 4.1 and 4.2 of real to movable properties and by the different correlation coefficients between real property and indebtedness for male and female lodgers respectively. The correlations show that for both men and women, owning real property tended to rank one higher economically than not owning property. Although both the men and women in this group tended to show their significant status as wage earners by displaying a reversal of the ratios between debits and credits from those that have appeared above for lower economic groups generally, the men were involved in the credit

97

market more favorably. The much greater scale of credit transactions and most particularly the consistent correlations between the debts and the assets of their households mark the
more confident and perhaps more "calculated" involvement of
male lodgers in the rural credit, labor, and commodity market.
These differences between the sexes occurred also among the
servant group.

Unlike the servants, lodgers did not depend on their employers for food and lodging and were at considerably greater
liberty to choose and change their employment on short notice.
Here is a clear instance of the relatively early development of
labor in rural industry combining with traditional forms of
agricultural labor to create a rural working class distinct from
the traditional field hands, stable help, and scullions. The lodgers, although belonging in terms of wealth and economic behavior to the lowest strata in the Upper Austrian social system,
displayed connections to the wealthier land-owning and commercially active peasantry. Not only could individual lodgers
be held in higher esteem as persons whose special skills made
their labor more valuable, but they were often also the offspring
of relatively wealthy families who had not inherited the family
farm but who had used their inheritance portion to create a life
of independence, relative prosperity, and well-being even at low
economic status. For example, one such lodger, a subject of
Schlägl, owned a meadow worth 80fl, which was probably a part
of an inheritance portion; in his inventory's property disposition
it reverted back to the original family farm. Another male lodger,
also from Schlägl, whose assets amounted to 632fl(!), owned
two meadows valued at 110fl and 40fl, two large oxen, two cows,
four sheep, and a pig. He was obviously from a prosperous
family and why he did not purchase a farm of his own remains
a mystery because he was wealthy enough to do it and, judging
by the activity of the land market, farms were available to those
who could afford them. Perhaps the life of the lodger had appeal
in terms of personal freedom that challenged the more responsible, legally supervised, and, possibly, risky life of the tenant
farm owner. In any case, this particular lodger had sufficient

means to become a significant creditor and to diversify his labor considerably. He loaned sizable amounts, owned a number of field tools, flax, linen, and two spinning wheels, and employed a female servant. The cost of his wake alone, 49fl, equalled the entire average value of a female lodger's household and is probably an accurate measure of the size and prestige of this man's "clan." The wealthiest female lodger in this inventory population (also from Schlägl) owned two meadows worth 50fl and 20fl respectively and among her items of extended credit was one unspecified 100fl debt owed by a burgher from the nearby market town of Aigen.[4]

The fact that many lodgers did not have these advantages and connections and displayed a bleaker and more isolated style of life, despite their diverse industrial and agricultural skills, raises questions concerning the social status of members of this group. Here were relatively well-off men and women, often the offspring of powerful and wealthy families, who had to live as diversified workers and who in some cases could not distinguish themselves economically from the less flexible and less independent servant classes. These instances of potential status discrepancy and status anxiety that are so evident among the lodgers suggest that the addition of an industrial sector to the rural economy of Upper Austria, while it removed social conflicts that arose from the scarcity of jobs in a more traditional agricultural economy, initiated at the same time a new period of more complex status distinctions and conflicts. To what extent did those children who had not inherited the home farm, but who could now remain in the area, continue to participate in and derive their social status from their primary family's wealth and status? Did their actual economic and occupational status alone define them socially? How were the flexible laboring activities of the lodgers viewed by those who entered the group from above and by those who entered from below? In order to throw these problems into sharper focus, we can compare the industrial and agricultural working class of lodgers to the older traditional working class of male and female servants.

TABLE 4.3
Inventory Breakdown. Male Servants (17 cases)

	Total Assets	Real Property	Movables	Loans	Debts	Freigeld
Sum	1,942	300	130	1,498	475	177
Mean	114	17	7	88	27	10
S.D.	73	35	6	46	13	8
Correlation Matrix						
Total Assets						
Real Property	.77					
Movables	.61*					
Loans	.88		.59*			
Debts	.44*	.45*				
Freigeld	.97	.74	.65*	.85	.55*	

TABLE 4.4
Inventory Breakdown. Female Servants (12 cases)

	Total Assets	Real Property	Movables	Loans	Debts	Freigeld
Sum	810	0	141	669	286	87
Mean	67		11	55	23	7
S.D.	32		10	29	14	4
Correlation Matrix						
Total Assets						
Real Property						
Movables						
Loans	.94					
Debts	.53*			.53*		
Freigeld	.79			.76*	.77	

100

Even the inventories of many poor to middling households show debts owing for the services of male (*Knecht*) and female (*Magd*) servants (Tables 4.3 and 4.4). These were the traditional field laborers, stable hands, kitchen and house servants who performed the char labors necessary to farming since its earliest days. Servants were hired by the year and became a part of their employer's household. While lodgers paid for their own lodgings in a tenant household, servants tended to sleep in one of their employer's outbuildings or, if the latter was wealthy, in a room and bed shared by all servants. The closest the servants came to participating in industrial labor was in such preparatory work as hackling flax or spinning. The actual number of people employed in this role must have been far greater than my inventory population indicates. As I have already suggested many members of this group probably had nothing worth inventorying, with the result that they are not represented here in their true proportional strength.

Although servants did not necessarily perform the same labor services as lodgers and did not, as a comparison of the tables shows, live at a comparable economic level, they nevertheless show some economic characteristics and behavior similar to the lodgers. Most striking is the similar economic inferiority for women in both working groups, a fact that further refines the questions concerning status discrepancy posed in regard to the status of the lodgers. A woman attaining lodger status from a starting point as servant would consider this a positive achievement, while a woman entering this status from a higher social position where sex was a less significant status indicator in economic and social life would no doubt feel the sexual inequalities within the working groups much more acutely. We will take up this theme again below.

None of the serving women in this inventory population owned any land whereas four male servants did own properties. The wealthiest member of the latter belonged in economic group three and came from what must have been a wealthy family. His real estate holdings were worth 120fl and consisted of two meadows; he owned 13fl and some change in cash and his one

101

"loan" was an inheritance portion of 218fl that was being held in trust by his godparents.[5] He was probably very young and his possessions make him a most unusual case at this low level of society. However, male servants displayed generally stronger economic characteristics than even female lodgers in terms of property ownership and "loans." Some of this is deceptive. For example, servants, like other members of the lowest economic groups, extended credit by working for deferred wages, often annual wages, and men tended to earn more than women;[6] therefore their inventories' total values were often inflated by unpaid wages. The consumption levels of the servant groups, measured by their movables, was extremely low. The higher average value for movables among serving women is puzzling and the only way to account for this may be that women from this group were more closely involved in the textile putting-out system than men and they show among their possessions the necessary yarn, linen, wool, spools, and even an occasional poor spinning wheel, all of which they had to supply themselves and which would drive up the value of their movables. The drover, field, and stable work performed by the men would require no possessions of this kind. It is noteworthy that at this lowest and most traditional laboring status, peripheral involvement in rural industry did not produce any market economic advantages. This was probably the result of both the small scale of involvement possible as well as of the generally low status of working women.

The correlations in Tables 4.3 and 4.4 among the possessions, incomes, and liabilities of the two servant groups are a weak reflection of the relationships that appeared for lodgers. Clearly, higher-valued property and loans for men and incoming debts alone for women correlated positively with a higher economic position. Women tended to be in a less favorable position on the credit market because men apparently tended to have more assets to cover their debts than did women. A lot of this was illusory, however, because men at this low level had a great deal of difficulty in calling in the outstanding loans and wages that were owed to them to cover their own debts when these were called in. Most of them did not possess any real estate for collateral and therefore were not necessarily in a better position than women. The several strong correlations between indebtedness and assets that appear for the lodgers are here replaced, if at all, by much weaker correlations. Calculability and economic adjustments were much harder to achieve for the servant population than for the more independent and generally wealthier lodgers. The strong correlation between the death tax (*Freigeld*) and debts for female servants is particularly remarkable. A working woman's death was often also her greatest expense. These women's inventories were charged, moreover, a death tax of 10.75 percent of their holdings and were proportionately the most highly taxed in the entire inventory population. The least taxed of these four groups was also the wealthiest; namely, the male lodgers. Even though male lodgers were obviously in a stronger economic position than the other three working groups discussed here, they were all four potential victims of the market. Their wages were low, their collective force in the market was negligible, and this, combined with their wage arrears and their significant indebtedness, gives us a measure of their economic vulnerability that must, in times of economic crisis, have reduced all four laboring groups to very similar economic straits. The social results of such hard times were, of course, considerably different for these groups than for the rest of the rural population.

COTTAGERS AND FARMERS

Even though their overall economic status still ranked them among the rural poor, the possession of a house made the cottagers (Table 4.5) of rural Upper Austria less directly dependent on favorable market events than the lodger and servant population. As their designation as *Häusler* or *Söldner*[7] implies, they were identified as a group by the small house and acreage they owned. The homestead seems to have been the most important part of the group's wealth, more than two and a half times more than the movables. They were not numerously represented in this inventory population and this reinforces the contention that unlike the cases of the Zürich Oberland and Bavaria, in Upper Austria the population that supported itself by a mixture of industrial and agricultural labor tended to become lodgers rather than cottagers.[8]

TABLE 4.5
Inventory Breakdown. Cottagers (12 cases)

	Total Assets	Real Property	Movables	Loans	Debts	Freigeld
Sum	1,217	785	297	133	542	50
Mean	101	65	24	11	45	4
S.D.	47	33	25	28	41	2
Correlation Matrix						
Total Assets						
Real Property						
Movables	.81					
Loans	.70	−.50	.86			
Debts		.82				
Freigeld		.56*		−.64*	.53*	

Cottagers made their living as gardeners or small agriculturists who often produced for the urban market or as textile workers and in some cases as specialized craftsmen. The strong correlation in Table 4.5 between movables and high overall economic status suggests that wealthy cottagers not only had more and better household goods but that they also tended to invest in tools and capital goods on a larger scale. The inventories of the wealthiest cottagers indicate that diversified industrial and craft functions were essential features of greater wealth. The wealthiest cottager in the inventory population was worth 225fl and possessed five spinning wheels, a considerable number of carpentry tools, two cows, and a great number of roofing shingles. He was also a major creditor.[9] Another cottager, a subject of the monastery Schlägl, held a meadow in addition to his house as well as a cow, a loom, and other weaving paraphernalia. Similarly, a cottager from the estate Schaunberg had a garden in addition to his house, as well as a considerable investment in spinning wheels and spools.[10] These were independent men who did not work for wages but might instead even have been small-scale employers. Among the servants and lodgers, "loans" tended to signify unpaid wages, but such was not the case for the cottage owners. The combination, in Table 4.5, of the significant inverse correlation between loans and real property with the strong direct relationship between loans and movables suggests two things about members of this group. Those who had a larger holding tended to be engaged in small-scale farming (or large-scale gardening) and sold their produce for cash. Those who had small holdings but had heavily invested in capital goods were involved in the industrial sector and tended to be active as creditors, no doubt letting finished goods go to market on a credit basis. It is significant also that those who had more real estate tended to be deeper in debt while for those who were involved in the industrial sector (as shown by the high value of movables) debt seems to have been of negligible importance.

The cottagers appear to have been a small and complex social group of petty landowners who followed diverse occupations simultaneously. The most successful among them were those who had begun to specialize for participation in the rural industrial sector. I doubt that the limited number under discussion here allows a complete or entirely accurate description of this group, which was in any case not particularly active in the rural politics of the period. Their relatively small number and their physically isolated as well as socially and often economically marginal position makes them difficult to place in the class and status structure of rural Upper Austria. The apparently incipient occupational division among the cottagers appears in far more developed form among those who owned small and large farmsteads, but there the level of involvement in the market was on a higher level and the risks and rewards of diversification into some industrial enterprise were much greater.

TABLE 4.6
Inventory Breakdown. Farmers (286 cases)

	Total Assets	Real Property	Movables	Loans	Debts	Freigeld
Sum	114,835	77,076	31,469	6,160	66,623	5,509
Mean	400	268	109	21	232	19
S.D.	174	124	68	43	177	20
Correlation Matrix						
Total Assets						
Real Property	.88					
Movables	.70	.41				
Loans	.32					
Debts	.41	.42	.23			
Freigeld	.50	.50	.28		.39	

Specialized farming was a significant occupation for many among Upper Austria's rural population during the seventeenth century (Table 4.6). While the 286 households whose resources were engaged in this livelihood were spread across all but the highest of the economic groups, they were concentrated most heavily in group three. Correlations in Table 4.6 suggest that only the wealthier farmers, probably those appearing in economic groups four and five, could afford substantial amounts of implements and livestock and could participate in the market as significant individual producers. Because they were all heavily in debt and because all but the wealthiest of them were incapable of extending credit, the group as a whole was in considerable economic danger. Their weakness as creditors, expressed best by the astonishing 11:1 ratio between debits and credits, and the narrow range of agricultural products to which they were committed combined with their dependence on other sources for a wide and varied range of necessities and made them a group that was extremely vulnerable to market crises. The cautious economic behavior contained in the string of correlations under the debt column indicates that increased risk was incurred only along with generally higher economic status and was secured by both real and movable properties. To hang on to their farms and to continue to live and perhaps even flourish by small progressions, these people required stable markets. In times of crisis they became either victims of the market or more dependent clients of their *Obrigkeiten* and creditors. Many of them courted the danger of overextension and the loss of their tenures. Their situation, grounded in never having quite enough and intensified by any shocking disequilibrium in the market, could lead them to support any cause, even a desperate one, if it held out hope for relief. They were prominent participants in the rebellions of the period and especially in 1626.

DIVERSIFICATION

Grafting various industrial diversifications or craft skills on to what was essentially a specialized agricultural operation was economically beneficial but could also be potentially dangerous (Table 4.7). The diversified farmers' higher placement in the

TABLE 4.7
Inventory Breakdown. Diversified Farmers (115 cases)

	Total Assets	Real Property	Movables	Loans	Debts	Freigeld
Sum	85,588	50,270	23,902	11,222	35,461	4,521
Mean	744	437	207	97	308	39
S.D.	269	142	118	185	207	37
Correlation Matrix						
Total Assets						
Real Property	.56					
Movables	.67	.30				
Loans	.62					
Debts		.56				
Freigeld	.56	.28		.46	.29	

hierarchy of economic strata, their greater average holdings of real property and movables, and the much more favorable balance between creditor and debtor status (1:3) mark these householders as middling peasants of a "better" sort. They were financially freer and the carefully controlled economic behavior expressed by the numerous correlations among the assets and obligations of the specialized farming group does not exist here. The adjustment that mattered most here was that between real estate holdings and indebtedness. Members of this group incurred capital debts and owed others for wages and industrial piecework. These debts were secured finally by real estate alone. While diversification no doubt increased this group's resilience in the face of market crises, it also increased the dangers of what has been called "rising expectations." Not only did these householders become accustomed to higher standards of economic action and living, but they became committed to expansion and greater risk-taking in terms of greater capital outlay and labor expenditures. In times of economic crisis this group tended to behave less desperately than the farmers. They tended more toward economic solutions, toward riding out a crisis by collecting what debts they could and by defaulting where possible. That these were only short-term possibilities and that they caused considerable further economic and social problems, especially among lower economic and occupational groups, makes these farmers a key group for peasant economic and political action during a more long-term crisis.

Among farmers, traditional agriculturalists were not as well off as those who had added some industrial enterprise to their farming activities. Not only did such diversification broaden the economic base of the farm, it also tied the farmer into different market and credit networks that allowed him to form new business and social relationships, thereby making new levels of social status possible in ways that were denied the traditional agriculturalist. Here industrialization clearly introduced vertical stratification into a broad occupation group by sharpening the economic and social differences among Upper Austria's farmers.

To investigate this problem of vertical against horizontal stratification further, we may compare two occupation groups:

millers, who were engaged in a long-established economic pursuit related to agriculture, and weavers, who were the core group in one of the more recently organized rural industries.

TABLE 4.8
Inventory Breakdown. Weavers (42 cases)

	Total Assets	Real Property	Movables	Loans	Debts	Freigeld
Sum	14,851	9,395	3,977	1,421	12,223	484
Mean	353	223	94	33	291	11
S.D.	351	224	100	77	588	15
Correlation Matrix						
Total Assets						
Real Property	.96					
Movables	.81	.72				
Loans	.66	.56	.30*			
Debts	.33*	.37*				
Freigeld	.26*	.26*				

To begin with the latter group, Upper Austria's seventeenth-century linen-weavers resided for the most part in the wooded Mühlviertel, north of the Danube and close to the flax and hemp fields, where they functioned as producers and, in some cases, had also become active as transporters and subcontractors in the textile putting-out system (Table 4.8). Their inventories were distributed throughout the lower five economic strata with no particularly heavy concentration at any single economic level. The high standard deviations for their inventories' main ingredients indicate a high degree of horizontal stratification for all aspects of weavers' economic behavior. Within the inventories, however, there appear some strong correlations among the assets of these householders. Weavers in both the highest and lowest economic groups were businessmen and calculating entrepreneurs of varying scale. Correlations suggest that the wealthiest landowning weavers were significant creditors as part of their industrial function. They were deeply in debt as a group, but these debts were very unevenly distributed and bore only a weak correlation to their overall economic status. This means that even though wealthier weavers and especially those with valuable property were more prone to risk greater indebtedness, these risks were also being taken by less economically powerful householders.

The two wealthiest weavers in the inventory population were both designated as weavers and as burghers in the market town, Aigen, subjects of the adjacent estate Schlägl. Here industrial occupation had led to a high legal status position. The one whose inventory amounted to 1,737fl owned 1,060fl in various real estate holdings and had a relatively large cash holding of 214fl. Along with two looms and several additional weavers' tools, he also owned two oxen and two excellent wagons and therefore must have combined weaving with a teamster function. It is likely that this householder was a major subcontractor. He also possessed such luxurious commodities as 80 pounds of pewterware and was a powerful godfather who administered a total of 400fl on behalf of his wards. This amount appears among the debts held against the estate. The second wealthiest weaver in this population also owned two looms and diverse tools accompanying them; he had less cash; his wagons, judging from their value, were only for short-range transport, and he owed one debt for 420fl. He was a minor cattle dealer with nine head of livestock (and two pigs); he had just sold a pair of oxen for 28fl and had bought four more at 50fl. Instead of being a diversified farmer, he was a weaver who had diversified as agriculturalist. Both these households had substantial debts at 897fl and 983fl respectively but were well within their limits of responsibility. By contrast, a poor weaver and burgher, also from Aigen, worth 278fl, had several smaller pieces of property, two low-quality looms, only one cow, no loans, but a number of debts, most of which were in the 10fl to 40fl range with one to three years' interest accumulated on them. He had a number of small consumption debts for meat and grain and firewood in addition to his greater and unspecified burdens. His clothes were of good quality at a total value of 9fl.[11]

Here status incongruence within an occupation group, which was partially the result of the manipulation by the estate of the legal status of the weavers under its jurisdiction, is most obvious. In terms of their occupational status and of their legal status as burghers, which was in the town of Aigen a part of their occupation's corporate status, these three weavers shared similar economic and legal privileges and concerns. At the same time, however, they were different economic and social actors who obviously did not share the same economic and social status. The poor weaver simply could not have participated in and could not have derived the benefits from the economic and social networks in which the wealthier and diversified weavers found themselves. Involvement in the weaving industry, even at the sophisticated and capital intensive level of master weaver, did not guarantee high economic or social status.

At the same time, authority relations were also of primary significance in determining differences in social position, especially among groups that did not uniformly participate in rural industries. While such groups as weavers built their class position on uniformly shared positions as householders, burghers, and guild members, and improved their social positions by their diversified involvement in the market, others, like the millers and, to some extent, the innkeepers, built their class positions primarily on unequal portions of authority granted them by or purchased from their overlords.

As a group, millers tended to live less spectacularly and seemed less inclined to incur risks than weavers (Table 4.9). The correlations suggest that the greater the value of a mill, the more household goods there were and the greater the overall economic status of the householder. The several other weak correlations indicate that there were no really serious attempts by members of this group to coordinate their assets and credit transactions. However, many millers were deeply involved in the illegal traffic in grains and other foodstuffs and it is possible that the information they gave to the inventory-takers, particularly in connection with the credit they extended to other producers and dealers, was incomplete. The richest of this group was a man whose mill was priced at 1,000fl and who had, besides 96fl in

111

TABLE 4.9
Inventory Breakdown. Millers (11 cases)

	Total Assets	Real Property	Movables	Loans	Debts	Freigeld
Sum	9,394	5,418	2,565	1,251	4,604	590
Mean	854	492	233	113	418	53
S.D.	793	351	320	186	344	47
Correlation Matrix						
Total Assets						
Real Property	.91					
Movables	.93	.82				
Loans	.73*		.56*			
Debts		.62*				
Freigeld	.90	.93	.74	.64*		

cash holdings, 61fl in gold and silver.[12] A wealthy miller from the estate Schlägl who was worth 2,121fl,[13] possessed firearms and a chest full of coins. When we compare these two to a poor miller whose mill was worth only 105fl, who had only 2½fl in tools, who had not been able to turn the 63fl brought into the household by a ward into any kind of profitable enterprise, and whose debts exceeded all of his assets by 70fl, then we see the range of economic possibilities open to millers as an occupational group.[14] Clearly, high and low economic and social status were not completely determined by whether or not a householder engaged in some form of industrial enterprise in addition to his more traditional occupation. Those millers whose mill was of sufficient size to assure them of a sizable scale of enterprise and volume of turnover could participate not only in the market but in social life at the highest levels, while those who operated small and marginal mills were involved with small quantities of grain and with a poorer and purely local clientele. Here was a situation of status difference within an occupation group that was related to the growth of bureaucratic capitalism not as an industrial but as a monopolistic enterprise. The millers with large mills who acquired the voluminous business of their estate authorities almost automatically achieved a relatively high economic and social status, one with which those who did not get seigneurial contracts could not possibly compete. While vertical stratification in the weaving occupation resulted from the weavers' differing levels of involvement with more distant and larger markets, similar stratification among the millers appears to have been dependent on the volume of trade and this was most significantly determined by the direct economic patronage of the estate owners and managers. Among the millers it was the great buying power of estates in the local markets that introduced new economic and social differences and raised the stakes for achieving higher status.

TEAMSTERS AND INNKEEPERS

The two occupational groups that occupied the pinnacle of Upper Austrian peasant society most consistently were teamsters and landlord-innkeepers. Both the agricultural as well as the industrial sectors of the rural economy were simultaneously in the hands of these two groups whose members managed to acquire seigneurial contracts and monopolies and to accumulate sufficient quantities of commodities in order to participate in a variety of markets at or very near the highest levels. They acted as brokers and middlemen, helped coordinate production and marketing, engaged in the widest variety of credit transactions both as creditors and debtors, and, in their capacities as employers and family heads, managed a considerable amount of Upper Austria's labor force and small capital. Finally, because their commercial and family connections followed the trade routes taken by Upper Austria's industrial and agricultural products, these two groups tended to develop a wider economic and social outlook than their fellow subjects. In short, not only did they act to maintain the inner cohesion of local rural society but they also linked that society with the authorities and with distant markets and communities. Here high economic and occupational status were derived from the mutually supportive agricultural and industrial sectors of the rural economy and cohered so well that the demands for a higher political status, which were advanced by the leading members of these two groups in the peasant rebellions of the sixteenth and seventeenth centuries, seemed to follow logically.

TABLE 4.10
Inventory Breakdown. Teamsters (52 cases)

	Total Assets	Real Property	Movables	Loans	Debts	Freigeld
Sum	63,258	35,675	18,290	9,290	23,602	2,619
Mean	1,216	686	351	178	453	50
S.D.	552	321	178	264	527	51
Correlation Matrix						
Total Assets						
Real Property	.82					
Movables	.66	.46				
Loans	.63					
Debts	.45	.71				
Freigeld	.47	.40	.58		.42	

Teamsters (Table 4.10) tended to be involved in some form of successful agriculture; the wealthiest of them invested in greater amounts of real property. Although they lived at a consistently higher level, they still displayed the internal economic controls that we have seen for most of the Upper Austrian peasant tenants. Their debts exceeded their loans—if only by two and one half times—and the correlations between debts and their overall wealth and particularly their real estate show that while this was an enterprising group it also exercised some

114

financial restraint and responsibility. Although members of this group were distributed throughout the three highest economic groups, they were concentrated, numerically, in groups four and five. Their average debt, however, was higher than that of either of these economic groups and, since debts at this higher economic level were not primarily consumption but capital debts, this greater indebtedness suggests that teamsters were greater investors, employers, and risk-takers. Conversely, diversified farmers and large-scale agriculturists would have had to incur even greater risks if they had wished to share in the several markets in which teamsters participated. The teamsters' diversification, the opportunity of the most successful members of this group to appear in the credit market as creditors, the privileges extended to this group by the authorities in recognition of their economic usefulness and, finally, the connections they maintained as a part of their business shielded many of them against adverse market conditions. On the other hand, their risk-taking made them dependent on the smooth functioning of all these safeguards.

TABLE 4.11
Inventory Breakdown. Innkeepers (10 cases)

	Total Assets	Real Property	Movables	Loans	Debts	Freigeld
Sum	23,247	9,243	4,998	8,994	6,864	830
Mean	2,324	924	499	899	686	83
S.D.	1,364	524	411	741	629	76
Correlation Matrix						
Total Assets						
Real Property	.78*					
Movables	.87	.80*				
Loans	.80*					
Debts						
Freigeld	.72*		.69*	.60*		

Innkeepers' importance as community leaders in peasant society has long been recognized by historians. The reasons for
this leadership role have been ascribed correctly to the fact that
inns were the peasants' meeting places, that innkeepers were
business leaders, and that they tended to have literacy skills
uncommon among peasants.[15] Table 4.11 points in particular
to the second of these characteristics and gives it considerable
substance. The average size of credit offered by innkeepers in
this sample is huge and outstrips their own dependence on
credit—although the debt carried by certain individuals in this
group was enormous as well. Real property was not as significant to members of this group as it was to property owners
who were dependent on agriculture. In other words, the state-
liness and size of an establishment was not necessarily a sign
of its economic success. As the single strong correlation suggests, the cash, commodities, and capital goods in the movables
were the most apparent product and producer of greater wealth.
These commodities not only included the obvious things connected with running a public house but also those capital goods
required to fulfill the additional economic roles of industrial
diversification and the carriage trade in which innkeepers were
involved. As for the other correlations among the innkeepers'
assets and obligations, this group displayed the same weak relationships that we have already observed for economic group
six. The abandonment here of those visible controls and careful
adjustments witnessed with the teamster group does not suggest, however, that this group did not possess calculating commercial instincts and practices. Its economic assets were such
that individuals were free to make economic and entrepreneurial
decisions that expressed their own choices and preferences and
did not follow any pattern or generally successful formula. It
is likely that they were in fact the most active and most intel-
ligent participants in the Upper Austrian rural economy. They
were the most significant beneficiaries among the Upper Austrian peasantry of over a century of rural economic development
that had seen the growing together of traditional agricultural
enterprise and labor with commercially innovative and sophisticated rural industries. That such a curiously "traditional" and

116

nonindustrial occupation could maintain its position of economic dominance in an industrializing countryside alerts us to the social limits of the capitalism practiced in early modern Austria.

SUMMARY

The traditional notion by which the peasant population of this region was divided into the stereotypically rich agriculturists of the Danube valley and of the Alpine foothills on the one hand and the poor weavers, woodworkers, and charcoal burners of the Mühlviertel mountains on the other[16] is clearly no longer tenable. Relative wealth and poverty were distributed throughout all the regions of the province and were not so much the result of regional resource endowment and occupational characteristics as of the economic choices individuals and households made within the range of economic and occupational options open to them. This chapter has shown that not only may the gradations of wealth from the previous chapter be thrown into much sharper focus by crosscutting them with occupational groupings but also that our perception of these occupational groupings may itself be further sharpened by analyzing them according to their relative degrees of internal specialization and diversification or, as with the laboring population, according to their gender divisions.

The general broadening of the Upper Austrian rural economy during the sixteenth and seventeenth centuries, brought about by an increasing investment of German and local capital in household industries, improved opportunities for traditional agricultural and craft occupations. Members of the laboring population found greater chances for mobility, albeit still within the framework of the traditional house administration, by expanding the skills and services they could offer. Cottagers and farmers could diversify their agricultural operations. Others who were already engaged in such industrial craft specializations as weaving, milling, and blacksmithing could diversify into agriculture or expand their teamster and marketing capabilities. These choices created the great differences we can observe in the economic character and behavior of the specialized and di-

117

versified members of the occupational groups in the inventory population. Those of the tenant farmers, for example, who remained traditional producers of grains and livestocks also remained trapped as the single most debt-burdened group; at the other end of the spectrum were those farmers who had not only engaged in both agriculture and industry but who had entered and profited from the market as transporters, enterpreneurs, and agents—and had been able to escape to various degrees the compulsions of the credit market. Nowhere do we see these differences between diversified and undiversified members of occupation groups more clearly than with the functioning of credit. For the undiversified, extended credit ("loans") was a liability and their uncollected wages and the unredeemed inheritance portions signified their economic and social victimization. For the diversified, loans were genuine capital investments from which they could gain direct economic and social advantages. At the same time, debts were for the undiversified a part of their consumption burden and signified the complete absence of any margin of economic safety; for the diversified they represented operating and investment capital, unpaid-for labor, and conspicuous consumption.

One of the great issues in peasant studies since the 1950s has been the special nature of the "peasant economy" and the unique qualities of peasant economic behavior. Rooted in the contributions of Polanyi, Mauss, Banfield, and Foster, opinion has most recently been divided between proponents, on one hand, of peasants as insecure economic actors eschewing profit-seeking for the "safety first" principles of a community- or state-directed moral economy that guarantees them survival through bad times[17] and, on the other hand, of peasants as amoral, risk-taking economic maximizers.[18] Not only does this debate appear misguided on conceptual grounds—it does not, for example, draw on Weber's valuable discussion of purposive and values rationality—but, as the analysis in this and the previous chapter has shown, such a need to develop general "social scientific" principles of peasant economic behavior does not assist us in unravelling the highly stratified variations and dynamics of economic action among specific rural people.

Some of the poorest peasant farmers in the inventory population remained traditional agriculturists, took no investment
risks, and yet, nevertheless, calculated and sought to balance
their assets and debits carefully—and lost their tenures when
their careful adjustments and economies proved insufficient.
The wealthiest farmers, by contrast, often abandoned the internal adjustments of assets to debits altogether and profited
greatly. In the specific circumstances of the Austrian peasant
economy it was the emphyteutic nature of tenure that compelled
all tenured subjects to be economic maximizers, at least to the
point at which their tenure was not in danger. Paradoxically,
those poor tenants who would, theoretically, be the greatest
adherents to conservative moral economy principles were forced
to be maximizers with very limited means while those wealthy
diversified householders who had profited from risk-taking max-
imization and estate monopolies could abandon the compulsions
of pure economic rationality and, as we shall see, could support
(and further profit from) the state and estate bureaucracies'
notions and practices of moral economy.

So far we have dealt with relative wealth and occupational
differences as means to stratify the rural population into various
groups. Occupational decisions were the key to economic success
or failure in this rural society, but the nature of these decisions,
with their intermingled elements of choice and compulsion,
remains a problem for analysis. The kinds of occupational diversification we have seen resulted not only from the addition
of various industries to the rural economy but were also governed by changes in the authority relations, in the class relations, of rural social and economic life. In the remaining chapters
we shall investigate the broader legal, social, and political framework in which the Austrian peasant economy operated and, in
the last chapter, we can return to reconsider the purposive and
values rational aspects of Austrian peasant life.

~ CHAPTER 5 ~

Peasant Classes

It is not uncommon to find country men and women living in Austria in the early seventeenth century referred to as the "vulgar" (*gemain*) and "inferior" (*schlecht*) peasantry. With such derisive, prejudicial terms those of higher status had traditionally distinguished themselves from their inferiors.[1] The peasantry was, in the eyes of the Imperial authorities, an unrestrained rebellious rabble[2] whose representatives could not be allowed to meet their prince in person.[3] This attitude that persons of subject or lower status were inevitably and congenitally deficient was carefully cultivated by Austrian authorities, and we must keep it in mind as part of the background to this discussion.

The Upper Austrian peasantry's attack on this dichotomous perception of human society in the early modern period was halfhearted, roundabout, and weakened by the stake the tenant-owners themselves had in it; but though their resistance was finally crushed, the social values and practices that produced it as well as the internal contradictions that spelled its failure remain of the greatest historical interest. In the face of a social dualism whose origins and traditions reached at least into the early medieval period of Bavarian lordship, and in the face of the persistent humiliations[4] that accompanied the authorities' practical reinforcement of the peasantry's inferior status, the upper status groups among the subject population of this period maintained, on the surface, a remarkable sense of their collective and individual worth. At the same time, as we shall see, they denied such worth and status to those below them.

THE COLLECTIVE STATUS OF THE PEASANTRY BY 1600:
THE EXAMPLE OF *Robot*

The collective status of the Austrian subject population changed with the successful emergence of new forms of estate-building and management as well as through sixteenth-century conflicts between Estates and crown. The social vision of the "whole house" that sustained both the growth of the new estates and, ultimately, their owners' more profound integration into the state during the seventeenth century also redefined the collective status of the subject population. A rejuvenated vision of a classical agricultural state extolled the collective functioning of the rural lower classes as the essential basis of all social and political life. At the same time, a relatively simple view of the composition of rural society ascribed the benefits of the subject population's collective status to a specific class of peasants, namely, the owners of tenures on farms, houses, mills, workshops, and inns.

It is possible to view the developments that sustained the economic pluralization among the rural population, which the inventories have revealed, in an altogether positive light by seeing the changes of the sixteenth century as the creative response of lords and subjects alike to pressures and economic opportunities among both Austrians and residents of neighboring German territories.[5] On the basis of the picture that emerges from the household inventories one might argue that rural society, under the double impetus of new estate management and the addition of an industrial sector to the rural economy, was able to exploit new opportunities for production and exchange as well as new tasks and functions in the commercial and service sectors. It appears that the market chances of the Austrian peasantry multiplied in this period: there was increased geographic and social mobility and the peasantry was able to generate new institutions in its stepped-up search for personal and collective advantage. Some of these social innovations were in turn codified and administered by the owners and managers of the emerging great estates who thus protected the efforts and advancements of a select group among their subjects while at the same time protecting and expanding their own controls over all their properties and tenants.

One could claim, moreover, that through the conflicts among the several Upper Austrian and Habsburg authorities as they unfolded during this period, the peasantry's elite achieved greater collective identity and higher and more significant political status. Not only did they seem to participate in and profit from their overlords' economic and political rivalries but they also apparently obtained their lords' support in maintaining the integrity and stability of their communities' social life as well as their dominance over it. One could say that they waged a partially successful legal and military struggle for equality under the law and occasionally for elective public control over their magistrates. At the same time, they continued to organize in associations of their various crafts, trades, and occupations, or of the parish churches and priests. At the larger level of the Upper Austrian Estates, the Interim Resolution of 1597 had formulated new guidelines for the treatment and administration of the Upper Austrian subject population and had thereby apparently raised the peasantry's collective legal status; at the more local level of the magnates' judicial authority many of the estate codes also required that their magistrates treat all subjects, rich or poor, equally and, in at least one case, the subjects were reminded that they ought to treat each other as it befits members of a Christian brotherhood.[6]

Such a "positive" perception of the collective status of the subject population may seek to give the post-1525 peasantry a creative role in the building of early modern society,[7] but it blocks a more detailed view of the history of the rural population in this period. We no longer need to be told that "only seldom . . . were the peasants objects of dominance, a dull amorphous mass, without initiative, frozen in political lethargy and impotence."[8] What we need rather is to understand precisely how the economically and socially differentiated rural population participated in and was shaped by the many changes that took place between 1500 and 1600. The ideal type of peasant society on which the interpretation outlined above rests is one that admits to the internal differentiation of the peasantry but that nevertheless perceives the units of analysis to be the entire, undifferentiated housecommunity and the village. We may well ask: Was there then a "dull amorphous mass" below the class of house and community heads?

To begin to view such an interpretation critically it is useful to turn to recent work by Alan Macfarlane, who cites English evidence to dispute the view that in England a "peasant" society existed before about 1350 and that a number of factors combined in the following period, to about 1700, to destroy the communal and familial aspects of rural society and give birth to a period of individualism and capitalism. Macfarlane's research into the records of two contrasting English communities suggests that a "communal" model is not supported by the English historical evidence and that "individualism" may be found in England as far back as the records can take us.[9] In the pages that follow we are going to argue in a somewhat similar fashion and maintain that what Macfarlane calls the "peasant" model (in which "the basic element of society is not the individual, but the family, which acts as a unit of ownership, production and consumption" and "parents and children are also co-owners and co-workers")[10] is also not applicable to the rural population of sixteenth and early seventeenth century Austria. We need to develop a new conceptualization of the collective status of the peasantry that can take into account the high degree of individual economic and social differentiation that existed within the housecommunity, the peasant family, and the surviving forms of community corporations.

There is a weakness in Professor Macfarlane's approach that severely limits its direct applicability to a Central European setting. To begin with, his "peasant" model is something of an oversimplification of what Marx, Weber, Chayanov, Wolf, and others have said about the internal social divisions of peasant communities and families. What he is in fact attacking is the chronology and the "whiggish" aspects of the history of English rural society found in some of these authors' writings. He, correctly, denies the periodization of the evolution from peasant communalism to capitalistic individualism; he also, however, drops altogether or simplifies to the point of caricature the so-

ciological concepts and methodologies developed by these theo-
reticians of rural society.[11] This is a dangerous step for him
because these authors are not positing as simple a "family"
model of rural society as he seems to think. Eric Wolf, for
example, in his classic text, is, among other things, primarily
concerned with "whether [the family] unit cannot be subdivided
conceptually still further, and whether such subdivisions do not
also occur 'naturally' ";[12] in his essay on "Closed Corporate
Peasant Communities in Mesoamerica and Central Java,"[13] he
posits a model for the "closing" and "opening" of rural communities that, despite recent criticisms of it, still offers a significant historical explanation for changes in rural communalism
without resorting to a long-term developmentalist periodization
of historical change.

The paradigmatic change that Professor Macfarlane offers us
is in reality limited to the history of England and there to a
change in periodization (with which one can agree). The sub-
stantive part of an alternative sociology of English rural society
is, however, not very well developed. The conceptualization of
"capitalism" and "individualism" on which he builds lacks the
complex insights and refinements of those very writers whose
chronology he has rejected. His idea of "capitalism," for example, is only loosely defined and is akin to the idealistic and
commercial definitions of the word that Maurice Dobb correctly
rejected long ago as leading "inexorably to the conclusion that
nearly all periods of history have been capitalist."[14] His evidence
concerning the primacy of individuals in the family and community, the land market, and the complexities of ownership
and inheritance, is all very significant and one suspects that it
is here that the chief value of Professor Macfarlane's work will
lie. His data still need to be compared to what other researchers,
most notably, for example, Margaret Spufford and Cicely Howell,[15] have found, and we need to see much more of what his
proposed exhaustive study[16] will reveal.

The expressed ambition of *The Origins of English Individualism* is a "'paradigmatic shift'"[17] and we cannot fault the author
for not offering much evidence at this stage, which must necessarily be theoretical; however, it is precisely in the theoretical

aspects that his attempt falls short. Most disappointing about what Professor Macfarlane proposes in *Origins* is that he in fact accepts and depends on the peasant model's relevance for other areas of Europe, especially east Central Europe. His study may actually be read as a nationalistic argument whose purpose is not a revision of the analysis of early modern rural society but a restatement of the difference of English history from that of the continent. So we learn that England had no "peasants"; but the "peasants" are defined in ways that anthropologists have not generally accepted for a number of years.[18] A genuine paradigmatic shift requires genuine conceptual innovations and these are conspicuously absent. Finally, nothing is said about "origins" except to remove them to some apparently prehistoric realm.

The specific subjects with which Professor Macfarlane concerns himself—the significance of individuals in relation to the nature of property ownership, inheritance, the land market, the mobility of people and labor—are, however, also of great significance for the study of continental, especially German and Austrian rural society in the early modern period. There is in progress a revision in the historiography of these early modern peasant societies that suggests that a transformation of the fundamental social relationships and the peasants' collective status was occurring in this period. According to this revision, we may hypothesize that the sixteenth century saw the disappearance of the substance but not the forms of power lodged in house-communities and in village commune and guild organizations (*Gemeinde* and *Genossenschaften*), while at the same time the primary focus of authority and other relationships shifted to individuals. Contrary to what Professor Macfarlane argues, the disappearance of a "peasant" society by the mid-seventeenth century and the appearance of "capitalist" and "individualist" forms seem certain, constituting an important change in the periodization of early modern Central European history. Moreover, some of the developments in Austria suggest that the anticommunal trend also had deep roots in landlord and peasant thinking and action before the sixteenth century, and we may eventually be able to push this periodization back in time much further. This chapter intends to show that at the latter end of the period, the "paradigmatic" concept that might explain these changes in Austrian rural history is not to be found in capitalism or individualism—although these play important parts—but in the development of the absolute state and, specifically, in the bureaucratization of individual, family, and communal life.

By about 1500, a new pattern of Austrian rural politics that would dominate the next century and a half had become apparent. Throughout east and south Central Europe those with some property and authority were trying to expand what they had, by any legal and quasi-legal means available or by outright usurpation. This was a period of interlopers, of invasion by sword and pen, of a testing of old rights against new interpretations and manipulations of old law; it was a period of communal and familial civil war, of betrayal of neighbor by neighbor and kin by kin for the sake of improving one's position and security. We may say that the peasant uprisings of the period were only a part of a contest for authority and advantage in which everyone participated either actively or by default and in which polyglot legal competence was as important as the violent and well-timed overriding of law. The initiatives and activities of ecclesiastical and secular lords aided by the collaboration of the state changed the status of the peasantry, reorganizing and decommunalizing the internal institutions and structures of peasant houses and villages. The year 1597 is, as we will see in a moment, of epochal significance in this transformation because it saw, finally, the assertion, however partial, of public law over private law and of state-guaranteed contract over usurpation and will.

An example of this process of change is the transformation in Upper Austria of labor service or *robot** from a medieval institution that was a part of the duties accompanying personal bondage (*Leibeigenschaft*) to a tax owed by all subjects of all

---

* The word *robot* is of Slavic origin and entered Austrian usage in the mid-fourteenth century. It existed alongside the older German *Werchart* and *Scharwerk* until the mid-sixteenth century when it was adopted officially by royal and estate officials as well as by peasant lawyers contesting estate and state claims.

126

seigneurial authorities and enforced by state law and estate authorities.

Two distinctly separate forms of labor service predominated in Austria during the Middle Ages.[19] Most prevalent, and most vaguely defined, were those services that the territorial authorities could demand from all subjects in case of emergency and war. Subjects could be called on by royal or other order to build fortifications, dikes, roads, and bridges, for example, as the need arose. This first kind of *robot* was not legally regulated and was potentially unlimited. The second form of labor service was a part of the contractually defined relationship between specific authorities (chiefly ecclesiastical in the Middle Ages) and certain of their subjects. From the Upper Austrian evidence of the thirteenth and fourteenth centuries it is clear that these specifically limited services could vary greatly from subject to subject, and that not all subjects owed these services. They were administered and accounted for by administrative units (*Ämter*) of the estates and houses could be variously grouped within these *Ämter* to render combinations of manual or draft services. In all cases the services required were spelled out in great detail. Furthermore, as the *robot* register of the abbey Kremsmünster from the year 1299 already indicates, the obligated subjects could negotiate through their bailiffs to substitute a cash payment for the actual rendering of service.[20] The fourteenth and fifteenth centuries saw the introduction, development, and expansion of similar rights by secular authorities, some of whom had acquired or sponsored ecclesiastical estates and institutions. Others attracted *Leibeigene* or other kinds of bound subjects to their estates and extracted labor services from them, or they simply asserted rights to the first kind of *robot* services as a part of their responsibility for the commonweal and, incidentally, to improve their estates and upgrade their value.

It was the deliberate confusion and blending of the two kinds of *robot* services by the state as well as by the authorities in the sixteenth century that produced the radically altered form of *robot* we find in Austria after 1600. In 1499, for example, the estate authorities of Freistadt near the Bohemian border demanded that their subjects, who were for the most part free tenants, collectively render, according to *Ämter*, such general services as woodcutting and hay and straw haulage; at the same time the estate administration left the way open for further *robot* demands to be made in the future "at the authority's mercy."[21] At about the same time *robot* services began to play a greater role in the pawning of estates (*Pfandherrschaft*) and it was increasingly to an estate owner's advantage to be able to offer the labor services—or the alternative labor fees—as one of the estate's incomes to a potential creditor. The subjects of the estate Windhag experienced this change in 1508 when they discovered that their labor services, measured by *Ämter* and requisitioned by the estate manager, were a part of a lien contract that stipulated also that the current owner of the estate could raise and lower these services at will. Such contracts were upheld by a royal order in 1522, contested by the peasant rebels in 1525, and, finally, upheld by another royal order in 1526.[22]

In the sixteenth century it was the royal treasury administration (*Hofkammer*) that took the lead in this process of transforming and combining the two kinds of *robot* to a universal and uniform obligation. For example, when treasury officials drew up an inventory for the royal estate Steyr in 1526 in preparation for its pawning (in 1533), they also included a list of *robot* services and their cash equivalents that were assigned to all individual houses or groups of houses. In 1535 this was supplemented with specified fines for failure to serve or pay. Also around 1500, the royal administration changed the character of the unspecified common welfare *robot*. Citing military needs (against the Hussites in the fifteenth century, the Turks, Hungarians, and Swedes in the sixteenth and seventeenth) the royal administration extended the call for *robot* labor to build fortifications to all royal subjects in 1487 and, by order of Archduke Ferdinand in 1526, to all subject householders in Upper Austria. Needless to say, estate owners as well as royal managers and lien holders exploited this general labor for their personal advantage when they could. By mid-sixteenth century it is not uncommon to find a general *robot* clause in various estates' rules and regulations similar to that in the 1553 *Taiding* of the estate Windhag according to which a magistrate or bailiff could request service as it was needed and fine those who did not comply.[23]

During the 1560s and '70s the "Lower Austrian"* treasury officials (*Kammerräte*) took decisive steps to create a uniform labor obligation and an alternative fee (*robotgeld*) for each subject house. By 1568 they required the Upper Austrian estate-owning authorities to extract *robot* or *robotgeld* from everyone, including those who had hitherto been exempt from such service.[24] This regulation was of course applied to such royal lien estates as Steyr, which the crown redeemed in 1569 and where a comprehensive program of administrative reform included the imposition of a *robotgeld* on all subject houses in preparation for a new pawn arrangement. When the estate's subjects were convened in 1588 to meet representatives of the "Lower Austrian" *Kammer* to negotiate the *robotgeld*, they sent representatives but refused, in effect, to participate in the negotiations or to render services.[25] Curiously enough, they thought that the royal officials were not acting on the emperor's authority—which they were—and sought Imperial intercession, but wholly in vain. The innovations were enforced after 1597 and by a special royal decree for Steyr in 1606.

Treasury officials sought also to set an example for other estate owners by raising uniform *robot* and *robotgeld* on their private estates—and here too they encountered peasant resistance. The most famous case is that of the royal *Kammer* official Ritter Christoph Haym, a Catholic immigrant from Styria who purchased the estate Reichenstein, to the northeast of Windhag, in 1567 and sought there to reproduce the more stringent subject relations that already existed in southern Styria. He introduced new *robot* regulations as part of stricter terms of leasehold when these changed hands through death and sale. His householders rebelled in the fall of 1568 under the leadership of a Protestant parish priest, Koloman Khunringer, and a well-known house-

---

* I.e., the state administrative division as defined by Maximilian I in the early sixteenth century. This included, besides Upper Austria, Lower Austria, Styria, Carinthia, and Carniola. The administrative "Upper Austria" consisted of Tyrol, Vorarlberg, and the Imperial holdings in Swabia and elsewhere. I use quotation marks when referring to state administrative divisions.

holder by the name of Siegmund Gaisrucker who attached a notice of personal feud to Haym's castle gate, by all accounts an anachronistic act even then. After the compulsory arbitration between Haym and his tenants left the latter worse off than before, the *Kammerrat* was assassinated by unknown assailants near his home in the early summer of 1571. Gaisrucker, the object of an Imperial manhunt, disappeared in the woods north of the Danube and the quarrel between the Hayms and their subjects dragged on through the remainder of the century—it was mostly in the hands of lawyers hired by both the peasants and the owners—until it was finally settled in 1597 by the Imperial Interim.[26] The royal treasury, of course, supported the Haym party throughout this period as a part of its policy to spread uniform *robot* throughout the duchies. Its direct orders, in 1579, to the abbot of Gleink instructing him to extract *robot* from all his subjects as it was "customary" elsewhere suggests the lengths to which they were prepared to go. The expressed reason for this direct order is interesting and revealing: *robot* was a measure of the subjects' obedience to authority and to central authority in particular. Implied as well was that it measured the obedience of lower to higher authority.

Robot and *robotgeld* were major points of contention in the uprising of 1595-1597. Seventy years before, the moderate party at the Innsbruck negotiations in 1525 had already accepted universal *robot* in principle and its concern with limiting both service and alternative fees to acceptable levels also dominated the negotiations of 1596 and 1597 in Prague. These latter negotiations on *robot* as well as on other issues that were raised in direct connection with *robot* services reveal the extent to which this process of what we may call the bureaucratization of labor services had progressed among the estate owners and the extent to which the state had drawn the peasant householders to its side in its larger struggle against the noble Estates. We also begin to get some idea of the extent to which this process had penetrated into the peasant housecommunity itself.

The representatives of the Upper Austrian Estates, headed by Georg Erasmus Tschernembl, the estate owner and Calvinist scholar who would lead the Upper Austrian Estates into a fatal alliance with the Protestant party and the Bohemian frondeurs in 1618, arrived in Prague with instructions to demand twenty-four days of *robot* labor (and settle for no less than twenty), to reserve for the owners the decision whether the service was to be performed or the money to be paid, to demand that a day of service be measured from sunup to sundown, and that extra days could be demanded in return for some compensation. The royal negotiators in the meantime had come to an agreement with the peasants (who had tried to reduce service to six days) that twelve days was a reasonable period and it was the royal position that determined the final outcome of the negotiations with regard to labor service. The final formulation of the Interim was decisively brief: "To begin with, as far as the *robot* is concerned, the subjects owe their lords and authorities fourteen days of work a year, and it is the estate authority's prerogative to demand either *robot* or *robotgeld* but not to burden the subjects with both simultaneously."[27] Although we can see how the state "protected" the peasants here, it also seems an excessively laconic conclusion to over a century of legal conflict and violence. It simply advanced the position of the state and of prior administrative practice. This is especially so if we consider what issues it did not address directly. No limit was put on *robotgeld*, for example. The peasants had complained, moreover, that some lords were beginning to demand that stem family elders and lodgers be considered separate "units" for purposes of labor services and fees, and that they either render such service or be charged an alternative fee. The Interim is silent on this issue and, as later evidence suggests, the practice continued wherever lords wanted to advance these claims.[28] In the case of the monastery Wilhering, women were declared a separate *robot* category in 1597.[29] Connected to this is the question of child labor services. The authorities had long held protective authority over orphans and illegitimate children and had increasingly come to interpret this as a priority right to the servant labor, as it was needed, not only of orphans but of the children of all subjects. The peasants protested in 1595 against this change from orphan labor (*Waisendienst*) to forced servant labor (*Gesindezwangsdienst*), performed for the most part by

131

children and adolescents,[30] but in this regard the Interim is also silent. An Imperial general order had, in 1582, required the Austrian subject population to offer their children's labor to the authorities and the drafters of the Interim saw no need to alter this.[31] Moreover, since the seigneurial and state demand for labor was not nearly as great as the Imperial regulations had stipulated, child labor went the way of *robot* service and was for the most part commuted into a release fee.[32]

The final stage in the transformation of *robot* to a generally applicable, centrally defined, and locally administered duty or tax began immediately after the publication and acceptance of the Interim on 5 May 1597. Its implementation began in September of the same year with the arbitration of 115 contracts between specific estate authorities and their subjects in which the labor services and fees were spelled out, and in which such other administrative innovations as child labor, the seigneurial supervision of inheritance and property transfer, the payment of transfer fees, personal individual exemptions from the inventorying process, the payment of new services in kind, ordinary and extraordinary state taxes, tithe payments, the feeding of the estate owners' cattle and dogs, payments for errand services, preemptive buying privileges for the estate owners, et cetera, were defined, regulated, and made subject to the state's administrative and criminal judicial authority. The actual implementation of these regulations and the contracts that grew out of them varied greatly from estate to estate. Some peasant subjects still had to be coerced into performing *robot* services, but now they confronted both the owner of the estate and the state.[33] During the seventeenth century, the estate owners progressed at their own pace in actually imposing the *robot*[34] and continued, for the most part, the experimental process which they had begun in the sixteenth century of calculating which combinations of service and payment worked best for them.[35]

Compared to Styria, Bohemia, and Lower Austria, the Upper Austrian subject population was relatively well-off as far as the weight of the *robot* burden was concerned; in Styria, for example, the *robot* burden, already greater in 1600, continued to expand so that by 1778 lords were empowered by the state to demand 165 days labor service a year from their subjects.[36] Demesne farming was not as well developed in Upper Austria as it was in the other duchies of "Lower Austria" and Bohemia and consequently the Upper Austrian demand for labor services was not as great.[37] It is noteworthy, however, that when estate owners in Upper Austria sought to copy the Bohemian or Styrian forms of estate management, they simply expanded their demands illegally and defeated their protesting subjects, who were reduced to lawsuits that they fought as *Ämter* (administrative units),[38] in the administrative and higher courts that the lords often controlled, both directly and indirectly; thus the Starhembergs, attempting to diversify into tobacco and silkworms, were able to raise the *robot* on their estate Schwertberg to 71½ days by the second half of the seventeenth century.[39]

The Upper Austrian type of estate management used its demesne farms (*Meierhöfe*) not for producing marketable grains and cattle but for maintaining a household and for growing such raw materials as hops and hemp needed for commercial brewing and textile enterprises.[40] Labor demands were small and *robotgeld* was consequently more significant than the actual performance of labor services. It is of some importance for us to look more closely into the function peasant *robot* actually performed in such an estate economy and into what group of incomes it belongs. Georg Grüll has already noticed that the *robotgeld* added up to a substantial portion of the incomes of those estates that collected it from all their subject houses. Thus we may see from his tables that the small estate Klamm, in the northeastern part of Upper Austria, obtained 11.7 percent of its 4,798fl gross income in 1660 from *robotgeld*; the much larger abbey estate Garsten with 1,258 subject houses collected 2,166fl in *robot* fees, or 21.1 percent of its gross income, in 1631.[41]

Elsewhere I have reconstructed on the basis of account books and accounting memoranda the annual incomes and expenditures of the estate Weinberg for the period around 1600[42] and my calculations support these impressions and enable us to refine them further. From this work I can select certain traditional and "new" incomes for certain years so that the changing significance of peasant *robotgeld* stands out much more sharply:

TABLE 5.1
Selected Weinberg Incomes
(in guilders)

Year	Rents	Robotgeld	Prov. Tax	War Tax	Gross	Net
1581	960	632 (7%)*	1,546		8,895†	3,424
1614	689	1,116 (11%)	1,103	2,247	9,936	1,691
1622	687	1,157 (7%)	1,079	2,247	16,392	2,994
1630	702	2,308 (14%)‡	1,086	2,269	17,570	5,853
1634	726	2,343 (15%)	1,121	2,315	15,592	9,060

SOURCE: Rebel, *Rural Subject Population*, p. 127.

* Percentage of gross.

† I selected only certain incomes to compare to each other and to the gross and net incomes and therefore these figures do not add up to the gross.

‡ The increase is accounted for by the addition of the *Fuhrgeld*, a fee substituting for *robot* in draft horses and cartage.

The majority of the incomes of an estate in the sixteenth century were from "new" sources, that is, from incomes that were the result of administrative innovations of the estate or state. From the table we can readily see that by the early seventeenth century the Upper Austrian estate was no longer dependent on the traditional rent incomes; such incomes as the *robotgeld* or the various forms of state taxes (which were passed on to the Estate and then the royal treasury but only after having become a part, for a time, of the estate owner's annual budget) far outstripped the chief traditional incomes in terms of the quantities of revenues they produced. This means we can no longer speak about a period of crisis in estate revenues because of an inflationary devaluation in rents. We must instead recognize that an entirely different kind of estate, one dependent on cash flow from state taxes and state-regulated fees, had come into being by 1600. Private and public estates functioned as administrative adjuncts to the state and derived their chief incomes from this functional change.

The new incomes, among them the *robotgeld*, ought collectively and individually to be held against the net rather than the gross incomes because, like the old rents, very little overhead went into producing these incomes. It is readily apparent that in some years without any two of them there would not have been a net income at all (in some accounts the state tax incomes were a part of the "expenditures" but in others they were not and they were not in fact passed on to the state).

If we look at the *robotgeld* specifically from this point of view we can come to a further conclusion about the significance of what was happening on these estates. There is an essential difference between requiring the actual performance of labor service and collecting a fee instead. While the *robot* services were legally restricted to only certain kinds of labor and indeed were spelled out in the private medieval *robot* regulations in minute detail, the *robotgeld* enabled the estate owners to pursue an entirely different strategy with labor. They could now purchase all of the estate's labor needs in the market and, at the same time, purchase much more varied and specialized kinds of labor than their traditional *robot* laborers were required (or able) to furnish. And in any case, some of the "old" labor service aspects continued, for the *robotgeld* was not collected from all subject houses and a few of the householders whose farms were in close proximity to the estate's limited farming operations continued to furnish the traditional services as these were needed. In 1635, the estate Weinberg paid in wages for all its hired help 636fl out of a total *robotgeld* income of 2,300fl.[43] For this it got not only the several hundred laborers it needed for harvesting but it also imported a Bohemian brewmaster and a Bohemian pond-builder for two of its commercial operations, paid its entire administrative staff, particularly the estate manager (*Pfleger*) and the gamekeeper and his helpers, as well as a number of servants, messengers, and guards. The costs of the estate owners' *entire* labor, craft, and professional needs—including vineyard laborers in the eastern provinces, lawyers on retainer in Vienna and Passau, craftsmen to keep their various *palazzi* in the provinces and in Vienna in repair, personal messengers and bodyguards—amounted to 2,800fl.[44] We may therefore say that in terms of the estate Weinberg along, the *robotgeld* produced an enormous profit; in terms of the owner's entire complex of estates, vineyards, toll houses, and *palazzi*, of which Weinberg was the major part, the Weinberg *robotgeld* covered 82 percent of the labor services, professional fees, expense accounts, tips, and maintenance labor costs.

What we have outlined here taking place in the course of the sixteenth century—the advent of a universally compulsory *robot*, the separation of *robot* from *robotgeld* (both based on state regulation by 1597), and the increasing adoption of the *robotgeld* by the estate-owning authorities after 1600—amounts to an epochal change. We see here a change in the legal character of *robot*, as it emerged from the private law of diverse authorities (including that of the royal treasury) and became a part of the administrative law of the absolute state. We also see, in the actual practice of estate administration, *robotgeld* as the capitalization of labor appropriation by the estate owners achieved with the assistance of bureaucratic regulation backed by the courts and by military coercion. In other words, in the sixteenth century the Austrian state was beginning to develop a legal-rational character with distinctly capitalist functions.[45]

What was happening to the *robot* was happening to the other "traditional" institutions of Austrian peasant life as well. Old forms and old names survived everywhere but their functions and meanings changed. It is clear that to characterize these changes as some aspects of "refeudalization," or "second serfdom," or even as "feudal capitalism" misses an essential feature: the momentum driving these changes forward did not originate from a feudal reaction by which individual estate owners tried to counter the inflationary devaluation of their rents, but came initially from a change in the fiscal policy of the crown by which the market value of royal estates and incomes was upgraded in order to increase their pawn value. In the process new incomes were invented and old incomes radically altered. It was the universalization and bureaucratization of these "reforms," for which we may take 1597 as the pivotal date, that determined the changes in the collective status of the subject population in the period of early Habsburg absolutism.

From the Upper Austrian experience with *robot* it is clear

that "capitalism" and "individualism" were at work in the transformation of rural life. The conversion of *robot* to *robot-geld* provides evidence for the former and the extraction of *robot* from individual houses and, beyond that, from specific individuals in the housecommunity (lodgers, stem family elders, and servants) suggests that the village and family "communities" were being penetrated by administrative policies—and, conversely, by economic calculations—whose focus was the individual. At the same time, however, it is also clear that something beyond individualism and capitalism, something that contained them, produced them, and limited them, was also at work reshaping the traditional institutions of rural life. It is to Leonard Krieger's great credit that, on the basis of Günter Franz's largely wrong-headed work on the German peasant uprisings of 1525, he was able to perceive that the areas of greatest peasant unrest were also those areas where state bureaucratization was most advanced.[46] Our account of the reform in the *robot* regulations has illustrated and supported this connection between later sixteenth century revolts and bureaucratization. However, Professor Krieger also made the mistake of ascribing great importance to a "feudal" component in this process of state-building instead of investigating more closely the actual form that this early modern bureaucratization took. If one wished to add to the "isms" that have been used to describe what is happening in this difficult period of mixed forms and transitions in Central Europe one could rather characterize the chief source of the peasantry's collective experience as "bureaucratic capitalism." In what follows we shall begin to explore the nature of Austrian bureaucratization of rural society, concentrating in particular on the changes it brought about in the internal affairs of the peasant housecommunity and on the interpretations these changes allow us to make regarding the household inventory data we have been able to analyze in previous chapters.

BUREAUCRATIZATION, HOUSECOMMUNITY, AND CLASS

While it is clear that Alan Macfarlane's contribution to English rural history concerning the extension of "modernizing" forces of individualism and capitalism backward into English medieval history is essentially correct, a problem remains with his idea that a "peasant" model survived on the Continent. Other writers have noted that such a model of analysis may in fact not be applicable to continental rural societies in the early modern period. Jan de Vries has suggested most succinctly that in a number of areas in seventeenth-century Europe

> . . . the 'farmers' acquired a mental outlook characterized by an interest in material comforts, status, and even urban influences plus a familiarity with the written word as it was used to familiarize contractual and market relations. The gap between these relatively secure cultivators and the supporting cast of rural dwellers was now such that the village and parish ties linking peasants together ceased to hold the moral authority they once had. And as industrial employment rose to become the chief support of many of this supporting cast, or caste, the poor, too, elaborated a way of life foreign to the peasant culture of earlier generations.[47]

The question arises: what "authority"—moral or otherwise—displaced the village and parish as the integrating element in the "peasant" society? There was a similar "gap" in Austria between "farmers" and a "supporting cast" of rural dwellers by 1600, as the findings from the inventories suggest, which emerged as a serious (and publicly recognized) moral dilemma by the mid-eighteenth century.[48] The cleavages were deep and bore no resemblance to traditional social divisions. We shall argue in the remainder of this study that the "moral" glue that tried to hold this rural society together after about 1600, with greatly varying degrees of success, was the bureaucratic and legal apparatus of the Austrian absolute state functioning through the mediating institutions of provincial administrations (*Landesregierung* and Estates), estate and market authorities, and, most significantly, the subject house and "family."

The concept "bureaucratization," as it is used here, is problematical because we are obviously not dealing with the centralized institutions and bureaus staffed by salaried civil servants that are the normal subjects of such inquiry. Our focus is instead on the housecommunity, whose membership appeared in chapter two and whose basic economic and occupational characteristics were analyzed in chapters three and four. How did that housecommunity, and the families and individuals within it, fare under the new collective status of the subject population? How do we define its new state-regulated character and functions? If we consider the subject house with its housecommunity as a quasi-bureaucratic unit, then we can apply to it Max Weber's concept of "bureaucratic authority" and tie it to his model of class structure, and thereby illuminate some new aspects of rural social relations under Habsburg absolutism.

It is doubtful that Weber would have sanctioned such an enterprise, but one may find in his writings sufficient elements of a sociology of the housecommunity to allow us to see it as a part of his sociology of class and bureaucratic dominance and to use it to interpret the social-historical significance of the data we have so far uncovered and analyzed. We may begin with his discussion of the process of "dissolution" of the housecommunity as "community of maintenance" (*Versorgungsgemeinschaft*), as it moves from a "production community," in which the various productive enterprises of the members are carried on and contribute to the collective welfare of the housecommunity and, beyond that, of the "neighborhood" or commune (*Gemeinde*), to a "consumption" community that no longer contains or coordinates its members' productive activities and members' security depends chiefly on the institutions of a larger polity.[49] The chief cause of this change, aside from such indeterminate and external factors as increases in economic opportunity and development of money economy, is what Weber calls the changes in the "accountability" (*Rechenhaftigkeit*) of the members of the housecommunity. For Weber this accountability was not of recent origin, or even part of the evolution toward modernity, but was found in antiquity. Initially this concept concerned the right of individuals to inherit weapons and tools and, later, came to include marriage relations that established legitimate heirs and took into account the dower rights of the wife. Accountability differentiated the relationships of members to the housecommunity and thereby undermined the egalitarian communal economics of the housecommunity.[50] Most significantly, such "accountability" not only introduced cleavages between the legitimate and illegitimate children in the housecommunity but also radically altered the terms of membership of the legitimate children. All members may be held to account so that

> the participation 'by birth' in the communal activities of the house with its advantages and duties is replaced by a rational socialization. The individual may still be 'born into' the housecommunity but he is as child already a potential 'worker' (Kommis) or 'partner' of the rationally ordered enterprise which is sustained by the community.[51]

It is precisely this division, based on a concept of accountability (in turn based on marriage and inheritance), that assigned individuals, their families, and households to their proper place in the rural Austrian housecommunity. As the inventories' existence and, more significantly, function, demonstrate, the peasant housecommunities, although still productive units, were penetrated and divided by concepts of accountability that not only took measure of the economic success of the family enterprise as a whole but that also updated the accounts between the various family and other members of the housecommunity on a continuing basis. For much of the remainder of this study we shall not only examine the penetration of accountability and its bureaucratic significance in greater detail but we will also focus on the two alternative career tracks (worker or partner) to which the members of the housecommunity were assigned as children.

Weber was aware that the divisions and "individualism" introduced by accountability into the housecommunity's inner life paralleled exactly that separation of the public from the private that accompanies the rationalization of production and "the obvious bureaucratization" of even private economic enterprise.[52] However, he saw these developments taking place in the commercial cities of northern Italy during the late Middle

Ages, and we must leave his discussion of the housecommunity's history at that point and look to other elements of his sociology to enable us to develop further the quasi-bureaucratic character of the Austrian peasant house as it appears in the sources. In order to understand the housecommunity in terms of bureaucratization and class, we need to understand better not only the divergent market situations it contained but also its internal authority relations. In this regard we may posit that the inhabitants of the peasant houses constituted what Weber called "imperatively coordinated" groups,[53] subject to the legitimate and legal-rational authority of the state. The peasant housecommunity, internally divided according to market and authority relations, was a class situation in which the individual and family units took their places according to both their market chances and their position in relation to the familial arrangements of the head of the house. The heads of the housecommunities were, in addition to being farmers, tenants, and parents, officially authorized administrators of the changing familial, personnel, and property relations contained by their house, and it is their family, property, and household relations that are of primary interest to this study.

If, as I shall argue in greater detail below, the bureaucratic functions and roles of the various members of the housecommunity were more important, from an analytic point of view, than their economic enterprises and occupations, their family position, and their relations with their village and parish communities, then we can argue further that from the point of view of bureaucratization all the house inhabitants constituted what Weber called an "acquisition class" (*Erwerbsklasse*).[54] Those few who had held, were holding, or were about to hold the headship of the house constituted what he called the "positively privileged" members of that class. Those whose family, employment, and property relations were administered for them were, then, the "negatively privileged." An entirely different conception of social class relations and conflict thus emerges. Wolfgang Mommsen has summed up Weber's distinctions as follows:

The concepts of 'class' and 'class struggle' apply more directly to the antagonisms within the [acquisition classes]. It should be noted, however, that Weber defines the class character of the [acquisition classes]—which include the enterpreneurs as well as the 'professions' *and* the workers—in a way which is very different from the Marxist one. The decisive criterion is not the ownership or the disposal of property but the actual degree of participation in the entrepreneurial management as such.[55]

In the pages that follow we will explore how the attempt to bureaucratize both royal and private estates along legal and rational lines created a positively privileged acquisition class (the masters of the house) whose members functioned as the lowest instance of bureaucratic authority, and as such determined the market situation and authority relations of the other members of the housecommunity (a minority of whom—the prospective heirs—were also positively privileged while the majority belonged to the negatively privileged). It is this class division, whose accountability cut through the housecommunity and the families and households it contained, that imposed a variety of often conflicting roles on the family and housecommunity members and it is here, finally, that we must look for the class conflicts and "psychological strains," mentioned earlier, which characterized the social life of the Austrian peasantry as it experienced the first extention of the absolute state.

The Housed and the Unhoused: The Bureaucratization of Property

The image we have so far from the household inventories of the peasantry's economic and occupational stratification deceives us, for the apparent continuum of strata conceals real discontinuities of a class character. There were in effect only two *kinds* of household inventories. One of these described the holdings of the nontenant subject population and the other those of the tenant population. We call the latter "housed" and the former "unhoused." What is also not apparent is that there was an

overlapping of the two so that the "households" of the unhoused, of the laboring population, of the lodgers and servants,
were actually intrinsic parts of the households of the housed
and as such were subject to the authority relations that directed
the economic and social goals of the tenant householders. The
breach introduced into rural social life by this kind of dualism
and overlap in household and, as we shall see, family enterprise,
undermined and distorted the apparent gains in collective status
made by the Austrian peasants in the sixteenth and seventeenth
centuries. What is also not apparent from the inventories is
that there were those who were never inventoried because they
lived entirely outside the order of officially recognized housecommunities. They are not crucial to this study but they deserve
brief discussion.

There were two important legal distinctions among Austria's
rural lower classes which continued to form the basis of their
social system throughout the period of the *ancien régime*. The
first of these was based on the separation of those who were
subjects of one or several of the Upper Austrian authorities
from those who were, in effect, "masterless." In a society where
legal and physical protection by one or another officially recognized authority continued to be the minimal requirement for
personal social status, the absence of such "protection" by authority not merely excluded one from enjoying the privileges
and "freedoms," such as they were, of the subject population,
but also forced one into a life of obscurity and marginal subsistence at the physical fringes of the rural economy and community.[56] Although members of this group might own a cottage
or simply live as a part of a housecommunity at a small farm
"in the woods," they were effectively excluded from the public
life of the estate and subject community.

How many such people there were by around 1600 and what
their condition was are matters on which we cannot obtain any
completely reliable information. The census investigation into
the bleak landscape along the Bohemian border, undertaken
jointly by the authorities of Weinberg and of the city and estate
Freistadt in the winter of 1615 turned up only 113 unregistered
houses—of which twenty-three had been built since 1560—and

these were headed by householders of whom only sixteen did not acknowledge the overlordship of any authority. Most of these houses were cottages evaluated at under 40fl, with only two houses worth over 80fl. The heads of these households were chiefly charcoal burners, woodworkers of various kinds, glass-blowers, basketmakers, and the like.[57] The existence of only sixteen "masterless" households in an area where authority was hard to assert and where three estate-owning authorities shared among themselves well over 2,000 subject houses suggests that this part of the population must have been relatively small. But we cannot really tell how intensively the authorities' census-takers searched for houses nor precisely what areas they covered; nor do we have any idea of what numbers and kinds of people were not heads of households and lived both as parts of unauthorized housecommunities and as transients, beggars, and "gypsies."

This "masterless" class marked the limits of a bureaucratic state whose lowest administrative units were the houses of peasant subjects. In the sixteenth and seventeenth centuries, the masterless were considered a nuisance and occasionally a threat to the social order, especially when they took the opportunities provided by what the householders considered to be legitimate protests to indulge in violence and destruction. As early as 1525, peasant householders asked that the authorities do something about them.[58] They were in effect useless people, who lived outside the newly emergent bureaucratic order; they had chosen to live as cottagers, beggars, and wanderers rather than suffer the conditions that the life of a servant or laborer in a proper peasant house offered. In the course of the later seventeenth and early eighteenth century the state could no longer avoid taking notice of the growing numbers of unemployed and un-attached persons in the countryside but it is significant that in "doing something about them" the state could not break free of its reliance on the house. State-managed factories such as the woolen mills in Linz or the workhouses of Vienna were in effect substitute house administrations for the unemployed and unattached. Beginning in the 1680s, masterless children were "legitimized," i.e., attached to peasant housecommunities by state and estate authorities where they could be supervised and put to work. Estate administrations were made responsible for the poor who had been assigned to one householder or another. Moreover, in 1727, after a royal investigating commission found in rural Upper Austria over 25,000 masterless persons, including over 7,000 children, in need of welfare assistance, the estate authorities were forbidden to increase the cottages available to this class of people. Charles VI decreed that the unattached were to become part of regular peasant houses and again forbade marriage to the unemployed.[59]

This drive to bring the masterless under the care of the "house" and thereby of the bureaucratic state proved to be inadequate to the growing numbers of destitute and by the 1770s the state was willing to assist in the expansion of the cottager class and to regulate expansion of its economic functions (such as allowing its members to keep and deal in livestock).[60] This was followed, in the 1780s, by Joseph II's largely unsuccessful attempts to centralize the welfare of the destitute and unattached. This Austrian welfare state, which worked by enlisting families, households, and publicly managed houses into its poor relief administration, survived until well into the nineteenth and, in some of its aspects, the twentieth century.[61] It was never able to overcome its fundamental contradiction already apparent around 1600: many of those who needed help had fled from or been forced out of families where life had become oppressive and intolerable and the families into which they were reenrolled were often no different. Their lives were treadmills of escape, starvation, reintegration, exploitation, brutalization, and escape.

The masterless class is outside the classes that are the focus of this study. Nevertheless, its presence is of some importance and must be kept in mind. Its numbers were increasing in this period, fed by escapees from the "house," by those who could have no hope of ever becoming a tenant-owner and head of a household and who did not wish to live as someone's private subject. The "masterless" were in effect the logical byproducts of a state based on a family life that was divided between those who had a position as heads (or prospective heads) of houses— and therefore occupied a position in the hierarchy of state

145

administration—and those who were excluded from ever achieving such status and on whom the entire panoply of administrative authorities came to fall. It is to this second division within communities and families that we now turn.

In a period during which the great landlords were reducing and eliminating the specially privileged and so-called "free" properties and tenancies by burdening them with all the normal rents, dues, and services, and at a time when the gentry were insisting that those of their properties that passed into the hands of persons of lower status should lose their third estate privileges, i.e., in a period during which the status of many privileged peasant holdings was in general decline, the desire to become a subject tenant seems actually to have increased. The reason for this lies not only in the pressure an increasing population placed on a limited number of available and impartible tenancies. The estate authorities were pursuing a twofold policy with regard to their properties that made them, despite increasing limitations and burdens, extremely desirable. Unlike their Bavarian counterparts, who were responding to population increase by breaking up larger tenancies and creating a special and large class of small holders and cottagers,[62] the Upper Austrian magnates developed a practice of estate management that relied to a great extent on two classes. Economically independent tenant proprietors paid relatively moderate amounts of traditional rents and not so moderate estate fees and state taxes, and a substantially growing class of nontenant subject laborers either rented their lodgings from one of the subject tenants or else were a part of the tenants' servant population (Gesinde). In addition, the Upper Austrian magnates "yielded" in the course of the sixteenth century to the demand for hereditary and freely disposable subject tenures that had been voiced strongly in Central Europe generally, and Upper Austria specifically, since at least the beginning of the sixteenth century.[63] Since the impartibility of the tenancy was one of the conditions of hereditary status, two broad and legally defined economic classes were created and perpetuated among the peasantry. On one hand were the tenant subjects whose status assured them of more or less secure material well-being and of a full participation in the life of the peasant community as well as of possible achievement of the highest status positions among the tenured peasantry. On the other hand were the dispossessed and the "propertyless" who confronted a lifetime of material scarcity and limited life choices, and whose chances for acquiring a holding and achieving the highest possible status positions were extremely slight. It was for these reasons that demand for subject tenancies remained high.

The process of eliminating freeholds by bureaucratic takeover and of transforming all peasant holdings into uniform tenancies was not done with the mere consent of the royal bureaucracy, but was initially driven forward by the emperor and his "Lower Austrian" officials.[64] In the first place, the royal treasury (Kammer), acting on behalf of the prince as ecclesiastical protector (Vogt), was entitled to the fees charged ecclesiastical estate subjects on receipt of their copyhold documents (issued by the royal bureaucracy), and in the 1570s the heads of monasteries were instructed to proceed with the issuing of these documents and with the collection of fees. The members of the first estate resisted this coercion because they feared loss of control over their peasant subjects and incomes, but with royal decrees guaranteeing them their rights and incomes and with the sale of copyholds extended to all royal estates and lien properties, the process of "levelling" proceeded relatively smoothly after the early 1570s. Private estate owners, who were in many cases also royal creditors and lien administrators as well as officials in the Kammer and in other central institutions, followed the royal lead, and by 1600 there existed a fairly uniform class of copyholding tenant-owners whose position was guaranteed by state law. On occasion, royal authorities acted in lieu of the estate-owning authorities; in some cases they summoned householders who were reluctant to pay their fees and threatened them with the death penalty if the moneys were not immediately forthcoming.[65] On the other hand, they also made certain that estate owners issued a copyhold documentation—and if they did not, Imperial commissars did—and passed the collected fees on to the royal Kammer.

It must be stressed here that, although the estate owners

continued to collect "feudal" dues and continued to exist as
members of provincial political corporations (the Estates) whose
origin was feudal, the changes discussed so far in this chapter
grafted a nonfeudal legal-rational state order to the estates,
making them administrative units, and their owners and managers administrators and executors of state regulations. The
compulsory extension and standardization of copyholds in effect
tied the estate owners even more closely to this bureaucratic
order not just by freezing the feudal incomes collected from
each holding and allowing increased incomes only through the
administration of such state revenues as the *Kontribution* and
Rüstgeld, as we have seen, but also by bringing the estate owners' subjects, both housed and unhoused, under the legal regulation of state administration. The lien administrators, estate
owners and their managers, became the transmitters of state
regulations to the peasant subjects; they carried through new
concepts of tenure and property and they provided the administrative and legal apparatus that the contractual relations arising
from their subjects' new property relations required. They could
no longer treat peasant houses as units in the communal and
estate orders alone but were required to administer them as
units of the state.

As late as the late nineteenth century, many Upper Austrian
peasants' surnames were derived from the names of the houses
in which they lived—and this, in some cases, without being a
member of or related to the residing tenant's family.[66] However,
a house bestowed its particular status as it was legally, economically, and politically defined only on the married couple that
owned it. More specifically, there was only one person in each
house, namely its tenant-owner, who personally represented
the house and all who lived there vis-à-vis the larger community. In return for this customary legal and protective role, the
tenant-owner also wielded disciplinary authority and legal responsibility within the household. Of all the Upper Austrian
subject peasantry, only the tenant-owner as head of a house
derived status from what was originally a position of patriarchal
and feudal authority[67] and became, in the period around 1600,
a bureaucratic function. The subject tenants' homes were places

of refuge and shared this function with the parish churches. It was traditionally the householder's responsibility to maintain and defend the sacred peace and tranquility of his house (*Hausfrieden*).[68] As in classical times, it was supposedly through the manner in which the householder carried out his duties as secular and spiritual lord of his house that an Upper Austrian tenant proprietor gained or lost social esteem.

To recapitulate, beginning during the second half of the sixteenth century, the function of the peasant house changed and with it the official character of the incumbent head of the house was transformed. New lines of communication brought cultural directives to the mass of the population through the incumbent tenant. Incumbency brought with it a host of new opportunities and responsibilities. Gaining and losing incumbency was, as we shall see, governed by precisely calculable economic criteria and surrounded by a series of contracts that assured an uninterrupted succession of heads of houses. Incumbency and the contracts it necessitated were entirely circumscribed by a growing system of administrative law focusing on estates, markets, and houses.

During the second half of the sixteenth century there were two developments that raised the peasant householders' legal responsibilities and opportunities and offered them greater chances for achieving higher social status. First, some estate owners designated certain houses—which had often already been houses of "special" status among the peasantry—as places of special political and administrative importance and made their incumbents potential stand-ins and deputies for the bailiff (*Richter*).[69] Other estate owners extended exclusive beverage-marketing concessions to certain houses, thereby changing them to taverns, or they gave certain mills exclusive contracts for handling the estate farms' milling requirements (*Standmühle*). These places were governed by new regulations and given additional administrative functions. As we saw in connection with the inventories of millers and innkeepers, holding tenure on one of these temporarily or permanently upgraded houses opened great opportunities for a better economic and occupational status; it also made it easier to obtain membership in one or another signif-

149

icant subgroup in the peasant community, a subject to which I shall return later.

The second development, more significant because it touched on all tenant houses, was the transformation of what had been the private "feudal" legal codes of estates, markets, and villages into increasingly uniform administrative law codes. There were at the end of the Middle Ages several sources of law for the Upper Austrian peasantry. Villages had occasionally their own codes, *Hauptmannbriefe*, which regulated the annual election of a village chief and spelled out the duties and rights of the inhabitants.[70] Though an increasingly rare and independent form of legal observance, where they survived the village codes continued to regulate the internal life of their communities' immutable custom.[71] At the other extreme was Imperial law, which had begun to gather momentum with the inquisitorial criminal code of Charles V of 1530; it had been adopted (and in some respects adapted) for the Austrian crownlands by Ferdinand I in 1542.[72] Between these two sources of law were the various authorities of Upper Austria: the members of the upper two Estates, the town councils of the cities and markets, and the *Hofkammer*, each of whom exercised precisely defined combinations of legal competence in relation to their own and each others' subjects, to each other, and to their prince. The prince remained the final source of law and his power to intervene in the legal affairs of Upper Austria had produced the regulation of the lord-subject relationship that occurred in 1597. During the sixteenth century, the estate owners of Upper Austria, particularly if they had acquired, through lien arrangements, the highest authority of royal provincial law, incorporated into their own codes the ancient village codes of their subjects, the codes of the market towns under their jurisdiction, as well as the Imperial regulation and criminal code. The *Landesgerichtsordnung* of Ferdinand I (1559) bureaucratized the administration of law by granting to the royal courts jurisdiction over capital crimes and to the estate owners jurisdiction over all other law. Royal courts, of course, could take over for estate courts that failed to perform. The regulations, together with such Imperial edicts as the 1597 Resolution, established the estate owner's right to be the subjects' immediate source of law; but at the same time, it asserted that the royal law of the land was the final legal authority, above and behind the evolution of all legal authority.[73] The estates were, in short, beginning to become units in the legal administration of the state. Their estate codes, despite many variations and inconsistencies, were the beginnings of a pervasive, state-wide administrative law. The control by the state's official bureaucracy over the estate owners and their officials would not become complete until after 1848, but this did not prevent the latter from standardizing and bureaucratizing regulations governing the peasant subjects. The rural subject population experienced law first and foremost under the jurisdiction of one of those members of the high nobility or clergy who had acquired the highest royal judicial authority (*Bann, Bannkreis*) and who issued annually reconfirmed police regulations for their estates (*Banntaidinge*) and markets (*Marktordnungen*).

Although the estate codes, called *Banntaidinge, Ehafttaidinge, Freiheiten*, and *Marktordnungen*, of late medieval and early modern Austria have long been discussed as a part of the *Weistümer* tradition, they were in fact very distinctive types of documents whose medieval origins and mature form in the late sixteenth and the seventeenth centuries had an entirely different character and purpose. *Weistümer* were actually only a relatively limited type of legal code from medieval Franconia by which the peasant communities there gave up "rights" to their overlords in annual reconfirmation ceremonies. In the areas of Bavarian settlement, on the other hand, the legal habits of the subject population were not concerned with a maintenance of "right" but rather with the maintenance of law and order.[74] It was the evolution of this latter tradition in Bavaria, Upper Austria, Styria, and Bohemia[75] that coincided with the development of early absolutist state formation. There were, of course, significant differences within these "Bavarian" areas as well. According to Stahleder, since the Bavarian tradition was, unlike the earlier Franconian *Weistümer*, not concerned with maintaining a sense of the origins of the law, it was much easier for the state and the estate owners and managers to let many of

151

the traditional regulations of peasant life lapse (or at least push them into the background) while at the same time introducing innovations and alterations that advanced their own commercial and political power. In other words, the ability of the state and the estate owners to draw the everyday lives of the subject population further into the legal and political bureaucratization of the estates was partly rooted in the authoritarian legal traditions of southeast Central Europe.

The *Taiding* was an annual meeting of the subject population, organized in village, market, or other administrative units (*Ämter*) that was occasionally visited by the lord but was administered chiefly by the estate manager and the appropriate bailiff or magistrate. All heads of subject households were compelled to attend—and often severely fined if they did not. Some kinds of *Taidinge* everyone had to attend. After the mid-sixteenth century advent of printed regulations, the law was simply read to the householders or, and this has been mistaken for a remnant of a *Weistümer* tradition, they were asked to give correct answers to a series of questions concerning the law of the estate.[76] By the mid-sixteenth century, all vestiges of medieval corporatism had been removed from the *Taiding* meeting and it was a one-sided process by which regulations and laws could be dropped from one year to the next and new law simply announced. The subject peasantry had to adjust to such innovations without question; they could test those to which they objected in court or reject them through rebellion but both processes were costly and often did not, even after interference by higher authorities, bring about a satisfactory settlement. Cases of dispute between subjects and disputes concerning the estate officials' administration of the law (but not its substance) could be raised at the *Taiding* meeting.

The law codes of several Upper Austrian estates from the fifteenth to the seventeenth centuries are available and give some indication of the types of changes that accompanied the evolution in the making and administration of law. For example, of the three versions of the "Ordnung und Gesetz des Marktes Ebelsberg" (a Passau holding near Linz), those dated 1439 and 1516 were essentially the same and were concerned with such market and village regulations as the control of fire, the quality of meat and bread, and the control of preemptive buying. While the 1546 regulation retained most of these measures and made some important additions such as granting the burghers of the market the right to trade in salt and grain in addition to the traditional wine, it also marked significant innovation in the *policing* of this market regulation. The estate manager and his bailiffs appeared prominently for the first time, and they were given extensive powers to punish and regulate. The 1546 version put teeth into the clauses of the older *Ordnung*. The estate officers were to supervise stringently such additions to the law as that forbidding the burghers to act as commercial agents for outsiders. Such a relatively innocuous clause as that compelling the bakers to furnish bread for the town was replaced completely by one that required the magistrates to supervise all the activities of the bakers on a continuous basis and threatened the latter with confiscation of their wares (and the partial distribution of these among the poor). The most interesting change of all was a new clause in the 1546 version that stated that although the custom concerning the freedom to trade with "foreigners" would be left intact, the owners reserved the right to change this provision; this clause was then crossed out and an entirely different one concerning the exclusive right of the magistrates to settle all disputes and the estate manager to handle appeals put in its place. Another new clause stated that it was the owners' right to amend or abrogate any clause they wished.[77]

To cite another example, similar and even more far-reaching innovations can also be observed for the estate Windhag between 1509 and 1553.[78] The code of 1553 was, unlike that of 1509, published and distributed among the officials of the estate. Much of both codes regulated the subjects' behavior, especially their petty and major crimes, working hours, the payment of their wages, how they must control the free movement of animals, and so forth. The 1553 code, however, introduced elaborate regulations concerning the bailiffs, and it designated the tenant-owners of several subject houses as stand-ins for the bailiffs. The powers of these magistrates were both increased and limited. In addition, millers were held responsible for building the gallows and the ladders required for executions. The code of 1553 also introduced, verbatim, many of the regulations concerning crimes and the criminal procedures found in the *Carolina* and in Ferdinand I's adoption of it. It introduced a great number of commercial regulations such as those governing credit, speculation in futures, the involvement of servants in trade, and the illegal use of back roads by teamsters carrying marketable goods. Almost as afterthoughts there were interspersed among these administrative innovations admonitions that neighbors were to treat each other according to ancient custom and that streets and houses should be kept up as was the custom.

Most of the legal innovations of the sixteenth and seventeenth centuries made the peasants' lives more complicated, piling regulation upon regulation, and making them increasingly subject to the possibility of fine, imprisonment, and inquisitorial procedure. For example, the Windhag code grew from 92 paragraphs in 1509 to 157 by 1553, and such acts as slandering the estate administration and having too costly a wedding suddenly became punishable offenses. That is not to say, however, that all innovations were additions to the law or that they all necessarily increased the burdens the peasantry had to bear. In its 1570 *Taiding*, the estate Frankenburg, for example, dropped all reference to the traditional prohibitions of preemptive buying.[79] This was in violation of royal law but was a measure that was surely welcome among some members of the peasantry such as those privileged innkeepers, millers, weavers, and teamsters who had the financial power and other means to participate in the market as both buyers and sellers.

Aside from the estates and their administrative subdivisions (*Ämter*), the fundamental administrative unit designated by these codes is the house under the management of the tenant-owner. Most codes took great care, for example, to distinguish the house as an independent legal entity, at whose entrance the specific authority of the estate managers and magistrates ended. In most of the *Taidinge* and *Ordnungen*, the house of the subject was declared his sanctuary not only against other men but also against the estate magistracy; in some cases he could only be arrested between the church door and his house door.[80] This right was abrogated in the course of the seventeenth century and the number of those to whom it was denied increased. At the same time, the codes broke the housecommunities down into their various constituent parts so that there were paragraphs detailing not only the required behavior and responsibilities of the heads of households but also of their children, lodgers, and servants, and of others who resided in their house or on their property under special protective arrangements (*Schirmknechte*). Heads of houses were required to collect such taxes as these other members of the housecommunity had to pay and they represented them legally vis-à-vis other individuals and administrative officials. At the same time, the "unhoused" could lodge complaints against the head of a house if the latter did not administer the house as the rules required.[81] A reading of the *Taidinge* reveals that, in fact, next to the paid officials of the estates, the heads of households are mentioned most frequently as persons with administrative responsibility, not the least of which was that they were to enforce the observance of the laws in general by the members of their families and housecommunities. It was through the *Taidinge* that the estate owners granted such special privileges and duties to particular houses (inns, mills), as we have noted above, thereby creating an administrative hierarchy among the "housed" which was a part of the official legal order.

It is wrong to see the increase in Austrian "*Weistümer*" in the sixteenth century as a codification of custom and as a sign of the uniformly increasing power of the peasantry organized in communes of parish, village, or guild.[82] The commune movement of the German peasantry after the great uprisings of 1525 took a variety of directions and met with varying kinds of success. For such specific areas as Swabia and Alpine Austria, we are able to determine that, with the exception of some specific estate administrations and regions, the movement achieved some limited success, and this not only with regard to resisting the extensions of authority by lords and princes but also with regard to ensuring and increasing existing domination over the servants, lodgers, artisans, and laborers by householders and village oligarchies.[83] The commune movement in Upper Austria, on the other hand, along with the movements of Bavaria, Salzburg, and Styria, did not meet with similar success. There the state and the Estates managed to displace the communes from the effective administration of the rural population. In this area of Central Europe, the growth in the number and the elaboration in the contents of the estate codes of the sixteenth and seventeenth centuries signified the initial stages of the victory of the legal-rational state and its administrative law.

When Ferdinand I's judicial reforms of 1559 gave to the owners of estates the power to administer all matters of "lower" judicial authority—a right that was specifically reaffirmed in the 1597 Interim—he had pulled off a considerable coup. At a stroke he had placed such matters as noncapital crimes, civil actions, and market regulations under the rule of the state's administrative law and had bypassed the communes and Estates by drawing the managerial and judicial employees and subjects of the nobility directly into administering centrally issued ordinances, guidelines, and directives that appeared as new law in the *Taidinge*.[84] By holding on to formerly acquired rights of highest judicial authority or by newly acquiring such rights through lien administration agreements with their prince, a few members of the nobility and their employees could achieve the administration of the complete corpus of secular law. Perhaps the two most significant areas of the law in which the state and the estate owners displaced the commune was in the administration of the rules governing the acquisition, use, and inheritance of tenure on a subject house as property and in the regulation of such household and family matters as headship, marriage, guardianship, retirement, and the division of labor.

As elsewhere in Europe, property ownership had never been an undivided right in the German crownlands of the Habsburgs and, as elsewhere, the "mix" of ownership rights peculiar to Austria went through some significant changes in the course of the early modern period. It is an oversimplification to suggest that a "reception" of Roman law concepts was the most important source of change and that it signified a privatization of property in houses and land.[85] The complexities of infinitely varied and individually "feudal" precedents and agreements aside, the legal arrangements associated with medieval conditional ownership of an Austrian peasant farm involved in effect three owners: the peasant tenant who used the farm; the estate owners who collected rents, tithes, and services; and finally, the incorporated communes who partially controlled an individual's or family's accession to incumbency as tenant-owner and wholly supervised the proper uses to which lands and farms could be put. By granting all lower judicial authority to the landlord-estate owners, Ferdinand I's judicial reforms of the mid- and late sixteenth century restricted and eventually eliminated not only the rival landlord authority of those who were the bond-lords (*Leibherren*) or judicial lords (*Vögte*) of the peasants but also the judicial rights exercised by the communes.[86] In a limited sense it is correct to say that here the modified "Roman law" dualism of *dominium directum* and *dominium utile*—with the former accruing to the landlords' advantage and the latter to the tenant-owners'—replaced the older forms of tripartite property ownership.[87] It is not, however, correct to claim that this change granted exclusive rights of property ownership to the landlord class and in effect dispossessed the peasantry.[88] Landlords in the Salzburg area had long been acting as if they were the exclusive owners of peasant farms but this did not mean that in law they were the exclusive owners.[89] *Dominium utile* in fact not only strengthened the tenants' legal position as user-owners of property vis-à-vis their lords but it also eliminated the controlling restrictions the communes could place on the way a tenant-owner used his property. Formerly, if a farm had been defined by communal custom as an agricultural enterprise alone, its owner could not enter into the kinds of industrial and craft diversifications that we have been able to document in previous chapters. By the late sixteenth century, the right to define the use to which a house could be put was taken over by the landlords, and it was in their interest to remove restrictions on the occupational characteristics of their houses and to tax householders for changing to new occupations.[90] In other words, industrial and craft diversification of the housecommunity became much easier.

Multiple, and not just dual, ownership remained in effect,

however, throughout the early modern and part of the modern history of the Austrian state. The dualistic relationship of *dominium utile* and *dominium directum* was shared with two other parties: on the one hand, the state could interfere directly in property relationships through the *Kammer* administration of royal domains and indirectly through its lien administrators and through the *Landgericht*'s appellate jurisdiction in landlord-tenant and other property- and family-related contractual disputes; on the other hand, there were the inheriting kin of the tenant-owners, godparents or trustees if the latter were minors, and, finally, those with major liens against the tenant-owner.

Taken together, these changes in ownership that took place during the sixteenth century represented what amounted to an administrative revolution of great importance. In some respects, the position of the housed peasantry improved markedly. Properties were freed from communal restrictions, a development of special benefit to those whose legal status had prevented them from becoming householders because they were not desirable or eligible members of a commune, and to those who sought to diversify their enterprises and turn their houses into inns, workshops, or other sorts of commercial establishments. The proliferation of cottages that were not proper subject-tenant houses seems to have been restricted, at least by standards being set elsewhere, and this also favored the housed.[91] Finally, the peasant householders, through their houses, retained control over the unhoused population. This remained in effect at least until "the house" proved inadequate to the population pressure and the lack of employment opportunities that characterized the later seventeenth and eighteenth centuries. In Upper Austria the desire by the housed for their communal liberties, which had animated the less radical faction among the peasantry in 1525,[92] was lost in the course of the sixteenth century, but the same legal changes that gutted communal institutions of their separate, if not independent, legal force also gave to the housed the authority over property and kin relations which, if we accept David Sabean's interpretation of 1525, had originally been their chief objective.[93]

There were, however, other aspects to these innovations that circumscribed the freedom of the housed and subordinated them to new rules and controls. Chief of these was assertion by the authorities of control over access to and continued possession of a house by a tenant-owner. Under the new legal auspices of the state and the landlord, the criteria for possession and dispossession changed not in terms of the value of managerial competence but rather in the way that competence was assessed and in who did the evaluation. Formerly the judgment concerning the performance of a householder was based on both publicly observable success or failure and on reputation, and the chief judges had traditionally not been the estate owners and their managers but neighbors and peers. The texts of many of the new estate codes of the sixteenth century appear to have kept the old communal criteria but in fact the inventories examined for this study reveal that the landlords dispossessed tenants for far more precisely calculable criteria than for the customary causes of their being "unjust and dishonorable"[94] or "unfit to own a house" (unhäuslich).[95] By 1600 the tenant-owners held their *dominium utile* under rights of emphyteusis, i.e., the tenant could enjoy the farm, and dispose of its substance as if it were his own, provided he did not lessen its value in any way.[96] Although emphyteusis as a condition of tenure in Austria (and Central Europe generally) has been played down in some of the literature on tenure,[97] the actual practices of the landlords—as these are revealed by the inventories—suggest that emphyteusis was of crucial importance both for them and for the tenant class. The Austrian landlords interpreted emphyteutic conditions as follows: if, at the death of a tenant or his spouse, the postmortem inventory showed liens in excess of the total value of all the assets, the estate authorities, with few exceptions, declared the tenancy bankrupt (*crida*) and could expropriate the incumbent tenant family. In other words, emphyteusis, as interpreted by the Austrian authorities around 1600, substituted a precisely calculable measure based on a compilation of intimate social, economic, and financial data from the householders' family contracts and accounts for an older and communally ascertained judgment based on opinions about a family's continuing qualification to possess and enjoy its hold-

159

ing. The expulsion of the commune from property ownership and, hence, assessment of tenant performance meant a shift toward different criteria of assessment based on legal-rational calculability. This in turn produced, as we shall see in a moment, accompanying shifts in the relations among the members of families and housecommunities.

The change toward a new kind of conditional ownership and toward accountability and surveillance brought with it more "individualistic" relationships between landlords and both their housed and unhoused subjects. The housed acquired and held their privileged position at the pleasure of their landlords who could not only dismiss them from tenure if they did not live up to expectations but could also force a subject to take on the headship of a tenant house.[98] As masters of the house, the incumbent tenants did, moreover, not always have complete control over the membership of the housecommunity: they could be forced by the authorities to take in lodgers though at the same time the number of lodgers especially protected by the housed subjects was often limited by law.[99] The state authorities were required by law to dispossess a householder directly in case he or she was convicted of such major crime as theft;[100] the estate authorities could expropriate for such additional infractions as the nonpayment of dues and taxes[101] and the nonregistration of property- and family-related transactions and contracts.[102] A further restriction, and perhaps the most fundamental one, on the freedom of the housed subjects was the impartibility of property. It was the commissars of Maximilian I who initiated and sought to enforce this policy for the first time early in the sixteenth century when they required the Imperial lien administrator Wolfgang von Polheim to reconstruct the numerous peasant holdings that had been broken apart by sale and inheritance, and to cease issuing contracts permitting their future breakup.[103] In the course of the sixteenth century the peasant houses became impartible administrative units, units of power as well as economic and social entities, and could be enjoyed and improved but not otherwise altered in any way by their tenants.

Accession to properties and their transfer through the property market and through inheritance were increasingly subject to state-regulated fees (*Freigelder*) that were derived from and analogous to those moneys levied on once "unfree" bondsmen (*Leibeigene*). Hannah Rabe has recently argued that it was the collection of these fees and of similar innovations that was one source for protest by the peasant rebels of 1525 against *Leibeigenschaft*. They saw this not as an extension of a feudal form of servitude but rather as the elimination of a communal legal sphere (*Rechtskreis*) in favor of an individualized legal relationship between lords and subjects.[104] It is wholly misleading to speak of a "second serfdom" for this period and interpret it as part of an aristocratic feudal victory over an "early bourgeois" urbanization of the countryside. There was nothing feudal about the new property relationships and the rules governing them. They were rather part of a centrally regulated and locally administered legal-rational system that treated both housed and unhoused subjects as individuals, albeit with differently graded legal rights, whose property-related rights and obligations were matters of private contract subject to administrative public law.

The chief surveillance instrument through which the authorities managed incumbency was, as we have seen, the household inventory and, specifically, the accounting it contained of a tenant family's property, inheritance, and credit relationships. The earliest inventory on record is from the estate Freistadt in the 1550s.[105] Beginning also about mid-century, authorities began to regulate the familial and other legal relations among their subjects with a series of contracts that accompanied the most important individual life stages, family events, and property transactions. These contracts, together with the inventories, were issued exclusively by the authorities as the only legal documents valid in the estate and royal courts, and copies of them were kept by the estate magistrates and bailiffs.[106] In other words, the private transactions and dealings of the subject population were increasingly required by law to be on file with the authorities who were thus not only in a position to supervise the managerial fitness of the housed but also to police the obligations among the housed and between the housed and unhoused. The bureaucratization of property ownership and property relations meant a penetration of the family's most intimate accounts by the state.

When an Austrian peasant couple was about to marry and inherit a holding they entered into a formal marriage contract that integrated the properties each brought to the marriage into what has been called a "conjugal community"; that is, the marital fund was completely integrated into one, and each spouse had the right of survivorship of the other and took precedence as chief heir over any children the marriage might produce.[107] In the absence of children, first the siblings and nephews and, secondly, the surviving parents of the deceased partner inherited his or her share in equal portions.[108] In the case of the *inter vivos* inheritance associated with stem families, the parents gave up the tenancy as a part of their marital fund to an heir and their *Auszug* household became their new marital fund. When a stem family elder (*Auszügler*) remarried, the new spouse assumed full rights on the *Auszug* household alone as well as on those residual rights that might still exist over the original tenancy. The heir and his wife had, in the meantime, integrated the tenancy, and whatever other properties and rights they had brought to the marriage, into a new conjugal community of their own. This meant, in effect, that in stem families the remaining children whose inheritance consisted of an equally divided sum of money worth half their parents' estate were no longer entitled to any portion of the tenancy as a whole but only to a portion based on the value of the *Auszug* household. Moreover, this latter sum was, in the case of children who had not gained majority, not paid immediately but usually "held" in trust by the chief heir who had to pay it out at a later date. In cases of a parent's death where *inter vivos* inheritance had not taken place, the siblings that did not inherit the tenancy were usually somewhat better-off, since the parental marital fund still contained all of the farm's properties and assets. In this way, the stem family as an institution increased and sharpened the economic class conflict within Austrian peasant families. On the one hand, it eliminated the inheritance claims of all but one person against the tenancy and forced the rest to accept a reduced portion, and on the other hand it increased the burden on the chief heir who, in practice, had to come up with his siblings' portions of the *Auszug* inheritance from his own incomes.

A disinherited child faced two possible courses. First he or she could leave the parents' or siblings' household, thereby becoming entitled to a single inheritance portion either on the entire farm, if no *inter vivos* inheritance had taken place, or on the *Auszug* household. It is doubtful that once a child had left he or she could lay claim to another portion. The inventories offer some evidence to support this.[109] The other choice was to remain in the inheriting brother's or sister's household, unmarried, and continuing to claim, if not a portion of subsequent inheritances, then at least a livelihood from the tenancy. From the inventories it is apparent that there were instances in which a sibling appeared as heir alongside the chief heir's children, but this was not a common occurrence and points to special family relationships rather than customary practice. In most cases the siblings departed from the stem family as soon as they could and, unless they married well or were otherwise able to acquire a tenancy, they joined the growing number of unhoused, those rural servants and laborers who worked for, and lived with, the families of tenant householders. Whether they stayed with their family of origin or worked in another household, the disinherited siblings, the unhoused, were members of an inferior social class, a distinction that drove siblings apart as their separate life courses progressed.[110] The feeling that existed between the housed and unhoused is perhaps best revealed by the Swabian peasantry who, in their protests of 1525, expressed the fear that their lords' policies were reducing them (i.e., the housed peasantry) to the level of their "servants and dogs."[111] As the sixteenth-century administrative revolution progressed, these feelings were fixed in new family regulations that elaborated family class distinctions in state-controlled contracts concerning marriage and inheritance.

What makes the bureaucratization of the property and family relationships among the Austrian peasants of the early modern period complete and a matter beyond dispute is the authorities' adjudication of contractual and other conflicts among the peasantry. From the administrative archives of the estate Weinberg we can draw ample evidence concerning the legal procedures governing property, family, employment, credit, and other contractually regulated matters. The unhoused clearly had no independent legal standing whatsoever. For example, in the cases involving the payment of back wages to servants and day laborers, it is the heads of households, acting either as godparents or other sponsors of the unhoused or simply as heads of houses in which the unhoused persons involved in litigation are residing, who act on behalf of the unhoused. Such action usually involved representing the case to the estate manager and speaking on behalf of the unhoused at the settlement of disputes during the *Taiding* meetings.[112] If the dispute involved subjects of different estates the estate managers settled it between each other in strictly administrative fashion.[113] Although the godparents of unhoused children were assigned the inheritance portions of their godchildren and wards in trust and were expected to defend their godchildren's legal interests, the actual records show that it was the heads of the houses in which the young lived and worked as servants or lodgers who most often represented the godchildren's legal rights against the godparents and trustees! The estate managers determined their subjects' legal rights to an inheritance as matters of internal administration and bureaucratic regulation.[114] Disputes between housed subjects were also wholly negotiated and adjudicated through the estate officials, or, if they involved housed subjects acting through the officials of separate estates, by the royal provincial courts (*Landgericht*).[115]

In other words, individual members of the peasant subject population could not confront one another in civil suits but were forced to communicate their complaints to those placed immediately above them, to housed subjects, to administrative employees of the estates, or to members of the royal courts. These "authorities" then adjusted disputes between their subjects among themselves or pleaded their respective causes for disposition before more highly placed and professional officials. Civil matters involving family, inheritance, or other contractual and essentially private litigation were therefore dealt with entirely within the framework of administrative law that was in turn based on royal patents and orders and on the *Taiding* regulations of the individual estates. Thus, in the period around 1600, a major turning point in the legal order and praxis of the Habsburg state as it affected the peasant population had been passed; the effects of this change, as the important study by Henry Strakosch has shown, were not overcome by the legal reforms of the Habsburg state in the modern period, and lasted even after its demise in the twentieth century.[116] The debates among Maria Theresa's reformers concerning the creation of private civil law within and yet separate from public law[117] did not seriously consider, for example, the disposition of inheritance cases among the subject population as a matter of civil law, and still later reformers similarly left the relations between employers and servant laborers wholly within the public law.[118] Although the predominance of public law and the professionalization of the administration of law in Central Europe has long been noted and contrasted to the English common law system of civil law administered by laymen,[119] it is worth noting that the Austrian form of public law differed in significant respects from that of, say, Prussia, where public law also triumphed in the early modern period. In Prussia traditional private law survived among the rural subject population insofar as the state did not appropriate areas of the law that did not suit its administrative, economic, and military purposes;[120] it was not until the eighteenth century, with the growth of the Prussian military-industrial complex, that the private affairs of the rural subjects were increasingly drawn into the public law.[121] In the German crownlands of the Habsburgs, on the other hand, the legal reforms that commenced in the 1530s and '40s and continued throughout the period of the *ancien régime* were more comprehensive in their subordination of all private and civil matters to public law, functioning through interlocking estate and royal courts; the former being restricted to civil cases and noncapital crimes among the subject population and the latter exercising appellate jurisdiction over all cases. It is interesting to consider that the medieval feud, legally prohibited to the subject population but in practice often the preferred means of

settling disputes among and between both the housed and unhoused, was the last means available to the Austrian peasantry
to deal with each other directly without the interposition of the
state. We may agree with Otto Brunner that the outlawing of
the feud at the beginning of the early modern period and the
assertion by the state of a monopoly on violence meant the end
of a deplorable means of settling differences and conflicts and
was one of the crucial beginnings of the new absolute state (and
therefore also the beginning of the modern state).[122] However,
we must at the same time not lose sight of the particular legal
forms that overtook the feud, forms that eliminated direct legal
confrontation and substituted for it bureaucratized forms of
mediation in which the conflicts and legal actions among inferiors were negotiated and settled by officially recognized su-
periors.

Judging by the nomenclature, there were numerous surviving
medieval institutions in this new system of public law: the
Taiding, Estates and estates, the magistrates (*Amtmänner*), and
the peasant house itself. Many of these institutions were, however, pressed into new service, their functions expanded and
their character altered beyond recognition, and it is wrong to
persist in talking about a surviving system of feudal law[123] and
a victory of a "feudal class" seeking the "consolidation of serfdom."[124] As we shall see in the final chapter, the military debacle
of the Estates in the 1620s sealed the century-old process of
bureaucratization at both the highest and at the lowest levels
of Austrian society and left nothing but the forms of the feudal
state intact.[125] There was nothing feudal about this paradoxical
state that sought centralization through that most decentralized
traditional institution, the peasant house, and sought to establish its official presence through an administrative class of unpaid private individuals, the housed subjects whose duty it was
to run an orderly and profitable house. This meant in practice
that the latter had to manage, under the scrutiny of and with
the legal means put at their disposal by the authorities, the
properties, welfare needs, and labor resources of their own families and of the other members of their housecommunities in
such a way that life plans and choices—the "chance in the

market"—of all the housecommunity's unhoused members were subordinated to those of the housed tenant-owners.

SUMMARY AND PROSPECT

Beginning with the appearance of royal commissars (*Umreiter*) on royal estates held in lien in the early sixteenth century and ending with the issuing of royal patents and orders concerning property, labor, family, and other relations and applicable to authorities and subjects during the last three decades of the sixteenth century—with the Interim of 1597 marking the decisive turning point—the Habsburg state invaded the everyday economic and social life of the rural subject population with a new legal-rational order. In the process it created a new class division as measured by market chances and authority relations among the subject population: the housed and the unhoused. To be sure, these categories had existed before the formation of the early Habsburg state, but under strict orders of impartibility of tenant holdings, of emphyteusis, and of contractual accountability, the functions of this social division were greatly expanded and its meaning radically altered. The housed acquired a new security in their holdings and new forms of authority, provided they could fulfill the state's and their authorities' formal expectations of what amounted to their "office." They were the lowest members of a "privileged acquisition" class whose tenure was akin to bureaucratic office-holding in that their duties were fixed and officially distributed, their authority to give the commands necessary for the discharge of their duties was supported by a state claiming a monopoly on violence, and, finally, their continuity in "office" depended on an ongoing successful discharge of their duties and periodic assessments of their qualification to hold their tenures.[126] The unhoused, as the "negatively privileged," were subject to the management of the authorities in general and, specifically, to the heads of households who acted as chief disciplinarians.

Because peasant holdings in this region were impartible (a restriction that remained in effect until 1868), historians have commonly emphasized the corporate character of its peasant families and households. These historians usually describe property as "family property"[127] and the household as "the whole house," an early modern administrative conception of the family that allegedly preceded the later bourgeois ideal of the family, and that included both kin and outsiders who acted and worked as members of the family.[128] This conception of the "whole house" is not entirely wrong, especially in the distinction it draws between those who leave and those who stay.[129] It was a moral concept that served an important ideological function in early modern Austria. However, as we saw, this family corporation was not a whole in its internal social functioning and effect, and we need to examine more closely the social historical significance of this internal division of families and housecommunities in order to achieve a better sense of the social and emotional relations such a system offered (or mandated).

In the chapters that follow we shall bring together the data and analysis derived from the inventories with the bureaucratically ordered family, property, and labor relations we have described in this chapter. We shall see how a family and housecommunity divided into two classes, consisting of those whose life chances were shaped around mutually held and contractually defined properties and those whose life plans were adjuncts of and subject to the contracts among parents and chief heirs, affected social life in the new state. The peasant stem family was, most notably, the culmination of these family and social divisions. If the disinherited children's life plans were subordinate to those of the chief heir, then the plans of the latter were in turn subordinate to those of the stem family elders who, as we shall see, could search for an heir to suit their needs and could grant or withhold as much as they saw fit. The chief purpose of the stem family was not to preserve the integrity of the "family property"; it did not seek to assure the future of all the children, nor indeed that of the "stem" or lineage. It was an evasion of emphyteusis. It was a family-role complex designed to support two conjugal units of which the unit of the elders was the more privileged and the less burdened with economic, social, and family responsibilities. It is true, in a sense, that the *Auszügler* were retired and had relinquished the plough to the next generation—but, as the next chapters seek to show, that was only so that they could do other things. It is only after such analysis that the questions of "psychological strain" mentioned earlier become genuinely interesting and historically significant.

~ CHAPTER 6 ~

Family Roles

"FAMILIES go through developmental cycles as the individuals who compose them go through their life cycles."[1] If the experience and character of family development sketched in the previous chapter is correct, then this perceived relationship between an individual's natural life cycle and the development of his or her family is quite misleading. We may argue instead that rural Austrian families in the period around 1600 no longer followed a "natural" life course like the organic evolution of their members; instead, they followed a pattern that was determined by the administrative demands the authorities placed on the housed peasants and by the social and economic demands placed in turn by the housed on the unhoused members of the housecommunity.

THE SEARCH FOR AN HEIR

The final and, for this study, the most important phase of the Austrian peasant family's "developmental cycle" was that of the stem family. "Retired"[2] householders passed the ownership of the tenancy to an heir in return for a place in or about the house, for what was in effect a mortgage on the holding and an annual stipend from the agricultural and, where possible, other enterprises of the housecommunity. In the history of the Central European family, these stem family elders have been pushed aside. They are often portrayed as quaint figures who are of no consequence for the real social and political life of the rural population. Historians have emphasized the incumbent tenants as the chief actors of this period and have not understood that tenant status was only a position along the way toward becoming a stem family elder, that it was the latter position that was in fact the more desirable because it offered release from the responsibilities of being head of the house without necessarily demanding a loss of influence and power. In terms of the bureaucratization of the family we can argue that the stem family elders were retired from their incumbency but continued to enjoy both the social and the economic rewards of their former position.

Austrian usage most often gives the name *Auszügler* or *Ausnehmer*[3] to those elderly who continued to live as members of their heirs' households. These terms are now translated as "a retired farmer (living on property reserved for himself)" and in modern everyday usage the terms have even been divorced completely from actual legal and social circumstances and have come to signify persons who have been excluded from participating in something;[4] such meanings of retirement and exclusion were not attached to the institution of *Auszug* when it first began to appear in the legal and administrative documents of sixteenth-century estates. The contemporary meaning of these terms can be traced to the Central European debates about social policy and welfare that took place in the 1880s and after World War I. At that time, and in contrast to social conservatives who idealized *Auszug*, liberal intellectuals and politicians saw this institution and the behavior associated with it as obstacles to the extension of state welfare for the aged to rural areas, and they stressed what they perceived to be the negative features of *Auszug*, especially the intergenerational conflicts and strains between the retiring parents and the prospective heir.[5] Their redefinition of *Auszug* as an inadequate form of retirement and old age welfare and their views on its psychological aspects continue to appear in some of the recent literature on the historical stem family. Thus Lutz Berkner, for example, opposes "the romantic's picture of the happy extended family," but then goes to the opposite extreme by using the opinions of two early twentieth-century critics of the stem family as a basis for evaluating its eighteenth-century character. He pictures a discordant intergenerational relationship in which retired elders competed with their heirs and denied them early access to the family farm.[6] Also exploiting the theme of what Berkner defined as "severe psychological strain," but doing so farther removed from the sources and less successfully, Edward Shorter, in his recent interpretation of the history of the Western family, presents what seeks to be an empathic but is really only a fanciful picture of the meager, anxious lives of the "retired" and aging peasant farmer. Nonetheless, despite his view of the hardships suffered by "retired peasants," Shorter too offers a romantic view of the stem family, comparing what he thinks was a psychologically and socially complex extended family life of the past with the privacy and loneliness of twentieth-century people.[7] It is only the false universalism of modern family studies and our modern stereotypes of the old that have pushed the stem family elders out of the picture. If we seek them out "as they really were" then somewhat different perspectives on the peasant family open up for interpretation.

During the late sixteenth and early seventeenth centuries the Upper Austrian peasantry was independent-minded and rebellious, and the Habsburgs continually had to enlist Bavarian help to keep their border subjects under control. In a compilation of Bavarian spy reports concerning the state of unrest in Upper Austria during the 1630s, we find what may be our only description of an *Auszügler* of the period:[8]

> There is still another peasant named Symondl im Tobl who lives near Brand whom I know personally. He has a number of powerful sons and served for a while on our side during the Geyersberg campaign. But he only stayed for six weeks to see what the outcome would be and then he deserted and went home. Now it's known that there was a Lutheran preacher's son by name of Colibalt who had gone to university, had been a leader of the peasants for a considerable time, and who was always well supplied with clothes and excellent horses. When the peasants were defeated at Wolfseck, he feigned Catholicism and became chief steward in Colonel von Tartenbach's employ. He didn't stay long in that service but left to come back to Upper Austria where

he roamed about among the lords as an elegant cavalier and recruited soldiers; where he took these I don't know. Colibalt liked to have the peasant *Auszügler*, mentioned above, along as his attendant. About four years ago he and this peasant disappeared . . . and after about four weeks had gone by the peasant returned accompanied by Colibalt's well-known horse, pistols, and clothes. He stayed at home a little while, served among us to see what we were doing and, after riding along with us for a few weeks, he deserted again. No authorities dare touch him because they're afraid of him and his brothers and he's now at home once more. I haven't found out who his overlord is.

The peasant *Auszügler* Symondl ("little Simon") was clearly not retired in our sense of the word—except perhaps insofar as he no longer had to live on and manage the home farm. Rather than restrict him to a quiet life of withdrawal, *Auszug* made it possible for Simon to venture into the world in order to engage in profitable, albeit shady, activities. Although he may have been extraordinary in a number of respects, his experience demonstrates that by going into *Auszug* an elderly householder did not necessarily go into retirement. The evidence we are going to examine momentarily suggests that Simon was not alone. The life plans of heads of other peasant households aimed at Simon's kind of active *Auszug*. The indications are that in early modern Austria, *Auszug* was not a social expedient for retiring the old and arranging a modicum of welfare for them but was rather a householder's option for exploring new economic and social activities beyond the sphere of home and family. It was around the exercise of this option that the lives of both the young and old members of the house revolved.

In Austria, as elsewhere in early modern Europe, individuals tried to exert control over their personal lives by controlling fertility. Whether they employed birth control techniques is uncertain,[9] but it is certain that they reduced births by means of late marriage and celibacy. This "remarkable trend" of marriage restriction was initially chiefly a decision of the young, who imposed late marriage or celibacy on themselves, perhaps in order to improve their chances for a higher standard of living.[10] By the later seventeenth century, state regulations imposed celibacy on those destined not to own a house or practice a trade. On the other hand, once a peasant had joined the ranks of married householders, then he or she tended to remain married, often remarrying after the death of a spouse.

Michael Mitterauer's analysis of the mid-seventeenth century soulbooks of two Austrian villages, which we used in chapter two, throws interesting light on these opposing forms of behavior of the young and old. In early modern Austria it was not customary for a prospective heir to marry until he or she actually inherited the farm, and this made the age of marriage generally very high. Those whose parents went into *Auszug* and who therefore probably inherited at a somewhat younger age, delayed their marriages until they were between twenty-nine and thirty-one years old.[11] It is not certain to what extent this delay imposed sexual restraints on prospective heirs[12] but, given the life expectancy rate of males in this society (about fifty-one years),[13] marriage delay meant that the heirs had to remain single and endure a subordinate family status until well into their adulthood. It is particularly noteworthy that the wealthier householders tended to enter into *Auszug* at an earlier age, possibly even in their late forties, and in such cases the strains of celibacy and dependence ended sooner, only to be replaced by those connected with supporting one's wife, siblings, parents, and, eventually, offspring.[14] In neighboring Bohemia the authorities tried to control the stem family in the early modern period by forbidding parents from entering *Auszug* at too early an age.[15] It was a parental decision that created stem families and their plans seem to have aimed at establishing such families as soon as this was feasible. They had to take into account not only the heir's age, maturity, and readiness to marry but also the farm's and household's potential capacity for carrying the heir's spouse, siblings, and children while the *Auszügler* were still alive. Given this complex interplay of necessary conditions, it is remarkable that there were as many stem families as Mitterauer's and Berkner's investigations have shown. Moreover, it was not *any* form of the extended family that

Austrian peasants settled for; there are no patriarchal stem families nor joint families in the soulbook and inventory samples from the early modern period. Of all forms of family organization, it is the stem-form based on *inter vivos* inheritance that offered aged parents the advantages of family and family property without the burdens of being responsible for and having to manage either.

An *Auszügler* enjoyed the freedom to remarry after the death of his or her spouse. Mitterauer's data show, for example, that in 61 percent of the marriages of male householders between the ages of twenty and forty-nine the husband was older than the wife by an average of 5.7 years. In marriages of males aged fifty to seventy-nine, on the other hand, the husband was the older partner in 83 percent of the cases, and this time by an average of 15.8 years. This suggests that older men, many of whom were widowed *Auszügler*, remarried with younger women. This is further confirmed with regard to the *Auszügler* specifically when we compare the ages of the heirs' wives and the *Auszüglers'* wives in any stem family household. There we find cases of the *Auszüglers'* wives being only two or four years older than the wives of the heir; in one case the heir's wife was actually seven years older than the heir's stepmother (40:33).[16] Remarriage among the male *Auszügler* would furthermore account for the high number of all the stem families (24 out of 68) in which the elder unit consisted of a widow. Mitterauer does not analyze his data in connection with widow remarriages, but the fact that in 39 percent of the marriages of men in the twenty-nine to fifty age group the wife was older than the husband suggests that marriages between stem elder widows and younger men might also have taken place, although less frequently. Not only did *Auszug* allow the remarrying widows and widowers to look for younger spouses but it also made it possible for them to improve their economic status. Among the household inventories of the estate Frankenburg, for example, there is the case of Hans Schrämbl whose wife Margaret died in 1610 when the couple was already living in *Auszug*. Then their jointly held properties consisted of an *Auszug* house worth 10fl and 24fl of movables, including two cheap looms, for an inventory total of 34fl. When Hans died in 1624 he left a new wife named Barbara, and his *Auszug* house was now worth 28fl. The movables of the couple were evaluated at 115fl and instead of looms they now included substantial quantities of flax, yarn, and cloth—a sign that Hans was no longer involved in the textile industry as a primary producer but rather as a dealer in raw materials and finished products. His and Barbara's goods also included a bed which, at 10fl, must have been extremely luxurious. Debtors owed the couple a total of 271fl and the total value of their inventory amounted to the sum of 445fl.[17] Remarriage with a younger partner who brought property and different connections to the household was something that the elderly *Auszügler* could hope for. Family reconstitution studies are needed along these lines to determine precisely the extent to which remarriage changed the economic and social status of the *Auszügler*.

Remarriage also accounts, in part, for another characteristic of the stem family that further reveals how that institution functioned in the life plans of the Austrian peasant householders. Mitterauer discovered that of his sixty-eight families in the stem phase, only thirty contained two couples with the same family name. Moreover, upon further investigation he concluded that only five of these households could be assumed to contain a patrilineally related stem family consisting of grandparents, parents, and children.[18] To account for this we can imagine cases in which, for example, the heir was the son from a previous marriage of the male *Auszügler's* second wife or the nephew (i.e., sister's son) of an *Auszügler*.[19] However, the most obvious behavior that explains the nonpatrilineal stem family was probably that form of the stem family that Mitterauer unaccountably excludes categorically, namely, the cases in which the inheriting couple consisted of a daughter and her husband. In one series of sale records from this period in which we find the sales transactions that took place between parents who went into *Auszug* and the inheriting couples, five out of eighteen sales of all kinds involved an elderly couple's daughter and son-in-law as the purchasers of the tenancy.[20] These *inter vivos* inheritance dispositions suggest that not only is it futile to discuss the Austrian peasant family's inheritance practices in this period in terms of primogeniture or ultimogeniture but that such structural concepts obscure aspects of family life that reveal how individuals, families, and households were functionally interrelated. The life plans of the peasant householder of this period were not governed by ideologies or rules of sibling preference but consisted instead of what may be called strategies of heirship that aimed at maneuvering children and other prospective heirs into a stem family.

It was a combination of the realities of restricted property ownership and of the parents' desire to unburden themselves of the formal responsibilities and limitations attached to a tenancy (while maintaining, as we shall see, a considerable measure of control) that governed the interrelationship of individuals and families. The parents' life plans were paramount and focused on finding a viable married male heir.[21] The immediate results of their strategy of heirship were twofold. First, it resulted in stem families that were often not a family composed of two or three biologically and patrilineally related generations, but were rather a family role complex in which outsiders could be called on to play the roles of son, daughter, and even parent. For example, when the *Auszügler* Hans Hiersch from the estate Frankenburg died in 1630 he left behind a widow, Maria, and five children; one of these, a daughter, had married and left the house (but got a share of her father's legacy) and another, a son, Balthasar, had taken over the farm with his wife Anna. According to the inventory's preliminaries, Anna was already in charge of Balthasar's remaining three young sisters, and her mother role was made legally binding by the contract that completed the inventory. According to this contract she and Balthasar agreed to "properly keep and maintain the three children until they came of age."[22] It is in such role relationships rather than in those between father and son that the potential for "severe psychological strain," noted by Berkner and others, lies. It is possible, for example, that if the widow Maria was the real mother of Balthasar's sisters then Anna might have found it difficult to exercise a mother's authority. Or, that if Maria was Hans's second or third wife, then Balthasar might have resented having to share some of the authority in the household (as the contract specified) with someone who was not his mother. The most severe potential strain existed in those stem families in which an outsider like a son-in-law or a nephew of the old parents was called in to become the heir and head of the household, and to assume the role of father for his wife's siblings or for his uncle's children. This was a particularly conflict-ridden form of the stem family, for it brought into full play the second consequence of the parents' strategy of heirship; namely, the division of the family into two social classes consisting of those who inherited and controlled the family's properties and those who did not.

Michael Mitterauer has suggested that the stem family was a result of the estate authorities' direct interference in the family life of their tenants,[23] but, given the conditions of tenure, such interference was not necessary at all. Emphyteusis and the surveillance of the tenant farms through post-mortem inventories compelled the tenant class to seek a process of *inter vivos* inheritance by which they reduced the chance that a death in the family would cause the entire tenancy to be inventoried. They could also, by this system, better manage their farms' assets, liens, and personnel in the incumbent tenants' and stem elders' favor. The bureaucratization of property ownership had brought about the bureaucratization of the family and the latter in turn served the interests of both the authorities and the housed peasantry. The result of the bureaucratization of family and housecommunity was a role family complex that placed the majority of the members of the housecommunity into a state of complete dependence on the smooth and conflict-free functioning of the material and administrative affairs of the housed. This is to say that the roles individuals were required to play did not serve the conflict-free integration of society as a whole, but rather served the interests of a specific class. The roles one played in relation to the "house," rather than the roles that connected one to one's kin took precedence, as is best illustrated by the strategy of heirship that went outside the family altogether to find someone to play the not always compatible roles of incumbent tenant, husband, son, father, and authority representative.[24] This notion—and the materials that support it in the remainder of this and the next chapter—tears asunder the positivist perceptions of the relations between role and kin relations at least as far as the society in question here is concerned. Relationships that appear to be personal—based on sentiment, shared beliefs, and the affectionate interplay of family members[25]—were in fact something different altogether. The Austrian peasantry in the period around 1600 did not in all cases substitute role-kin for family members, but the fact that they not only could and did but also were compelled to do so by the prevailing system of property management suggests that the peasant family represented, in Marxian terms, the "disintegration" of a new set of class relations "into a general form" so that "individuals come into relation with one another only in a determined role [and] . . . are now controlled only by abstractions, whereas earlier they depended on one another."[26] "Family" members were primarily members of different property-related groups in the housecommunity and performed different roles in connection with their group membership. Eric Wolf once remarked on the need for a theory that connects rural social groups to classes.[27] It would seem that role theory and family and household analysis provide such connectors.

In order to develop a more detailed understanding of the interrelations between role and group, between individual and housecommunity, we need to do much more work reconstituting families and their networks. Only such inquiries will reveal such things as the full extent of role relations, the length of time spent in role positions, and the criteria and directions of choice for finding role players.[28] For the time being, however, the material and role relations within households, as these are shown by the inventories, permit us to reflect on the quality of human relationships that existed behind the inward-looking, defensive visages of the great peasant houses of this region.

THE STEM FAMILY ELDERS

The nuclear unit of elders in the stem family stood in a highly ambiguous position vis-à-vis the younger members. With regard to the children, spouses, grandchildren, lodgers, and servants that made up the rest of the housecommunity, it was at once both dependent and independent, supportive and exploitative. In order to unravel these relationships and interpret them, we need to show how the unit of elders functioned as a separate household within the housecommunity. From such an examination we can learn what kinds of livelihoods the elders managed to extract from the main household and in what kinds of activities they were involved; what their occupational and economic status was in relation to the peasant population as a whole and to specific groups in that society; and finally, whether their primary social allegiance was to their families or to their class.

The notion of retirement has influenced not only the way historians have described the social significance of the elders in general, but also the way they have imagined the details of their everyday lives. Added to the general picture of a withdrawal from life is, as we have seen, the idea that the lives of the elders were on the whole poor and ascetic; the elders in the stem family have been drawn as plain and simple folk who did not need much and did not ask for much.[29] In some cases this picture was undoubtedly accurate, and among the inventories of the *Auszügler* we find several examples of poor and modest lives. However, in the majority of cases the actual circumstances were rather different, and, just as the life plans of the elders had not aimed at a simple withdrawal from life but rather at a calculated change in their position as an active member of their family and society, so too was their new position in the family based on a more or less carefully calculated transfer of properties and obligations, a transfer whose purpose it was to provide themselves with a life of comfort and to support a continuing personal drive for economic and social status.

To assure themselves of a dependable livelihood for a long period of time, the parents, when they passed the household on to an heir, had to evaluate its economic future. At the time the *inter vivos* inheritance took place, there were two opportunities for the parents to adjust their needs and desires to the heir's ability to meet them. First, they could reduce the price of the tenancy to below its market value and in effect give the heir a discount and an advantage in the real estate market. It is difficult to tell from the sources how often or what kind of reductions took place in the transactions between tenants going into *Auszug* and their heirs, for most properties are usually mentioned only once in the sales records that remain from this period, and there is usually no comment regarding the relationship between the sale price and a property's supposed market value. There are, however, exceptions, and these provide some interesting insights into the financial transactions that accompanied *inter vivos* inheritance.

There were a few cases in which the reduction in price was substantial.[30] Thus, for example, one Hans Peundtner bought the Fuettergut in Eferding parish in 1608 for 450fl but turned it over to his son in 1627 for 160fl. Similarly, in 1618 Hans Pichler and his wife Maria bought the parental farm, the Pichlergut in Valentin parish, for 530fl when the authorities had evaluated it at 850fl; in 1646 Hans's widow turned the farm over to her son for 600fl. And in 1647 a hammer mill worth 900fl according to the authorities was turned over to the heir for 590fl. The Häckelgut was sold by a father to his son in 1647 for 190fl; a mother had sold the same farm, however, to her daughter and son-in-law in 1627 for 300fl (and at that time the estate authorities had put its value at 400fl). However, most properties that were sold to heirs went at or near the going market value. In one case, an heir whose wife died and who could no longer hold the parental farm, which was worth 900fl, turned it over to his sister and brother-in-law for 860fl. A similar circumstance might account for the sales history of the Schachnergut near Enns; it was sold to an heir in 1616 for 324fl and turns up later in the hands of a brother of the original heir. The new owner also failed to hold on to the farm and sold it to an outsider for 350fl in 1619. The Nebleckhengut in Hörsching parish near Linz was worth, according to the authorities, 180fl, and a widower sold it to his son for 155fl in 1614. The son in turn sold it to an outsider in 1624 for 207fl. Hans Paur bought the Pichlergut in Sierning parish for 500fl in 1614 and sold it to his son-in-law and heir for the same amount six years later. In one case the sale price to the heir actually exceeded the market value of the property, but this did not involve a tenant farmer; instead, it was a poor carpenter and his wife who went into *Auszug* and sold their cottage, the Färberhäusl, to their son, also a carpenter, for 75fl when subsequent sales showed that the house was worth closer to 55fl. It is extremely rare to find a stem family among the Austrian cottager class in this period and the somewhat different economic relationship between the Färberhäusl heir and stem elders supports the thesis that in areas (and times) where these kinds of families were more prevalent among cottagers, different kinds of family relations existed.[31]

The parents' purpose in setting a sale price on the tenancy was not to make things as easy as possible on the heir, but rather to adjust the price to the heir's ability to pay for the property while he was also supporting them. There are cases in the records that show that this could be a risky calculation and that the burden could prove too much for the heir, who then would have to sell to a married sibling or cousin, who could continue the stem family, or to an outsider who would have no obligation to the parents in *Auszug*. In other words, if the parents miscalculated in selling the property to an heir, they risked losing their position in the family and in the community as elders in a stem family. Such might have been the case with the Schachnergut and the Nebleckhengut mentioned in the previous paragraph. In some cases, such as that of the Steinmässlgut in 1627, the parents lost their *Auszug* status when the heir and his wife both died and the farm had to be sold to an outsider. In 1609 Stefan Meister sold the Meistergut in Neukirch parish to his son Leopold at the market rate of 910fl; ten years later, Leopold and his wife Anna could no longer hold the farm and sold it through an agent at an enormous loss for 300fl. A widow sold the stately Meierhof at Haag near Linz in 1622 to her son and his bride for 1,200fl. This was considerably below the market price of 1,500fl but the heirs still went too deeply in debt and were removed by the authorities; they profited, however, when they sold the farm to their chief creditor, an outsider, for 1,630fl. Although it is not clear from the sources whether in each of these latter cases the parents lost their *Auszug* status, it is certain that the transfer of a tenancy in *inter vivos* inheritance involved some risk, especially if the elders sought to secure their own financial future by selling the farm to their heir at a price near or at the going market value. On the other hand the fact that there were relatively few stem family-related bankruptcies suggests that in some cases *inter vivos* inheritance sales did not overburden the heir; in any event there were other means by which the *Auszügler* could adjust the burden on the heir after inheritance had taken place in order to prevent the loss of the farm.

The second adjustment the parents could make at the time of the initial transfer of the farm was in the annual living stipend they extracted from the farm. Obligations concerning shelter, foodstuffs, and other materials were governed by a separate contract and a look at a number of such contracts reveals that here too the parents adjusted their demands to what they thought the heir could afford. To begin with, the demands seem to have varied over time according to changing economic conditions, and hence changing personal fortunes. Georg Grüll, in his investigations into the Upper Austrian peasantry's social position in the sixteenth century, has suggested that when the *Auszug* contracts first begin to appear in the sources in the 1540s (the first ones on record are from 1548) they contained demands for a relatively modest and well-balanced rural life; in the period between 1570 and 1590, the *Auszüglers'* pressure on their heirs increased considerably but declined again as the seigneurial pressures on the tenant class also increased.[32] These observations suggest that the elders' demands on the heirs' households were adjusted not only to an heir's economic and managerial abilities but also took into account such external factors as the general condition of the rural economy and the changing policies of the landlords with regard to their properties and tenants. While we may agree with these conclusions in general, the causes for the actual fluctuations of the elders' demands remain open to question because there are a number of factors, including above all the correspondence between the total value of the heirs' households and the extent of the elders' demands, for which Grüll did not control. His impressions concerning the fluctuations over time in the *Auszüglers'* demands are without a doubt correct but need to be studied much more closely on the basis of family reconstitution and in connection with the short and long range secular changes in the Austrian rural economy.

A look at the contents of the *Auszug* contracts during the first half of the seventeenth century without reference to changes over time is sufficient for our present purposes because it allows us to compare the standard of living the elders continued to enjoy with that of other members of the rural population. There are contracts from the late sixteenth and early seventeenth centuries which specify the living arrangements and privileges of the elders in the family household.[33] Most *Auszügler* secured for themselves a room or two in the main house along with use rights in the main living areas and the kitchen. This tended to be the minimum arrangement; more extensive demands also appear in the sources. One widower from the Mondsee region, in a contract from the year 1561, reserved for himself one-quarter of the living and utility spaces of the main house; another did the same in 1578 and yet another from the same area in 1558 took over half the top floor of the main house. In addition, several of the *Auszügler* claimed contractually specified use-rights on such outbuildings as wagon sheds, stables, and granaries. As a corollary to these guarantees of living and utility space, most contracts contained an additional provision by which the elders could demand that the heir build them a separate house; in one of these contracts, that of a widow in 1594, the heir did not have to pay for the actual construction of the house but had to supply the building materials and haul them to the site.

The clauses specifying the living stipends of the stem family elders contained similar dual arrangements by which the *Auszügler* reserved a place at the family table but also kept open the option that if they did not like the family's fare then the heirs had to provide them with specific staples and foodstuffs so that they could cook for themselves. In that case the heir also had to supply the hearth, kindling, and firewood for cooking and baking. The lists of alternative foods suggest that the elders did not live badly at all. Grains were the staple food in the peasant diet and of these the *Auszügler* demanded all the varieties, from wheat, still a luxury grain in this period, to the more common rye, barley, and oats. Most of the children and servants in the peasant household lived on a bread made from a mixture of lentils and oats, and ate meat only on rare feast days during the year. The *Auszügler*, by comparison, had substantial quantities of meat or heads of livestock written into their contracts, and must have eaten meat several times a week. Just as with the grains, they demanded no less than the best for themselves and, while others in the family went without meat altogether, they had veal, beefsteak, lamb, and suckling pig. In addition, many of the contracts guaranteed them such additional foods as eggs, fruit, honey, whey, and cheese.

The claims the elders placed on the farm's produce were not only on the cream of the crop but must also in many cases have exceeded the personal needs of the elderly couple. Several of the contracts required the heir to give up, in addition to food and shelter, one-quarter of the harvest or the crop from precisely defined portions of existing fields; others wanted at least one-third or, in some cases, all of the fruit harvest (for making ciders and wines, no doubt) as well as the harvest from specified hemp and flax fields and pasturage for their livestock. In the alpine regions the harvest request could include all of the summer's cheese production. One *Auszügler* whose heir's farm manufactured ceramics demanded, in addition to the usual agricultural goods, an unspecified portion of the total annual output in tiles. This leads to the conclusion that the elders did not simply extract a living from the main household but must, in fact, have gotten a share of the marketable surplus.

Several of the *Auszügler* also put special provisions into their contracts, and these confirm the general impression that they continued to live both luxuriously and actively. Some, for example, stipulated that their daily pail of milk come from the

185

farm's best cow. Others reserved the best bed and bedding for themselves. Still others had their contracts specify that a servant bathe them daily and do their laundry. Requests for haulage services were common, and clothing materials (cloth and leather) and articles of clothing such as shoes also turn up in the contracts. Taken altogether, the annual provisions for the elders indicate neither an ascetic life nor one of withdrawal; they supplied the means for a life of well-being and commercial activity. These provisions must have engaged between one-quarter and one-half of the productive capacity of the heirs' households—and given the relatively early age at which the elders tended to enter *Auszug* as well as their tendency to remarry, this burden often weighed on the heirs for a long time. In one case on record from the estate Frankenburg in 1632 the heir's household had to support two generationally separate *Auszug* households. *Auszug* meant, in short, that at reaching a certain age, a tenant householder was assured of a cash income from his or her heir, could get the best in food and shelter the household had to offer, and could, in many cases, market a share of the household's output—and all without investing time or labor. The result of this relative luxury and freedom was that the stem family elders formed a separate occupational and social status group within the class of housed peasants and maintained a style of life and economic and social activities that were distinctly different from those of the tenant farmers who were their heirs.

The contents of the *Auszügler's* household inventories that were taken at the time of their death verify in general that they had received the goods that the contracts guaranteed them and that they had used these to build an independent and active life for themselves. The following tables are based on the information in the inventories as these were analyzed in previous chapters and, by holding them against values taken from the fifty-one *Auszügler* inventories available for this study, we may compare the *Auszügler's* material conditions to those of the peasant population as a whole, as well as to those of specific occupation groups in that population.

TABLE 6.1
Economic Status. *Auszügler* and the Subject Population

Inventory Mean Values	Population	Auszügler
Total Assets	467	405
Real Property	266	61
Movables	120	62
Loans	78	259
Debts	220	80
Freigeld	22	16

NOTE: All amounts in guilders.

The average total value of the *Auszug* inventory places the
elders very close to the middle ranks of Austrian peasant society,
especially when we consider that the majority of the peasantry
were poorer than the mean indicates (the median value for the
population was 363fl). But while a number of *Auszug* households were wealthier than many among the poorer farmers,
cottagers, and lodgers, this did not mean that as a group they
belonged exclusively to the middle or even the upper economic
groups among the peasantry. More than any other occupational
group in this entire peasant society, they could be found at all
economic levels, with the poorest *Auszug* inventory worth only
11fl and the wealthiest valued at 2,103fl. Although we do not
have the data with which to test the proposition, it is likely that
there was no correlation or only a low correlation between the
values of the *Auszug* households and the values of the larger
households of which they were a part; a wealthy *Auszug* household did not necessarily originate in a wealthy tenancy, since,
as we saw above in the case of Hans Schrämbl, whose *Auszug*
household went from 34fl in 1610 to 445fl in 1624, there was
a chance that *Auszügler* could improve their lot through remarriage and a successful change in economic pursuits. Family,
kin, and network reconstitution studies are needed to fill this
gap. However imperfect a measure of social mobility it might

be, the fact that out of the twenty-seven occupations that appear in the inventories the *Auszügler* were the only group to exist at all levels of economic status suggests that all classes of tenants must have sought this status when it became economically and socially possible for them to do so and that some of them used it to improve their personal economic status.

The further components of wealth in the inventories clearly separate the economic character and activities of the stem family elders from those of the rest of the population. The 61fl in real estate assets that appear for the *Auszügler* group consisted of two kinds of property: on the one hand there were small but comfortable houses[34] that were usually worth 25fl to 30fl, and on the other there were such fields and meadows as they could dispose of and even subdivide for sale or rental. Such independent properties were especially prevalent among the *Auszügler* of the Mühlviertel near the Bohemian border, a frontier area of sorts where peasants could still clear small fields and other grounds from the hilly woodlands. While the average real estate figure for the rest of the population reflects the value of a poor to middling tenancy, that of the *Auszügler* represents cottages and a few small but choice pieces of land that were unencumbered and freely disposable.

The movables of the *Auszügler* were also fundamentally different from those of the population as a whole, and from those of other specific occupational groups. Neither the basic holdings of livestock, implements, and grains of the farmers, nor the collections of agricultural and craft tools of the lodgers and cottagers account for the 62fl worth of movables found among the stem family elders. Rather we find items that reflect the contents of the *Auszug* contracts—foods, bedding, household utensils, a still (illegal; the fine appears among the debts), carpenter and wheelwright tools, and flax, hemp, yarn, and cloth in various stages of preparation. The industrial and commercial activities implied by these latter items were on a relatively small scale compared to those of some farming households that had diversified in the direction of the textile industry; at the same time these activities must have been disproportionately profitable for the *Auszügler* since they could shift the overhead costs of labor and transport to the heirs' households. The relative position of the stem elders vis-à-vis the other economic groups we have examined so far in this study bears out the advantages they enjoyed.

TABLE 6.2
Economic Status. *Auszügler* and the Dispossessed

Inventory Mean Values	Female Servants	Male Servants	Male Lodgers	Auszügler
Total Assets	67	114	123	405
Real Property	0	17	36	61
Movables	11	7	24	62
Loans	55	88	60	259
Debts	23	27	48	80
Freigeld	7	10	7	16

The data from the inventories have already revealed that female servants were the poorest and probably the worst treated group in this peasant society. They were, for example, the only group who actually had to pay the legally prescribed 10 percent transfer fine when most other groups, including poor male servants, had to pay less. The *Auszügler* were specially privileged in this regard as well, paying a tax of only about 4 percent. They were clearly wealthier than any members of the dispossessed groups, including the male lodgers. What the stem family elders had in common with the dispossessed was the fact that unlike the population as a whole, their loans were greater than their debts (see also Table 2.4 above), as well as the fact that loans made up the largest part of their total assets. It is precisely in this similarity, however, that the greatest economic and social difference between the *Auszügler* and the dispossessed lies. For the latter "loans" were, for the most part, moneys owed them by members of the tenant class, including the *Auszügler*, who not only controlled their inheritance portions in trust funds, but who also tended to owe them their wages in sums that often amounted to arrears of several years at a time. For the *Auszügler*

loans were investments; for the dispossessed they were the
badges of their economic and social weakness and vulnerability.

TABLE 6.3
Economic Status. *Auszügler* and Tenants

Inventory Mean Values	Farmers	Diversified Farmers	Teamsters	Auszügler
Total Assets	400	744	1,216	405
Real Property	268	437	686	61
Movables	109	207	351	62
Loans	21	97	178	259
Debts	232	308	453	80
Freigeld	19	39	50	16

The three tenant groups compared in Table 6.3 to the *Auszügler* represent the majority of the tenant population among
the Austrian peasantry. We may recall that the farmers, who
were the most numerous group, were engaged in agriculture,
selling their grain and livestock on the market; diversified farmers were those who, in addition to the normal agricultural pursuits, had also become involved in the growing and processing
of industrial raw materials as well as in the manufacture of
textiles; teamsters, finally, were those agriculturists who also
engaged in the transport of agricultural and industrial products.
All of these three groups borrowed more often than they lent,
and among them, the worst-off were the farmers, who were so
deeply in debt that they could not have covered themselves with
their liquid assets. These three groups were also the heirs and
debtors to the *Auszügler*.

The debts of these three tenant groups in Table 6.3 like those
of the *Auszügler*, included, to varying degrees, the inheritance
portions, trust funds, and wage arrears of the dispossessed children, servants, and lodgers who made up the greater part of the
peasant household. In addition, even though they were no longer
officially leaseholding tenants and heads of households, the *Auszügler* continued to share in one of the tenants' most important

class characteristics, namely, the manipulation of the inheritance and sale of leaseholds for the purposes of borrowing and lending. The *inter vivos* inheritance was a sales transaction that created a debt obligation for the heir and lending capital for the *Auszügler*; post-mortem inheritance created an inventory valuation that in turn, through the trust funds of the dispossessed, became buying and lending capital for both tenants and *Auszügler*. Inheritance created value, and eventually an exchange of cash; and it was the tenant class generally and the *Auszügler* in particular who controlled these transactions. For example, the inventory contract following the death of the *Auszügler* Hans Hiersch between Maria, the widow, and Balthasar, the chief heir on the farm, shows how complicated these transactions could be and to what extent the stem family elder who survived his or her spouse controlled them. The inventory's total value was 396fl, and there were 100fl in liens against the estate, which left a net worth of 296fl. Half of this amount, 148fl, was the widow's portion and the other half was assigned to the children. The contract reads as follows:

Agreement

Between the widow and the heirs; the widow, in good will, agrees to the *Auszug* arrangements and the movables that go with it. In return, she remains entitled to the outstanding loan of 90fl owed by Hanns Wibmer at Obermühlhamb; and the owner of the farm, Balthasar Hiersch shall pay her 25fl for the farm on Candlemas 1631. In addition the widow agrees to receive for the 148fl mentioned above 115fl and reduces her portion by 33fl 3s 22d which are added to the heirs' portion of 148fl 2s 22d making altogether 181fl 5s 14d of which each heir gets a fifth portion, 36fl 2s 20d. The four heirs agree to leave the estate intact for their brother Balthasar Hiersch and each agrees to reduce his portion by 6fl which makes 24fl altogether. In return Balthasar must pay them, without interest, 120fl, 30fl each, on Candlemas 1631. In addition he must properly keep and maintain the three younger children on the farm until they reach majority (*Vogtbarkeit*). He alone must pay the authorities their dues and fees and pay and account for all current expenses.[35]

Here the widow turned all but one of the loans made by the *Auszug* household over to the chief heir, thereby increasing his estate substantially; moreover, Balthasar still owed 125fl on the farm and Maria reduced this debt to 25fl to take a further burden off her heir and supporter. At the same time, a new burden was placed on Balthasar in the form of his four siblings' inheritance portions, which were in effect increased by the widow, who decreased her own entitlement of 148fl so that those of the dispossessed heirs might be larger—but *these* portions were then again reduced somewhat in Balthasar's favor. Balthasar was both beneficiary and benefactor in this agreement whose net effect was that he had to come up with 145fl in one year in order to own the farm clear of all family obligations. Of course, the terms of this agreement could be changed in subsequent contracts and the payment of the inheritance portions to the dispossessed heirs extended indefinitely. The widow was the benefactor in this agreement, and her role demonstrates that in cases of post-mortem inheritance and credit arrangements involving stem families, it was the surviving elder who controlled the arrangements by increasing or reducing his or her portion of the inheritance, and thereby maintaining a measure of authority over and prestige in the household as a whole. We must keep these kinds of transactions in mind in the next chapter when we see how the *Auszügler* specifically, and the tenants generally, together created and maintained their class and status positions by means of a credit market that was in effect a further reification of their leases and of their children's and siblings' inheritance claims on those leases.

The changes in property ownership that we observed in the previous chapter not only imposed certain options on the rural subject population but obviously also created new advantages and opportunities for certain of its members. The advantages were open only for *individuals* and not for their families as a whole and this introduced sharp cleavages and anomalies into the personal relationships of the housecommunity. Family roles were at once expanded and reduced. Thus, for example, the family role of "grandparents" fell to the stem family elders and it was open to them to play that role not only with regard to their own grandchildren but also with regard to all the children in the housecommunity—and, of course, in those cases where the cycle of family *roles* (as opposed to the cycle of the family)[36] had brought another person into the stem unit to replace a deceased spouse, the grandparent function became, in effect, a "pure" role. It was what that role allowed one to do that made it such a desirable social status position in the family and housecommunity. In the description and analysis of the stem elders that we have been able to draw together there is little to suggest any of the traditional attributes of grandparents. Rather they appear to have played out a complex of both familial and non-familial roles that served above all to release them, a small and select number of individuals in the subject population, from the constraints of economic responsibility and surveillance under which the tenants labored and also to reduce the chances for the terms of emphyteutic tenure to come into play.

It is in this light that the resistance of the Austrian peasant rebels of 1595-1597 to the separate bureaucratic definition and accounting of stem households gains new significance.[37] It was not an attempt to shield older members of the peasant family from the burdens of taxation and labor dues nor was it an attempt by the rural commune (*Genossenschaft*) to protect its members and its collective prerogatives for, as "retired" tenants, the stem elders were no longer members of the official commune. As a career group they had moved beyond the commune and house and the family itself but had maintained much of their former authority and continued to derive their income and status from these institutions. It was rather an attempt to place limits on the *further* bureaucratic penetration of the house and family in order to maintain the class interests of the housed, generally, and of the stem elders specifically. It would be false to characterize the family relationships we have outlined to this point as "natural" or as tending toward the "individualistic" family life of the modern state. Under the auspices of the early modern Habsburg state "individual" and "family" relations were redefined and recreated according to the needs and language of the bureaucratic authorities. What may to an outsider—and this includes the modern historian—have looked like a tranquil conflict-free peasant family, with the young working and producing and the old sunning themselves and telling stories, was in fact something else altogether. The apparently "natural" family relations were the roles that masked the existing class situation.[38] Nowhere is this more evident than when we compare the position of the "children" of the house to that of the stem elders.

The Dispossessed

In strictly legal and financial terms the group I call the "dispossessed" was of course not entirely dispossessed. They shared in inheritance as the previous chapter has outlined. I use the term here to indicate those who could never hope for a house. They were what I have also called the "unhoused" and were, in particular, the younger (but not that much younger) members of that class. As the remainder of this and parts of the next chapter will show, their economic, social, and psychological condition can only be described as one of dispossession.

The struggle for the legal control over the unhoused was one of the major issues of Austrian peasant politics in the second half of the sixteenth century, one that was not completely settled until the state authorities determined that the heads of houses were in control of the labor power of both kin and nonkin children in the housecommunity but had to offer these to the authorities from time to time so that the latter's needs for servants and labor could be fulfilled (1582). Needless to say, wealthier householders could, for a standardized fee, free such children as they chose from this service. It is to the credit of certain of the peasant rebels and negotiators of 1596 and 1597 that they demanded a proper wage for those who were thus called on to serve, but the Interim of 1597 simply referred back to the 1582 Resolution that had made no such provision. In the individual negotiations between estate owners and subjects that immediately followed the royal ruling, several of the subjects of specific estates obtained the concession of a wage for drafted servants from the owners.[39] Having fought for the payment of wages to those children who served their authorities does not, however, signify that the housed were representing the class interests of the unhoused: as the next chapter shall show, they often did not themselves feel compelled to pay wages to their servants and laborers. Moreover, the housed had an indirect interest in the wages paid to those who went to work for the authorities since they were ultimately in control and disposed of their unhoused wards' assets until these reached majority at age twenty-one and could press a claim for their own. This was perhaps the most significant ruling in the 1597 Interim as far as the inner life of family and housecommunity was concerned: "The authorities shall no longer appropriate assets of wards but the guardians shall instead invest these in the interest of the wards and under the supervision of the authorities."[40] When we consider that it was common practice for the housed to exchange their children with other housed peasants as "wards" (transforming biological children into legally exploitable role children) then this ruling takes on great significance.[41] Of course, as the typical contract attached to the inventory of the *Auszügler* Hans Hiersch in the previous section of this chapter demonstrated, the inheriting tenant and the surviving stem elders exercised control over the inheritance portions of the stem elders' biological and role children.

Bureaucratic regulation of the housecommunity had, by 1600, created a class of both biological and role children in the "families" of the housed and they formed a class of the truly dispossessed. They were no longer in control of their own labor power nor of those properties and assets to which they were entitled. Their extraordinary poverty, which the inventories have revealed in such detail, cannot simply be accounted for by a general widespread poverty in this rural society. It is rather the result of their deliberate exploitation by their own families and by role-kin who had been empowered by the state. This vast legal dispossession—and one is tempted to say dehumanization—of the 1580s and '90s found no significant reversals in the eighteenth and nineteenth centuries, when the tides of new social thought, reform, and even revolution reached into the Danubian states.[42] No doubt it is here that we must begin to look for the deeper currents of social and political despair that tore apart these areas of Europe during the first half of the twentieth century.

It is the labor function of "children" and "servants" that has most recently attracted the attention of historians. Lutz Berkner, in his important analysis of eighteenth-century peasant families in Lower Austria, has suggested that "the servants' main function in the peasant household was as a labor substitute for children."[43] Servants joined the household while the children were too young to work and then decreased in numbers while the latter were in their teens only to increase again as children left the household.[44] The problem with this neat distinction between children and servants is that it did not actually exist that clearly in the life of the peasant housecommunity. It is wrong to assert that what determined a child's "class" character was the class to which the parents belonged. Without detailed family histories, it is not at all clear that the children of the housed, for example, ceased to be servants once they received their marriage portions and that the children of lodgers were inevitably destined for a lifetime of servant status.[45] And in any case, even if we proceed by this logic, then servants are still more than merely "young persons engaged in certain economic functions in another person's household for a limited amount of time";[46] as grandchildren of the dispossessed children of the housed, they are on the bottom rung of the social ladder after two generational steps instead of one.

Another way of interpreting Lutz Berkner's findings is this: children performed the role of servants and laborers in their own families and when they departed to become servants in another housecommunity they continued to have the legal status of and play the social role of children. What one may term the exchange of children for servants seems to have occurred while the children were anywhere from their preteens to their early twenties,[47] while at the same time "childhood" did not always officially end with the attainment of majority but could go until about thirty years of age.[48] The paths of mobility from child to servant and from there, when possible, to either tenant or lodger overlapped and did not often move in that direction, as the next chapter shall suggest. The growing limitations on marriage for the unhoused hindered an easy evolution to the attainment of "full" majority for even lodgers. As Mitterauer has observed, the lines between children, servants, and lodgers were blurred and in actual social praxis servants were not a homogeneous age group.[49] "Child," "servant," and "lodger" were often interchangeable and always overlapping roles one played as a member of the unhoused class, of the dispossessed. The lodgers had the most control over their labor and assets but until one became a married lodger (if one became one) at, say, age twenty-four, one's labor power and one's inheritance portion or other incomes had been exploited for over a decade by one or another of the tenants or by stem family elders.

From the point of view of the family and housecommunity, it appears that the stem family was a strategic institution, one that guaranteed small measures of status increase for the family of the housed as a whole over an extended period of time. It was, to some extent, an occupational-functional division of the farm into two units, one of which, the heir's, continued the farm's normal operations and the other, the elders', became, as we shall see in the next chapter, a lender in the credit market; when one of the elders died, a portion or all of their loans and incomes from loans could be reintegrated into the main household whose economic and social status would thereby rise. In actual familial, economic, and social terms, however, there was no house "community." Rather, as we have seen, the Austrian peasant family was sharply divided between those who inherited and those who did not, those who could make their own life plans and those whose life plans depended on property, credit, and inheritance agreements among others, those who could marry and those who could not, those who stayed and those who left, those who lent and borrowed and those who worked for deferred wages. All of these differences were contained by the roles one played in the "house" and not by one's natural family ties to grandparents, parents, siblings, or other kin.

To restate the thesis, the Austrian peasant family was a class situation in which a tenant class exploited their role families in order to engage in competition for status within their own class. Such status competition took place not only in the larger society, in villages and communities, but within the family as well; the community of conflict and interest within the stem family—between the heir and his spouse on the one hand and the elders on the other—contained one of this society's most fundamental status (but not class) conflicts. The *Auszügler* combined a controlling interest in the land and credit markets with consumption patterns and life plans freed from the restrictions and responsibilities that burdened their tenant-heirs, and had, therefore, a good chance for acquiring a personal status and honor that raised them above most other members of the tenant class. The status tactics of the tenants and stem family elders were for the benefit of individuals and not for their entire families. Dispossessed children and siblings lived in a world of their own in which they were exploited as servants and day laborers by the tenant class with whom they shared family and household. Of course, all of them, tenants and dispossessed alike, shared also a single social fate in that their class and status relationships were based on legally defined and bureaucratically administered leases and not on freely disposable property. We must continue to bear in mind that the reifications that split apart Austrian peasant families and villages were a result of the economic and social policies of the state and of the cooperating authorities who together manipulated and restricted their subjects' property rights to suit their own interests.[50] Nevertheless, the peasant tenant class, wholly absorbed in its internal status tactics and maneuvers, not only accepted the new conditions under which it was required to live, but rebelled in the sixteenth century only when changes in estate management threatened their authority and collective class positions in their families and houses; they fought very hard for control of the labor and properties of their dispossessed children. In the bureaucratized peasant family of the early modern Habsburg state, bureaucratic roles and their prerogatives, duties, and disabilities had superseded the affective ties binding together children, parents, and siblings.

~ CHAPTER 7 ~

Social Mobility and Conflict

THE NEW REGULATION of property ownership by the state radically altered relations within the peasant family and housecommunity and enforced a new set of role relations that coincided only in appearance with the traditional roles of parent, child, sibling, and grandparent. In this chapter we shall see how the patterns of social mobility and social failure derived from these changes were experienced not by families but by individuals. The causes for social mobility and failure were to be found in the degrees to which individuals could manage and exploit their familial roles to favor their occupational and bureaucratically defined social roles.

The Austrian peasant family was not a harmonious, conflictfree institution. It experienced an internal role conflict in which the individual's self-interested search for social status through the acquisition of new occupational, economic, and administrative roles clashed with his or her search for affection and nurture in the family group. Life-plans were not worked out in harmony with the other members of the family but instead individuals were tracked into what were in effect "careers" (tenants or dispossessed) at a fairly early stage in life. These tracks determined whether one would occupy, usually for the rest of one's life, an exploited or exploitive position vis-à-vis one's family and community. As we shall see momentarily, nowhere are these role conflicts more in evidence than in the credit relations that permeated rural family and communal life at every level and that replicated, in effect, the system of lien administration on which the higher public finances of the entire state rested. It is on the basis of such role conflicts that we are also able to examine more closely the nature and quality of "psychological stress" that characterized life in the Austrian peasant house-community. The deepest sources of this stress were to be found in the dualistic system of roles, one based on family and work, on the natural and universal needs for love and self-esteem, and the other based on the values of career and social advancement within a bureaucratized peasant housecommunity. The constant threat of social failure as well as the desire to advance directed the inhabitants of the house to make choices in which the values of family and of intimate personal relations had to be repressed in favor of the values of career and social position. The bureaucratized peasant family was the war of all against all and there were no alternative social institutions that provided any sources of relief: the house, where families lived in intimacy, was also the main battleground of social and economic conflict. When the stresses and failures intrinsic to this system of family relations were worsened by the crises of the economy and of the Habsburg state in the first half of the seventeenth century, the class differences that severed the family found expression in the rebellions and social warfare of 1626 and the 1630s.

OCCUPATIONAL MOBILITY

Although it is not possible to reconstruct for seventeenth-century Austrian rural society the kind of occupational ranking scales that have been drawn up for modern industrial societies,[1] it is nevertheless possible to determine what types of occupations offered chances of social success and mobility and which ones did not. On the basis of the analysis of the inventories, it is possible to assert that there were four occupational status ranks by which an individual, whether a propertyless subject or a tenant, could be identified: unspecialized, specialized, diversified, and legally privileged. Moreover, the class distinctions between the housed and the unhoused were of great significance for occupational status. For the unhoused, occupational status could only adhere to the person, while for the tenant-proprietors occupational status adhered to both the house as a whole and to the individual as head of the household. In this section we shall examine these differences further and go on to a discussion of how diversification in its broadest sense, i.e., in the sense of combining all four of these forms of occupational status, contributed to one's social status.

The most menial tasks, the lowest wages, the most crowded and squalid living quarters, and the least nourishing fare were the lot of the servants, stable and field hands, scullions, and other helpers that drudged in Upper Austria's peasant households. The economic profiles of the *Knechte* and *Mägde* that I presented above suggest that they were members of an unspecialized occupation group that wielded virtually no economic and social authority of any sort. They were often not paid their wages and their employers often "owed" them these for several years. They were under the full bureaucratic authority of the tenant they served, and their property was often in the hands of a sibling, godparent, or guardian who used it as he would his own—and, as some court records show, often neglected to pay even the interest.[2] They were used by some householders to carry out illicit smuggling and black-market operations and were thus placed in danger of imprisonment and interrogation.[3] Members of this group could better their lot through some sort of specialization, particularly in the direction of performing services in the industrial textile or in the transport sectors. Some form of industrial activity appears to have helped women in this low status group in particular, even to the point where, if they were sufficiently well connected to a wealthy house, they could achieve a relatively comfortable position.[4] If some form of craft or industrial or other specialization was relatively rare among the servants, then diversification in the form of combining two or more occupational specializations seems to have been beyond members of this group altogether. In any case, all that occupational specialization seems to have offered to members of this group is a slightly better material standard of living. The higher forms of economic and social status among the unhoused subjects went to the generally wealthier and more consistently diversified lodgers.

Occupational mobility from such servile status as I have just described to the more independent life of the lodger was often

merely a matter of reaching majority and receiving one's inheritance portion as well as of acquiring additional skills and
maturity. Their relative mobility, their contractual relationships
with their landlords, their higher incomes and more substantial
possessions, and finally the more flexible use of their labor
services all set the lodgers apart socially from the servant population. Not only do we find that many of these men and women
added some traditional skill such as carpentry, pottery, or tai-
loring to their manual labor services, but several of them specialized to a higher degree to support one of the particular
industries of their estate or community. For example, two lodgers under the monastery Schlägl, renowned for beer of the very
highest quality, achieved a comfortable life and no doubt considerable social respect in the community as brewer and cooper
respectively.[5] Beyond such traditional specializations, there were
also several functions that the lodgers performed in the growing
industrial sectors. I have found, for example, a number of lodgers with looms, other textile paraphernalia, agricultural implements, and such other implements as brandy stills and carpenter's tools.[6] There are others with a considerable number of
preparatory and finishing tools who must have been employers
in the textile trade in their own right.[7] Finally and most significantly, several individuals in this group, most notably men,
reached a point in their occupational development where they
were no longer just diversified laborers and producers but were,
in addition, dealers and brokers in a variety of credit and commodity transactions. For example, in such traditional fields as
wine production and transport we find an occasional teamster-
lodger controlling and dealing in substantial amounts of wine.[8]
Most often it was in the industrial sectors and the textile trade
in particular, however, that lodgers achieved this highest form
of occupational diversification. They were employers who both
participated in and organized primary production among the
servants and other lodgers; they engaged in the distribution of
raw materials and finished items; most significantly, they extended credit within this system of production and distribution
on a considerable scale.[9] There can be no doubt that such dealer,
broker, and creditor services placed a lodger into a position of

higher economic and social status and this not only in terms of the acquisition of acreage, of better clothes and foodstuffs, and other items of relative luxury, but also and primarily in terms of "better" social relationships. Such lodgers could even function, for example, as godparents and as holders of wardships.[10] Moreover, since commerce and distribution were jealously guarded personal rights and privileges, such commercially active lodgers often stood under the personal protection of the householders and dealers for whom they acted as organizers of production, as business agents, and as creditors.[11]

The various functions performed by those lodgers who served as brokers between unpropertied labor and the tenant employers were of vital importance to the functioning of this highly competitive rural economy and were not without risks and physical danger, and it is for both these reasons that certain of the lodgers were raised in legal status to *Schirmleute* or *Vogtknechte*. These terms designated lodgers who were under the special protection of one or another of the tenant householders and it was a means by which a tenant could identify "his people" in the marketplace and community; conversely, a lodger's special status, which was either formally recorded as *Schirmmann* or else was simply a matter of an informal but widely known personal arrangement, allowed him to identify with and publicly represent the house or group of houses he served. Although this is a matter for further investigation, I would think that the dispossessed sons and a few of the daughters of wealthy and highly placed householders would have the inner track for reaching this higher form of social status among the propertyless. Coming from an economically diversified household themselves, they would enter the class of the unhoused as lodgers with relatively large inheritance portions and with the added advantage of finding a good position among their parents' and affines' commercial associates. At the same time, further research might reveal that lodgers of relatively poor origins also succeeded in reaching these highest forms of occupational and economic status among the nontenant subject population. In either case, while the chances for finding traditional and innovative forms of employment expanded on the whole for the unhoused peasantry, competition for the highest occupational status positions and the economic and social status they made possible continued to be fierce. The addition of several industrial sectors and the increasing need for the use of agents, brokers, and petty financiers in the expanding Upper Austrian rural economy created among these lower occupational classes new status possibilities and new ambitions, but accompanying these were new social conflicts, anxieties, and great potential discrepancies, as we shall see in a moment.

It is possible to imagine an unpropertied subject in this rural society advancing in a single lifetime from unspecialized servant through various occupational endeavors to the highest legal status possible to members of his class. Very few, if any, advanced to tenant status. The great majority of the tenants, on the other hand, could experience status mobility on an intergenerational basis in that they gained their legal, economic, and occupational status chiefly through the evolving status of their house as a whole. There were exceptional individuals among the Upper Austrian tenant class who advanced in their life-time to the highest status positions, even to the point where they left behind them their subject status and acquired the status privileges of burghers or even of the highest estate officials. Such men were, however, extremely rare and had considerable notoriety.[12] At the same time, however, for members of an Upper Austrian tenant family to acquire, over a period of several generations, the highest forms of economic and occupational status and to achieve a similar departure from subject status was not as impossible a feat as it has been claimed for peasantries elsewhere during this period.[13] Of course, as we shall see below, what they advanced to after having reached the highest occupational positions available to tenants is a matter of great importance.

Tenants and their households achieved social mobility by similar stages of occupational status development as we have observed for the servants and lodgers. We have examined, on the basis of the inventories, the connections between economic and occupational status, and there the economic advantages of specializing, diversifying, and, finally, of becoming privileged dealers and brokers were evident. To improve his or her status, the tenant landowner had to take some risk and at least specialize for the cattle and grain markets. The great majority of the householders in my inventory population had taken this initial step. Beyond the raising of livestock and grains there were further opportunities; the economic base of the household could be strengthened through a variety of diversifications. The householder could develop already existing features of his holdings such as the presence of particular kinds of workshop facilities or flax-processing houses, or he could attract one or more persons with such special skills as weaving, tanning, or carpentry to his house. He could employ members of his or another household, including members of the immediate family as well as fictive kin, lodgers, and other hired labor, in one of several operations in the textile or metal putting-out systems. These efforts at diversification involved the tenant households in various sectors of the growing rural economy and this increased their commitment of greater amounts of labor and capital to the market. It is evident, moreover, from the inventory population, that the risks of such commitment to enterprise were not so great that a substantial number of the tenants did not take this further step toward a higher occupational and social status. Diversification of this sort was for some only a prelude to their involvement in the transport of agricultural and industrial products. Investment in the prerequisite wagons, horses, oxen, and other teamster paraphernalia meant a further and deeper and riskier involvement in the Upper Austrian market, but the potential reward for success in the carriage trade was the achievement of the highest occupational and social status.

Diversification and the teamster function could combine to give a tenant access to such legally privileged functions in the economic and administrative bureaucracies of the seigneurial estates as weaver, textile distributor, innkeeper-landlord, miller, grain dealer, or some other combination of such commercially active and privileged positions. Broker and dealer functions on this most significant scale were beyond the reach of most of the normal peasant tenancies and advancement to this highest form of occupational status involved, besides the purchase of a legally privileged mill or tavern or otherwise distinguished house,[14] the extension of loans and deferred payments to the managers and owners of one's own and other estates as well as to other persons of higher authority and status.[15] In return for such transport, brokerage, and credit services, Upper Austria's teamsters and innkeepers and the others who performed these functions received legal privileges from their estate authorities and business contacts that further enhanced their social status. While the traditionally specialized occupations were strictly controlled and supervised by their estate authorities and guild organizations,[16] teamsters and innkeepers, although they were admonished to use the legally approved highways[17] and to keep order and seemly hours and behavior in their establishments,[18] were not subject to bureaucratic supervision in the same degree as other members of the subject population. Not only could teamsters expect the service of other housed and unhoused subjects in keeping the roads in good repair and passable,[19] but they could also demand exclusive carriage rights within the legal jurisdictions of their lords.[20] Most teamsters exercised de facto rights of preemptive buying and selling and in at least one case, namely that of the estate Windhag, this right was written, in direct violation of state regulation, into the estate's code, the *Taidingbuch*.[21] Teamsters and innkeepers were in some respects above bureaucratic regulation while in other respects they enjoyed special advantages in the prosecution of the law. According to the Frankenburg *Taiding* of 1570, for example, a teamster who defaulted or made a bad delivery could be held to account by the damaged party but the latter could not count on the assistance of the authorities.[22] At the same time, there is on record in at least one estate code a law by which debts owed to an innkeeper, if they remained unpaid, became the legal equivalent of theft and were punished accordingly.[23] Finally, innkeepers in the countryside exercised monopoly rights in the sale of wine and beer and their rights were protected by estate laws.[24]

There was little possibility for social mobility from one class to another in this rural society. Only the designated heirs and those fortunate enough to espouse an heir made the transition from unhoused to housed subject. The general drift was always in a downward direction.[25] Within these two classes, however, the analysis of the inventories has revealed a surprising similarity in the paths of upward occupational advancement. Occupational mobility reflects not only the general pattern of a limited industrial diversification of the rural economy but also of the bureaucratic regulation of rural economic and social life. At the occupational and economic bottom of one's class, whether housed or unhoused, one felt the full weight of those above and of the regulations that favored those who had advanced to higher positions. For the unhoused, this meant that both the youngest children and those least capable of advancing beyond the meanest chores performed by servants experienced the domination of their socially mobile kin and role kin and, conversely, that those who advanced did so only over and at the expense of their less fortunate siblings and housemates. The housed, on the other hand, had to pass through stages of occupational specialization and diversification—which they could only do, as we shall see next, by investing and risking their own as well as their children's labor and properties—before they could reach the point at which they were relatively free from working for other more privileged householders and from feeling the full weight of the bureaucratic regulation of property and family. Only at the highest occupational levels could the housed subjects restore to their families a measure of intimate, loving, and nurturing relationships that contemporary social values concerning house and family called for.

CREDIT, AUTHORITY, AND ROLE CONFLICT

The limitations in the divisibility and availability of property that had accompanied the bureaucratization of leaseholding and the administrative redefinition of rural houses placed increasing emphasis on occupation and occupational improvement as the chief avenue for social mobility. Even the ownership of land and success in farming no longer represented the high point in a peasant's possible career development; they were more like way stations along the path to higher social status and had, in fact, to be left behind by anyone intent on achieving the highest social positions available for rural subjects. The ownership of a lease on various kinds of rural or village property and the uses to which one put one's properties were actually only signs of one's occupational status and success. Another such sign was how an individual extended and used credit: specific kinds of borrowing and lending were intrinsic to different kinds of occupational status and behavior and were essential activities for achieving any kind of social mobility.

The analysis of the inventories has revealed that it is too simplistic to equate poverty and low occupational status with indebtedness on the one hand and property ownership and relative wealth with creditor status on the other. Everybody both loaned and borrowed but did so under different circumstances. The housed and the unhoused both extended and used credit at different times in their life course and for different purposes. Status was measured by one's particular mixture of debts and loans. Questions concerning the social significance of the kinds of credit relations we found in the inventories cannot simply deal with the commercial aspects of those relations and we can not confine ourselves to questioning only after the relative economic success brought about by various kinds of borrowing and lending. Economic success due to the skillful management of one's resources in the credit market was of great significance for achieving a higher social status but this is only one of the social aspects of credit relations in early modern rural Austria. The bureaucratization of property and family relations had introduced a new factor: regulated and enforced authority relations. This meant that one's status was not merely determined by the relative size and commercial success of one's credit transactions but also by whether one could "borrow" by acquiring more or less temporary control over the assets of those under one's jurisdiction or by whether one was forced to "lend" because one could not resist the "borrowing" demands of those in positions of authority.

When one reads the lists of creditors and debtors attached to the household inventories, the most noticeable feature of the peasant credit system was, besides its ubiquity, its geographic dispersion. A single individual's creditors and debtors were to be found among his or her neighbors in the immediately surrounding community and also, in some cases, from places several hundred kilometers away. Since much of Upper Austria's commercial and productive capital came from areas outside the province and since much of Upper Austria's trade was between peasant dealers and brokers from Upper Austria and their counterparts elsewhere,[26] these transactions were reflected in the lists of debtors and creditors that were an intrinsic part of the inventories. For example, a weaver from Perkham, subject to Schlägl, owed 100fl as a godfather to a shoemaker's heirs in Munich.[27] A teamster from Carling, also under Schlägl, owed a total of 151fl to his creditors in Bavaria as well as nearly fifty *Gulden* to a "Frau von Starhemberg."[28] In the long and detailed list of moneys still owing to the "most honorable and wise Conrad Prauhinger, Imperial excise agent (*khayserlicher Aufschlags Einnehmer*) and chief innkeeper of the earldom of Frankenburg" there appear several large loans totaling 2,336fl for which the debtors are not even disclosed—a degree of confidentiality that was not common in the inventories generally—but among the few of his transactions that were recorded in full there is one that connects him, through the estate manager (*Pfleger*) of Frankenburg, to the textile trade with the Bavarian weavers from the Ried area.[29] We might pause here to point out that although such transactions in which the amounts were large and the debtors not disclosed were rare, they do occur throughout the inventories and almost without a doubt signified loans to persons of high estate. Such loans, in all cases, were made by members of the subject population who had reached the highest occupational positions possible and whose privileged commercial and administrative positions as innkeepers or millers or, as in the case of Prauhinger, as innkeeper and royal official, required them to act as business partners and agents of their authorities.

There are more examples of long distance credit transactions. In the 1631 inventory of a tanner's deceased wife there appears a debt of 35fl owing to one Hans Wolf, a metal dealer (*Eisenmann*) in Regensburg. The tanner, named Christoff Schwaiger, had disappeared in the previous year into Bavaria with his wagon and a load of unspecified goods worth 100fl but had never made restitution to those whose goods he had thus transported on consignment. We must note here also that the estate authorities saw themselves forced to remove his family from the tenancy and replace him with a new tenant.[30] A wealthy *Auszügler* (a former miller) listed among his credits a 100fl debt owed by an unspecified person from Mosberg in Upper Bavaria and, among his debts, the small sum of 1fl 2sh owed to someone in Salzburg.[31] Wolf Nader, a Frankenburg teamster whose movables included substantial amounts of textile materials at every stage of production, from raw and hackled flax to yarn, cloth, and drill, had a total of thirty-four debtors, one of whom was in Nuremberg and owed him 40fl.[32] Finally, there is the example of Hans Riedter, a "burgher and innkeeper" of Frankenburg who had in his inventory 1,000fl in assorted cash (*"in allerlei Münz"*), gold, silver, and pewter dishes, several rooms with beds, a substantial quantity of drill and linen, and a general store (*Crämerei*) with an inventory worth 25fl, had also among his outstanding loans the following: 28fl owed by a burgher of Bruck in Styria, 70fl by a patrician of the same town (*"rathsburger alda"*), and 20fl by another resident of Bruck. Among his own debts we find him owing 24fl to one resident of Salzburg, 49fl to another, and 22fl to yet another; in addition he owed sums of 21fl and 20fl to two residents of Nuremberg and a single debt of 19fl to a creditor in Augsburg.[33] Riedter's case illustrates very well the actual flow of petty credit from the great financial centers of southern Germany to southeastern Europe.

The manifest relationship that appears in these examples between several of the highly placed legal and occupational status groups I have described and long distance trade and credit transactions deserves to be studied in far greater detail; however, for the purpose in hand of describing the important features and some of the weaknesses of the Austrian rural credit system and the social status problems connected with it, the examples I have just cited suggest that high social status was somehow related to one's ability to engage successfully—and, one might add, on the basis of sound currency—in commercial and other transactions that linked the Upper Austrian peasant economy directly with its foreign markets. The economic and social relationships of a significant minority among the Upper Austrian peasantry were not contained by their local communities nor even by the boundaries of Upper Austria itself. This connection between high status and long distance credit was of considerable social importance. Not only was the peasant economy as a whole vulnerable to a closing of the Austrian borders to such long distance commercial transactions, but the inheritance, *Auszug*, and other commercial and social relationships of those among the peasantry who engaged in this trade as dealers, creditors, and brokers could also be adversely affected. Moreover, a credit system of this nature, in a period when travel on the roads was extremely risky and judicial authority was still localized and fragmented, placed a high premium on the mutual trust between creditors and debtors who were often not only from different social classes and different estate jurisdictions but from different principalities altogether. Persons who occupied high positions of social status were officially and in estate documents addressed with such terms as "honorable" or "trustworthy," qualities that were directly related to their involvement in both short and long range credit transactions. If such a person did not or could not fulfill his or her obligations in this dispersed credit network, then this could result in a loss of reputation and a relative loss of status that no amount of wealth or legal privileges could offset.

Somewhat below this group of highly placed subjects—but also including members of it—was another group of subjects active in the credit market, the stem family elders. I have discussed many of this group's unique economic and social characteristics and their special role in the family elsewhere but they also deserve special note in this discussion of the connections among credit, authority, and social mobility. Indeed, the greatest difference between the elders' economic behavior and that of the subject population in general lay in the former's economic and social role as moneylenders. The Upper Austrian peasant economy of the early seventeenth century was remarkably similar to the early modern British peasant economy in this respect: it too was thoroughly saturated with large and small credit transactions that were, for the most part, outright loans, but that also took the form of marketable goods given on consignment, or were socially disguised through *inter vivos* or postmortem inheritance agreements.[34] Loans accounted for 16.7 percent of the assets of the rural population in my inventory population—compared to 13 percent in rural England[35]—and loans made by the *Auszügler* alone accounted for almost 20 percent of the amount loaned by the population as a whole. This places them second only to the true village plutocrats of this area, the innkeepers, who made up only 1.2 percent of the inventory population but accounted for 13.3 percent of the loans. *Auszügler* and innkeepers are the only occupational groups in the tenant class of this society who reversed the normal relationship among the peasant population, evident in Table 2.4, between loans and debts; both were specialized creditors, even though they most likely engaged in different areas of the rural credit market. Despite the generally dispersed nature of that credit market, there were clearly specific individuals and groups who controlled a significant share of it, and their presence contradicts the notion that in this kind of situation cadres of professional moneylenders could not develop. Among the Austrian peasantry of this period they did develop, and the *Auszügler* were the most numerous and widely dispersed of them.

Despite the Central European economy's long secular downswings and rapidly bursting inflationary bubbles, the rural market of this part of Austria remained, in the decades before and after 1600, hungry for capital; deference and prestige went to those who could feed that hunger. As we saw, social prestige was further increased for those who could supply the capital that linked local village markets to each other and to those in other regions. The lists of debtors in the inventories make it clear that although the *Auszügler* were chiefly involved in the local credit market, supplying neighbors and kin with building and purchasing capital, they were also connected to the credit market in more distant villages. Thus, for example, in the case of a former miller and *Auszügler* under the jurisdiction of the estate Frankenburg, we find sizable loans and debts involving individuals as far away as Upper Bavaria.[36]

Moneylending is one of the ways in which wealth can seek

legitimation and social prestige, and the *Auszügler's* position
in the never-ending battle for capital in a rural economy that
lacked official credit institutions assured them of such prestige
in their kin groups, their villages, and even beyond. At the same
time, moneylending and investment were the most important
aspects of the *Auszügler's* high economic status, and it is likely
that moneylending helped them become economically and socially mobile.

TABLE 7.1
Auszügler. Wealth and Credit Relationships

Total Value of Inventory	No. of Cases	Loans Individual Mean	Group Total	Debts Individual Mean	Group Total
0-99	12	15	182	19	231
100-199	9	55	492	73	656
200-499	17	210	3,569	38	638
500-999	8	481	3,851	256	2,049
1,000-	5	1,023	5,116	107	535

NOTE: All amounts in guilders.

The population as a whole had 16.7 percent of its wealth in
loans, while tenant farmers as a group had only 5.25 percent
of their assets in the form of loans. The stem family elders, by
comparison, had 64 percent of their wealth at work in the credit
market.[37] The Pearson correlation coefficient between the total
wealth and the loans of the *Auszügler* was, at .91, the highest
single correlation among the various assets of any group in the
inventory population.[38] This relationship between high wealth
and increased moneylending is evident in Table 7.1, which breaks
the population of the stem family elders down into wealth groups,
and shows how much money they lent and borrowed both collectively and as individuals. The obvious relationship between
wealth and loans takes on a more complex social significance
when we take the debts of the *Auszügler* into account as well.
Their debts were of two kinds. On the one hand there were

213

small debts for commodity, foodstuff, livestock, and raw material purchases, while on the other there were larger debts that were usually moneys held in trust for the disinherited children of other tenant families. For example, the elders in the stem families often acted as godparents and guardians for the children of their kinsmen, neighbors, and other social allies, and this involved administering large and small trust funds until the godchildren came of age or married. These trust funds show up as debts in the elders' inventories. We ought not, therefore, to take "debts" as automatic signs of "indebtedness" or poverty; here they are sources of lending capital with which the *Auszügler* could improve their economic and social status. The debt figures in Table 7.1 suggest, in addition, that the acquisition of such trust funds was the means by which the poorest members of the *Auszügler* group moved to the middle ranks, while those with middling wealth made the transition to the highest economic and social status on the basis of greater indebtedness. The assets of the dispossessed were, therefore, essential funds in the credit market, and served the elders in their occupational specialization and in their rise in status.

The *Auszügler's* exploitation of their families and fictive kin for the purpose of dominating a substantial part of the credit market is of great significance for a wider intrepretation of the Austrian peasantry's family and social life. Not only did capital emanate from those who were wealthy and who thus acquired social status but, more significantly, credit and capital also moved in the other direction. People of low economic and social status extended credit to those above them in the hope of improving their status by becoming a part of the networks of those who had better connections and more authority in the community. There was a striking precedent for this type of credit transaction that we noted above in the *Pfandherrschaft* relationship between the Habsburgs and their service nobility, by which the latter lent the former great sums of money in return for administering in lien a portion of the royal family's possessions. By the late sixteenth and early seventeenth centuries under the administrative social system of the estates, this practice had grown to the point at which credit flowed from the very lowest economic and occupational levels of this society to its very peak. As we have seen, servants and other laborers extended "credit" and secured thereby their employment, by working, often for a period of several years, for deferred wages. Lodgers, if they were involved in some form of transport or industrial production and wished to achieve a higher status as dealers and brokers, lent or advanced sums of money to their landlords or employers or to whoever occupied an immediately higher position above them in the putting-out network. The subject tenants in their turn rose to the top of their class by extending credit in several ways to the officials, managers, and, in some cases, even the owners of the great estates. The estate managers and the other administrative officials of the great and small estates were significant creditors to the estate-owning magnates who employed them and who, in their turn, provided credit to the Habsburgs and to other prominent secular and ecclesiastical princes in southeast Central Europe.

At each stage of this credit system, the creditors gained, in return for their services, such specific privileges and commercial advantages as their debtors would grant. They also entered into such official and unofficial protective relationships as these latter, on the basis of their legal and political status, could extend and enforce. Extending credit to those in authority was the surest way to secure the protection of authority. Taken together, commercial and protective relationships could yield a higher social status than was otherwise possible to individual members of both the unpropertied and tenant classes. At the same time, however, this was a way of linking status mobility and credit relationships that was not only punitive and debasing to the lowest classes of creditors but one that was also potentially disastrous to their welfare as well as to the advances in social status that creditors had achieved. According to this practice, the debtors were simultaneously the arbiters of status as well as the wielders of authority and the result was that they could default on their debts without serious fear of prosecution from their socially and politically inferior creditors and dependents. Particularly during periods of economic and political crisis, when defaults or other disruptions at or near the top of this credit

215

system triggered further waves of default down the line among the lower classes, the many members of the lowest status groups could give up hope of ever recovering the moneys or merchandise that were held in trust by or that they had advanced to parents, inheriting siblings, godparents, guardians, employers, putters-out, teamsters, innkeepers, and others. A failure of the credit system in this particular rural society meant not only desperate and extreme physical hardship at the lowest social and economic levels but it also meant severance from and a loss of faith and trust in those persons on whom one's social position and identity had largely depended. Individuals of the lowest social status groups were cut adrift from their social connections and they experienced this trauma with the bitter knowledge that the years of hard labor for wages they had never received or that the small inheritance portions that their inheriting siblings or their godparents had held in trust—their once-in-a-lifetime stake for social and economic improvement—were irretrievably lost. We shall consider the social revolutionary implications of these aspects of socialized credit relations in the next chapter.

Although the interlocking credit and social systems of the Austrian peasantry alone constitute a remarkable feature of everyday life in this period, we must also continue to remember that this relationship rested on the bureaucratic regulation of tenure and of the relations between the inheritors and the dispossessed. The considerable social significance of peasant credit transactions has long been established by researchers into subcapitalist economic formations. The exchange of social communication disguised behind economic exchange in the classic works of Mauss, Polanyi and Chayanov and, more recently, in the anthropological researches of Foster, Geertz, Mintz and Wolf, and many others has been one of the most fruitful concepts for penetrating to the key institutions of village societies and for forming explanations of peasant social and even religious behavior.[39] At the same time, the stress placed in these studies, especially in the earlier ones, on the discontinuities between folk and urban culture and on the potential significance of traditional social economies for the humane development of modern industrial society, lessens somewhat the value of these conceptualizations for our purposes.

In the case of early modern Austria (and, by implication, of other parts of Central and East Central Europe as well) we are dealing with something besides socially organized patterns of accumulation, distribution, and exchange; we are dealing with a transformation of social relations in which traditional relations of credit and of community and family membership were absorbed by a system of rationally ordered property and credit relations that replicated a significant part of the state's system of public finance in the family and housecommunity. The fundamental framework of the Habsburg state of the early modern period consisted of a bureaucratically regulated but decentralized system of public finance in which property use-rights and authority were exchanged for credit—and at the bottom of this system was a class of disinherited "children" who were forced to give up their wages, their labor, as well as their birthright to the capital requirements of the housed subjects who exercised authority over them. Authority *roles* were paramount in credit relations at this lowest social level. This does not merely mean the kinds of relations we have already observed earlier in this study in which housed subjects simply abused their authority and refused to pay the wages owing to a servant, forcing the latter to "sue" through the intervention of another housed subject with the authorities, but it also means that the moral authority of the house could be invoked to deny a servant his or her wages. In a letter dated 21 June 1635, the estate manager of the estate Reichenstein requests that Sauracher, estate manager for Weinberg, look into the case involving a servant girl, godchild to a subject of Reichenstein, and the bailiff of Kefermarkt who had not paid 12fl for two years' service because the girl had allegedly misbehaved while in service. The Reichenstein manager justified his interference in this case because he had heard reports that the bailiff's claim was false.[40] No evidence concerning the disposition of this or any of the other such cases has survived but the implications of this letter alone are clear: if the servant girl *had* somehow disobeyed her employer and if there were no evidence to the contrary, then the employer, as ruling authority in the house, had acted correctly. At the same time, Sauracher's managerial correspondence also reveals that a tenant could be held responsible for wage arrears incurred by a previous owner of a tenancy who had been forced out of his position on account of the Counter-Reformation or who had left illegally for some other reason.[41] In such cases the house authority was liable but no evidence has turned up so far to tell us what restitution, if any, was made in such cases.

The cases in the managerial papers of Weinberg involving simply the unexplained withholding of a wage or an inheritance portion from a servant by someone in authority, sometimes even by a subject in a high position in the local royal market administration,[42] are by far the most common; however, it is of considerable significance for understanding the interrelations between membership in the house community and bureaucratic authority that in at least some of these cases the rationalizations associated with house administration were invoked to justify payment or a refusal of payment in credit relations between the housed and the servant population. In other words, house authority significantly helped the housed members of a family separate themselves from their unhoused kin in credit matters and indeed strengthened their control over the labor and possessions of the latter. If we recall that Alan Macfarlane's separation between an "individualistic" English rural society and a European "peasant" society rested in part on evidence that social mobility in the latter involved the family as a whole while in the former "families did not move in a block but shed some of their younger or less talented children,"[43] then the Austrian subject population's experiences clearly place it outside the realm of Macfarlane's European peasant model. At the same time, if we are dealing with an "individualistic" society in rural Austria, then it is an individualism outside of Macfarlane's understanding of the term. In Austria, it was the specific social roles played by individuals in the service of the bureaucratic order that gave them advantages in the credit market and supported their occupational and social mobility versus those members of their families and housecommunities who could not serve authority but merely obeyed it.

Having discovered by an analysis of credit relations that peasant social relations in the emergent Habsburg state can only be fully understood by focusing on the individual, we have opened our subject for a different kind of analysis—and we have shown that Macfarlane's perceived distinction between "individualistic" and "communal" rural societies in medieval and early modern Europe is perhaps a real distinction only for the intellectual historian concerned with dominant social norms but not for the social historian concerned with an analysis of actual social relations. As Ralf Dahrendorf has suggested, the smallest unit of social analysis is not the individual but the social role and individuals are identified by the combinations of roles they have to play. So far in this study we have ascertained what the chief roles—or, as sociologists would call them, role-sets[44]—in the Austrian peasant family and housecommunity of this epoch were and how they related to each other. Now it remains for us to seek to understand how individuals experienced these role relations. What is needed to do this problem full justice is much more research with various kinds of "household" data to produce family reconstitution studies as well as the statistical reconstruction of the flow of individuals into and out of family and housecommunity roles, as Tamara Hareven has suggested[45] and as Michael Mitterauer has begun for rural Austria.[46] For now, I shall develop, in the next few pages, a theory of role relations and, specifically, of role conflict that is appropriate to the more sharply focused image of the family authority and credit relations that we have developed up to this point. Its purpose is to allow us to make a statement about the experience of social conflict in this time and place and to propose, in the next chapter, an explanation for the roots of social pathology in the Austrian peasant household that differs from the one offered by Berkner and others.

The economic, occupational, familial, and bureaucratic roles we have discussed in this study were the basis of each subject's social identity and experience. The deep significance of role relations for understanding individual experience cannot be overemphasized. Again we may cite Ralf Dahrendorf to point out that one's social roles are not merely masks that conceal nor are they controlled by a separate and intrinsically complete individual but must rather be considered as a part of the individual's constantly changing self.[47] "Cultural resources are ingredient, not accessory, to human thought"[48] and individuals are not complete until they interpenetrate with their culture by building for themselves an identity composed of social roles. Moreover, behind the play-acting in the *theatrum mundi*[49] is not a personal space free of roles but rather a deadly serious conflict in which the self has to adjust continually and balance and harmonize the demands its many roles make against each other.

Where roles conflict, either in terms of divergent demands within a role (called by sociologists intra-role conflict) or in terms of conflict between roles (inter-role conflict), individuals suffer.[50] The prevailing structural-functional perception of this suffering—expressed in the terms "sociological ambivalence"[51] and "role strain"[52]—is not really adequate to what social actors feel because, first, it does not fully acknowledge the nontheatrical and existential dimensions of role-play. That is to say that the structural-functional view of role conflict depends on a vision of role choices made to gain social rewards and does not help us comprehend what has been one of the results of this study, namely that the assumption and enactment of roles are often not a matter of choice and are, in any case, primarily experienced in terms of negative sanctions.[53] Secondly, in the structural-functional view, role conflict occurs when there are conflicts in and between the cultural norms that govern role expectations. Merton and Barber refined this idea by pointing out that in any social encounter there is a dominant set of "major norms" and a subordinate set of "minor counter-norms" which define the situation and govern the roles individuals must assume in the encounter. Role conflicts are avoided when the individuals in the situation (and in particular the dominant individual) adjust their role behavior in such a way that the "ambivalence" produced by the conflicting norms is neutralized. In other words, *individuals* must manage the contradictions in their roles "to cope with the contingencies they face in trying to fulfill their functions."[54] This view, most useful for dealing with intra-role conflicts, avoids questions about the historical development of the existing hierarchy of "major" and "minor" norms and whether the conflicts between them are sufficiently under the control of individuals to be managed at all. It not only implicitly favors the authority of dominant norms and ignores the lack of choice that may exist in role situations but it also shifts attention away from institutions and class differences and places the responsibility for adequate role performance squarely on the individual. Individuals are judged and ranked according to their "natural" ability to assume roles and to absorb or overcome role conflict.[55]

Structural-functional analysts view role conflict in a positive light because it requires individuals to break through the blocks of indecision if they are going to carry on social life at all. Individual role conflict becomes a source of social adjustment and historical change and serves to integrate social groups and systems—provided that the social actors recognize the ultimate necessity of authority and of the dominance of certain kinds of norms and role-sets over others.[56] The choice of examples of role conflict by Merton and others is most instructive in this regard. Merton's studies, for example, focus on the role experiences of those who exercise authority: doctors, "scientists," and business executives who must all accommodate major norms derived from their base of authority with minor counter-norms derived from the public service aspects of their positions. Thus, for example, doctors assert their dominant norms of detachment by accommodating them with the patients' needs for sympathy and their resulting role behavior vis-à-vis the patient is governed by "detached concern."[57] Not only is it difficult to see how the intra-role conflict of norms is adjusted by stringing together two essentially contradictory words (detached concern) but the participant in the role-set who is outside the structure of authority, in this example the patient, is only taken into account as a victim of his own ambivalences that cause him or her to make essentially irrelevant "affective demands" on the doctor. Although socially important as a source for "counter-norms," the anxieties and hostilities of the patient are ultimately of secondary importance because they derive chiefly from anxieties aroused by the "functionally appropriate and role-prescribed behavior by the professional" that is of course beyond challenge because it is essential to the successful functioning of the relationship whose "real" purpose is the healing of the patient's illness.[58] But, on this point, Merton and Barber have engaged in conceptual sleight of hand. By emphasizing the objective purpose of the social encounter between doctor and patient and identifying the authority of the doctor and the subordinate role of the client with that purpose, they deny their own original concern with the *social* aspects of role relations and their original intent to explore "how and to what extent ambivalence comes to be built into the very structure of social relations."[59] They do not do full justice to the sociological aspects of "sociological ambivalence." The dimension of the role relations between doctors and patients that Merton's analysis does not therefore take into full account is that the patients' awareness of the potential and actual exploitation of role relations by those in authority may be the chief source of their anxiety and hostility and hence of the affective demands the patient may bring to the encounter. In other words, the minor counter-norms the patients bring to the social encounter with their doctor are not really dealt with properly when they are only given an ultimately integrative function that causes doctors to adopt an attitude of "detached concern." That the clients may be attempting to forestall malpractice or the exploitation of their needs by the authorized professional is dismissed by Merton and Barber as "socially important but analytically trivial."[60] Their role analysis denies, in effect, the exploitive features and class aspects of authority relations and is theoretically incapable of dealing with role conflicts that cannot function to integrate social relations but must simply be understood as sources of social conflicts—conflicts that may be repressed behind an appearance of mutually integrative major and minor norms but that remain conflicts nevertheless.

Finally there remains one further aspect of the structural-functional view of role relations to which we must address ourselves before returning to the social life of the Austrian peasant house. One of the ways in which social actors can, according to the theatrical and functional view of roles, diminish the suffering they experience as a result of playing contradictory roles is to maintain "distance" from one or another of these roles. They simply deny that the role in any way defines the actual self of the role actor.[61]

Again, the concept seems to apply to—and serve—the need of those in positions of authority to diminish the vexations, ambiguities, and discomforts their authority-derived roles force on them. For example, in his classic discussion of "merry-go-round role distance," Erving Goffman remarks on how "some adults, riding close by their threatened two-and-a-half-year-old, wear a face that carefully demonstrates that they do not perceive the ride as an event in itself, their only interest being their child."[62] Here the parent controls his or her affect to gain distance from the (ostensibly childish) act of riding the merry-go-round. But does this kind of "role distance"—which is not too far from Merton and Barber's "detached concern"—overcome role conflict? And the answer, of course, is that it does not, for the kind of detachment described by Goffman serves merely to cloak the continuing role conflict that the merry-go-round riding adult must feel (especially if he or she feels it necessary not to react to the merry-go-round at all). In other words, this kind of behavioral analysis of role-distancing behavior by someone in authority or "in control" simply persists in separating the inner from the outer person; it does not help us develop an analysis of the nature of role conflict but rather only helps us judge the abilities of individuals to endure the suffering contradictory roles force on them. Thus "the act through which one can afford to try to fit into the situation is an act that can be styled to show that one is somewhat out of place. One enters the situation to the degree that one can demonstrate that one does not belong."[63] In this paradox it is the individual who is again burdened with the task of overcoming conflicting role demands and the question of the existence of irreconcilable conflicts in the social norms governing role behavior is not broached. Moreover, in the merry-go-round example, the repression of the child's needs in the role relationship with the parent is completely ignored. The parent, presumably taking as his or her primary reference group the merry-go-round watchers, places the child-companion into a secondary or minor role position and displays a parent role that, while appropriate to the spectators, only addresses itself to one of the needs of the child (safety). The child suffers because the situation is diminished by the presence of a parent who can only supervise but who cannot be a companion; the parent suffers because he or she feels compelled to place the imagined role expectations of a group of strangers above the relationship with the child. Role distance, rather than overcoming and diminishing the experience of conflict within and between roles, can actually increase it.

In most cases of "role distancing" the role partner who is in a position of authority also controls the amount of "distance" that exists in the relationship. The parent on the merry-go-round, for example, dominates the social relationship with the child, in the sense that the parent can adjust his or her role behavior so that the child's needs are balanced against the supposed norms about "parenting" of the spectators—and indeed, the parent can overthrow the spectators as a reference group altogether and deal exclusively with the role partner on the merry-go-round. The child, on the other hand, is entirely subject to the parent's decision about the existence and relative degree of role distance and may therefore be defined as the *negatively privileged* member of the role set in Goffman's example. The only choice open to the negatively privileged role partner is to withdraw from the role relationship entirely.

There is one additional aspect of role distancing that goes beyond the merely behavioral discussion of control of affect or the display of "detached concern." The only role distancing that can somewhat alleviate the ambivalence felt by the person in authority is to separate physically the "theaters" where roles of one kind or another are played. Structural-functional analysts recognize this kind of role distance but are reluctant to discuss its deliberate creation or institutionalization. Thus, in his seminal study of the English working class family during industrialization, Neil Smelser demonstrated that the role conflict between home and work increased as the forces of industrialization separated the two, but that the net effect of this distancing was to reduce pressure on the working parent as the expectations placed on the familial roles were reduced.[64] Similarly, Peter Berger applauds bureaucratically institutionalized role distance as a "defense against plurality," that is, as a means to master the inevitable proliferation of life worlds that accompanies modernization.[65] These approaches to institutionalized role distance further trivialize the experience of role conflict and ignore the problems that arise in situations in which persons in positions of authority create institutions and adopt a rationale of norms to produce specific kinds of role distance that diminish the experience of role conflict only for the persons in positions of authority—and do so without eliminating the actual conflict itself and without diminishing the suffering experienced by the negatively privileged partners in the conflict-ridden role relationship. It is precisely this kind of role conflict and role distancing that we find in early modern rural Austria.

As we have repeatedly pointed out, authority relations governed the economic and family life of the Austrian peasant house and, consequently, authority-related roles took precedence over familial roles. The role families we have described were marked by the search for an heir, by the evolution of the family to the stem family and by the reification of the leases in the contracts following the inventories; and all of these were products of the bureaucratization of property ownership. The creation in the sixteenth century of a relatively uniform class of tenant farmers who were in effect managers and not owners of property created a new set of "major norms" governed by the requirements of good management implicit in the emphyteutic terms governing the leasehold. In order to avoid negative sanctions (i.e., the loss of the tenancy) and consequent downward social mobility, the heads of households no longer had to satisfy the scrutiny of their community as a reference group; estate owners and their managers were the only referents who counted and the avoidance of "observability of role performance"[66] became the chief objective of the tenant class. Emphyteusis made such avoidance specific and, theoretically, easy. Tenants could create stem families and we have observed how the state authorities supported such family formation—presumably because a householder who could establish such a family form was managing his affairs well. Tenants who could not avoid the inventorying of their entire household could still juggle their loans and debts as well as the inheritance portions of their siblings and wards in such a way that their assets would outweigh their debts in the final accounting. The Austrian case is a clear example of what happens when the choices actors have in playing their roles—that element of individual choice being so essential to the theatrical and/or functional point of view—is severely restricted. Members of the tenant class *needed* to reify their leases and exploit their positions of authority, their bureaucratically defined and maintained family roles, not simply in order to achieve upward social mobility but in order to avoid a loss of tenancy and status. At the same time, they were required to extend credit when they could to those with greater authority in return for pieces of that authority—and they treated those below them, specific members of the dispossessed class, in the same way.

Trade-offs between credit and authority relations permeated this society from top to bottom. At the bottom levels of society, the role-playing associated with these relationships ceased to be a matter of choice and became a necessity, with the result that individuals must have experienced extreme social "ambivalence," if not outright pain, at the contradictions this coercion produced in family life.[67] Fathers were also heads of houses and as such they confronted a different reference group—the estate owners and their managers, acting for themselves and for the state. The negative sanctions that threatened a tenant's social relations ensured that authority-related roles received primary attention and that familial roles became secondary. The situation was, in its undisguised terms, nearly intolerable. By 1600, Austrian rural society had already begun to advance, long before the advent of industrial technology and the social forms and ideologies associated with it, toward a destruction of affective human relations in the family and toward an instrumental rationality that subordinated those relations to its own purposes. Everyone, both the masters of the house as well as the dispossessed, suffered under this invasion of family relations by the state. House parents suffered because they bought their security and social position with the love and trust of their siblings and children. The dispossessed, however, bore the brunt of this system's incongruencies: married lodgers suffered when they sent the children they could not maintain to become servants in the houses of the tenants and the children of both the housed and of the lodgers suffered when they were cut loose from the family house in which they spent their earliest years. What made the social suffering of the dispossessed doubly great, however, was that there were role-distancing mechanisms at work that not only eased the conflict between authority and parental roles for the heads of houses but also broadened the latter's hold on the inheritance and other moneys owed to the dispossessed.

Michael Mitterauer has done much to deepen our insight into the meaning of "childhood" as a status position in the Austrian peasant family of the early modern period. Among the several types of individuals who were considered "children" in the house, he points to one group who were called, in the soulbooks, *Zuchtkinder*; these were wards of a house. Another, and colloquially more common name for them was *Pupillen*. The numbers of wards in the housecommunities of the peasants is still uncertain. Mitterauer does not give us any exact figures but only tells us that there is "frequent" mention of them in the soulbooks and that, in any case, they blend in and overlap with the servant population to an extent that makes it nearly impossible to get a realistic estimate of their actual numbers.[68] While it would be instructive to know how many wards there were, what trust funds they brought with them, and what their social origins and ultimate destinations were, we do not need to have that information to make a point about the use of wardship as a role-distancing device in the Austrian peasant family.

Alfred Hoffmann, Lutz Berkner, and others have suggested that sending one's children to live in another's house—from the inventories it appears that children frequently went to the house of their godparents or appointed guardians—to work and learn was a normal part of Austrian social and family life.[69] It is not entirely clear that all children employed in this fashion automatically became wards of their new "housefather," but it is clear that not only orphans became wards (although orphans were a significant group among the wards), for the legal and social language of the time distinguished between wards and orphans. From the inventory contracts we may deduce that children who had become entitled to an inheritance portion (either through *inter vivos* or post-mortem inheritance) but who were no longer living in their house of origin and who had not yet come of age were considered the ward of the person in whose house they resided and worked. The reader may recall that the peasant rebels of 1595-1597 had fought hard and successfully for the control of the inheritance portions of the *Pupillen*; the Interim of 1597 had explicitly removed the control of these funds from the hands of the estate owners and had placed them in the hands of their guardians.[70] It is finally here in a discussion of the relationship between credit and role relations that this clause of the 1597 Interim acquires its full historical importance.

The actual prevalence of wardship and the fluctuating size of the funds associated with it will have to be investigated further because they will have some bearing on the overall historical significance of this institution, but, for now, there is no doubt that we can interpret it as a means by which role-distancing behavior was not only uniformly and legally regulated but also encouraged by placing the funds of wards in the hands of their role parents. Most significantly, and Mitterauer's data about the distribution of servants support this,[71] those tenants who had turned their farms into diversified enterprises or who had gone even further and received the privilege of running a mill or an inn and who could therefore profitably employ more children and youths, benefited more from this institution than the average poor tenant who could not maintain a large housecommunity and *had* to send his children or siblings away. The incomes derived from controlling wards' inheritance portions and labor went to those who were already upwardly mobile. At the same time, the swapping of dispossessed children among those tenants who could exploit their labor and inheritance portions greatly reduced the "role strain" tenants experienced when they, as heads of a house, had to exploit their children or siblings. In other words, wardship in conjunction with the absorption of inheritance portions into the credit market helped create a purer form of the bureaucratized role family in the early modern Habsburg state. (We have already noted the function of the stem family in this regard as well.) By physically separating the housed from the unhoused members of a family, wardship reduced the inter-role conflicts experienced by the housed; but this does not mean it reduced role conflict and social conflict in this rural society. The young wards, as the negatively privileged participants in this role-distancing behavior, did not feel such relief; instead, cut off from their house of origin and from parents and siblings and, theoretically only temporarily, from their inheritance, their social suffering increased as they were required to treat as their parents relative strangers or outsiders who were exploiting their labor and inheritance. It would be interesting to know what happened to this institution in the later seventeenth century and in the era of "reform" that begins in the mid-eighteenth. We know, of course, that relations between the heads of houses and their servants (including orphans and wards) continued to be a part of the bureaucratic and not civil law even after the legal reforms of 1811. But we have as yet no work on the possible further bureaucratic regulation of wardship and the inheritance funds of the dispossessed under the Habsburg state. It is, however, interesting in this regard to point to the comparable case of Upper Swabia where, as Peter Blickle has observed, the inheritance portions of orphans were, by the eighteenth century, administered by state lending institutions to assist "needy" members of the tenant class.[72]

229

The Impact of the Counter-Reformation State on Peasant Tenure and Social Relations, 1620-1636

To DISCUSS in terms of economic stratification, occupation, social mobility, role conflict, and role distance a society that may still appear to our eyes merely backward and feudal is to commit onself to the view that categories of social science may appropriately be used to analyze "premodern" societies. The most telling argument against such an approach is not that the language of social science distorts the way historical social reality was perceived by contemporaries; the argument that only the language of contemporaries discloses social reality denies the epistemological and social limits of all language. Moreover, not all actual historical or other experience finds its way into direct language or even into any language at all. Such experience would therefore be closed to us if we denied ourselves the use of a theoretical language that allows us to draw inferences from existing data we might not be able to otherwise. In this section, we shall return to "contemporary language" in the form of the peasantry's expressions of discontent in 1626 and the 1630s but we shall be able to interpret these grievances and programs for change in ways not possible until now.

A more serious threat posed by social science appears to be directed against historical narrative, as Alan Bullock has recently observed.[1] Under the impact of an analytical language aimed at understanding the structure of social relations, the successive events around which our remembrance of the past is necessarily organized are in danger of becoming mere superficial chronology, not nearly as significant as the structures that move invisibly and slowly below the surface occurrences. This view, however, is an unnecessarily limited vision of what constitutes historical narrative, for it is true not only that time occurs in layers, of which each requires its own methods of analysis and narrative, but also that by placing event and structure in opposition to each other (events are told; structure can only be described) we separate narrative and description.[2] Events constitute the medium through which structures express themselves and through which they may be detected. This is not to say, however, that structure can ever provide a complete explanation for events; nor do events disclose entire structures.[3]

In the remaining pages of this study we shall look at some of the events in the history of Upper Austria that followed the defeat of the allied Bohemian and Upper Austrian Estates at the battle of White Mountain in 1620. Our particular concern will be to bring together the structural narrative (concerning the process by which property and family were "bureaucratized" between 1511 and 1597) that we have developed thus far and some of the statements, personalities, and events connected with the Upper Austrian peasant rebellions of 1625 to 1626 and of 1632 to 1636. In the light of the preceding analysis, what new meaning can we ascribe to these uprisings? Where can we place the leaders and their followers in terms of the class and role relations we have been able to determine? How are we now to interpret the expressions of discontent and the political desiderata of the peasants that these rebellions brought forth; and, in particular, what are we to make of their apparently religious and "Estate" (*ständisch*) character? Were these merely traditional anachronistic demands or did they demonstrate that the politically and militarily active peasant subjects understood their new position in the growing Habsburg state?

"Now they have chosen a King they must chiefly address themselves to Kings and absolute Princes," wrote James I's ambassador to The Hague after the Bohemian Estates and leaders of the Bohemian Confederation dethroned Ferdinand II of Habsburg and accepted Frederick of the Palatinate as their king in August of 1619.[4] Ambassador Dudley Carlton's sympathies were with the Bohemian frondeurs, and he covered his disappointment at their conservative path with the apology that the reason for their failure to carry through on their professed allegiance to the Dutch example or to the anti-Habsburg traditions of the Swiss cantons was that they were isolated and needed allies. And indeed, if only to prove their isolation, we may point to the Protestant Elector Frederick, soon to be the "Winter King," who was voting at Frankfurt to confirm Ferdinand of the Habsburgs' Styrian line as possessor of the Bohemian crown at the same time as the Bohemians chose him as king.[5]

To dwell on their diplomatic isolation as a cause for their commitment to absolutism is to preserve to some extent the myth that the Bohemians and their confederate Estates in the Austrian crownlands represented a genuine democratic movement that was the forerunner of modern parliamentarism.[6] In fact, we must note authoritarian and bureaucratic tendencies in the Estates' history that reached back into their sixteenth-century evolution and that favored the royalist solution to the Bohemian constitutional problem. The Bohemian and Austrian aristocrats who organized the Confederation were themselves absolutists in their estate domains; their Confederation was never intended to be a republican movement. They were against Habsburg rule, not absolutism.[7] A recent investigation into the early modern history of Upper Austria's clerical Estate suggests that, if anything, the secular nobility, the *Herren* and *Ritter* (emphatically the former), collaborated with the crown around the turn of the century to centralize the legal organization of the Estates. For example, in the reconstruction of the uniform Upper Austrian legal code, a process that took from 1568 to 1618, the clergy were consistently pushed into a subordinate place by the noble "political Estates."[8] The nobles' maneuvers show their recognition, even before the forfeiture of Estates' liberties after 1620, that the Estates were becoming a part of a hierarchic state bureaucracy[9]—and that position *within* the Estate ranks was of paramount importance. That the Estates would never be an independent institution was obvious at least as early as 1608, when the Upper Austrian Estates treasury stood on the brink of bankruptcy, due, ironically, to lack of support by the noble Estates—a situation that had not found its remedy when the province fell without offering significant resistance to Maximilian of Bavaria's League Army in the summer of 1620.[10] The rural subjects were never a serious party to the allied Estates' constitutional plans except as disposable instruments. Speaking more like a cynical oligarch than the aristocratic magistrate he was, the Calvinist leader of the Upper Austrian Estates, Georg Erasmus Tschernembl, urged his Bohemian counterparts to liberate their peasant bondsmen shortly before the outbreak of hostilities with the emperor and thus turn the common man's willingness to die for his freedom to their own political use.[11] As the representative of the noble Estates party in the negotiations that preceded the Interim of 1597, Tschernembl had had a direct hand in the developing bureaucratic integration of subjects, estates, and state. Writing from exile in 1622, he asserted that the peasants could still be used because they were completely under the political control of the Estates, and despite the emperor's victory, might offer hope for continued resistance.[12] Indeed, a case can be made that the peasant guerrilla resistance of 1620, the parish rebellions against the reinstallation of Catholic priests in 1624 and 1625, and the full-scale revolt of 1626 (whose expressed purpose was to throw out the Bavarian occupation armies, to restore Protestantism, and to gain the tenants a place among the Estates in lieu of the clergy) were all a part and continuation of the larger Estates movement. It may be argued, for example, that the peasant subjects were beneficiaries of the Estates' religious politics after 1568 and 1571, when the nobility won from Maximilian II their right to Protestant worship in their own houses, a right they expanded in 1609 to include the women, children, and subjects under their authority. The peasants' resistance to the Counter-Reformation during the 1620s may be seen as a continuation of this struggle for Protestantism, if not for outright religious self-determination. A further argument can be made that the leaders of the revolts, particularly those of 1626, were both high and low ranking members of the administrative personnel of such important noble frondeurs as the Polheim and Jörger families and that they were merely incited to rebellion by their lords. One can even give some credence to the speculations one finds in the diplomatic and spy correspondence of 1626; namely, that the emperor himself, in order to keep the Bavarian occupation in disarray and drive the nobility into his camp, had an interest in the continuation of the peasant rebellions.[13]

The peasants' political and military acts during the 1620s and after were not, however, the result of manipulations by those in authority, or merely the prolongation of the nobility's struggle. It would also be wrong to ascribe to them the same principles—anti-Bavarian patriotism, religious self-determination and Estates freedom—that the majority of their lords professed but scarcely believed. The peasants had a politics of their own, rooted in their economic and social milieu, which changed with the progress of the Austrian state. What Professors Polisensky and Snider have shown for Bohemia, that the "dynamic" period of social change at the top of society in response to a developing Habsburg state reached well back into the sixteenth century, was also true of the Bohemian Estates' Austrian allies. The defeat of the allied nobilities in 1620 and the reconstruction of the next three decades meant not a radical new departure in the Austrian provinces but rather an acceleration of the bureaucratizing and centralizing tendencies of the absolute state.[14] The vision of an aristocratic republic failed, but once the nobilities of the crownlands were integrated more completely into the state's civil and military apparatus, their superior status over clergy, gentry, bourgeoisie, and subjects in the bureaucratized Estates hierarchy was assured—and this outcome only solidified the social regulations and institutions that the Interim of 1597 had imposed on rural subjects and landlords alike. Why should the peasants rebel if nothing of significance to them had really been decided by White Mountain?

While the structured world of the peasantry remained essentially the same, there were short-term changes such as the Bavarian occupation and the monetary devaluation and price inflation of 1622 to 1624, as well as such permanent changes as the mandatory return to Catholicism, that confronted the peasant population with difficult problems of adaptation and even outright economic and social survival. The peasant rebellions of the 1620s and '30s may be seen as the reactions of specific classes and groups among the rural subject population to specific changes in the state and the social structure that made life for the rural population even more difficult than it already was. The prayers on the peasant banners of 1626 may have appeared as popular adherence to the principles of the noble frondeurs:

> From Bavaria's yoke and tyranny
> and its great oppression
> free us, dear lord.
> Because we've staked our properties and souls
> we'll stake as well our lifeblood!
> Dear Lord, grant us heroic strength.
> It has to be!

But this was not merely a low culture parroting the aristocracy's opposition to tyranny. Evidence suggests that in the mouths of the peasant rebels of 1626, the patriotic, confessional, and libertarian slogans of the age had more than straightforward universalistic appeal. They referred rather to specific problematical aspects of the tenants' class position.

Finally, the rebellions of the dispossessed that occurred later during the 1630s, can not be identified, even superficially, with the nobles' revolts. These later revolts not only gave a millenarian and anarchist cast to the peasant movement, causing it to split along class lines, but they exposed as well the desperate negations and hopes to which the dispossessed had to resort to give meaning to their lives and actions. It was only at these lowest levels of protest that an urgent cry against the system as a whole finally arose; and it should come as no surprise that the institution that drew the greatest opposition of the dispossessed was marriage.

What did the Bavarian occupation of the period 1620 to 1628 and the Counter-Reformation of Ferdinand II mean to the peasant subjects? The fall of the Bohemian aristocratic republic did not entail an automatic defeat for Protestantism in the Upper

Austrian countryside and towns. To accomplish this, Ferdinand had to resort to more roundabout and long-range plans. His rule has been identified as an ideal of absolutism shaped by a praxis whose core was the prince's striving for the unity of confessional with political action.[15] Deeply religious since his earliest years, Ferdinand was afraid of committing sin and surrounded himself with learned casuists who aided him in his struggles with his conscience. He brought his training in the arts of government into the service of his religious purposes. Determined to bring together *ragione di stato* and the functions of the prince as *advocatus ecclesiae*, Ferdinand was both consummately skillful, and unrelentingly severe in subduing both the Upper Austrian nobility and subject population. The taming of the Upper Austrian nobility had been relatively easy for him if only because behind the fanciful flights of Tschernembl's frondeur diplomacy there stood Estates that could not pay their bills and a military force whose leader, at the critical moment of the Bavarian invasion in 1620, lapsed into a state of drunken lassitude and failed to exercise the most elementary strategic foresight.[16] The peasantry was another matter, and one wonders if it was Ferdinand's experience with Inner Austria's Catholic restoration that led him to anticipate that the goals he meant to pursue in Upper Austria—the complete extirpation of Protestantism in the countryside as well as the strengthening of Vienna's hold on the Austrian lands—would be a difficult and messy business in which he would be advised to keep a low profile.

Diplomacy offered a solution to his problem. In order to repay his cousin and ally, Maximilian of Bavaria, for furnishing the money and troops that defeated the Bohemians, Ferdinand placed his Upper Austrian *Kammergut* and the confiscated seigneurial holdings of the Upper Austrian leadership and emigrés under the administration of the Bavarian prince in what was one of the largest *Pfandherrschaft* transactions of its time. By the same token, however, he also repaid Maximilian for his policy in the Empire, which challenged his own, by placing him and his occupation troops in a position to bear the main burden of the conflict that the pacification of Upper Austria was sure to unleash.

Had Maximilian of Bavaria been interested only in recouping his Bohemian expenditures and carrying on the Catholic cause, one could say that he was badly served by Ferdinand. Though some contemporary observers thought he was primarily interested in money and intended to bleed the province dry,[17] Maximilian was in Upper Austria chiefly for his own political purposes, whose ambition far exceeded Upper Austrian revenues and, indeed, Upper Austria itself. In an agreement "concerning war costs" concluded in 1623 and intended to clarify not only the financial but also the political aspects of Maximilian's lien administration in Upper Austria, Maximilian's real interest appears clearly. For him Upper Austria was not primarily a source of money nor was it security for the 12,000,000fl that Ferdinand owed him but rather the means by which Maximilian secured Ferdinand's promise to follow through in a sale of privileges and properties that would give Maximilian control of the Upper Palatinate.[18] For this Maximilian was willing to endure, in absentia, the abuse of the Upper Austrian peasantry.

Maximilian never pushed too energetically for the incomes from the Upper Austrian *Kammergut* that he was entitled to, even though his representatives in Vienna notified him of their continuous frustration by the evasive tactics of the highest economic and political officials at court. His letters in response advise a policy of persistence tempered by restraint.[19] The Bavarian prince never actually controlled many Upper Austrian institutions or agencies. For example, the 300,000fl per annum that were his due were to come from the *Salzkammergut*, but he managed to place only one official at Gmunden to represent his interests in the salt trade, that otherwise remained in the hands of the Lower Austrian official, the *Salzamtmann*, in Vienna. Although the Upper Austrian Estates were suspended by Maximilian, their standing committees, and particularly the finance committee, remained in session and played an important mediating role among Ferdinand, Maximilian, and the inhabitants of Upper Austria.

Maximilian's representative in Upper Austria was Adam von

Herbersdorf, an ambitious convert to Catholicism,[20] who combined his authority as *Generalwachtmeister* in the League army with that of *Statthalter* in Upper Austria to pursue an independent and self-serving role that leaned, finally, toward Habsburg service. Much of the peasants' anger in the rebellion of 1626 focused not only against Maximilian, the Bavarian "tyrant," but also—and more properly—against his agents, who exploited the incomes and seigneurial estates that flowed through their hands and reaped the rewards for implementing the confessional and economic plans Ferdinand II had in store for the province. Count Adam von Herbersdorf was one of the most successful of these agents to emerge from the period of the Bavarian lien administration, and he represents the new generation of Austrian high service nobility. The criteria for belonging to this group, applicable to both established and immigrant nobility, appears to have been the acquisition of estates in the Habsburg domains, which entailed the administration of royal seigneurial holdings, contribution to royal finances by entering into arrangements of lien administration with the prince, representation of the royal party in local and Estate politics, and, above all, enforcement of the Catholic restoration among the peasantry.

Herbersdorf performed all these functions. The son of a Lutheran baron (*Freiherr*) from Styria, he had risen rapidly in the service of Philip Ludwig von Neuberg, and converted to Catholicism under the influence of the Jesuits in 1611. In the service of Maximilian of Bavaria, he was a part of the invading force that arrived in Upper Austria in the summer of 1620 and he was named *Statthalter* on 1 February 1621. At the conclusion of the Bavarian *Pfandherrschaft* period in 1629 he had acquired three estates in Bohemia, two in Upper Austria and one in Styria; when the Upper Austrian Estates received back their constitution and privileges with the Edict of Restitution in 1629, Herbersdorf became chief officer of the Estates, *Landeshauptmann*, which made him the highest Habsburg administration official in Upper Austria. It was the activities of this highly ambitious and, when the occasion demanded it, ruthless aristocratic bureaucrat on behalf of the Habsburg state that threw the recently established rural social order into disarray and burdened it with an even more contradictory set of rules and conditions than it normally had to bear.

During the period 1622-1624 there occurred in all the Habsburg territories a drastic reduction of the silver content in the most common coin in circulation, the kreutzer. This devaluation was intended to ease the strain on the royal treasury that resulted from the initial financing of the Thirty Years' War; in Upper Austria it threw markets into a frenzy of exchange speculation and an equally frenetic and speculative commodity price inflation.[21] Herbersdorf carried out Maximilian's policy by lowering, temporarily, the value of small Bavarian coins in order to ease the strain the inflation caused among the province's laboring population and, in particular, among the salt workers.[22] But the emperor's as well as Bavarian interests were served by Herbersdorf's first measures concerning the trade and commerce of the Upper Austrian peasantry, allegedly intended to control an inflationary market. With patents that foreshadowed in several striking respects the policies that the Imperial *Kammer* would pursue shortly in regard to Austria's economy as a whole, Herbersdorf tried to assert a degree of control over certain key aspects of Upper Austria's commodity and specie market that was unprecedented. As early as November 1620, for example, he placed a prohibition on the export of textile products, which he later relaxed somewhat to permit their sale on the open market (the sale of textiles in the homes of the peasantry continued to be forbidden). He also permitted textile exports under license granted by him.[23] After the publication of several such prohibitions, which, as he noted, were not being obeyed, Herbersdorf published a major and comprehensive list of price ceilings in which he clearly stated the controls that were to be imposed. He asked the Estates, their magistrates, and the city administrations to form committees to control the movement of raw materials and finished products on their markets, to inspect the books of tradesmen, and, in particular, to exercise strictest controls on the trading and craft guilds, the teamsters, and the innkeepers.[24]

The Estates complained to Maximilian and to the emperor

against Herbersdorf's inspection of their granaries and against his threats to reassess and update the tax base.[25] He had gone so far as to visit their grain depots in order to verify their claims concerning the grain reserves that were actually present, and his zeal in these matters threatened some traditional economic liberties when he attempted to conduct a proper census in order to establish what taxes were actually owed by the Estates. Ferdinand forbade Herbersdorf to carry out these plans since they also threatened his royal rights.[26] There was no one, however, to intercede on behalf of the peasantry, with the result that the troops and collaborators of Herbersdorf were free to enforce such controls in the countryside and in the rural markets. Moreover, Herbersdorf placed roaming patrols on Upper Austria's roads and stationed his troops at mountain passes and border crossings; these were measures that hit the Upper Austrian peasant traders and brokers particularly hard since they bore the risks of actual transport in the overland commodity and credit markets.

The details of the commodity price inflation and its effects on Upper Austrian rural economy in the period 1620-1625, and the full extent of the state's counterinflationary measures need to be studied further before definitive statements can be made about their impact. We may deduce some of the effects of these measures on the economic and social life of the Upper Austrian peasantry, however. The Estates complained in 1622, 1623, and 1624 that Herbersdorf's attempts to lower prices were "forcing" peasant traders and brokers to withhold their goods from the market in the hope of further price rises that would allow them to profit. They also complained that the closing of the borders caused many of the peasant traders heavy financial losses.[27] The impression one gets from the inventories is that the inflation of the early 1620s, particularly during its peak period between 1622 and 1624, had triggered a wave of investment and credit transactions among the Upper Austrian peasantry. Price fixing and martial law on roads and in markets combined with the stringent Counter-Reformation measures of 1625 to cause prices to decline sharply in Upper Austria's markets with the result that many among the peasantry who had speculated on the inflation could not meet their debts. Waves of default and bankruptcy lasted through at least the remainder of the 1620s and the next decade.

In this latter regard especially, we may turn once again to the evidence contained in the household inventories. Figure 2 shows the fluctuations in the annual percentages of inventories in which the liens were equal to or greater than the assets, i.e., inventories of tenancies that had been declared, or could legally be declared, bankrupt and forfeit. The function of a trend line— aside from making the direction and slope of the data immediately clear—is to introduce visual order to the fluctuations of a time series, to group the data above and below a line so that the character of spans of time *within* the time series stands out

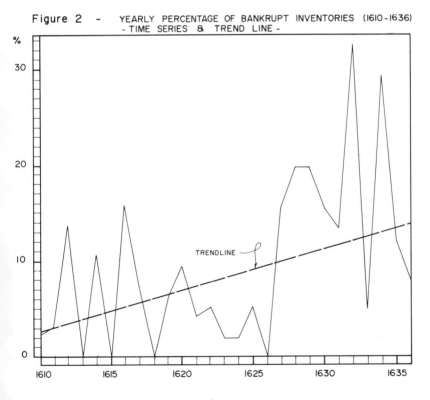

Figure 2 - YEARLY PERCENTAGE OF BANKRUPT INVENTORIES (1610-1636) - TIME SERIES & TREND LINE -

more clearly. Not only is there, in the case illustrated in Figure 2, a general trend of increasing bankruptcy, but the trend line also causes the decade that begins in 1617 and ends in 1627 to stand out sharply in contrast to the period before and, in particular, to the decade following. A period of moderate and relatively low fluctuation gives way to a few years of almost no bankruptcies which are in turn followed by a period during which tenants lost or were in danger of losing their farms at a sharply increasing and wildly fluctuating rate. The strikingly different shape of the data in the 1620s is particularly noteworthy. The average annual failure rate for the last two decades of the sixteenth century was 4 percent[28] and was the same as for the period from 1617 to 1626; in the decade after 1626 that rate jumped to 16.5 percent! The years from 1625 to 1627 clearly constituted a transition period for the peasants of Austria during which they saw not only the onset of the Counter-Reformation, the assertion of control by the state over rural markets and market prices, and the most important Austrian peasant uprising of the entire century, but also a sudden sharp increase in the inability of the members of the tenant class to live up to the emphyteutic terms of their tenure and to hold on to their farms.

A small number of inventories for tenants who died in the peasant war of 1626 has survived and the characteristics of this group (Table 8.1) allow us to draw suggestive conclusions concerning the social significance of the time series in Figure 2. The immediately striking collective characteristic of those who died during the uprising of 1626 is of course their astronomical indebtedness (the debt to loan ratio is 50:1!) and the extraordinarily high correlation coefficients between debts and wealth in property. But before we jump to the conclusion that a purely economic motive, high indebtedness, was the primary reason for a peasant tenant's participation in a desperate cause, we ought to consider what else we know about this group. They were all male tenant farmers and of the upper middling sort with regard to average total wealth and the average value of their farms. From the contents of their inventories we may deduce that they were undiversified farmers and, indeed, the relatively low value of their movables as well as the movables' simple contents both further suggest that their agricultural operations were down to bare essentials, below the norm for farms

TABLE 8.1
Deceased in 1626 Peasant War (12 cases)

	Total Assets	Real Property	Movables	Loans	Debts	Freigeld
Sum	6,448	5,050	1,272	126	6,181	401
Mean	537	421	106	11	515	33
S.D.	394	303	97	24	0	22
Correlation Matrix						
Total Assets						
Real Property	.99					
Movables	.96	.95				
Loans						
Debts	.93	.95	.88			
Freigeld	.78	.77	.75			

NOTE: all amounts in guilders.

of this value. It is this latter characteristic that, when combined with their near-bankruptcy indebtedness, suggests to us a possible course of developments preceding the involvement of these men in the armed conflict of 1626.

The period of inflation between 1622 and 1624 promised a high rate of return for agricultural production as well as for the various kinds of industrial specialization and diversification. It was during this period that a good number of undiversified peasants sought to improve their position by investing in the equipment, raw materials, and labor necessary for industrial diversification, most likely from some form of participation in the textile industry organized by south Bavarian putters-out. When Herbersdorf's measures concerning the abrupt fixing and lowering of market prices and the enforcement of controls on trade routes and tolls took full effect in late 1625 and the spring of 1626, they destroyed chances for profits for members of this group of peasants and with that destroyed their chances for improving their economic and social position. We remarked earlier in our discussion of undiversified middling peasants (see Table 7.1) that their inventories showed an acute dependence on the market for a very limited range of agricultural products and that, given their weak credit position, they had very little chance to move out of their unspecialized occupational status. The inflation of the early 1620s, stimulated by an increased military demand for agricultural and industrial products, gave them such a chance. Not only would the capitalization of their farms for increased output have yielded a greater income from an inflationary market, but labor costs were also greatly reduced by the drastic devaluation of those coins in which labor was paid. However, the restoration of the "normal" order in the marketplace in 1625/26 meant a sudden return of the undiversified peasant to his normal position, only now with a vastly greater overextension of debts than normal. The result was what Figure 2 and Table 8.1 combine to show us. Those tenants who died in battle in 1626 and whose inventories have survived had not only failed to move upward but had lost the game altogether and were about to lose their social position as tenured heads of houses.

The inventory data that gave us the preceding analysis therefore do not simply signify an economic crisis for the tenant population but a deep-reaching social crisis as well. It was a crisis of tenure. At stake were the headships of households and the economic and social fates of the inheritors and the dispossessed associated with a particular tenant family. We cannot forget that a substantial part of the massive debts that caused the waves of bankruptcy in Figure 2 and that threatened the families of the deceased in Table 8.1 consisted of the inheritance portions of the dispossessed children, the trust funds of wards and orphans, and the wages of servants and laborers. The crisis of tenure that resulted from the economic instability of the early 1620s necessarily unleashed economic and social disaster among the disinherited, whose exploitation, with the failure of their "house family," became complete. We can illustrate this in part if we treat the inventories of both the male and female

244

servants from the period 1625 to 1627 as one group and compare it to the group formed by the inventories of male and female servants for the period 1609 to 1624. Most of the total value of the inventories in both groups was still made up of various kinds of moneys owed, but there was an increase in such extended credit for the 1625 to 1630 group, up to 71 percent from 66 percent for the servant inventories from before that period. Not only did the amounts owed to servants increase but their debts increased even more, going from 32 percent for the period before 1625 to 43 percent after that date. In other words, the disinherited were being exploited at an increasing rate and inflation had forced them into deeper debt. At the same time, we must keep in mind that the worsening economic position of this servant group after 1625 was only one aspect of their deteriorating social position, which was linked to the social failure of members of the tenant class.

The crisis of tenure for the housed peasants arose not only from economic and social causes but also from the onset of the Counter-Reformation, which, though threatening since the last decades of the sixteenth century, did not begin in earnest until 1625. The first attempt at installing a Catholic priest at Natternbach in January 1625 had been a complete failure in face of the determined resistance of the leading members of the parish and their followers. Having learned their lesson, the Emperor's *Reformationskommission*, headed by Herbersdorf, tried again at the estate Frankenburg, where they could count on the cooperation of its absentee owner, Franz Christoph Khevenhüller, and his chief manager, Abraham Grünpacher, both of whom were, like Herbersdorf himself, converts to Catholicism. Again the installation of the new priest met with resistance. There was an attempt to murder *Oberpfleger* Grünpacher whose new parish priest was badly beaten and driven away; this time Herbersdorf retaliated in a most deceptive and cruel fashion. Long before he arrived in the parish with his troops, cannon, and executioner's paraphernalia, the peasant crowd dispersed. Herbersdorf, upon his arrival, sent out a proclamation calling for an assembly of the inhabitants of five of the surrounding parishes. He promised mercy to those who complied and threatened forfeiture of properties, family, and life to those who did not. Then, with over 6,000 members of the peasantry assembled under the guns of his troops, Herbersdorf asked the estate bailiffs, village councillors, and parish guildmasters to step forward and assemble so that he might address them. This done, he berated them severely for allowing such criminal behavior to occur and concluded that, since the perpetrators escaped, the bailiffs and council of Frankenburg as well as the parish councils and guildmasters of the surrounding countryside would have to suffer criminal punishment instead. These men, already separated from the crowd, paired off, and were made to roll the dice against each other. Those who lost, with the exception of two for whom Grünpacher interceded, were bound and executed. Their bodies were left to hang for three days and then impaled on pikes alongside the Imperial road near the market at Vöcklabruck.[29]

Herbersdorf's actions have been explained, if not excused altogether, as the normal procedure of military discipline in the era of the Thirty Years' War.[30] One could maintain, moreover, that the cruel rolling of the dice not only allowed half of the "guilty" to escape but introduced an element of chance that brought into play the ancient theory of trial by ordeal, according to which an evil act entered the world again to strike the evildoer. Herbersdorf was acting as the head of an occupying army, and precedents dating from the Romans to current seventeenth-century practice indicated that the principle of decimation decided by lot was often called on to deal with massive mutiny among soldiers, when it was expedient to have only a few experience the punishment of all. In this view, the "dicing" at Frankenburg, an event that has retained a prominent place in Austrian popular history and mythology, did not warrant the outraged reaction of the peasants to what appeared as the infernal cruelty and tyranny of Herbersdorf's regime, since this action was a "normal" part of military life. We must however remember that the parish leaders and peasant officeholders who were singled out at Frankenburg were not soldiers and that they represented not mutineers, but an active, if somewhat passionate and even violent, opposition to the coerced transformation of parish organization and ministry. We cannot simply assume that the peasants were only capable of an emotional reaction to what they perceived as cruel and unjust punishments; there were cooler heads among them for whom the legal and social implications of the bizarre events at Frankenburg were perfectly clear. It was they who would be the targets of discipline in the state's new religious order. The new regime was not punishing a few recalcitrant and particularly rebellious individuals; in fact, it ignored these. Instead, it directed itself against those who had achieved the highest offices and positions of esteem and respect among their fellow subjects and parishioners and threatened them, first, with the loss of tenure if they did not comply with the order to assemble. By executing men who were not personally responsible for the resistance, Herbersdorf was flinging the gauntlet in the face of the peasantry's leading groups and persons, and holding in opposition to their demands for religious self-determination his authority to deny them even the most fundamental processes of civilian law. Under the Counter-Reformation the new bureaucratic order for tenants and estate officers was enforced by military rules backed by the powers of the absolute state. It was this essential "lawlessness" of the Counter-Reformation process, especially when we consider it in a context of bureaucratically regulated tenure and social mobility, which, as we shall see in a moment, acted in concert with the economic plight of certain members of the peasantry to interfere with tenure and upward movement through the occupational ranks.

With the peasantry of Frankenburg temporarily pacified and the installation of Catholic priests slowly gaining momentum in the rural parishes, the *Reformationskommission* felt sufficiently secure to let the other shoe drop; on 10 October 1625, they published a *Reformationspatent* whose nine articles did not threaten the peasantry with merely religious but also with social reprisals.[31] According to this patent, the parishes were required to give up immediately not only their Protestant clerics, key figures in the social life of the parish, but also their control over the endowments and treasuries of the parish churches,[32] which had been a vital part of each rural parish guild's banking and commercial functions and had also supported the parish schools and their teachers. The Counter-Reformation state clearly aimed to bring under control the last of the previous century's "independent" communal organizations and politics. Also in the area of education, the *Reformationspatent* forbade the keeping of private tutors, disbanded the women's social circles that had formed to read and interpret sermons, attacked the sale and ownership of proscribed heretical literature, and, finally, forbade the education of children in schools outside Upper Austria. All of these were important institutions and practices serving both peasantry and townsmen. Furthermore, the commercial, craft, and labor guilds were required to participate in their parish's Corpus Christi parade and were otherwise required to participate in the Catholic liturgical year. The most serious clause in this new religious order was, however, directed at the broad mass of the subject population. Everyone in Upper Austria had until Easter of 1626 to do one of two things: they could either convert to the Roman Church and display, when required, the documents proving they had attended confession,[33] or they could choose to leave Upper Austria, after paying the customary 10 percent *Freigeld* as well as a further 10 percent tax on their assessed properties.

This clause of the *Reformationspatent* confronted the peasant householders with a frustrating dilemma. On the one hand, if they chose emigration and exercised a tenant's "freedom" to move, they took a bad financial beating; according to the grievances of June and July 1626, under Herbersdorf's administration of the *ius emigrandi*, other charges were imposed on top of the two 10 percent fees so that by the time a tenant received his permission to leave and his passport, he had often forfeited over 50 percent of his properties.[34] In other words, they not only gave up tenure and the social position they had built in Upper Austria but their chances of getting away with enough to purchase and maintain tenure elsewhere were not good.[35] On the other hand, if they took the *politique* course as Abraham Grünpacher and others had done,[36] and changed their religion to retain their tenured status, they denied many of the collective political and legal gains they appeared to have made since the latter decades of the sixteenth century, most notably, that no authority could determine *directly* a subject's religious choice[37] and that the maintenance of tenure over several generations guaranteed a kind of "residency" that even the terms of emphyteusis could not touch.[38] The *Reformationspatent* of 1625 triggered the revolt of 1626 because it constituted the culmination of the state's long policy to gain control over the terms of tenure and over the bureaucratic duties imposed on and the privileges dependent on tenure; it overthrew once and for all any illusion that the authority behind the position of the tenured class carried any kind of feudal or Estate-derived legality, and clearly demonstrated that it rested rather on bureaucratic rationality that was in turn wholly subject to the charismatic authority of the prince and his state.

To make this point more forcefully, we can briefly examine the social positions and activities of the peasant leaders who organized the resistance armies of 1626 and follow this with an analysis of the peasant grievances that were sent to the emperor in July of 1626. Some analysts of the period might consider the motivations of a handful of peasant leaders a trivial matter, but in the light of the purposes we stated at the outset concerning the social integration of the Austrian absolute state and the analysis of the development of mass social relations under absolutism, what these men represented, their resistance, and their defeat are all of central importance. The best-known leaders, and those about whom we have the most information, are Stefan Fadinger and Christoph Zeller, who led the peasantry in the early phase of the war, and Achaz Wiellinger, who held the high command until the end of the rebellion.

Fadinger and Zeller,[39] both of whom were subjects of the estate Aschach-Stauf, led the peasant band from the parish St. Agatha, which had defeated *Statthalter* Herbersdorf at Peuerbach on 21 May 1626. They became the elected leaders of the peasant army that formed after this initial victory. Stefan Fadinger (in the popular consciousness of Upper Austria today still the most remembered figure from the year 1626) was, like so many other peasants of his day, the subject of several authorities. The original owner of his tenancy was the Protestant

Freiherr Johann Karl Jörger who lost his properties and life for the role he played in the 1620 fronde. Fadinger's new landlord, after 2 June 1622, was Count Carl von Harrach, one of the chief executors and beneficiaries of Ferdinand II's Counter-Reformation. Fadinger's judicial overlord was the Protestant Christoph von Hohenfeld, owner of the market town Peuerbach, to which Fadinger paid his tithe until 1618, when the *Pfleger* of Peuerbach bought the tithe for 120fl and resold it to Aschach-Stauf.[40]

Fadinger's tenancy is invariably described as the "handsome estate" Fatting am Walde[41] and had been, significantly, in the hands of his family since the days of his great-grandfather in the early sixteenth century, when the family was subject to the estate Schaunberg. Stefan, the youngest of three sons, took it over in 1616/17 from his father Paulus. His brothers Moritz and Hans appear not to have been active in the 1626 uprising; the latter was deeply involved in the textile trade and died in 1637, a moderately wealthy man.[42] The fixed property of Stefan's tenancy was assessed at 800fl and his indebtedness after his death amounted to 1,300fl; the value of his movables and outstanding loans must have been quite high, for his inventory showed a surplus of 174fl.[43] The question of Stefan's occupational status is problematical since the sources are not in agreement. Stieve, in his authoritative history of the peasant war, felt he had to debunk what he considered to be false and confused perceptions of Fadinger's occupation.[44] A Protestant contemporary from Wels who kept a chronicle of the war identified Fadinger as a charcoal burner and this does seem to miss the mark—although it certainly arouses one's curiosity about why he thus identified the rebel leader. Stieve also discounts the report of the Venetian ambassador to Vienna who declared Fadinger a former military man. Carafa's description of Fadinger as a hatmaker and the description of him by Raupach, an eighteenth-century historian of Austrian Protestantism, as a cloth dyer, are considered equally false by Stieve. These three occupational descriptions may, however, not be as far-fetched as Stieve thought nor are they, in the light of the present study, incompatible with the role of simple farmer for which Stieve finally settles. Fadinger's wealth, his indebtedness, and, as we shall see, his overall social status were completely out of character with that of a "simple" farmer. Perhaps most telling in this regard is the actual size of his farm which at about 17 acres arable, 8½ acres of meadowland, and a little more than 7 acres of woods,[45] was at best modest for a farmer of this period and could certainly not have accounted for his wealth and social status.

Stefan Fadinger's overall social status is hard to assess since little remains in the archive of the estate Aschach-Stauf that might give us further clues.[46] Of his transactions there remains only one record of a debt, 24fl, and one instance in which Fadinger witnessed a receipt. There is, however, one fragment of evidence concerning Fadinger that places him squarely among the legally privileged members of the tenant class. When the Steyr lawyer and manager of the Polheim estate Parz, Lazarus Holzmüller, was interrogated after the peasant war, he claimed that he, together with Wolf Madlseder (a magistrate of Steyr and, as we shall see, connected to Achaz Wiellinger as well) and Johann Grenner (the estate manager of Peuerbach), had helped to direct the peasant war and that the latter had held Fadinger's signet ring.[47] Among the Upper Austrian peasantry of this period signet rings (Petschaften) were complex instruments not only of personal and public correspondence but also of commerce.[48] They were exchanged as signs of mutual trust between parties engaged in private commercial and credit transactions as well as in official affairs. As we have noted, in their correspondence and even in the inventories, the highly placed and commercially active subject tenants were identified by such respectful terms of address as noble (ersam) and steadfast (vest), qualities that were of utmost importance in a cosmopolitan rural society where the wheels of commerce moved on hubs of trust, loyalty, and rank—and it was the use of personal signet rings that backed up these forms of address and that identified their bearers and holders as men of particularly good reputation involved in important commercial and public affairs. To "hold" another man's seal, as Johann Grenner held Fadinger's, permitted the holder to affix that seal to an official document.[49]

Signet rings therefore functioned as bureaucratic instruments denoting chains of authority and privilege. With his signet ring in the hands of the estate manager of Peuerbach, Fadinger was clearly not the simple peasant farmer that Stieve imagined but was rather an ally of a significant commercial and political figure. He stood above the common tenant farmers and had moved to the highest position of legally privileged occupational status to which a subject could aspire.

Stefan Fadinger's brother-in-law and second-in-command, Christoph Zeller, led the peasants from north of the Danube (even though he too lived south of the Danube in the parish St. Agatha and was a subject of the estate Stauf). He was an innkeeper in the town of Haibach, which was a Protestant center and had been a focal point of the 1595-1597 rebellion.[50] It was the Protestant *Pfarrer* Hans Cummerer whose church and school at Haibach the parishioners of St. Agatha generally patronized, and since Zeller's tavern was next to the church, it was a natural meeting place for the Protestant peasantry of the surrounding countryside. There is little information concerning Zeller's economic position, but it must have been quite high since the tavern alone, in two transfers during the late sixteenth century, was valued at 1,400fl. The earliest Zeller incumbent of the tavern at Haibach was Christoph's great-uncle Michael who appears in 1530; Christoph's father, Siegmund Zeller, was the tenant innkeeper of a tavern at Haichenbach. Christoph's brother George held tenure on the Haibach tavern during the first two decades of the seventeenth century and Christoph himself took it over in 1618 when it was sold by Peuerbach to the estate Stauf.[51] According to the estate protocols, Zeller was a moneylender. He appears there also eight times, with three requests to hold a ceremonial feast (*Zehrung*), with four marriage sponsorships, and once as holder of a wardship.[52] The most telling document concerning Zeller is a description of him by the Upper Austrian knight Erasmus von Rödern who claimed to know Zeller very well. Somewhat witheringly he identified Zeller as the former innkeeper at Haibach who now liked to be called "Your Honor" (*Ir Gnaden*). He described him also as an equestrian sort ("*ein reiterischer Kerl*") and a teamster.[53] The most significant piece of information in Erasmus's description of the rebel chief is that the latter had been under the special patronage and in the administrative service of one Hieronymus Schluchs zu Grueb and Haglau, a *Ritter* whose seat Grueb was near Kirchberg in the Mühlviertel. It was as a member of Hieronymus's personal retinue that Zeller travelled in Upper and Lower Austria when the former performed his duties as provost in charge of rents and tenancies (*Lehensprobst*) for the Starhemberg family.[54] This connection with Schluchs places Zeller in the same privileged occupational group as Fadinger, and, as we shall see, Achaz Wiellinger. After Schluchs's death in 1603, Zeller, according to Erasmus, went into military service, and that is all we know of him until he turns up as innkeeper in 1618 and as military organizer and peasant leader in 1626. In the course of the rebellion itself he appears to have been a ruthless and self-serving extortionist who used his status as supreme military commander to confiscate livestock, grains, linens, and properties of Catholic priests in order to sell these for his personal gain.[55]

Fadinger was shot and mortally wounded during the early phase of the peasants' siege of Linz by one of Herbersdorf's snipers, and Zeller, who did not have sufficient stature to control the peasants of the Hausruckviertel, lost his supreme command. There was a short-lived attempt on the part of the St. Agatha party to elect Fadinger's personal bodyguard—who is referred to as the "Bauernsohn Egger" from Haibach and whose father was probably the Georg Egger who appeared among Zeller's debtors with a cancelled 200fl debt[56]—to the post of supreme commander. This attempt to retain control failed in the face of the rise of another party whose geographical center lay further to the south, around the great commons known as the Weiberau. The leader of this group, Achaz Wiellinger "von der Au," was a reputed member of the third Estate.[57]

The Wiellinger family appears as incumbent on the Gatringerhof near the estate Starhemberg and the market town of Haag in 1480. In the course of the next century, members of the family achieved several positions of prominence. In 1550/51, Kristoph Wiellinger, Achaz's uncle, became estate manager (*Pfleger*) of the seigneurial possessions of the city Steyr, while two other members of the family, Caspar and Wilhelm, whose relationship to Achaz is not ascertainable, managed to achieve admission to the *Landtafel* by means of skillful purchases and fortunate marriages.[58] Achaz, who was born in the year 1595, took over the Gatringerhof from his father in 1612/13(!) and he too married well, to Johanna Stauff von der Stauff who was connected to the Polheim family. Despite all of these favorable signs, the achievement of noble status eluded Achaz and it is around this failure that much of his story seems to turn. There had occurred at the time of the Bavarian invasion in 1620 an incident at the estate Starhemberg that involved Wiellinger and from the subsequent events and from the correspondence between Maria Fink, the manager of the estate, and various authorities as well as Wiellinger himself, we can piece together the social status and better gauge the disillusionment of this figure whose fall in effect ended the rebellion of 1626.

When word reached Upper Austria on 15 July 1620, that a Bavarian invasion army was massing at the town of Ried in the nearby Innviertel, over five hundred peasants from the parish Gaspoltshofen, led by a blacksmith and religious fanatic named Sebastian Stix and his brothers,[59] appeared at the Gatringerhof, where Wiellinger organized them into military order. From there they staged a raid on the Bavarian border and damaged and closed the access roads. On their return they raided castle Starhemberg, a property of the bishop of Passau, where they committed extensive thefts and other damage. As part of the investigations that followed, Achaz Wiellinger was arrested in September of 1621 along with a number of other suspects and interrogated. In order to secure his release, he invoked a claim to nobility and protested his innocence and maltreatment through his solicitor and attorney, a Hans Bernhard Adler of Linz, to *Statthalter* Herbersdorf, who in turn reprimanded the estate manager Fink and ordered Wiellinger released. Fink held Wiellinger while she consulted further with Passau and finally released him on his own recognizance on 6 October 1621.[60] In the course of these proceedings Passau issued a request to Fink to furnish some precise information concerning Wiellinger's actual legal status and privileges.[61] Although there is some discrepancy in the dates between the request and the reply,[62] the description Fink gave of Wiellinger is enlightening. She identified the Gatringerhof as a former Hohenfelder peasant tenancy (*"ain plosses Bauerngut"*) under the estate Aistershaim. Achaz's father, whom she identified only as "old Wiellinger," was the owner of the tenancy and she could affirm that he had achieved admission to the *Landtafel*, i.e., that he had achieved Estate status. When Achaz took over the tenancy he bought only the usual tenant rights from Ludwig Hohenfelder for 1,000fl, but he did not acquire his father's legal status—although it was assumed by some that he did. As far as she knew, he had no noble seat, nor a noble estate, nor did he have any subjects of his own.[63]

Achaz was probably not the nobleman he claimed to be, but he was extremely well connected. Fink's letter also contained the following information concerning Wiellinger's occupation and personal affairs: he was a traveller and dealer who counted among his contacts the *Pfarrer* at Hofkirchen; he served, in addition, on the administrative staff of his brother-in-law, one Wolf Gästelsperger, who was the *Bestandinhaber* (a type of manager cum lien administrator) for Helmhard Jörger's seat at Groebming and was a dealer in grains and linens.[64] One can add to this evidence of high occupational status the following: a letter from Abraham Grünpacher, the Khevenhüller chief manager, to Maria Fink interceding, as the brother-in-law of Wiellinger's wife, on Achaz's behalf;[65] Wiellinger's own testimony that he had served in the administrations of the Lady von Königsberg and of Helmhard Jörger;[66] the personal support that Wiellinger received in order to become the supreme commander of the Weiberau camp from the Steyr *Stadtrichter* and *Rathsbürger* Wolf Madlseder.[67] All of these facts together also place Wiellinger in the highest social circles among the Upper Austrian peasantry. At the same time, however, Wiellinger had not managed to sustain his father's leap across Estate boundaries and, though he acted like a nobleman and received a nobleman's treatment even from those who knew better,[68] his aspirations to become legally "resident" (*landsässig*) remained frustrated.

The leaders of the 1626 uprising offer to the analyst an interesting combination of economic and social characteristics. In terms of the economic and occupational groupings drawn from the inventories, all of them had reached the highest ranks possible for a tenant subject. They were all wealthy and their economic positions were derived from the most privileged occupations possible, i.e., from a combination of services such as innkeeper, dealer, lender, and broker, and from employment as agents of estate and state officials. Why would these men, who had achieved high social status, lead a rebellion? It would not be entirely wrong to suggest that their motives were those of a group of socially mobile rural "bourgeois" with "rising expectations" who were trapped in the incongruities arising from their attachment to "feudal" institutions that on the one hand gave them the authority that allowed them to advance economically but that also blocked their full political emancipation and self-determination.[69] We have already suggested how the Bavarian occupation and inflation brought havoc to peasant entrepreneurs. Also detrimental, particularly to the upper strata among the successful and upwardly mobile tenants, must have been the Counter-Reformation's assumption of control over and use of parish guild treasuries;[70] gone also were the pastors who recorded contracts without the knowledge of estate and state officials[71] and the free-trade privileges adhering to the churches and their attached farms, which had been in the hands of lay brotherhoods and parish guilds.[72] Parish schools were placed under the control of the state church and the free-lance teachers who had offered preparatory education for peasant sons intending to go to university and also provided personal contacts and introductions to educators, officials, and professors at Wittenberg, Rostock, and Jena,[73] were expelled and persecuted.

At the same time, one must consider the Twelve Articles of 1626, which include peasant demands calling for the displacement of the clergy as an Estate and the installation in their stead of the peasants in some official capacity to "protect" the territory.[74] Such demands supply the archaic and reactionary side of the peasant leaders' apparently paradoxical position. They may have been upwardly mobile subjects whose movements had stalled; however, it is precisely with this latter point, concerning their apparently reactionary stance, that the analysis and conclusions we have drawn together so far in this study begin to contradict this initially attractive interpretation of the peasant position in 1626.

We know that the feudal appearance of Estates institutions was, since at least the latter half of the sixteenth century, increasingly mere appearance, and that Estates institutions no longer represented erstwhile provincial corporate liberties but were rather a part of the state's apparatus for assigning positions to fulfill bureaucratic prescriptions and administrative needs. The interpretation that sees the peasant leaders only as feudal reactionaries defending and seeking to enlarge their vested status denies them any understanding of their actual position in the state. It also places them outside the liberal traditions of Central Europe by assigning to them a role of reactionary opposition to a state that is perceived to be moving ultimately toward emancipation and citizenship.[75] The fact of the matter is that the peasant leaders understood their position fully and their requests, far from being reactionary, were fully appropriate to the existing institutions and implicitly envisioned a path of development that was at least politically, if not socially, progressive.

Their actual demands and grievances (some 138 items alone in the *gravamina* sent to the emperor in July 1626) were couched in the terminology of established state law and, lapsing only occasionally into emotionally charged and indignant language, demanded that the state authorities obey the laws, follow procedures of accepted administrative practice and adhere to the terms of the Imperial religious constitution of 1555 on which the *Reformationspatent* of 1625 itself was explicitly founded. They did not challenge the existing structure of authority in any way whatsoever but repeatedly stressed their obedience to the emperor, and this not in the general terms common to many peasant rebellions, but specifically asserting that they did not rebel because they did not wish to remain subjects ("zwar nicht zu dem ende . . . das wir im stande der untertanen nit verbleiben") nor to seek another Estate ("keinen andern stant suechen").[76] They rebelled because of the *Reformationspatent*, and not merely because it assured the failure of Protestantism. The way it was administered, they felt, unleashed chain reactions of dangerous and incongruous administrative turmoil particularly in connection with the official, household, and family affairs of the tenured. They wished it known that their grievances referred to a specific time, beginning with the publication of the *Reformationspatent* in the previous year, and their chief complaint (*"hauptbeschwer"*) was that to adhere to their religion meant that they had to forfeit their social position and that even after such renunciation, their exit was being obstructed and exploited by the present regime acting contrary to law.[77]

The stress, in 1626, on the *Reformationspatent* and its many consequences, suggests that bourgeois social and reactionary political motives were not really what were at work. The peasants' objections to specific changes in religious regime have to be accounted for. In addition, many of the tenants who participated in the war represented a group who had not even gained a foothold among the occupationally privileged subjects who made up the leadership. The followers of Fadinger (Table 8.1) were certainly not upwardly mobile feudal enterpreneurs. In order to explain as fully as possible the mixture of religious, political, economic, and social grievances that brought together the rebels of 1626, we must first consider whose problems the *gravamina* of 1626 expressed.

One explanation (a corollary to the "entrepreneur" thesis) that might serve to link Fadinger, Zeller, and Wiellinger to the unfortunates whose condition is demonstrated in Table 8.1 has been developed in recent years by anthropologists studying the function of certain "mediators" or "brokers" who link peasant society to the larger units of civilization of which they are a separate and only partially congruent part.[78] We might be tempted to call the leaders of 1626 *mafiosi* functioning as links between the subjects and the state authorities in general as well as the special personal agents of specific authorities. For example, the historical circumstances in which Anton Blok's *mafiosi*[79] appear might at first glance be comparable to the events and structures we have set forth in this study:

Mafia emerged in the early 19th century when the Bourbon state tried to curb the power of the traditional landowning aristocracy and encouraged the emancipation of the peasantry. . . . The gradual emergence of what came to be known only later on as *"mafia"* can be understood in the context of this development in which the central government, the landlords, and the peasants arranged and rearranged themselves in conflict and accommodation. I have referred above to this pattern as *modus vivendi*, in which mafiosi were recruited from the ranks of the peasantry to provide the large estate owners with armed staffs to confront both the impact of the State and the restive peasants, especially in the inland area of the island where the Bourbon State failed to monopolize the use of physical power.[80]

But while this might indeed have been the situation in Sicily around 1800, it does not help us understand what was going on in Austria two hundred years earlier. While such characters as the Stix brothers who had raided the Bavarian border in 1620 and the innkeeper Zeller probably were "violent entrepreneurs" who no doubt employed their public and quasi-public authority to use force for their personal advantage, this does not explain why the peasant leadership as a whole would mobilize a large number of the tenants against the state, especially after the "resistance" of the nobility was broken.

The comparison does help to distinguish the connection of the events of 1626 to earlier developments in the Habsburg heartland. By 1600, the progress of bureaucratization in Austria had eliminated one of the conditions that characterize a society where *mafiosi* can "exploit the gaps in communication between the peasant village and the larger society" and "ensure and buttress their intermediate position through the systematic threat and practice of physical violence."[81] The peasant leaders were themselves members of the tenant class that did not make up a separate society, representing purely localized part-systems of the whole state, but rather functioned as the lowest level of a statewide system of administration in which the lines of authority, while still defined by the institutions and language of part-societies, i.e., of Estates, flowed in one continuum from household to estate to state bureaucracy. The one thing the leadership had in common with their followers was that they held tenures as state posts on terms controlled, ultimately, by state authority. Seen in this context, the peasant leaders of 1626 and their followers were not engaged in a class struggle of the tenants as a class against, say, the noble estate owner class (as they had been in 1525 and 1595). Now they were members of a bureaucratic hierarchy objecting to changes in state administration.

Ralf Dahrendorf's further remarks on Max Weber's conceptualization of bureaucracy help to clarify what this view of the leaders of 1626 and their tenant followers means in terms of social conflict:

> . . . whereas industrial organizations are . . . dichotomous, bureaucratic organizations typically display continuous gradations of competence and authority and are hierarchical. Within dichotomous organizations class conflict is possible; within hierarchical organizations it is not. . . . This means that all incumbents of bureaucratic roles in the association of political society belong on the same side of the fence that divides the positions of dominance from those of subjection. . . .
>
> . . . Bureaucratic roles are roles of political dominance. . . . Nobody in particular seems to exercise the authority and yet authority is exercised, and we can identify people who do not participate in its exercise. Thus the superficial impression of subordination in many minor bureaucratic roles must not deceive us. All bureaucratic roles are defined with reference to the total process of the exercise of authority to which they contribute to whatever small extent.[82]

To be sure, some of the peasant leaders were involved in social conflicts that separated them from their poorer followers. Achaz Wiellinger's struggle for the recognition of his "nobility," for example, demonstrates what personal conflicts happen when "there are in a bureaucratic hierarchy several points of entry which divide the total career into subsections separated by insurmountable barriers."[83] His was a personal crisis, a product of his "family's" specific social mobility that none of his fellow leaders, let alone his followers, shared. What Wiellinger did share with Fadinger and Zeller and the other poorer tenants who arose in 1626 was a position in a bureaucratic order under pressure to conform to an abrupt change at the top levels of the state. Far from being conservative entrepreneurs or violent *mafiosi* exploiting the synapses between a tenant class and the state, the leaders who arose in 1626 stood at the head of a party within the administrative hierarchy of the Habsburg state, a party of tenants that sought "to influence the existing dominion"[84] in order to prevent or at least ameliorate what it saw as the imminent downward mobility of a good number of its members; it was a party of quasi-bureaucrats who objected to the radical changes in the rights and status of incumbents and who protested that the responsibilities of office could not be carried out under the new conditions.

A more detailed examination of the July grievances (*Beschwerden*) bears out this view of the peasant rebels of 1626 as a political party acting in the defense of a particular vision of the bureaucratic state. The picture that emerges there of what was on their minds contradicts sharply any notions that we are dealing with an illiterate mass of simple peasant farmers, conservatively and inflexibly committed to feudal values and a particular confessional orthodoxy. Their sole objection to the Counter-Reformation that reveals any kind of connection to agricultural production is that the insistence by the Catholic administration on the observation of the hours of mass on feast days was interfering with such essential work and marketing processes as the delivery of milk and the milling of grains.[85] But this was a minor aspect of the many objections to the *Reformationspatent* of 1625. Of primary importance was the disruption it caused in the province's good government and welfare ("*zerruettung gueter polizei*") and this disruption was blamed on the fact that the Counter-Reformation state placed the eradication of Protestantism above the efficient conduct and continuity of administrative processes—and primary evidence for this was that experienced administrators were removed from office, their desks and papers ransacked, some put under house arrest in their places of office or in their homes and others publicly chastised (or even unjustly murdered, as at Frankenburg). There was, significantly, also objection raised that their replacements had not previously held tenure on a house or farm (*"unbegueterte"*) and were therefore, according to the accepted rules, unqualified to hold office.[86] Particularly objectionable to the peasant leaders, for reasons we have already considered, was the incompetent and tyrannical administration by the new Catholic clergy of parish schools and churches.[87] They noted that these unheard-of procedures (*"unerhörte procedere"*) could be resisted better in the towns and cities but that the rural population was an easier victim of this administrative disjunction.[88] Finally, administration of the courts suffered under the new regime: those plaintiffs who had not converted to Catholicism and had experienced harassment by occupying troops could not get their cases heard in court while cases in which Protestants were the defendants were expedited.[89]

Taken altogether, such protest amounts to much more than what one might expect from traditional peasant rebels. There was, for example, a considerable difference between the July grievances of 1626 and the Twelve Articles of 1525 in that the former no longer expressed the point of view of the tenant class as a village commune[90] but rather as individuals and groups singled out for bureaucratic harassment. Those who bore the worst of these torments were those Protestants who tried to exercise their right to emigrate. The July grievances not only present a detailed account and numerous examples of the treatment of these would-be migrants, they also place the difficulties of the emigrés in a context of constitutional law and administrative regulation. The Catholic state authorities, preferring conversion to emigration, apparently obstructed the process of emigration as much as possible. Potential emigrés had trouble getting passports; they were subject to verbal and physical abuse, and were occasionally imprisoned until they converted; the items inventoried in the migrants' liquidation assessments often included personal and other goods declared exempt by the 1597 Interim; aside from placing numerous extra charges and taxes on the liquidated assets, the authorities often refused to accept the debased legal tender for which the migrant had agreed to sell his properties—and which the state itself had authorized and issued.[91] Most troubling of all was that the way the state administered the *ius emigrandi* violated administrative regulations securing the self-rule of families and households. If an emigré was single (and therefore "unhoused") the authorities took this as an occasion to investigate the holdings of housed kin, ostensibly to determine the full value of all the emigré's assets; children were occasionally not allowed to leave with their parents and this, the peasant leaders claimed, violated the constitution of 1555 according to which husbands held authority over wives and parents over children; the violation of this house authority on occasion went so far that the wives of those migrants who had gone ahead to establish themselves elsewhere were forced into marriages with converts.[92]

In other words, the subject tenants objected strenuously to the *Reformationspatent* not on religious grounds as such but on the grounds that in practice it contravened many rights concerning inventory-taking, control over inheritance portions and children, and over family relations generally, that the tenants had acquired during the sixteenth century through state intervention and bureaucratization. Most illustrative of this is the rebels' objection to the harassment of potential emigrés specifically and of the tenant class in general by the quartering of soldiers in peasant houses. Aside from the fact that in some cases such postings of soldiers were punitive and that the soldiers allegedly carried on as is reputedly (but sometimes not in actuality) their wont, the chief objection was that the soldiers interfered with the tenants' obligation (or right) to administer welfare, especially as this affected orphans, the simple-minded, and widows (viz., *Auszügler*).[93] This objection does not necessarily mean that the soldiers stretched the welfare duties of most tenant houses beyond their capacities—although the 1626 grievances made such a claim that was, in specific cases, no doubt appropriate. The tenant class benefited, as we saw in this and earlier chapters, from the administration of the properties of wards of various types and of the *Auszügler*, whereas soldiers were only a liability and brought nothing of any account to the tenant householder with which to improve his or her social position or to meet the terms of emphyteusis. Soldiers lodging in tenant houses, though required to pay small sums for their room and board, occasioned a disruption of the administrative functions of the house as well as of the assembly and maintenance of "role families" with which the tenured maintained, in part, their social position.

It is to this increasing insecurity of the individual's tenure that the *Beschwerden* against the *Reformationspatent* make, finally, their most deeply cutting objection. No longer free to argue as members of a parish or village community, the tenured peasants pointed instead to their years of service as tenants (claiming not only individual terms of tenure lasting from thirty to over sixty years but also terms lasting through several generations of a family) and to their assistance to the House of Habsburg in the "building" of the territory. They claimed this entitled them to some security as resident "members of the state" ("*lantsmitglieder*"). They claimed also the rights of private persons ("*privatpersonen*")[94] and remonstrated that because it was not possible for some to renounce their religious beliefs they should not be penalized with loss of tenure and status. They demanded a free conscience ("*freistellung des Gewissen*") and rejected the *politique* alternative.[95]

But, as in Habsburg and Bourbon territories everywhere,[96] it was the age for *politiques* like Wiellinger's in-law Abraham Grünpacher, a peasant tenant who had advanced in the bureaucratic hierarchy to become Francis Khevenhüller's highest estate official. In their belief that they could base their rights to tenure on administrative law and on proven records and seniority of service, the peasant rebels of 1626, both leaders and followers, fell victim to an illusory perception of their position in the state. Once the tenant class had submitted to uniform subject status, had been forced to accept, by 1600, the state's maintenance and regulation of property and family life; and had been required to assume and use for their own purposes administrative functions and roles, they also had to accept, knowingly or not, the logic of bureaucratic politics. They had accepted dominant roles and belonged "to the ruling political quasi-group. However, being a reserve army of authority, the bureaucratic members of this quasi-group are not potential members of an interest group of those in power. . . . The bureaucratic reserve army of authority is a mercenary army of class conflict; it is always in battle, but it is forced to place its strength in the service of changing masters and goals."[97] Far from being reactionary entrepreneurs in a distant time and place, the Austrian peasant rebels of 1626 were the first modern men, fighting one of the first battles in a political struggle that has lasted into and flowered profusely during this so-called "post-capitalist" (Dahrendorf) period of Western history. Fadinger, his fellow leaders, and their followers wanted an ongoing separation between conditions of tenure and such private rights as freedom of conscience and an independent family and household life. The faith they professed in the legal-rational practices of their system and in the rights that such major constitutional documents as the Interim of 1597 guaranteed them was seriously misplaced. We cannot fault them for misunderstanding their position or for maintaining "bureaucratic" values in the face of a victorious state; the fact that the regulations governing station, competence, equality, and rationality of advancement present an illusory security for those required to play bureaucratic roles often is not understood even in the present day.[98] The legal-rational appearances of administrative institutions and processes are at all times subject to the reason of hierarchy and domination and are ultimately subject "to an extra-and superbureaucratic power—to an 'unbusinesslike' power. And if rationality is embodied in administration, and *only* administration, then this legislative power must be irrational. The Weberian conception of reason ends in irrational *charisma*."[99] By appealing to the young legal and bureaucratic traditions of the Habsburg state, the peasant rebels of 1626 took the only path open to those tenants who did not wish to convert and whose emigration was beset by chicanery and violations of law pretending to be accepted administrative practice. The irony of their position was

that their new prince, intent "on creating a new kingdom that
conformed to his image of royal prerogative and Christian
duty,"[100] had at his disposal the same bureaucratic apparatus,
created by his forebears during the previous century in negotiations with peasants and nobility, that now allowed him to
realize his values and make them a reality in every house of
the province. In this situation, the theories of magisterial resistance and even tyrannicide, which had seriously occupied
some Austrian peasant rebels in 1511 and 1525 and whose formulas cropped up again in 1626, were almost entirely irrelevant.
Notably, at the same time in England, where the state had
evolved in a different bureaucratic direction (one is almost tempted
to call it nonbureaucratic) such theories had evolved into a relevant and effective revolutionary theory.

The victory of the Counter-Reformation by no means meant
a suspension or alteration of the nature and direction of development of the Austrian state. The legal-rational rules of calculable emphyteusis and house administration that, by 1600,
had given rise to the patterns of family life and mobility that
we have examined in this study all remained intact and continued to furnish the basis of rural economic and social life until
the modern era. What happened in the 1620s was that the prince
had asserted the prerogatives of his charismatic authority and
had added a religious condition to the holding of tenure. Once
that revolution was completed and only genuine Catholics or
politiques held tenure, the state returned to its "normal" legal-
rational operations. We will probably never be able to tell how
many tenants went into battle—or sent someone from their
house—in 1626 nor how many finally left the province, but by
the time Maximilian of Bavaria gave up his lien administration
in 1628 and the Estate constitution, now even further integrated
into the state apparatus, was restored, the process of religious
conversion was well under way and the majority of the tenants
and their "families" had become Catholic. Given the continuation of secret Protestant meetings, of the administration of
the sacraments by itinerant and lay preachers (which, as we
shall see in a moment, was an important aspect of the uprisings
of the 1630s), and of the need for state censorship of both

religious and secular works,[101] we must assume that many of these conversions were insincere, that is, that they were *politique* conversions done for the sake of maintaining the convert's position as tenant or officeholder in a state that had not, after all, changed that much.

The continuation of what has been called Austria's "secret Protestantism" (*Geheimprotestantismus* or *Kryptoprotestantismus*) until well into the eighteenth century suggests that *politiques* made up an important segment of Austria's officials and householders.[102] Although the term *politique* was born in the context of the French religious wars to signify someone for whom the "primacy of the demands of the state over those of religion" was self-evident and was part of a necessary "disentanglement of religious and political dissent" and a release from the "nonsense of civil war,"[103] it is worthwhile to take it out of its context of origin in political and intellectual history and to consider it briefly from a social historical perspective as an element of the social relations of absolutism. At the outset we must keep in mind that because the Austrian state had managed to penetrate the peasant house and family even before the Counter-Reformation could be implemented, the *politique* type (in Austrian: *Konvertit*) was a mass phenomenon and not merely someone who appeared among the governing nobilities and patriciates of early modern Europe. How are we to judge the effects of widespread *politique* behavior on social life? In the Austrian case, we may simply lament, as Robert Kann does,[104] that "the choice—reconversion with its social advantages, or their rejection at the price of discrimination and persecution—influenced not only public but also private morale for the worse." This view, which sees the success of the Counter-Reformation as a destructive and negative discontinuity in the life of the individual under absolutism, stands in sharp contrast to Reinhard Koselleck's positive version of the meaning of *politique* behavior. Koselleck, following Hobbes's lead and starting from the necessity to end civil war by excluding religious morality from political action, sees a shift in the burdens of guilt and responsibility that amounts finally to a general unburdening of the individual. The state, guiltless because it acts on the basis of secular morality alone, claims a monopoly and assumes responsibility for the consequences of political action, and the only burden of guilt the subject is required to bear is that of acting against state authority or of withdrawing from participation in public life.[105] In this view subjects are no longer required to act morally at all in the political sphere except to follow the state's mandates; the state takes responsibility for secular morality and religious morality was in any case inadmissible.[106] Here we are looking at the beginnings of the separation of the public from the private individual and of the state from society. Whatever price individuals had to pay for enduring this split, they were rewarded by religious and moral peace and by the benefits of the progress of the state.[107] This view fits the claim that any discomforts that resulted from *politique* dualism were, in terms derived from Gerhard Oesterreich's functional view of the absolute state, only one aspect of the "social discipline" necessary to drive early modern rural populations away from their self-indulgence and toward modernity and rationality.[108]

We must reject this version of the social effects of *politique* behavior in the absolute state both on general theoretical grounds and on the basis of the empirical findings of this study. Earlier we followed Ralf Dahrendorf's lead and explicitly rejected any analysis of roles that sees an independent and integrated person behind and outside each individual's role complex.[109] The *politique* rationalization in which a person is "secretly free" and "only in secret human"[110] is the door by which the repression of publicly inadmissible conflicts enters the private world and becomes the burden of each individual who wishes (or is required) to participate in public life. The prescribed role complex and not the person is integrated and governs the person's decisions and choices according to its interplay of dominant and secondary values.

In early modern Austria the problematical aspects of the *politique* solution to role conflict in a bureaucratized state are especially evident. There the necessity to convert, whether one wanted to or not, was intimately bound up with the private sphere of home and family. The state, unwilling to tolerate religious conflict, expected individuals to repress that conflict within themselves as a precondition of participating in the state—and to have any kind of family or successfully mobile social life one had first to participate in the state as tenant householder. So the burden of repressed values conflict is not removed from the subject and placed on the state, as Koselleck has suggested, but quite the reverse. The state, having penetrated the peasant family and indeed, the subject individual, by acquiring control over key institutions of property, family, and welfare could now shift the burden of religious conflict downward. The Counter-Reformation that followed the victories of the Habsburg state in the 1620s was not a radically discontinuous change (as Kann imagines) but another step, albeit an important one, in the further bureaucratization of the peasant family. The tenant families had long ago acquiesced in the state's invasion of family life. Where the rigors of tenure, emphyteusis, and social mobility for the tenured had required for some time a repression of personal and familial needs in favor of the state-contolled norms, the acquiesence in *politique* behavior during the 1620s was not, once initial objections to procedural changes had been overcome, a great issue. The tenant class, long helpless against the invasion and incorporation of family life by the state, understood and accepted that one simply had to endure the internal split that was covered over by *politique* behavior not only to participate in a limited public sphere as subject or "citizen," but to play even those most elemental of social roles of spouse and parent.

And what of those rural masses who were entirely below the bureaucratic apparatus, those dispossessed who were wholly subject to authority in the house because they had lost their tenured position or because they were children who could never hope to have one of the limited number of tenant houses and who would become servants and lodgers and live all their lives under the house authority of another? They made up a good part of the peasant armies of 1626; under orders of their house lords and without a leadership of their own, they fought for the bureaucratic order whose irrationalities had severed them from their families of origin and had excluded them from founding a family life of their own. As members of one suppressed class, as "incumbents of roles of subjection,"[111] the dispossessed fought in 1626 as a class-by-itself ("*Klasse an sich*") for the goals of their immediate oppressors.

If we continue to follow Ralf Dahrendorf's modification of Max Weber's class concept, as we have done throughout this study so far, the difference between the actions of the dispossessed in the rebellion of 1626 and in those that followed in the 1630s (and which we'll examine in a moment) become apparent:

. . . of the two aggregates of authority positions to be distinguished in every situation, one—that of domination—is characterized by an interest in the maintenance of a social structure that for them conveys authority, whereas, the other—that of subjection—involves an interest in changing a social condition that deprives its incumbents of authority.[112]

Hans Sturmberger has described the uprisings of the 1630s as aftershocks of the great rebellion of 1626[113] and in one sense they were that. As we shall see, some of the participants and leaders of the '30s were socially uprooted and cast adrift, both physically and, in some cases, mentally, by the events of the previous decade, and their small roving bands, led by self-styled prophets carrying millennial banners, were signs of unsettled times and of numerous individual social disasters. However, the rebellions of the 1630s also differed significantly from the great armed conflict of 1626; they were the one occasion in the seventeenth century when the dispossessed became a class-for-itself ("*Klasse für sich*") and demanded change in a particular social condition which they saw (in part, correctly) as *the* social condition that deprived them of humanity and authority. Among the religious protests and millennial fantasies of 1632 and 1635/ 36 we find a hard nugget of genuine social insight in the peasant rebels' explicit opposition to the institution of marriage—and, simultaneously, in their own elaborate marriage ceremonies. The tragic contradictions and repressions of these last uprisings that concluded the formative period of the Habsburgs' absolute state in Upper Austria epitomize the social development of that state and make a fitting conclusion to this study. The story of these uprisings needs to be told again because it reveals best the structure of social relations in the new state with all its unshakeable moral rigidity, its denials, blind alleys, and murderous pressures.

The 1630s saw a different kind of peasant movement. Gone were peasant armies numbering in the thousands with their tents, stacked rifles and pikes, their horses and cannon all spread over great common meadows in the lowlands south of the Danube. In their place there appeared millennial preachers dressed in garish fantasy uniforms behind whom trailed ragtag bands bearing aloft large white banners embroidered with magic formulas and stars, singing to the accompaniment of drums, pipes, violins, and trumpets. While on the march, they never numbered more than a couple of hundred souls and their colors and music must have been all but lost along the windy tracks that crossed the spacious green mountain saddles and wooded granite summits north of the Danube. The first of these gangs of irregulars emerged in 1630 in the vicinity of Freistadt, led by an unordained peasant preacher (*Rebellenprädikant*), Jacob Greimbl, who had made his first appearance in 1626. Greimbl was then arrested for preaching his personal creed of Protestantism and for administering the sacraments. He converted to Catholicism to shorten his term of imprisonment in Vienna, and upon his release, he settled in Prague. There, after Protestant armies occupied the city, he was recruited as a provocative agent by the Swedish party in the winter of 1631/32. He returned to Upper Austria in the spring of 1632 to recruit another armed band that he took south of the Danube to join in the minor rebellion of the housed peasantry of the Hausruck quarter in August 1632. Imperial troops made short work of this uprising and Greimbl fled into the woods of the Bohemian borderlands where he was arrested in October as a result of police work by the abbot of Schlägl. His beheading followed at Linz in February of the next year.[114]

At the same time as Greimbl was gathering his followers to lead them into the Hausruck quarter, another figure, who was to have much greater significance as a rebel leader, began to wander about the area south of Freistadt and Weinberg, preaching and gathering followers. Martin Aichinger, known for his farm as "Laimbauer," was arrested for his activities by his landlord but released as mad; he lost his house for failing to obey religious and other royal directives. For the next three years, Laimbauer stayed with whoever would shelter him and he preached and developed further his personal theology. He emerged from his underground activities with a band of several hundred followers in the spring of 1635 in the hills north of the Danube, near the Lower Austrian border. The authorities, puzzled by Laimbauer's apparently aimless wanderings, tried to establish contact but were violently rebuffed. The Imperial authorities, fearing that the Laimbauer band would travel south to join the peasant rebellions then in progress in Styria and Carinthia, ordered that Laimbauer's activities be confined to his present area in the Machland quarter. The Laimbauer group dispersed after its initial, and violent, encounter with the authorities at Gusen but surfaced again on Whitsuntide in 1636, to recommence revivalist processions through the countryside. Again the authorities surrounded the band and, after one militia (composed of housed peasants and officials recruited from the surrounding estates) was defeated in an armed encounter at Neumarkt on 8 May 1636, proceeded to organize a serious military effort under the leadership of the Estates and royal officials. On 12 May the Estate troops, over 1,000 strong, cornered Laimbauer and about 400 of his followers on the heights above the Danube and across the Gosen valley from where the remaining barracks of the slave labor and death camp Mauthausen now extend. After a three-hour house-to-house gun battle, the houses in which Laimbauer and his followers hid were burned. Herded into the ruined church of Frankenberg, Laimbauer was wounded and arrested and the remainder of his band massacred and burned inside the church. Laimbauer's own memorably gruesome torture and death on the scaffold in the Linz marketplace took place on 20 June 1636, ten days after he had converted to Catholicism. His name—"Laimbauer!"—entered popular usage and has survived to this day as an epithet for someone unreasonable and quarrelsome.[115]

The two movements of the 1630s appeared to contemporaries as tragic aberrations and are still treated as such in the literature on peasant rebellions, the more so because from the view of social and political development they were historically inconsequential. Part of the reason for this judgment is the apparent insanity of the two leaders and their followers. Greimbl and Laimbauer were, unquestionably, religious fantasists who claimed supernatural powers for themselves and lived generally erratic and disorderly lives. On the other hand, they have been attributed with an evil intelligence—Laimbauer appeared to contemporary authorities as the agent of the devil (*"der mit teiflischer Zauberei verblente Laimpaur"*)[116]—because they understood how to play on the fears and superstitions of allegedly simple and superstitious country folk and thus obtained their following. But if we look more closely at the leaders of the millennial gatherings in the 1630s and consider what linked them to their followers, their dismissal as mad or simpleminded seems at least partially wrong and also analytically unsatisfactory.

Greimbl dressed more like a mercenary soldier than a priest and lived "in sin" (*"in Unzicht"*) with the daughter of an official and these oddities, combined with his personal theology, his religious services, and administration of the sacraments in barns or in open fields at night make him an unusual figure, but it is doubtful that he was in any way mentally incompetent. It appears that he was a successful recruiter for the Protestant cause, although only of the young and unattached; the housed rejected him for reasons we shall see in a moment. Laimbauer's appearance was rather different from the somber exterior Greimbl affected. Laimbauer limped, wore his light-brown hair to his ankles and dressed in white suits set off by a tri-colored sash and gaudy feathers in his hat. His mental state was probably unstable but some of his concepts, images, and activities do have bearing on the objective situation of those he was leading. The authorities knew that he probably had a genuine grievance himself because his estate authorities had extorted money from him.[117] His response to his troubles, however, was unusual, to say the least. He claimed visitations by angels and by God himself who had passed on to him the power to forgive sins until Judgment Day. On occasion he had his followers stand in a circle, then sprinkled them with water he had blessed to make them invulnerable. He promised them that if their cause should fail, the Emperor Frederick (Barbarossa) would ride out of the mountains at the head of thousands of horsemen to aid them. On a more prosaic level, he, along with a dozen of his followers, dressed in sheets to resemble spirits, then visited villages and farmsteads to announce Laimbauer's coming. And so on.[118]

As much as all this may seem to come from Laimbauer's and his followers' shared delusional worlds, we must also see that there is some sense and even humour in all this nonsense. For example, there is Laimbauer's claim that God had appeared to him and nominated him to replace Christ until the Judgment Day because the latter had gotten too fat to lead mankind out of sin.[119] Not only is this an obvious dig at an opulent Catholic church, it is an appropriate analogy for a social world in which reified fathers exchanged their real sons for "role" sons, pushing the former into the class of dispossessed so that they could secure their own social status further and perhaps advance to the position of stem elder. Another example of such appropriate "delusion" may be found in the visionary experiences of a twelve-year-old girl who was "in service" to her uncle before she joined Laimbauer's troops. In her interrogation by the authorities she explained that an angel appeared to her several times when she went to the stable to feed the animals and told her that it was time the head of the house stopped treating the servants so badly and that it was wrong to feed the animals with grains that were intended for human consumption. She and the daughter of another householder then ran away to join Laimbauer because the angel had warned them that any servants who stayed in the house would die.[120] These were delusions, perhaps, but they point to real situations, to the contradictory and exploited role life of the dispossessed in the housecommunity.[121]

It would be wrong to see these forms of social withdrawal as purely regressive and delusional. It is true that both movements, and Laimbauer's in particular, refused to have anything to do with the authorities. They would not respond, for example, to the authorities' requests for statements of grievances that could be negotiated, because they understood that this would not get at the problem. According to one witness, the chief point of one of Greimbl's sermons was that they were all stuck under the oppression of "the authority" ("*wie sie unter der Obrigkeit stecken*").[122] Similarly, on the occasions when representatives of the authorities spoke with Laimbauer personally, they were quickly surrounded by an angry mob and forced to retreat in the face of incoherent shouting, gesticulating, and guns pointed at their heads. Several dead were invariably left in the field after these encounters.[123] Although they knew they had to stop Laimbauer's organizing efforts because they seemed dangerous and disorderly, the authorities had to admit that they could not fathom what Laimbauer's band was up to. This does not, however, mean that the movements of the 1630s were without purpose and direction; it only means that their purpose was outside the authorities' universe of discourse.

The clearest example of this is the view of marriage that found expression both in Greimbl's and Laimbauer's sermons and in their relations with their followers. Greimbl was an outspoken opponent of marriage who practiced what he preached; he lived, as we already quoted the authorities, "in sin" with a young woman, reputedly the daughter of someone in authority. It is significant that his common-law marriage prevented Greimbl from finding allies among housed peasants who might have agreed with his religious politics. When Greimbl tried to win a guild master in the metal trade over to his movement the latter rejected the alliance because in his mind a proper preacher lived with his wife and not with a "whore." Another housed tenant, this one in textiles, also repudiated any connection with Greimbl and his "slut" ("*Vetl*"). These vehement epithets seem to have been somewhat mistaken. Maria Nötztaller, Greimbl's common-law wife, was clearly much more than a common camp follower. She was Greimbl's personal letter-carrier, a dangerous task for someone connected with a Protestant spy. Also, the authorities took her seriously, referring to her as a woman soldier ("*soldatin*").[124] She eventually left Greimbl's group, escaping to Lower Austria, where she lived with one of her brothers. It is apparent that the tenants who so vehemently denounced her actually opposed her and Greimbl's refusal to be married; it is noteworthy, of course, that she was the primary target of their insults.

Laimbauer's conception of marriage was more complicated than Greimbl's and, as a result, allows us to see beyond the mere fact of opposition. Although Laimbauer also preached against marriage, he was married himself. In a ceremony born of his own liturgical imagination, he married Barbara Mayin, the daughter of one of his supporters, and he performed weddings for wards (*Pupillen*), young servants, and lodgers who had run away from their house authorities.[125] The water of "invulnerability" played a role in at least two of these ceremonies: in Laimbauer's own, where it was part of the marriage sacrament and passed among the circle of participants, and again in a later marriage between a carpenter and a tenant's daughter, where it was used to exorcise the demons that beset the groom. The message of these apparently contradictory beliefs and activities concerning marriage is quite clear. Laimbauer and his followers did not oppose marriage on principle but rather opposed what marriage had become under the regime of a house-based bureaucratic state. In a state where marriage was thoroughly bureaucratized and had become a class privilege of the housed, where it could only occur between unhoused lodgers after the authorities had attested to the religious, economic, occupational, and other qualifications of the couple and where, finally, most of the dispossessed could not marry at all, the denunciation of marriage and the simultaneous performance of illegal marriage ceremonies were logical, human, and politically appropriate responses.

There is much evidence to suggest that both Greimbl's and Laimbauer's movements were "youth movements," especially appealing to those young people who, for one reason or another, could not aspire to the tenant class or who had lost their tenant position. The interrogations of those who had contact with Greimbl disclose, for example, that his followers consisted of old single men, boys and girls in their teens, and a few poor householders who had accompanied their hired hands to one of Greimbl's services. [126] During the interrogations that followed Laimbauer's uprising, one housed witness stated that his servants (*Gesinde*) prevailed on him to attend one of Laimbauer's meetings. [127] The twelve-year-old girl whose visions of angels is mentioned above, and who ran away with a friend to join Laimbauer, testified that young lodgers and the sons of a weaver were followers from her area. When the authorities estimated Laimbauer's strength in the spring of 1635, they noted that of 300 to 400 followers, only sixty were armed men and that the rest were women and boys. Other authorities dismissed these "malicious people" (*"böse Leut"*) because they were, after all, only "women, children and boys" and still others spoke of them contemptuously as a ragtag rabble (*"Pöfel* [i.e., *Pöbel*], *Gesindel"* [the root of this latter word is Gesinde]). [128] Finally the massacre in the church ruins of Frankenberg was chiefly of women and children (Laimbauer himself was found hiding under the skirts of two seated old women). Most of the people in the lists drawn up for the purpose of dividing the belongings of the dead among various authorities, were poor young people or lodgers, unmarried servants who had not been paid in years, tenants' children who had not inherited, children of lodgers, or former tenants who had lost their holding (*"abgehauste"*). [129] For reasons I will go into in a moment, the preponderance of young people on these lists might not be entirely accurate but it is a fact that after Frankenberg a number of children in their early teens were arrested, incarcerated, interrogated, and even executed. One boy, possibly Laimbauer's son, was made to watch Laimbauer's dismemberment on the marketplace at Linz before experiencing the same fate himself. [130]

The savage spirit with which these protest movements of the young were crushed is all the more remarkable when we consider that those doing the actual fighting and killing were not imported professional soldiers but amateur militia units composed of city and estate officials, peasant tenants, and a few urban householders. What this suggests is that, far from being the insignificant aftershocks of 1626, as they have been presented, Greimbl's and, especially, Laimbauer's movements pitted, for the first time, the classes that divided the bureaucratized peasant family, the housed and the unhoused, against each other. Insofar as the disinherited recognized the institutions that created their suffering as a class (and their views and actions regarding marriage demonstrate that their class situation was at least partially apparent to them) to that extent the events of 1632, 1635, and 1636 were a genuine class struggle. To be sure, the small bands that roamed the windy high roads of the Mühl and Machland quarters in the 1630s never numbered more than several hundred and were all but lost against the landscape and in the vast slow history of their world, but the scale or success of their movement does not enter into a question of class warfare. On this we can only agree with Professors Piven and Cloward when they regret that "the movements of the people disappoint the doctrine, and so the movements are dismissed" and when they contend that "what was won must be judged by what was possible."[131] What is remarkable is not only the fact that armed class warfare took place but that in the midst of and even as part of the millennial frenzy a genuine class consciousness formed and found active expression. The dispossessed were a class of subjects who bore the full weight of an exploitive and individually destructive state apparatus; they were, in a bureaucratic "market-situation" sense, a genuine proletariat. At the same time, their class position was fragmented and masked by their class situation in dispersed rural housecommunities, each of which functioned as a bureaucratically regulated role family. In this connection, we can appreciate Sidney Mintz's conclusion that

> Peasant communities . . . may include in their membership some or many persons who are landless and even wage-earning; but their proletarian status is cloaked by the many relationships they have with the landed. On these grounds, and on others, peasant communities may be economically much more heterogeneous than rural proletarian communities; but the landless within peasant communities are not so likely to develop the consciousness of class membership common to those who live in rural proletarian communities.[132]

It was just such an unlikely class consciousness that we see taking shape in the rebellions of the 1630s. The failure of these rebellions to affect appreciably the course of history in this part of the world and the wasteful and tragic destruction of young lives that concluded these episodes should not deter us from grasping their historical significance. The year 1636 saw the final victory of the Habsburg absolute state as a social system and the events of that year demonstrate clearly how vicious and destructive a regime it was. The young who died in the skirmishes and on the scaffolds were only the new system's most visible victims.

Finally, nothing illustrates the victory of the state better than the smoothly interlocking functioning of the authorities as they hunted down and destroyed Greimbl, Laimbauer and the runaways and social failures who gathered around these "charismatic figures." The model of police cooperation that the provost of the monastery Schlägl and the housed subjects of the border town of Höritz displayed in arresting and bringing Greimbl to trial was followed on a much larger scale in the suppression of Laimbauer's uprising. The participants in this ranged from royal officials in Vienna and the chief of the Estates (*Landeshauptmann*) through the various estate owners, their managers and magistrates to the housed subjects. Some officials of Linz participated as individual subjects and not as official representatives of the city corporation. The chief form of communication among these various authorities was by way of letters carried by individual messengers and was speedy and effective, judging by the fact that a number of widely dispersed authorities organized the encirclement of Laimbauer's band, cut the flow of foodstuffs into the rebel area, and raised and organized a force of over 1,000 men and horses to crush the movement and carry out a number of arrests, all in the space of one week. In their letters they addressed each other as "colleagues" ("*Collega*") and their prevailing discourse about the uprising concerned a fire that had to be confined and stamped out before it could spread. The few times they managed to address themselves to Laimbauer's group directly, they did so, not unexpectedly, as parents addressing children with stern but "fatherly" benevolence.[133]

When one reads the correspondence that organized Laimbauer's downfall[134] one gets the impression that to the state
authorities this was an exercise with live ammunition. It was
an opportunity to test the obedience and effectiveness of the
housed—they were threatened repeatedly with regular troops
if they failed—and to refine and stake out in greater detail the
proper channels of command and areas of competence among
the various levels of state and estate officials. Officials near the
top of the pyramid, such as Abraham Wibmer who acted simultaneously as the estate manager of Freistadt and as chief
administrative officer of the provincial court (*Landgerichtver-
walter*), did their utmost to contain Laimbauer, although, not
surprisingly, there was considerable bickering and blame shifting among them when this took longer than the royal court
would have liked. Nothing was done to punish or pressure
seriously those authorities who, for reasons of health or distance
from the scene of the action, did not participate in the mobi-
lization of 1636. Below this level of estate-owning or managing
authorities, individuals were drafted to serve in the effort against
the rebels. A burgher and official of Linz was drafted by the
Landeshauptmann personally to lead the expedition, and the
quotas of foot and horse soldiers that the provincial authorities
demanded from the several estates they deemed responsible for
putting down the uprising were filled by subject tenants who
were drafted and threatened with the loss of tenure if they did
not comply immediately.[135]

The most interesting developments from our point of view
took place in the aftermath of the 1635/36 uprisings when the
various authorities quarreled among themselves about the administrative issues raised by those who were arrested, killed,
or executed. These issues already surfaced in 1635 after Laimbauer's band first appeared and dispersed after a bloody clash
with the authorities; the provincial administration was faced
with a decision about who had the right to punish and to claim
the properties of those who had been arrested or were known
to have joined Laimbauer. One of Laimbauer's followers, for
example, was a subject ward (*Pupill*) of the estate Riedeck and
in this case his guardians were required to forward his inher-

itance portion of 200fl to the estate authority.[136] The provincial
authorities (*Landesregierung*) at the same time issued an order
that all those who were convicted of participating in the uprising
without bearing arms should be fined four Imperial dollars and
that the estate authorities should forward this amount to Linz.[137]

When the state authorities made moves toward claiming the
confiscated houses and other properties of the convicted peasant
rebels, the estate-owning authorities sought the advice of the
Estates' provincial attorney, Dr. Joachim Enzmilner. This provincial *syndikus* was a learned *politique* humanist and lawyer
and had hardly made his brilliant career by swimming against
the stream of absolutist state-building. He had risen from com-
moner in Bavaria through the *Reformationskommission* of 1625
to state attorney, to nobility, and ownership of an estates complex centering on the *palazzo* and gardens of Windhag.[138] His
famous apologia of 1626 that had exonerated the Upper Austrian
nobility by denying the significance of the Counter-Reformation as a cause for the peasant war and that placed the blame
for that war squarely on the insubordination of the tenants, had
helped him in attaining his position as the Estates' lawyer.[139]
Now, true to *politique* careerist form, his legal opinion concerning the peasant rebels' properties sided, subtly, with the
state. He referred back to the revolts of 1525, but, significantly,
sought applicable legal precedents only since the 1595 to 1597
uprising. Moreover, he suggested a compromise according to
which, on one hand, the estate authorities should only have the
right to dispose of the properties of those who had not carried
arms and that, on the other, the state should take over those
properties whose owners had carried arms and had therefore
committed a "*crimen laesae majestatis.*"[140] Although on one
hand Enzmilner advised the Estates to put forward this compromise proposal and also to claim compensation for administrative costs against the properties confiscated by the state, on
the other hand, by conceding that the state took precedence in
cases of treason against the crown, he inevitably also conceded
the properties of housed rebels to the state because it was much
more likely that these would be armed.

The Viennese authorities formally rejected the Estates' (i.e.,

Enzmilner's) proposal in December of 1635 but then accepted many of its procedures as guidelines after the Laimbauer rebellion was crushed in the spring of 1636. The royal administration recommenced the quarrel over legal competence when it issued an edict for the confiscation of rebel properties in July of 1636. Again the Estates objected that such a demand was outside the administrative jurisdiction of the state authorities because, and this is noteworthy, peasant farms came explicitly under the law of emphyteusis ("*bona emphyteuticum*")[141] and were therefore a part of estate administration that was responsible for the compilation and disposition of the liens against a peasant house. The state again asserted its position on 26 August 1636, this time by claiming that all males who were of age and had participated in the rebellion were guilty of treason against the crown and had, therefore, lost their properties to the crown; at the same time, however, the estates were to administer these confiscations for the crown and pay for the expenses in this police action—and "expenses" were to include compensation for widows and orphans whose husbands or fathers had lost their lives fighting for the authorities at Frankenberg.[142] In October, the Estates countered with an argument that conceded the legal point but that made more sense from a practical point of view. The lists of rebel properties that the various estate administrators had drawn up in response to state instructions confirmed the Estates' earlier predictions that most of the participants had been unhoused and therefore had little property. Those who had been housed had been due to lose their farms anyway because they were overburdened with liens and therefore would not yield much income for the crown.[143]

It was characteristic that once the Habsburg state authorities had staked out their area of competence as a precedent in administrative law, they should yield on the actual carrying out of the law—and that the law should work, finally, against those on the lowest rungs of the bureaucratic hierarchy and altogether against those below it. In November, Emperor Ferdinand himself gave the Estates the authority to supervise the confiscations of all the rebel properties and, at the same time, shrugged off on to the Estates any responsibility for the expenses incurred in the course of the rebellion's suppression. This meant, of course, that the state had given the various estate authorities a carte blanche on what to do with the rebel properties; it also meant that tenants who had furnished horses, supplies, weapons, and hired hands received none or very little compensation and that tenant widows and orphans who had lost their husbands and fathers at Frankenberg also lost any chance for a compensatory award. The Emperor issued a final decree in December 1636 in which he reiterated his earlier position and urged the estate managers to make the compensation payments to widows to which his administrative authorities had committed themselves in August but there is no evidence that such payments were ever made.

The revolutionary process of rural bureaucratization and the development of social and economic forms associated with it that had had their beginnings during the second half of the sixteenth century had drawn to a close by 1640. The royal state authorities used the events of the 1630s to consolidate further the process of administrative centralization by which the housed peasantry, their families and housecommunities, the estates and their owners, and officials and the provincial *Stände* were all integrated more closely into a state-wide administrative structure. Having, by 1600, raised the principle of emphyteusis to primary importance as a uniformly administered qualification for tenure, the royal authorities by the 1630s also established that religious qualifications and crimes against the state overrode emphyteusis. In 1636 it was also apparent that there were few rewards to be had in this system. The dispossessed suffered their punishments and the widows and orphans of those tenants who had died in state service went empty-handed. The *syndikus*, Dr. Enzmilner, continued his social advance and eventually received a promotion to Imperial *Freiherr*,[144] while the estate owners and managers had to be content with administering the forfeited properties of their disobedient tenants. The only non-noble participant in the events at Frankenberg who is on record with a reward for special service is a Linz tavernkeeper who, in 1638, received a coat of arms with which to grace the entrance of his establishment.[145] For the other tenants who had fought for the state at Frankenberg, police and military duties on a provincial level had clearly become one of the responsibilities of the housed and for these subjects the continuing privilege of holding a tenant farm and the opportunity to serve the state had become their own rewards. Advantaged by and disciplined to perform in the pseudo-families of the emergent legal-rational absolute state, the housed could never again hesitate in their stifling of the protests of those dispossessed children and laborers who had grasped the terrifying fact that they were the necessary victims of the new order.

~ ABBREVIATIONS ~

AHR	*American Historical Review*
AÖG	*Archiv für Österreichische Geschichte*
JOÖMV	*Jahrbuch des Oberösterreichischen Musealvereins*
JSL	*Jahrbuch der Stadt Linz*
MOÖLA	*Mitteilungen des Oberösterreichischen Landesarchivs*
OÖH	*Oberösterreichische Heimatblätter*
OÖLA	Oberösterreichisches Landesarchiv
PSN	*Peasant Studies Newsletter*
VSWG	*Vierteljahrschrift für Sozial- und Wirtschaftsgeschichte*
WG	Max Weber, *Wirtschaft und Gesellschaft*
ZAA	*Zeitschrift für Agrargeschichte und Agrarsoziologie*
ZbL	*Zeitschrift für bayerische Landesgeschichte*
ZfG	*Zeitschrift für Geschichtswissenschaft*

~ NOTES ~

INTRODUCTION: PEASANT WARS AND PEASANT SOCIETY

1. This overview was assembled from the following detailed accounts: Alois Zauner, *Vöcklabruck und der Attergau*, Vienna, 1971; Albin Czerny, *Der erste Bauernaufstand in Oberösterreich, 1525*, Linz, 1882; idem, *Der zweite Bauernaufstand in Oberösterreich, 1595-1597*, Linz, 1890; idem, *Bilder aus der Zeit der Bauernunruhen in Oberösterreich, 1626, 1632, 1648*, Linz, 1876; Helmuth Feigl, "Die befreiten Ämter der Herrschaft Steyr in den Bauernkriegen des 16. und 17. Jahrhunderts," *MOÖLA* 6 (1959); Georg Grüll, *Der Bauer im Lande ob der Enns am Ausgang des sechzehnten Jahrhunderts*, Vienna, 1969; idem, *Bauer, Herr und Landesfürst*, Graz, 1963; Felix Stieve, *Der Oberösterreichische Bauernaufstand des Jahres 1626*, 2 vols., Linz, 1904; Julius Strnadt, *Der Bauernkrieg in Oberösterreich im Jahr 1626*, Wels, 1924; Hans Sturmberger, "Der Oberösterreichische Bauernkrieg von 1626 im Rahmen der Landesgeschichte," and Alfred Hoffmann, "Zur Typologie der Bauernaufstände in Oberösterreich" in *Der Oberösterreichische Bauernkrieg; Ausstellung des Landes Oberösterreich*, Linz, 1976; Friedrich Schober, "Zur Geschichte des Bauernaufstandes, 1632," *MOÖLA* 2 (1955); Franz Wilflingseder, "Martin Laimbauer und die Unruhen im Machlandviertel, 1632-1636," *MOÖLA* 6 (1959).

2. The most important articles and reviews summarizing this debate are in Rainer Wohlfeil, ed., *Reformation oder Frühbürgerliche Revolution*, Munich, 1975; H. A. Oberman, ed., *Deutscher Bauernkrieg, 1525*, Stuttgart, 1972; Janos Bak, ed., *The German Peasant War of 1525*, special issue of *The Journal of Peasant Studies* 3 (1975); H.-U. Wehler, ed., *Der deutsche Bauernkrieg, 1524-1526*, Göttingen, 1975; Rainer Wohlfeil, ed., *Der Bauernkrieg, 1524-1526*, Munich, 1975; Günther Franz, ed., *Bauernschaft und Bauernstand, 1500-1700*, Limbach-Lahn, 1975; Bernd Moeller, ed., *Studien zum Bauernkrieg*, Gütersloh, 1975.

3. For a shrewd summary and critique of social historical attitudes and writings about the Central European peasantry in this period see Robert Scribner's excellent article, "Is There A Social History of the Reformation?" *Social History* 4 (January 1977).

4. There have been a number of imaginative and original contributions to the history of the 1525 Peasant War which do not repeat the formulas of the Great Debate. In this regard see Heide Wunder, "Zur Mentalität aufständischer Bauern," and Thomas Sea, "Schwäbischer Bund und Bauernkrieg: Bestrafung und Pazifikation" both in *Bauernkrieg*, ed. Wehler. See also the interesting, if flawed, study by Hannah Rabe, *Das Problem Leibeigenschaft*, Wiesbaden, 1977.

5. David Sabean, *Landbesitz und Gesellschaft am Vorabend des Bauernkriegs*, Stuttgart, 1972. See also his articles "Family and Land Tenure: A Case Study of Conflict in the German Peasants' War (1525)," *PSN* 3 (1974) (this is a translation of an article that appeared in the *Annales* family issue, Vol. 27, no. 4-5, 1972); also his "German Agrarian Institutions at the Beginning of the Sixteenth Century: Upper Swabia as an Example," in *German Peasant War*, ed. Bak; "Aspects of Kinship Behavior in Rural Western Europe Before 1800," in *Family and Inheritance: Rural Society in Western Europe, 1200-1800*, ed. Jack Goody et al., Cambridge, 1976; "Problems of Nominal Data Linkage Using Württemberg Village Records from the Sixteenth to the Nineteenth Centuries," paper presented at the Nominal Record Linkage Conference, Institute for Advanced Study, Princeton, N.J., 24-27 May 1971.

6. Thus for example Peter Blickle, *Die Revolution von 1525*, Munich, 1975, does cite Sabean throughout but has not fundamentally altered his interpretation which, in effect, conflicts with Sabean's in many points. See also Rainer Wohlfeil, "Neue Forschungen zur Geschichte des deutschen Bauernkriegs (Part IV)" in *Bauernkrieg*, ed. Wehler, pp. 304, 330. Other researchers, for example, John C. Stalnaker, "Auf dem Weg zu einer sozialgeschichtlichen Interpretation des deutschen Bauernkriegs, 1525-1526" in *Bauernkrieg*, ed. Wehler, have, however, recognized the significance of Sabean's work for putting the history of the German peasantry on a new track.

7. Wohlfeil, "Neue Forschungen," p. 354. The contribution by Jürgen Bücking, "Der 'Bauernkrieg' in den hapsburgischen Ländern als sozialer Systemkonflikt, 1524-1526," in *Bauernkrieg*, ed. Wehler, uses the term in an unconvincing analysis.

8. Gerhard Heitz, "Zu den bäuerlichen Klassenkämpfen im Spätfeudalismus," *ZfG* 23 (1975).

9. Günther Franz, "Die Führer im Bauernkrieg," in his *Bauernschaft*, p. 13. This idea of complete political *Gleichschaltung* is a corollary of his idea that the peasants' social and economic life was fixed

in rigid forms after the defeat of 1525. It appeared in the first edition of his *Der Deutsche Bauernkrieg* in 1933.

10. Scribner, "Social History"; Rainer Elkar, "Geschichtsforschung der frühen Neuzeit zwischen Divergenz und Parallelität," in *Bauernkrieg*, ed. Wohlfeil. The article by Ernst Nolte, "The Relationship between 'Bourgeois' and 'Marxist' Historiography," *History and Theory* 14 (1975), is also relevant to these issues. See also the excellent article by Norman Birnbaum, "The Crisis in Marxist Sociology," *Social Research* 35 (1968). This has been reprinted by J. David Colfax and Jack L. Roach, eds., *Radical Sociology*, New York, 1971.

11. Helga Schultz, "Bäuerliche Klassenkämpfe zwischen frühbürgerlicher Revolution und dreissigjährigem Krieg," *ZfG* 20 (1972); see also Heitz, "Zu den bäuerlichen Klassenkämpfen."

12. Blickle, *Die Revolution von 1525*, pp. 241-242.

13. See the works of Sabean cited in note 5. In this connection see also the article by Lutz Berkner, "Inheritance, Land Tenure and Peasant Family Structure: A German Regional Comparison," in *Family and Inheritance*, ed. Goody. Also, in part, Grüll, *Bauer*.

14. For a discussion of the varying kinds of macroanalysis of rural social and economic developments see Robert Brenner, "Agrarian Class Structure and Economic Development in Pre-Industrial Europe," *Past and Present* 70 (1976).

15. Heitz, "Zu den bäuerlichen Klassenkämpfen," pp. 776-778; R. F. Schmied, "Der Bauernkrieg in Oberösterreich von 1626 als Teilerscheinung des dreissigjährigen Krieges," Ph.D. dissertation, University of Halle, 1963, claims to deal with the resistance of the peasant "masses" against the absolute state and military taxation but his analysis fails to use Upper Austrian archival materials and does not analyze Austrian peasant society as such.

16. See Günter Vogler's contribution to the symposium, " 'The Peasant War in Germany' by Friedrich Engels—125 Years After," in *Peasant War*, ed. Bak, pp. 108-116; also Scribner, "Social History," pp. 484-487. The urban revolts of the period have elicited a more detailed Marxist analysis. See Johannes Schildhauer, *Soziale, politische, und religiöse Auseinandersetzungen in den Hansestädten*, Weimar, 1959, and R. W. Scribner, "Civic Unity and the Reformation in Erfurt," *Past and Present* 6 (1975). The latter contains an excellent brief description of Erfurt's experience with the peasants.

17. Birnbaum, "Crisis," pp. 115-116; Rodolfo Stavenhagen, *Social Class in Agrarian Societies*, Garden City, N.Y., 1975. See also Scribner, "Social History," pp. 489-492.

18. See, for example, Immanuel Wallerstein, "From Feudalism to Capitalism: Transition or Transitions?" *Social Forces* 55 (1976).

19. Otto Brunner, *Land und Herrschaft*, Darmstadt, 1965, pp. 118-119, 398.

20. Ibid., pp. 254-257, and idem, "Das 'ganze Haus' und die alteuropäische 'Ökonomie' " in his *Neue Wege der Verfassungs- und Sozialgeschichte*, 2nd ed., Göttingen, 1968.

21. See, for example, the uses of the term by Lutz Berkner, "The Stem Family and the Developmental Cycle of the Peasant Household: An Eighteenth Century Austrian Example," *AHR* 77 (1972). See also Michael Mitterauer, "Zur Familenstruktur in ländlichen Gebieten Österreichs im 17. Jahrhundert," in *Beiträge zur Bevölkerungs- und Sozialgeschichte Österreichs*, ed. H. Helczmanovski, Munich, 1973.

22. But note Karl Marx, *Das Kapital*, Vol. 1, chap. 13, pt. 8; also Stavenhagen, *Social Class*, p. 68.

23. A. V. Chayanov, *The Theory of Peasant Economy*, Homewood, Ill., 1966. In this connection see also the use of the idea of "moral economy" in conjunction with Chayanov's idea of "self-exploitation" in James C. Scott, *The Moral Economy of the Peasant: Rebellion and Subsistence in Southeast Asia*, New Haven, 1976, p. vii.

24. Thus, for example, Heitz, "Zu den bäuerlichen Klassenkämpfen," p. 780; but see also the exploratory article by Hans Medick, "The Proto-Industrial Family Economy: The Structural Function of Household and Family during the Transition from Peasant Society to Industrial Capitalism," *Social History* 3 (1976):297-300.

25. In this connection see Stanislaw Ossowski, *Class Structure in the Social Consciousness*, New York, 1963, chap. 8.

26. Roland Mousnier, *Social Stratification*, New York, 1973, pp. 35, 39.

27. Ibid., p. 41.

28. For example, Lawrence Stone, *The Crisis of the Aristocracy, 1558-1641*, New York, 1967, passim.

29. See, for example, the articles by Margaret Spufford and E. P. Thompson, in *Family and Inheritance*, ed. Goody.

30. Mousnier, *Social Stratification*, pp. 42-44.

31. For theoretical works on this subject see John P. Davis, *Corporations*, New York, 1905; John R. Commons, *The Legal Foundations of Capitalism*, New York, 1924; Henry Kariel, *The Decline of American Pluralism*, Stanford, 1961; James S. Coleman, *Power and the Structure of Society*, New York, 1974; David Bazelon, *Power and American Society*, New York, 1971. Historical studies that are directly relevant

to Mousnier's point about American society are Stephan Thernstrom, *Poverty and Progress: Social Mobility in a Nineteenth Century City*, Garden City, N.Y., 1970; Grant McConnell, *Private Power and American Democracy*, New York, 1970; James Weinstein, *The Corporate Ideal in the Liberal State*, Boston, 1969; Gabriel Kolko, *The Triumph of Conservatism*, Chicago, 1965.

32. Mousnier, *Social Stratification*, p. 45. For a discussion of the theoretical weaknesses in Mousnier's stratification scheme see Armand Arriaza, "Mousnier and Barber: The Theoretical Underpinnings of the Society of Order in Early Modern Europe," *Past and Present*, in press.

33. Max Weber, "Class, Status and Party," in *From Max Weber: Essays in Sociology*, ed. H. H. Gerth and C. Wright Mills, New York, 1958, p. 194.

34. Ibid., p. 181.

35. Ralf Dahrendorf, *Class and Class Conflict in Industrial Society*, Stanford, 1959, pp. 234-238.

36. Weber, "Class," pp. 186-188, 190-194.

37. Ibid., p. 194.

CHAPTER 1: SETTINGS

1. Georg Grüll, *Weinberg; Die Entstehungsgeschichte einer Mühlviertler Wirtschaftsherrschaft*, Graz, 1955, pp. 31-32.

2. Werner Stark, "Die Abhängigkeitsverhältnisse der gutsherrlichen Bauern Böhmens im 17. und 18. Jahrhundert," *Jahrbücher für Nationalökonomie und Statistik* 164 (1952):270, and his *Ursprung und Aufstieg des landwirtschaftlichen Grossbetriebs in den böhmischen Ländern*, Prague, 1934, p. 28.

3. Alfred Hoffmann, *Wirtschaftsgeschichte des Landes Oberösterreich*, Vol. 1, Salzburg, 1952, pp. 88-99; Alfred Hoffmann's later article, "Die Grundherrschaft als Unternehmen," *ZAA* 6 (October 1958), developed the original formulation considerably.

4. Eckart Schremmer, "Agrarverfassung und Wirtschaftsstruktur. Die südostdeutsche Hofmark, eine Wirtschaftsherrschaft?" *ZAA* 20 (1972); Ferdinand Tremel, *Der Frühkapitalismus in Innerösterreich*, Graz, 1954; Anton Spiesz, "Die neuzeitliche Agrarentwicklung der Tschechoslowakei: Gutsherrschaft oder Wirtschaftsherrschaft?" *ZbL* 32 (1969), discusses recent Czech literature on the subject; Hans Rosenberg, "The Rise of the Junkers in Brandenburg-Prussia, 1410-1653," *AHR* 49 (1943-1944):228-236, describes developments somewhat similar to those in southeast Central Europe.

5. Hoffmann, *Wirtschaftsgeschichte*, pp. 76-79, 88-93; see also Stark, *Ursprung*, pp. 18-26, and Rosenberg, "The Rise of the Junkers," pp. 230-231.

6. Hoffmann, *Wirtschaftsgeschichte*, pp. 92, 99; see also Stark, *Ursprung*, pp. 29-30.

7. Hoffmann, *Wirtschaftsgeschichte*, p. 78.

8. In the early seventeenth-century library inventories of two Upper Austrian country squires who were economically very active and quite wealthy, there was not a single book dealing with economic subjects. See Laurenz Pröll, *Ein Blick in das Hauswesen eines Österreichischen Landedelmannes*, Vienna, 1889, 2:1-12.

9. Stark, "Abhängigkeitsverhältnisse," p. 271.

10. Oberösterreichisches Landesarchiv (OÖLA) Weinberg Archive, Vol. 370, file B/1/c. For a discussion of the cultural circumstances surrounding seventeenth-century Austrian economic thinking, see Otto Brunner, *Adeliges Landleben und Europäischer Geist*, Salzburg, 1959, pp. 237-312.

11. Hermann Kellenbenz, *Der Merkantilismus in Europa und die Soziale Mobilität*, Wiesbaden, 1965, pp. 51-52; see also Rosenberg, "The Rise of the Junkers," pp. 16-17.

12. Schremmer, "Agrarverfassung," p. 57, discusses similar developments for Bavaria.

13. For the complex property dealings and legal battles that accompanied the pawning of royal estates, see Alois Zauner, *Vöcklabruck und der Attergau*, Vienna, 1971, pp. 198-206; see also Grüll, *Weinberg*, pp. 13, 16-17, 20, 31-32, 34, 37. Lien administration was also a feature of Prussian absolutism, but since royal and public finances developed in a different, highly centralized direction there, it probably had a less significant long-range influence on the Prussian aristocracy's economic and political sense than in Austria. Rosenberg, "The Rise of the Junkers," p. 22; idem, *Bureaucracy, Aristocracy, and Autocracy: The Prussian Experience, 1660-1815*, Boston, 1966, p. 49.

14. Grüll, *Weinberg*, pp. 45-90, has reconstructed this extraordinarily complex history for one Austrian estate.

15. See Hermann Rebel, *The Rural Subject Population of Upper Austria During the Early Seventeenth Century: Aspects of the Social Stratification System*, Ann Arbor, 1976, chaps. 2, 3.

16. For somewhat analogous developments in sixteenth-century Swabia see David Sabean, *Landbesitz und Gesellschaft*, Stuttgart, 1972, passim.

17. Georg Grüll, *Bauer, Herr und Landesfürst*, Graz, 1963, p. 60.

18. Georg Grüll, "Die Herrschaftsschichtung in Österreich ob der Enns, 1750," *MOÖLA* 5 (1957):314, 317.

19. Alfons Dopsch, "Agrarian Institutions of the Germanic Kingdoms from the Fifth to the Ninth Century," in *Cambridge Economic History of Europe*, 1:184-185; Marc Bloch, "The Rise of Dependent Cultivation and Seignorial Institutions," in *Cambridge Economic History*, Cambridge, 1941, 1:225, 233, 275-276; Zauner, *Vöcklabruck*, p. 383.

20. Zauner, *Vöcklabruck*, p. 406.

21. Ibid., pp. 407-410.

22. In my sample of seventeenth-century peasantry there appear no persons of this legal status.

23. Grüll, *Bauer*, pp. 227-228; Helmuth Feigl, *Die Niederösterreichische Grundherrschaft*, Vienna, 1964, p. 20; Alois Mosser, "Beiträge zur Geschichte in Oberösterreich unter besonderer Berücksichtigung der Herrschaft Ott am Traunsee," Ph.D. dissertation, University of Vienna, 1964, p. 305.

24. Zauner, *Vöcklabruck*, p. 411.

25. Otto Brunner, *Land und Herrschaft*, Darmstadt, 1965, p. 356.

26. J. Strnadt, "Die Freien Leute der alten Riedmark," *AÖG* 104; Heinrich Wurm, "Die Weiberau. Geschichte einer Gemeinweide," *OÖH* 1 (1947); Othmar Hageneder, "Die Grafschaft Schaunberg," *MOÖLA* 5 (1957):76; Grüll, *Bauer*, pp. 227-228; Zauner, *Vöcklabruck*, p. 413.

27. Hoffmann, *Wirtschaftsgeschichte*, pp. 89-91; Georg Grüll, *Die Robot in Oberösterreich*, Linz, 1952, pp. 54-174; idem, *Bauer*, p. 141; Bloch, "Rise of Dependent Cultivation," pp. 275-276.

28. Grüll, *Bauer*, pp. 132-137, 227-229.

29. Amilian Kloiber et al., "Die neolithische Siedlung und die neolithischen Gräberfundplätze von Rutzing und Haid, Ortsgemeinde Hörsching, Politischer Bezirk Linz-Land, Oberösterreich," *JOÖMV* 115 (1970):33-34.

30. Othmar Hageneder, "Die spätmittelalterlichen Wüstungen in der Grafschaft Schaunberg," *Jahrbuch für Landeskunde von Niederösterreich*, Neue Folge 33 (1957):65-71; Hans Krawarick, "Die Besiedlung und Verödung der Rosenau," *OÖH* 22 (1968).

31. Felix Stieve, *Der Oberösterreichische Bauernaufstand des Jahres 1626*, 2 vols., Linz, 1904, 1:2; Hoffmann, *Wirtschaftsgeschichte*, p. 243; Heinrich Ferihumer, "Eine Beschreibung der Bewohner Oberösterreichs (1771)," *OÖH* 4 (1950).

32. Based on data from the Mühlviertel parishes Kreuzen, Dimbach,

Gallneukirchen as compiled in J. Heider, "Tabellen zu den Kirchenbüchern Mühlviertler Pfarren," unpublished typescript, OÖLA, Linz.

33. For example, when the communities around the parish of Pergkirchen lost their Protestant priests through enforced emigration, the ranks of the communicants at Pergkirchen swelled dramatically from 358 in 1617 to 456 in 1620, 517 in 1621, 1,441 in 1622, 1,503 in 1623, and diminished to 1,214 in 1624 when Pergkirchen's own priest was finally also forced to leave. It is important to point out, however, that these figures which were inflated by the participation at communion of outsiders are not reflected in the parish's baptismal, marriage, and burial records for the same years. Georg Grüll, "Pergkirchen. Beiträge zur Geschichte eines Dorfes," *Heimatgaue* 2 (1930):131-136.

34. Ferdinand Wiesinger, "Die Stadt Wels zur Zeit des Bauernkrieges, 1626," in *Das heldenmütige Martyrium von Anno 1626*, ed. H. Zötl, Linz, 1927, pp. 90-91.

35. Heinrich Wurm, "St. Georgen bei Grieskirchen. Beispiel einer Dorfentwicklung im Hausruck," *OÖH*, 22 (1968), pp. 151-152.

36. Engelbert Koller, "350 Jahre Salinenort Ebensee," *OÖH* 11 (1957): 88-89.

37. Wurm, "Weiberau," pp. 6-14.

38. Georg Grüll, "Die Leute im Walde. Ein Beitrag zur Geschichte des Freiwaldes," *OÖH* 1 (1947):209.

39. Ibid., p. 210.

40. OÖLA, Windhag Archive, Hs. 9, *Urbar* for the year 1672.

41. OÖLA, Windhag *Protokolle*, Vols. 1932, 1933, 1935.

42. OÖLA, Frankenburg *Protokolle*, Vols. 265-268; Schaunberg *Protokolle*, Vols. 280, 281.

43. OÖLA, Garsten Archive, *Verkaufsprotokolle*, Vols. 22-24, 29.

44. Walter Lehnert, *Die Oberösterreichischen Exulanten im ehemaligen Ansbachischen Oberamt Stauf-Landek*, Freie Schriftenfolge der Gesellschaft für Familienforschung in Franken, Neustadt/Aich, 1962, 14:63-64; Gilbert Trathnigg, "Wels und Regensburg," *Jahrbuch des Musealvereins Wels* (1957):190-192.

45. Ferdinand Tremel, *Sozial- und Wirtschaftsgeschichte Österreichs*, Vienna, 1969, p. 129; Helmuth Feigl, "Die befreiten Ämter der Herrschaft Steyr in den Bauernkriegen des 16. und 17. Jahrhunderts," *MOÖLA* 6 (1959):211-214; Friedrich Schmidt, *Die freien bäuerlichen Eigengüter in Oberösterreich*, Breslau, 1941, pp. 87-89.

46. OÖLA, *Landschaftsakten*, Vols. 1227, 1228, Katastralsachen; see especially Vol. 1228, Hs. 10, the 1623-1627 correspondence between the Upper Austrian Estates and the magistrates of Haag con-

cerning the deletion of fifty-nine taxable "hearths" (*Feuerstätten*) from the tax rolls; see also Vol. 1333, Hs. 12, the abbot of Lambach's request for a reduced tax assessment because of several abandoned homes.
47. Schremmer, "Agrarverfassung und Wirtschaftsstruktur," p. 42.

CHAPTER 2: CHARACTERISTICS OF PEASANT HOUSEHOLDS

1. Georg Grüll, *Bauernhaus und Meierhof*, Linz, 1975, pp. 2-3, 173-174.
2. Ibid., pp. 228-279.
3. Unless otherwise noted, all the information concerning household size and composition in this section is taken from Michael Mitterauer, "Zur Familienstruktur in ländlichen Gebieten Österreichs im 17. Jh." in *Beiträge zur Bevölkerungs- und Sozialgeschichte Österreichs*, ed. Heimold Helczmanovszki," Munich, 1973, and idem, "Auswirkung von Urbanisierung und Frühindustrialisierung auf die Familienverfassung an Beispielen des österreichischen Raums" in *Sozialgeschichte der Familie in der Neuzeit Europas*, ed. Werner Conze, Stuttgart, 1976. I have used here only a small part of Professor Mitterauer's findings. His researches are of the greatest importance for social history and the wealth of information he has uncovered and his interpretations of the "soul books" and other sources must be read in detail to be fully appreciated.
4. The first two terms are used by members of the Cambridge group to describe families. See Peter Laslett and Richard Wall, eds., *Household and Family in Past Time*, Cambridge, Mass., 1972, passim. The latter is used by Hilda and Clifford Geertz, *Kinship in Bali*, Chicago, 1975, passim.
5. The Upper Austrian peasant household inventories I examined for this period and for areas somewhat further east yield similar information. Although the household inventories are not a good survey source for demographic data specifically, they do reveal the number of children per family in the lists of heirs. For the inventory data, the differences observed by Mitterauer between a rural farming area and an urbanized industrial area exist in the difference between areas of large farms in the flatlands and of smaller farms, workshops, and cottages in hilly areas. The former, represented by inventories from the estates Frankenburg and Aistersheim, had average family sizes of 5.1 and 5.9 individuals respectively; the latter, represented by inventories from the monastic estate Schlägl, had an average nuclear family

size of only 4.0 individuals. For more extensive information about the inventories used in this study see notes 18 and 19 below.

6. Tamara K. Hareven, "Family Time and Historical Time," in *The Family*, ed. Alice Rossi et al., New York, 1978.

7. Michael Mitterauer is presently engaged in such studies of early modern and modern villages in Austria. He discusses the problem of individual and family interaction in "Familiengrösse—Familientypen—Familienzyklus. Probleme Quantitativer Auswertung von österreichischem Quellenmaterial," *Geschichte und Gesellschaft* 1 (1975): 244-245; see also his "Auswirkungen," pp. 134-137. See also his recent article, with Reinhard Sieder, "The Developmental Process of Domestic Groups: Problems of Reconstruction and Possibilities of Interpretation," *Journal of Family History* 4 (1979).

8. For a role analysis of families see Marion Levy, Jr. and L. A. Fallers, "The Family: Some Comparative Considerations," *American Anthropologist*, n.s., 61 (1959):647-651; see the discussion by Raymond T. Smith, "Family: Comparative Structure," *International Encyclopedia of the Social Sciences* 5:303-304.

9. Peter Berger, *The Homeless Mind*, New York, 1974, pp. 72-73.

10. Frank E. Manuel, "The Use and Abuse of Psychology in History," in *Historical Studies Today*, ed. Felix Gilbert and Stephen Graubard, New York, 1972, p. 227; Else Frankel-Brunswick, "Adjustments and Reorientations in the Course of the Life-Span," in *Middle Age and Aging*, ed. Bernice Neugarten, Chicago, 1968; Tamara K. Hareven, "The History of the Family as an Interdisciplinary Field," *Journal of Interdisciplinary History*, 2 (1972).

11. Lutz Berkner, "The Stem Family and the Developmental Cycle of the Peasant Household: An Eighteenth Century Austrian Example," *AHR* 77 (1972); Jack Goody, ed., *The Developmental Cycle in Domestic Groups*, Cambridge, 1958.

12. Wolfgang Brücker, ed., *Volkserzählung und Reformation*, Berlin, 1974, passim.

13. In this regard see the discussion of "role" in Ralf Dahrendorf, "Homo Sociologicus" in his *Essays in the Theory of Society*, Stanford, 1968; also, the critical remarks by Hans-Peter Dreitzel are worth noting, *Die gesellschaftlichen Leiden und das Leiden an der Gesellschaft*, Stuttgart, 1968, pp. 114-115.

14. OÖLA, Frankenburg *Protokolle*, Vols. 248, 249, 250, 252, 254, 256, 260, 261.

15. Ibid., Vols. 262, 264-268.

16. Ibid., Vol. 253.

17. Similar use of the inventories was made in the *Urbaria*, the

compilation of registers of the estate's farms and their changing market value; e.g., see OÖLA, Windhag Archive, Hs. 9, *Urbar* for the year 1672.

18. Inventories have traditionally been used to capture and describe through records of properties and goods the details of extinct ways of life; see for example Wilhelm Ramsauer, "Das Inventar eines deutschen Marschbauernhofes aus den letzen Jahren des dreissigjährigen Krieges," *VSWG* 7 (1909); G. H. Kenyon, "Kirdford Inventories, 1611 to 1776," *Sussex Archeological Collections* 93 (1955); Barbara Cornford, "Inventories of the Poor," *Norfolk Archeology* 35 (1970). More recently there has been added to this essentially archeological and antiquarian concern an interest in the inventories as sources for describing and understanding the long-term development of past rural economies. When this interest has been pursued with the help of some basic statistical techniques such valuable studies as Walter Achilles's *Vermögensverhältnisse braunschweigischer Bauernhöfe*, Stuttgart, 1965, have been the result. Although my concern with status differs from both these approaches, I have learned from them. I must here also acknowledge a debt to Oscar Lewis for his article, "The Possessions of the Poor," *Scientific American* 211 (October, 1969).

19. The estate archives with substantial numbers of inventories for this period on which I drew for this study were the following: OÖLA, Frankenburg *Brief- und Inventurprotokolle*, Vols. 248-250, 252-254, 256, 260-262, 264-269; Schaunberg, *Brief- und Inventurprotokolle*, Vols. 278-281; Schlägl *Brief- und Inventurprotokolle*, Vols. 434-437; Aistersheim *Inventurprotokolle*, Vols. 90-91; Windhag, *Brief- und Inventurprotokolle*, 1932-1941.

20. OÖLA, Windhag Archive, Hs. 9, *Urbar*, 1672; Alfred Hoffmann, "Die Agrarisierung der Industriebauern in Österreich," *East European Quarterly* 3, (1970):455.

21. I did not find a single case of a farming household that had diversified into the rural metal industries. Such diversification was carried out by smiths who performed diverse metal manufacturing and repair functions and whom I classified under that title among my occupational groups. When there was no house or agricultural enterprise behind this kind of industrial involvement, then I classified the householder either under the categories of servant, lodger, or cottagers—terms that I will explain in chapter five below—or I simply called them "pail-maker," "rake-maker," etc. Weavers were in almost all cases identified as such.

22. The household in the appendix to chapter 2 had a business radius of about 150 km.

23. Hermann Kellenbenz, "Rural Industries in the West; From the End of the Middle Ages to the Eighteenth Century," in *Essays in European Economic History 1500-1800*, ed. Peter Earle, Oxford, 1965.
24. Georg Grüll, *Bauer, Herr und Landesfürst*, Graz, 1963, p. 81.
25. Hermann Haibock, "Kerbhölzer und Zehentstecken. Hauprequisiten der 'Buchhaltung' früher Jahrhunderte," *OÖH* 18 (1964).
26. E. Strassmayer, "Wohlstand in einem alten Greiner Bürgerhaus," *Heimatgaue* 14 (1933).
27. Laurenz Pröll, *Ein Blick in das Hauswesen eines Österreichischen Landedelmannes*, 2 vols., 1:7.
28. Georg Grüll, "Die Herrschaftsschichtung in Österreich ob der Enns, 1750," Vienna, 1889, *MOÖLA* 5 (1957):317.
29. Grüll, *Bauer*, pp. 75-84.

CHAPTER 3: ECONOMIC GROUPS

1. Georg Grüll, "Die Leute im Walde," *OÖH* 1 (1947):210.
2. Alfred Hoffmann, *Wirtschaftsgeschichte des Landes Oberösterreich*, Vol. 1, Salzburg, 1952, p. 95.
3. OÖLA, Schlägl *Inventurprotokolle*, Vol. 435 (1620).
4. OÖLA, Frankenburg *Inventurprotokolle*, Vol. 248 (1609).
5. Ibid., Vol. 261 (1624).
6. For these two householders, see ibid., Vol. 248 (1609) and Vol. 249 (1610).
7. Ibid., Vol. 268 (1636).
8. The one householder in this group who might be expected to contradict this assertion was the vintner; however, he conforms very closely to it. The real and movable properties of this householder were relatively modest at 895fl and 767fl, respectively. The real income was from the vintner's creditor function which accounted for 1,225fl of his assets. Moreover, the vintner function was combined with considerable involvement in cloth and yarn production which also helps account for the high creditor status. OÖLA, Schaunberg *Inventurprotokolle*, Vol. 279 (1619-1628). This particular inventory was taken in 1624.

CHAPTER 4: INDUSTRY AND OCCUPATIONAL GROUPS

1. Rudolf Braun, *Industrialisierung and Volksleben*, Zurich, 1960; see also Hermann Kellenbenz, "Rural Industries in the West," in *Essays in European Economic History 1500-1800*, ed. Peter Earle, Oxford, 1965; Franklin F. Mendels, "Proto-Industrialization: The First

Phase of the Industrialization Process," *Journal of Economic History* 32 (1972).
2. See also Hans Medick, "Proto-Industrial Family Economy," *Social History* 3 (1976).
3. Braun, *Volksleben*, pp. 36-47, traces these antagonisms in the Zurich example to dire political conclusions; see also Kellenbenz, "Rural Industries," p. 76.
4. OÖLA, Schlägl *Inventurprotokolle*, Vols. 434, 435. The years in which the inventories cited were drawn up were 1619, 1623, and 1621 respectively.
5. Ibid., Vol. 435 (1622).
6. From the inventories as well as from the estate accounts of Weinberg, OÖLA, Weinberg Archive, Vol. 368, file B/1/a, I can determine that male servants' wages fluctuated between 7fl to 10fl a year while women's wages between 3fl to 7fl.
7. "*Söldner*" is here derived from "*Sölde*," meaning a small isolated house, and has nothing to do with the ordinarily military meaning of the word.
8. Braun, *Volksleben*, pp. 33-34; Eckart Schremmer, "Agrarverfassung und Wirtschaftsstruktur," *ZAA* 20 (1972).
9. OÖLA, Frankenburg *Inventurprotokolle*, Vol. 249 (1610).
10. OÖLA, Schlägl *Inventurprotokolle*, Vol. 434 (1615); Schaunberg *Inventurprotokolle*, Vol. 279 (1621).
11. OÖLA, Schlägl *Inventurprotokolle*, Vol. 435 (1620, 1622, and 1620 respectively for the three cases cited).
12. OÖLA, Schaunberg *Inventurprotokolle*, Vol. 279 (1621).
13. OÖLA, Schlägl *Inventurprotokolle*, Vol. 434 (1619).
14. OÖLA, Aistershaim *Inventurprotokolle*, Vol. 91 (1634).
15. Georg Grüll, *Bauer, Herr und Landesfürst*, Graz, 1963, p. 71; Alfred Hoffmann, *Wirtschaftsgeschichte des Landes Oberösterreich*, Vol. 1, Salzburg, 1952, p. 235.
16. Ernst Bruckmüller, "Die Lage der Bauern um 1626," in *Der oberösterreichische Bauernkrieg 1626. Ausstellung des Landes Oberösterreich*, Linz, 1976, p. 101.
17. James C. Scott, *The Moral Economy of the Peasant*, New Haven, 1976.
18. Richard Popkin, *The Rational Peasant*, Berkeley, 1979.

CHAPTER 5: PEASANT CLASSES

1. Thus, the Imperial commissar Herbersdorf's correspondence and patents, OÖLA, Wagrain Archive, Vol. 18, file QII.

2. Felix Stieve, *Der Oberösterreich Bauernaufstand des Jahres 1626*, 2 vols., Linz, 1904, 1:129.

3. Ibid., pp. 139-140.

4. Some authorities, for example, maintained lists of the "disobedient" and pursued them capriciously, vindictively, with chicanery and with imprisonment, expropriation, excessive taxes, lawsuits, and, in some cases, execution without process or cause. Alois Zauner, *Vöcklabruck und der Attergau*, Vienna, 1971, p. 527; Georg Grüll, *Bauern, Herr und Landesfürst*, Graz, 1963, pp. 32, 49, 104.

5. Eckart Schremmer, "Agrarverfassung und Wirtschaftsstruktur," *ZAA* 20 (1972):42.

6. Ignaz Nösslböck et al., eds., *Österreichische Weistümer*, Graz, 1960, Vol. 14, pp. 308-309.

7. Peter Blickle, "Bauer und Staat in Oberschwaben," *Zeitschrift für Württembergische Landesgeschichte* 31 (1973):117-120.

8. Ibid., p. 117.

9. Alan Macfarlane, *The Origins of English Individualism*, Oxford, 1978, especially pp. 94-101; Professor Macfarlane's argument is summarized in his "The Origins of English Individualism: Some Surprises," *Theory and Society* 6 (1978).

10. "Origins," p. 255.

11. Cf. Macfarlane's discussion of Weber's concept of "household," *Origins*, p. 51, with Weber's actual chapter on "housecommunity" in *Wirtschaft und Gesellschaft*, Tübingen, 1925, pp. 194-215.

12. Eric Wolf, *Peasants*, Englewood Cliffs, N.J., 1966, p. 61.

13. *Southwestern Journal of Anthropology* 13 (1967); reprinted in Jack Potter, May Diaz and George Foster, eds., *Peasant Society: A Reader*, Boston, 1967.

14. Maurice Dobb, *Studies in the Development of Capitalism*, London, 1946, p. 7; cf. Macfarlane, *Origins*, pp. 98, 195-196, 201, and "Origins," pp. 256-260, 268-269.

15. Margaret Spufford, "Peasant Inheritance Customs and Land Distribution in Cambridgeshire from the Sixteenth to the Eighteenth Centuries" and Cicely Howell, "Peasant Inheritance Customs in the Midlands, 1280-1700," both in *Family and Inheritance*, ed. Jack Goody et al., Cambridge, 1976.

16. Alan Macfarlane, *Reconstructing Historical Communities*, Cambridge, 1977.

17. Macfarlane, "Origins," pp. 266-267.

18. See, for example, John Cole and Eric Wolf, *The Invisible Frontier*, New York, 1974; Sydney Mintz, "The Rural Proletariat and the Prob-

lem of Rural Proletarian Consciousness," *Journal of Peasant Studies*, 1 (1974); William Roseberry, "Peasants as Proletarians," *Critique of Anthropology* 11 (1978).

19. This account of *robot* in Upper Austria is based chiefly on Georg Grüll's monograph *Die Robot in Oberösterreich*, Linz, 1952; for his discussion of the two kinds of *robot* see pp. 28-34.

20. Ibid., pp. 37-42.

21. Ibid., p. 53.

22. Ibid., pp. 56-58.

23. Nösslböck, *Weistümer*, Vol. 12, p. 626; Grüll, *Robot*, p. 62.

24. Grüll, *Robot*, pp. 65-66, 75.

25. Helmuth Feigl, "Die Befreiten Ämter der Herrschaft Steyr," *MOÖLA* 6 (1959):239. This sort of action was not unique and throws a somewhat different light on the "positive" and cooperative interpretation Peter Blickle wishes to impose on state, estate, and subject relations in the sixteenth century, *Die Revolution von 1525*, Munich, 1975, p. 117.

26. The story is told more fully in Grüll, *Robot*, pp. 67-73.

27. Grüll, *Bauer*, p. 243.

28. Grüll, *Robot*, pp. 135, 140, 144.

29. Ibid., pp. 268-276.

30. Ibid., p. 134; idem, *Bauer*, pp. 193-195; Alfred Hoffmann, *Wirtschaftsgeschichte des Landes Oberösterreich*, Vol. 1, Salzburg, 1952, pp. 93, 246-247.

31. Grüll, *Bauer*, p. 193; Hoffmann, *Wirtschaftsgeschichte*, pp. 247-248.

32. Grüll, *Robot*, pp. 35-37; idem, *Bauer*, p. 238.

33. Grüll, *Robot*, p. 109.

34. See the correspondence between the abbots of Kremsmünster and Mondsee, cited ibid., pp. 109-110.

35. Zauner, *Vöcklabruck*, pp. 431-432.

36. Grüll, *Robot*, p. 250.

37. For comparisons of Upper Austrian estate management with Bohemian and Bavarian forms see Hermann Rebel, *The Rural Subject Population of Upper Austria during the Early Seventeenth Century*, Ann Arbor, 1976, chaps. 2, 3.

38. Feigl, "Befreite Ämter," pp. 253-257, documents the harassment, delays, expenses, and debts experienced by subjects seeking to defend their "freedoms" against bureaucratic encroachment.

39. Grüll, *Robot*, pp. 134-139; these 71½ days on the books did not include additional *robot* extracted for tobacco farming.

40. Rebel, *The Rural Subject Population*.
41. Grüll, *Robot*, p. 142.
42. Rebel, *Rural Subject Population*, p. 127.
43. OÖLA, Weinberg Archive, Vol. 370, file B/1/c.
44. Ibid.
45. In this connection see the interpretation of Austrian state development in this period in Hans Sturmberger's essay, "Dualistischer Ständestaat und werdender Absolutismus" in *Die Entwicklung der Verfassung Österreichs vom Mittelalter bis zur Gegenwart*, ed. Institut für Österreichkunde, Vienna, 1970, pp. 34-41.
46. Leonard Krieger, *The German Idea of Freedom*, Boston, 1957.
47. Jan de Vries, *The Economy of Europe in an Age of Crisis, 1600-1750*, Cambridge, 1976, p. 83.
48. Hoffmann, *Wirtschaftsgeschichte*, p. 249.
49. Weber, *WG*, p. 208.
50. Ibid., pp. 207-208; in this connection it is interesting to compare Weber's account to the housecommunity perceived by Engels's *The Origins of the Family, Private Property and the State*, cited in Marx and Engels, *Selected Works*, New York, 1968, pp. 493-499, and to Henry Adams's pessimistic and cyclical vision of family development, "The Primitive Rights of Women," in *The Great Secession Winter of 1860-1861 and Other Essays*, New York, 1963, pp. 351-357, 359-360. Because Engels makes no distinction between the various economic functions of the housecommunity, he sees the "dissolution" as economic unit only within the fully egalitarian socialization of the labor of both men and women, pp. 510-511.
51. Translated by the author from *WG*, p. 209.
52. Ibid., p. 211.
53. Ibid., p. 29.
54. Ibid., p. 177. Even though I am uncomfortable with the term "acquisition classes" for Weber's "Erwerbsklassen," I have used this translation by A. M. Henderson and Talcott Parsons, *Max Weber: The Theory of Social and Economic Organization*, New York, 1947, p. 424, rather than "professional classes," which is the translation used by Wolfgang Mommsen, *The Age of Bureaucracy: Perspectives on the Political Sociology of Max Weber*, New York, 1977, p. 60. Mommsen's exposition illuminates the apparent ambiguities of Weber's use of the term very well, see pp. 60-62.
55. Mommsen, *Age of Bureaucracy*, pp. 60-61.
56. Otto Brunner, "Die Freiheitsrechte in der altständischen Gesellschaft," in his *Neue Wege der Verfassungs- und Sozialgeschichte*,

2nd ed., Göttingen, 1968, p. 193; Georg Grüll, "Die Leute im Walde,"
OÖH 1 (1947):209.
57. Grüll, "Leute im Walde," pp. 209-210.
58. Hoffmann, *Wirtschaftsgeschichte*, p. 247.
59. Ibid., pp. 248-249.
60. Ibid., p. 289.
61. Franz Innerhofer's autobiographical novel *Schöne Tage*, translated by Anselm Hollo and published under the title *Beautiful Days*, New York, 1976, gives a graphic account of the life of the "outsider," the "role child," in a modern postwar Austrian peasant house.
62. Schremmer, "Agrarverfassung," pp. 47-51; idem, *Die Wirtschaft Bayerns*, Munich, 1970, pp. 349-358.
63. Grüll, *Bauer*, pp. 227-228.
64. Ibid., pp. 131-140.
65. Ibid., p. 134.
66. Laurenz Pröll, *Das Obermühlviertler Bauernhaus*, Linz-Urfar, 1902, p. 88.
67. Otto Brunner, "Das 'ganze Haus' und die alteuropäische 'Ökonomik' " and "Die Freiheitsrechte in der altständischen Gesellschaft" in his *Neue Wege der Verfassungs- und Sozialgeschichte*, Göttingen, 1968, pp. 108-109, 193.
68. Brunner, "Haus," p. 108.
69. Nösslböck, *Weistümer*, 12:604-605.
70. Georg Grüll, "Der Hauptmannbrief von Ohnersdorf," OÖH 8 (1954), describes and lists the articles of one such code.
71. Ibid., p. 226; the Ohnersdorf *Hauptmannbrief* was dated 1662 but claimed to have been unchanged from a 1583 version; it threatened any chief who attempted to change it with a fine of five Hungarian ducats. It too was clearly enforced by the new bureaucratic authority of state and estate.
72. For a recent study in English of the *Carolina*, its significance for the legal development of the German Empire, and its place in the legal development of Western Europe generally, see John H. Langbein, *Prosecuting Crime in the Renaissance*, Cambridge, Mass., 1974. The penetration of state regulations into estate codes after the early sixteenth century is investigated in Helmuth Feigl's important study *Rechtsentwicklung und Gerichtswesen Oberösterreichs im Spiegel der Weistümer*, Vienna, 1974, see pp. 132-137.
73. There was a project underway around 1600 for a separate Upper Austrian provincial code (*Landtafel*) that was especially supported by the rebellious high nobility led by Tschernembl, but it never succeeded

in receiving royal validation. Hans Sturmberger, *Georg Erasmus Tschernembl*, Graz, 1953, pp. 248-251. For details of the 1559 regulation see Feigl, *Rechtsentwicklung*, pp. 46-57.

74. Helmuth Stahleder, "Weistümer and Verwandte Quellen in Franken, Bayern und Österreich," *ZbL* 2 (1969), has dealt with this question in a critical and comparative framework; see especially pp. 877-879, 884-885. Stahleder's work has encountered sharp but unacceptable criticism from Hannah Rabe, *Das Problem Leibeigenschaft*, Wiesbaden, 1977, pp. 79-80, and Feigl, *Rechtsentwicklung*, p. 78, n. 22.

75. Werner Stark, *Ursprung und Aufstieg des Landwirtschaftlichen Grossbetriebs in den böhmischen Ländern*, Prague, 1934, pp. 11-12.

76. Nösslböck, *Weistümer*, 14:290-298; Georg Grüll, "Geschichte des Schlosses und der Herrschaft Windhag bei Perg," *JOÖMV* 87 (1937):207-208, describes a Taiding meeting. See also Feigl, *Rechtsentwicklung*, pp. 66-107.

77. Nösslböck, *Weistümer*, 12:97-104.

78. Ibid., pp. 591-644.

79. Ibid., 14:290-298.

80. Ibid., 12:280, 601; 14:290, 296.

81. Ibid., 12:607, 616, 625, 632.

82. See, for example, Barrington Moore, Jr., *The Social Origins of Dictatorship and Democracy*, New York, 1967, pp. 465-466.

83. Both Blickle and Sabean come to these conclusions, although from different perspectives and with differing implications. For an unnecessarily contentious critique of Sabean, see Rabe, *Das Problem Leibeigenschaft*, p. 54, n. 112.

84. Feigl, *Rechtsentwicklung*, pp. 46-52; for the larger background to Ferdinand I's reforms see Friedrich Walter, *Österreichische Verfassungs- und Verwaltungsgeschichte von 1500-1955*, Vienna, 1972; also Zauner, *Vöcklabruck*, pp. 162-173.

85. Perry Anderson, *Lineages of the Absolute State*, London, 1974, pp. 25-26.

86. Cf. David Sabean, "Family and Land Tenure," *PSN* 3 (1974).

87. Dieter Schwab, "Eigentum," in *Geschichtliche Grundbegriffe*, ed. Otto Brunner et al., 2 vols., Stuttgart, 1975, 2:69-72.

88. Anderson, *Lineages*.

89. Rabe, *Das Problem Leibeigenschaft*, pp. 56-59, 101-102.

90. Nösslböck, *Weistümer*, 14:305, 310; Zauner, *Vöcklabruck*, p. 486.

91. Schremmer, "Agrarverfassung."

92. Zauner, *Vöcklabruck*, pp. 512-520.

93. For a different evolution of multiple ownership, see R. S. Neale's suggestive description of English developments, "The Bourgeoisie, Historically, Has Played a Most Revolutionary Part," in *Feudalism, Capitalism and Beyond*, ed. Eugene Kamenka and R. S. Neale, New York, 1976, pp. 96-97. Here both the individual and the crown are pushed out of property relations with dynastic and familial considerations gaining ground through the expanding role of the "trust." In Austria, kin, mortgage-holders, and fictive kin also gain considerable ground but do so, as the text demonstrates, under the aegis of estate and crown.

94. Nösslböck, *Weistümer*, Vol. 14.

95. Zauner, *Vöcklabruck*, p. 418.

96. Schwab, "Eigentum," pp. 69-72; Henry Campbell Black, *A Law Dictionary*, 2nd ed., St. Paul, 1910, p. 421.

97. For example, F. Lütge, *Deutsche Sozial- und Wirtschaftsgeschichte*, Berlin, 1966, p. 127.

98. Nösslböck, *Weistümer*, 14:290; Zauner, *Vöcklabruck*, p. 409.

99. Zauner, *Vöcklabruck*, p. 409; Nösslböck, *Weistümer*, 14:291.

100. Zauner, *Vöcklabruck*, p. 167.

101. Nösslböck, *Weistümer*, 12:625-626.

102. Ibid., 12:629; 14:294.

103. Zauner, *Vöcklabruck*, pp. 507-512.

104. Rabe, *Das Problem Leibeigenschaft*, p. 79, passim.

105. Grüll, *Bauer*, p. 73.

106. Nösslböck, *Weistümer*, 14:304; attempts were made to centralize the issuing and filing of private contracts at the provincial level but this proved unworkable and these functions were returned to the estate managers in 1569. Zauner, *Vöcklabruck*, p. 442.

107. For a discussion of this terminology and these relationships see David Sabean, "Aspects of Kinship Behavior," in *Family and Inheritance*, ed. Goody, pp. 108-110.

108. This was the practice as revealed by the contracts attached to the inventories. See e.g., OÖLA, Schlägl *Inventurprotokolle*, Vol. 434; or Frankenburg *Inventurprotokolle*, Vols. 253, 261, 265.

109. OÖLA, Frankenburg *Inventurprotokolle*, Vol. 262; see also David Sabean, *Landbesitz und Gesellschaft*, Stuttgart, 1972, p. 40.

110. Cf., Sabean, "Kinship Behavior," pp. 110-111 and idem, "German Agrarian Institutions," pp. 82-83; Cole and Wolf, *Frontier*, pp. 242-243.

111. Cited in Rabe, *Das Problem Leibeigenschaft*, p. 46; see also p. 54.

112. OÖLA, Weinberg Archive, Vol. 1063, file B/73.
113. Ibid., Vol. 150, file A/1/b.
114. Ibid., Vol. 950, file B/35.
115. Ibid., Vol. 1061, file B/70; Vol. 148, file A/5⅚.
116. Henry E. Strakosch, *State Absolutism and the Rule of Law*, Sydney, 1967.
117. I am using private and public law according to the distinctions established by Max Weber, *WG*, p. 675. The latter governs relationships between authorities and between authorities and subjects while the former governs only relationships among the ruled.
118. Strakosch, *State Absolutism*, pp. 75-76, 213.
119. Hans Rosenberg, *Bureaucracy, Aristocracy, and Autocracy*, Boston, 1966, pp. 50-52; Langbein, *Prosecuting Crime*, passim.
120. Rosenberg, *Bureaucracy, Aristocracy, and Autocracy*, p. 47.
121. Otto Büsch, *Militärsystem und Sozialleben im alten Preussen, 1713-1807*, Berlin, 1962.
122. Otto Brunner, *Land und Herrschaft*, Darmstadt, 1965, pp. 106-110.
123. Strakosch, *State Absolutism*, passim.
124. Anderson, *Lineages*, p. 195.
125. Sturmberger, "Ständestaat," pp. 38-40.
126. Weber, *WG*, p. 650.
127. Lütge, *Wirtschaftsgeschichte*, pp. 126-127.
128. Brunner, "Haus"; Lutz Berkner, "The Stem Family," *AHR* 77 (1972):411-412.
129. Cf. Chie Nakane, *Japanese Society*, Berkeley, 1972, pp. 4-7.

CHAPTER 6: FAMILY ROLES

1. Lutz Berkner, "The Stem Family," *AHR* 77 (1972):405.
2. Ibid., pp. 400-401.
3. Other common Austrian synonyms for *Auszügler* are *Austräger, Ausdingler, Nahrungsmann (-frau)*. See Georg Grüll, *Bauer, Herr und Landesfürst*, Graz, 1963, pp. 92-93, and Michael Mitterauer, "Familiengrösse—Familientypen—Familienzyklus," *Geschichte und Gesellschaft* 1 (1975):233-234.
4. *Langenscheidt's New Muret-Sanders Encyclopedic Dictionary of the English and German Languages*, Berlin, 1974, Part II, 1:69. The Austrian *Auszug* and *Auszügler* are discussed as a part of the more common German term *Altenteiler*. See also *Wörterbuch der deutschen Gegenwartssprache*, 2 vols., Berlin, 1961, 1:114.

5. For a discussion by one participant in this debate see A. von Miaskowski's article, "Altenteil, Altenteilsverträge," in *Handwörterbuch der Staatwissenschaften*, Jena, 1898, 1: especially pp. 272-275; for the continuation of the debate in the 1920s see W. Wygodzinski's revision of the original article in the 1923 edition of the *Handwörterbuch*, 1:252-257; see Donald Rohr, *The Origins of Social Liberalism in Germany*, Chicago, 1963, pp. 110-111 for the earlier nineteenth century. Also, Hans Rosenberg, *Grosse Depression und Bismarckzeit*, Berlin, 1967, chap. 6.

6. Berkner, "Stem Family," pp. 401-405, cites Peter Rosegger's *Volksleben in Steiermark*, Leipzig, 1914, and Heinrich Rauscher's "Volkskunde des Waldviertels," in *Das Waldviertel*, ed. Eduard Stepan, Vienna, 1926. For Upper Austria there is a similar source in Laurenz Pröll's *Das Obermühlviertler Bauernhaus*, Linz-Urfar, 1902, pp. 11-12, that takes a, for the time, socially conservative line and idealizes *Auszug* as an idyllic form of retirement.

7. Edward Shorter, *The Making of the Modern Family*, New York, 1975, pp. 31-39.

8. F. Stieve, ed., "Bericht eines bairischen Adlichen über die Bauerschaft in Österreich ob der Enns [1641], Februar 14," *Mitteilungen des Instituts für österreichische Geschichte* 5 (1884):626.

9. Paul Demeny, "Early Fertility Decline in Austria-Hungary: A Lesson in Demographic Transition," *Daedalus* 97 (1968):511, 514.

10. Jan de Vries, *The Economy of Europe in an Age of Crisis*, Cambridge, 1976, pp. 9-12.

11. Michael Mitterauer, "Zur Familienstruktur in ländlichen Gebieten Österreichs," in *Beiträge zur Bevölkerungs- und Sozialgeschichte Österreichs*, ed. H. Helczmanowski, Munich, 1973, pp. 197, 200. By contrast, Berkner has found that in the eighteenth century there were some married children living in their parents' household and that the age of first marriage had declined, with some notable exceptions, to about twenty-five. "Stem Family," p. 405. Also, see the well-known article by H. J. Hajnal, "European Marriage Patterns in Perspective," in *Population in History*, ed. D. V. Glass and D.E.C. Eversley, London, 1965.

12. Austrian peasants sought relief from sexual restraints in "clandestine" marriages or in premarital sex after an exchange of vows and the proclamation of the banns. See Albin Czerny, *Aus dem geistlichen Geschäftsleben in Oberösterreich im 15. Jahrhundert*, Linz, 1882, pp. 28-32.

13. Mitterauer, "Familienstruktur," p. 200.

14. Ibid., p. 199; Berkner, "Stem Family," p. 408.

15. Werner Stark, "Die Abhängigkeitsverhältnisse der gutsherrlichen Bauern Böhmens," *Jahrbücher für Nationalökonomie und Statistik* 164 (1952).

16. Mitterauer, "Familienstruktur," pp. 187, 197-200.

17. OÖLA, Frankenburg *Inventurprotokolle*, Vols. 249, 261. The amounts shown in the second inventory add up to only 414fl but the total is given as 445fl. This is a not uncommon occurrence in the inventories and it does not mean that the estate's agent could not add. It usually means that a loan or a piece of property owned by the deceased was kept out of the official record but its value included in the final accounting. In all cases I have used the data found in the inventory and have not altered them.

18. Mitterauer, "Familienstruktur," pp. 198-199.

19. On the maternal uncle-nephew relationship in traditional German society see David Sabean, "Aspects of Kinship Behavior," in *Family and Inheritance*, ed. Jack Goody et al., Cambridge, 1976, p. 100.

20. OÖLA, Garsten Archive, *Ver kaufsprotokolle*, Vols. 22-25, 1602-1648.

21. Jack Goody, "Strategies of Heirship," *Comparative Studies in Society and History* 15 (1973).

22. OÖLA, Frankenburg *Inventurprotokolle*, Vol. 262.

23. Michael Mitterauer, "Arbeitsorganisation und Altersversorgung nach dem Mittelalter," *Beiträge zur historischen Sozialkunde* 5 (1975): 6.

24. We may cite the maintenance of the Balinese "houseyard" and the necessary strategy of heirship and the primacy of role over kin relations which that maintenance requires as a significant comparison to the Austrian case. It is, however, important to point out that the political and cultural settings are vastly different and that the effects of the two kinds of "role" families on individual and communal life are therefore also considerably different. Clifford Geertz and Hilda Geertz, *Kinship in Bali*, Chicago, 1975, especially pp. 53-54.

25. See the discussion in chapter two above; also, Christopher Lasch, *Haven in a Heartless World: The Family Besieged*, New York, 1979, pp. 31-33.

26. Karl Marx, *The Grundrisse*, ed. and trans. David McClellan, New York, 1972, p. 73.

27. See Wolf's review of T. Shanin's *The Awkward Class* in *Journal of Peasant Studies* 1 (1974).

28. Mitterauer, "Familiengrösse," pp. 244-246, 251-254.

29. Shorter, *Modern Family*; Grüll, *Bauer*, pp. 208-209.

30. All the sales data in this chapter were found in OÖLA, Garsten Archive, *Ver kaufsprotokolle*, Vols. 22-25.

31. Hans Medick, "The Proto-Industrial Family Economy," *Social History* 3 (1976).

32. Grüll, *Bauer*, p. 99.

33. My sixteenth-century examples are from Grüll, *Bauer*, pp. 92-93 and the seventeenth-century ones from OÖLA, Frankenburg *Inventurprotokolle*, Vol. 265.

34. Max Kislinger, *Alte Bäuerliche Kunst*, Linz, 1963, pp. 14-17.

35. OÖLA, Frankenburg *Inventurprotokolle*, Vol. 262.

36. Mitterauer, "Familiengrösse," pp. 254-255.

37. Grüll, *Bauer*, pp. 208-209, passim.

38. Marx, *Grundrisse*.

39. Grüll, *Bauer*, pp. 194-195.

40. The 1597 Interim, cited ibid., p. 243.

41. Mitterauer, "Familienstruktur," p. 205; idem, "Auswirkung von Urbanisierung und Frühindustrialisierung," in *Sozialgeschichte der Familie in der Neuzeit Europas*, ed. Werner Conze, Stuttgart, 1976, pp. 85-89, 95, 101-103; Berkner, "Stem Family."

42. Henry E. Strakosch, *State Absolutism and the Rule of Law*, Sydney, 1967.

43. Berkner, "Stem Family," p. 413.

44. Ibid., p. 414; Mitterauer, "Auswirkung."

45. Berkner, "Stem Family," p. 411.

46. Ibid.; on p. 418 Berkner leaves those who do not inherit out of his discussion of the cycles experienced by individuals and families.

47. Ibid., pp. 413-414; Mitterauer, "Familienstruktur," pp. 194, 205.

48. Mitterauer, "Familienstruktur," pp. 193-196.

49. Mitterauer, "Auswirkung," p. 106.

50. David Sabean, *Landbesitz und Gesellschaft*, Stuttgart, 1972, p. 101; also, idem, "Family and Land Tenure," *PSN* 3 (1974); Lutz Berkner, "Recent Research on the History of the Family in Western Europe," *Journal of Marriage and the Family* 35 (1973):401.

CHAPTER 7: SOCIAL MOBILITY AND CONFLICT

1. Cf., for example, National Opinion Research Center, "Jobs and Occupations: A Popular Evaluation," in *Class, Status and Power*, ed.

Reinhard Bendix and Seymour Lipset, Glencoe, Ill., 1953, pp. 411-426, or Bendix and Lipset, *Social Mobility in Industrial Society*, Berkeley, 1964, pp. 13-17; an interesting recent methodological contribution is William H. Hubbard and Konrad Jarausch, "Occupation and Social Structure in Modern Central Europe: Some Reflections on Coding Professions," *Quantum Information* 11 (July 1979).

2. OÖLA, Weinberg Archive, Vol. 950, file B/35; Ottensheim Archive, *Briefprotokolle*, Vol. 072a.

3. OÖLA, Weinberg Archive, Vol. 820.

4. OÖLA, Schlägl *Inventurprotokolle*, Vol. 434.

5. Ibid. (1614, 1615).

6. Ibid. (1611).

7. Ibid. (1613), contains an inventory of a deceased female servant in which a lodger appears as employer owing her 15fl in wages; see also, ibid. (1616, 1619), and Frankenburg *Inventurprotokolle*, Vol. 256 (1616).

8. In one such case a "Ladtsknecht" and lodger counted among his possessions 100fl worth of wine. OÖLA, Schlägl *Inventurprotokolle*, Vol. 434 (1610).

9. There were several such lodgers in the Mühlviertel around the monastery Schlägl. Ibid. (1611, 1614, 1616); see also OÖLA, Schaunberg *Inventurprotokolle*, Vol. 279 (1619, 1623, 1624, 1625, 1627).

10. OÖLA, Schlägl *Inventurprotokolle*, Vol. 434 (1616).

11. Ibid., Vol. 435 (1621); OÖLA, Schaunberg *Inventurprotokolle*, Vol. 279 (1627).

12. Alois Zauner, *Vöcklabruck und der Attergau*, Vienna, 1971, p. 454; Georg Grüll, *Bauer, Herr und Landesfürst*, Graz, 1963, pp. 166-167.

13. Hermann Kellenbenz, "Rural Industries in the West," in *Essays in European Economic History*, ed. Peter Earle, Oxford, 1965, p. 77.

14. Laurenz Pröll, *Das Obermühlviertler Bauernhaus*, Linz-Urfar, 1902, p. 38; Zauner, *Vöcklabruck*, pp. 150-151.

15. OÖLA, Weinberg Archive, Vol. 368, file B/1/a, 1628; Vol. 369, file B/1/b; and Vol. 1033, file B/57.

16. Ignatz Nösslböck et al., eds., *Weistümer*, Graz, 1960, 12:4, 9-12, 98-99, 154, 294, 296; 14:314-317.

17. Ibid., 12:642.

18. Ibid., pp. 623-624, 617-618.

19. Ibid., p. 638. "Es soll ain ieder underthann woo der weg mit schnee verwäht ausscharren und mit vleisz machen, damit die furleut nit ursach haben zu schaden zu faren. . . . . Fuer aber ein fuermann

über solliches in das traid zu schaden, ist er [i.e., the householder who did not clear the road] zu wandl verfallen."

20. Ibid., 12:289; 14:311.

21. Ibid., 12:615.

22. Ibid., 14:292.

23. Ibid., 12:635.

24. Regulations of such sales differed widely in specific terms and this particularly with regard to the burghers of rural market towns who often, with some notable exceptions, could all hold the privilege of serving wine and beer. Ibid., 12:49; 14:311.

25. As the first part of chapter two shows, the size of the rural Austrian family in this period was small and this suggests that the rate of downward mobility was, despite its persistence and pervasiveness, relatively slow, compounding significant social effects only over periods of decades and even centuries. The fact that the dispossessed did not band together for political action until the 1630s, a full century after the state's initiation of those processes of impartible and bureaucratized tenure that produced dispossession, seems to confirm this. The precise "rate" of downward mobility remains an open question. Rates differed according to regional variations in family size. The rates of in- and out-migration and the downward mobility of formerly tenured individuals (which, as chapter eight will show, fluctuated and increased in cyclical fashion) also have to be taken into account.

26. A. Marks, "Das Leinengewerbe und der Leinenhandel im Lande ob der Enns von den Anfängen bis in die Zeit Maria Theresias," JOÖMV 95 (1950). Alfred Hoffmann, Wirtschaftsgeschichte des Landes Oberösterreich, Vol. 1, Salzburg, 1952, pp. 103-109; idem, "Die Hütten und Stände am Linzer Bartholomäimarkt des Jahres 1583," JSL (1953).

27. OÖLA, Schlägl Inventurprotokolle, Vol. 435 (1621).

28. Ibid. (1631).

29. OÖLA, Frankenburg Inventurprotokolle, Vol. 265 (1632).

30. Ibid., Vol. 264 (1631).

31. Ibid., Vol. 268 (1636).

32. Ibid., Vol. 254 (1614).

33. Ibid., Vol. 266 (1634).

34. Credit for goods on consignment was what M. M. Postan called "sale credits." See his valuable article, "Credit in Medieval Trade," in Essays in Economic History, ed. E. M. Carus-Wilson, 3 vols., London, 1954, 1:65-71. The classic and, for a long time the only, work on English rural credit in the early modern period was R. H. Tawney's "Introduction" to Thomas Wilson's Discourse on Usury, New York,

1925. Now there is also the excellent brief analysis by R. B. Holderness, "Credit in English Rural Society before the Nineteenth Century," *Agricultural History Review* 24 (1976).

35. Holderness, "Credit," p. 101.

36. OÖLA, Frankenburg *Inventurprotokolle*, Vol. 268 (1636).

37. Holderness, "Credit," p. 102, shows that in early modern England "widows and single people" had, collectively, 45 percent of their assets in outstanding loans while farmers had 10 percent.

38. The Pearson correlation coefficients measuring the relationship between total wealth and loans are .66 for the Upper Austrian peasantry as a whole and .8 for the other specialized group of moneylenders, the innkeepers.

39. Marcel Mauss, *The Gift: Forms and Functions of Exchange in Archaic Societies*, Glencoe, Ill., 1954; Karl Polanyi, *Primitive, Archaic, and Modern Economics*, ed. George Dalton, Garden City, N.Y., 1971; A. V. Chayanov, *The Theory of Peasant Economy*, ed. Daniel Thorner et al., Homewood, Ill., 1966; May Diaz, "Introduction: Economic Relations in Peasant Society," Sydney Mintz, "Pratik: Haitian Personal Economic Relationships," Eric Wolf and Sydney Mintz, "An Analysis of Ritual Co-Parenthood (Compadrazgo)," and George Foster, "The Dyadic Contract: A Model for the Social Structure of a Mexican Peasant Village," all in *Peasant Society*, ed. Jack Potter et al., Boston, 1967; also, George Dalton, ed., *Tribal and Peasant Economics*, Garden City, N.Y., 1967; Clifford Geertz, "The Rotating Credit Association: A 'Middle Rung' in Development," *Economic Development and Culture Change* 10 (1962).

40. OÖLA, Weinberg Archive, Vol. 1063, file B/73.

41. Ibid.

42. Ibid.

43. Alan Macfarlane, *The Origins of English Individualism*, Oxford, 1978, p. 69.

44. For conflicting views concerning the appropriate uses of such terms as "role-set" for a critical social analysis compare Albert Szymansky, "Toward a Radical Sociology," with Allen H. Barton, "Empirical Methods and Radical Sociology: A Liberal Critique," both in *Radical Sociology*, ed. J. David Colfax and Jack L. Roach, New York, 1971, pp. 96, 460-462.

45. Tamara K. Hareven, "Family Time and Historical Time," in *The Family*, ed. Alice S. Rossi et al., New York, 1978.

46. Mitterauer, "Auswirkung," pp. 136-137.

47. Dahrendorf, "Homo Sociologicus," in his *Essays in the Theory*

of Society, Stanford, 1968, p. 32; Hans-Peter Dreitzel, *Die gesell-schaftlichen Leiden*, Stuttgart, 1968, pp. 116, 124.

48. Clifford Geertz, "The Growth of Culture and the Evolution of Mind," in his *The Interpretation of Cultures*, New York, 1973, p. 83; in this connection, see also the discussion of biosocial factors by Alice S. Rossi, "A Biosocial Perspective on Parenting," in *The Family*, ed. Rossi et al.

49. This seems to be a little understood aspect of role analysis even in the more radical American sociological literature. Richard Sennett, for example, claims to be concerned with experience of roles as a moral problem but does not, in fact, go beyond the theatrical and, hence, "presentational" aspects of roles. See his introductory remarks on "Roles" in *The Psychology of Society*, ed. Sennett, New York, 1977, p. 92.

50. Dreitzel, *Die gesellschaftlichen Leiden*.

51. Robert K. Merton and Elinor Barber, "Sociological Ambivalence," in *Sociological Theory, Values and Sociocultural Change: Essays in Honor of Pitrim A. Sorokin*, ed. Edward Tiryakian, New York, 1967; the concepts presented in this article were later developed further in Merton's volume *Sociological Ambivalence*, New York, 1976.

52. Chalmers Johnson, *Revolutionary Change*, Boston, 1966, pp. 32-33.

53. Dahrendorf, "Homo," pp. 38-39.

54. Merton and Barber, "Sociological Ambivalence," p. 104.

55. For a classic sociological experiment that sets an extreme example in this direction see Robert F. Bales, "Status, Role and Interaction" in *Readings in Modern Sociology*, ed. Alex Inkeles, Englewood Cliffs, N.J., 1966; see also Merton and Barber, "Sociological Ambivalence," pp. 114-115, and Johnson, *Revolutionary Change*, p. 34; for a critical examination of the general trend in American social science that focuses on adjusting the individual rather than the institutional or social circumstances see Lasch, *Haven*, p. 83.

56. Merton and Barber, "Sociological Ambivalence," pp. 104-105; see also Lewis Coser, *The Functions of Social Conflict*, New York, 1964, p. 72.

57. Merton and Barber, "Sociological Ambivalence," p. 105.

58. Ibid., pp. 108-109.

59. Ibid., p. 92.

60. Ibid., p. 109.

61. Erving Goffman, "Role Distance," in *Psychology of Society*, ed. Sennett, p. 108.

62. Ibid., p. 109.
63. Ibid.
64. Cited in Dahrendorf, "Homo," p. 72.
65. Peter Berger, *The Homeless Mind*, New York, 1974, p. 114.
66. Merton and Barber, "Sociological Ambivalence," p. 104.
67. Dreitzel, *Die gesellschaftlichen Leiden*, p. 1.
68. Michael Mitterauer, "Zur Familienstruktur in ländlichen Gebieten Österreichs," in *Beiträge zur Bevölkerungs- und Sozialgeschichte Österreichs*, ed. H. Helczmanovski, Munich, 1973, p. 196; idem, "Auswirkung," p. 103.
69. Lutz Berkner, "The Stem Family," *AHR* 77 (1972):44; Hoffmann, *Wirtschaftsgeschichte*, pp. 249, 494.
70. Grüll, *Bauer*, p. 243.
71. Mitterauer, "Auswirkung," pp. 103-115; idem, "Familienstruktur," p. 204.
72. Peter Blickle, "Bauer und Staat," *Zeitschrift für Württembergische Landesgeschichte* 31 (1973):119.

CHAPTER 8: IMPACT OF COUNTER-REFORMATION STATE

1. Alan Bullock, *Is History Becoming A Social Science?*, Cambridge, 1976.
2. Reinhard Koselleck, "Ereignis und Struktur," in *Geschichte—Ereignis und Erzählung*, ed. Reinhard Koselleck and Wolf-Dieter Stempel, Munich, 1973, p. 565.
3. Ibid., pp. 565-566.
4. Cited in J. V. Polisensky, *War and Society in Europe, 1618-1648*, Cambridge, 1978, p. 60.
5. H. G. Koenigsberger, *The Habsburgs in Europe, 1516-1660*, Ithaca, 1971, p. 225.
6. See the recent collection of articles edited by Karl Bosl and Karl Möckl, *Der Moderne Parlamentarismus und seine Grundlagen in der ständischen Repräsentation*, Berlin, 1977.
7. Polisensky, *War and Society*, p. 57.
8. Wendelin Hujber, "Der Prälatenstand des Landes ob der Enns, 1600-1620," Ph.D. diss., University of Vienna, 1972, pp. 363-384.
9. Hans Sturmberger, "Dualistischer Ständestaat," in *Die Entwicklung der Verfassung Österreichs*, ed. Institut für Österreichkunde, Vienna, 1970, pp. 38-40.
10. Herta Eberstaller, "Zur Finanzpolitik der oberösterreichischen Stände im Jahre 1608," and Hans Sturmberger, "Melchior Haimhofer's

'Christliches Wesen.' Ein Finanzprojeckt aus dem Jahr 1620 für die oberösterreichischen Stände," both in *MOÖLA* (1964).

11. Hans Sturmberger, *Georg Erasmus Tschernembl*, Graz, 1953, p. 354.

12. *Consultationes Oder Underschidliche Rathschläg Der maisten und wichtigsten sachen welche von Anfäng der Böhemischen und andern folgenden Auffständ fürgangen und zu Werck gericht worden oder werden sollen*, 1624, pp. 329, 332. On Tschernembl's authorship of this privately edited and published manuscript, see Sturmberger, *Tschernembl*, pp. 336-340.

13. Walter Goetz, ed., *Briefe und Akten zur Geschichte des 30. jährigen Krieges*, 3 vols., Leipzig, 1907, Part II, 3:209, 246-247.

14. Polisensky, *War and Society*, pp. 199-206; for Professor Snider's work see his "The Restructuring of the Bohemian Nobility, 1610-1656," Ph.D. dissertation, University of California at Berkeley, 1972.

15. Hans Sturmberger, *Kaiser Ferdinand II und das Problem des Absolutismus*, Munich, 1957, pp. 10-13, 44-45.

16. Wurm, *Die Jörger von Tollet*, Graz, 1955, pp. 172-173; Alois Zauner, *Vöcklabruck und der Attergau*, Vienna, 1971, pp. 242-243.

17. Anton Ernstberger, ed., *Ludwig Camerarius und Lukas Friedrich Behaim, Ein politischer Briefwechsel über den Verfall des Reiches, 1636-1648*, Munich, 1961.

18. This document is reproduced as no. 48, "Ferdinand II und Maximilian I. Übereinkunft hinsichtlich der Kriegskosten," in *Briefe und Akten*, ed. Goetz, Part II, 1:137-144. Maximilian did make money in Upper Austria. The account book of the League has a single entry for incomes from Upper Austria for the entire period between 1619 and 1627 and it reads 1,001,807fl. Compared to the 6,000,000fl that were supposed to come from Upper Austria or to the 20,000,000fl that came out of Maximilian's treasury, this is a small sum, but it does compare favorably with the 877,021fl collected from the Electorate of Mainz or with the 1,287,039fl donated by the Papacy. F. Stieve, "Das 'Contobuch' der deutschen Liga," *Deutsche Zeitschrift für Geschichtswissenschaft* 10 (1893).

19. Goetz, ed., *Briefe und Akten*, Part II, Vols. 1-3; see especially the correspondence between Maximilian and Dr. Leuker.

20. Protestant spies reported that Herbersdorf was not only disliked among the League's military leaders but that of all of these, it was Herbersdorf who crowed the loudest about acquiring properties and wealth in the defeated territories. "... sie mit bistumbern und andern ansehnliche güttern zue begeben, wie dan auch irer vil, sonderlich aber

der obangedeute abgefalne Herbersdorfer solches offentlich ganz un-
gescheucht reden, alle evangelische potentaten ganz schimpflich ver-
achten und sonsten also braviren sollen, als ob sie albereit ein gewunen
spiel in handen." Goetz, ed., *Briefe und Akten*, Part II, 1:90. For an
exhaustive biographical treatment of Herbersdorf's career see Hans
Sturmberger, *Adam Graf Herbersdorf: Herrschaft und Freiheit in Konfessionellen Zeitalter*, Munich, 1976.

21. Concerning the separation of the monetary from the commodity
price inflation, see Hermann Rebel, "Probleme der oberösterreichischen Sozialgeschichte zur Zeit der Bayerischen Pfandherrschaft,
1620-1628," *JOÖMV*, 115 (1970).

22. OÖLA, Wagrain Archive, Vol. 18, file QI.

23. Ibid., Adam von Herbersdorf, "Müntz und Fürkauf Patent," 9
March 1622.

24. Ibid., Adam von Herbersdorf, "Höchste Preise," 12 December
1622.

25. OÖLA, *Annales*, Vol. 77, fol. 560. *Beschwerdeschrift*, 1 June
1623, signed by representatives of all four Estates, including Gundacker
von Polheim.

26. A. Gindeley, "Die Gegenreformation und der Aufstand in Oberösterreich im Jahre 1626," *Akademie der Wissenschaften, Sitzungsberichte der Phil.- Hist. Klasse*, Abhandlungen, VI, Vol. 118, Vienna,
1889, p. 50.

27. OÖLA, *Annales*, Vols. 77, 78.

28. Calculated from the information in Georg Grüll, *Bauer, Herr
und Landesfürst*, Graz, 1963, p. 232.

29. Felix Stieve, *Der Oberösterreichishe Bauernaufstand des Jahres
1626*, 2 vols., Linz, 1904, 1:60-64; Julius Strnadt, *Der Bauernkrieg in
Oberösterreich im Jahre 1626*, Wels, 1924, pp. 42-46.

30. Sturmberger, *Herbersdorf*, pp. 242-246.

31. Stieve, *Bauernaufstand*, 1: 38-39; Strnadt, *Bauernkrieg*, pp. 46-
49.

32. The Estates' great school at Linz had already lost its endowment,
on 15 July 1625, to the Jesuits for the construction of a school and
seminary of their own. Stieve, *Bauernaufstand*, p. 37, n. 3.

33. Such *Beichtzettel* or *Absolutionsscheine*, as these documents
were called, were introduced in 1598, after the pacification of the peasant uprising. Strnadt, *Bauernkrieg*, pp. 47-48. A three-time offender
against the forced attendance at confession could lose his farm as early
as 1598 but this was not enforced until after 1625. Albin Czerny, *Der*

zweite Bauernaufstand in Oberösterreich, 1595-1597, Linz, 1890, p. 6.

34. Stieve, *Bauernaufstand*, 2:252, 263-264.

35. There were some emigrés who did very well in their new homes but they were exceptions and were among the wealthiest of the emigrants. See Walker Lehnert, *Die Oberösterreichischen Exulanten*, Neustadt/Aich, 1962, and Gilbert Trathnigg, "Wels und Regensburg," *Jahrbuch des Musealvereins Wels* (1957).

36. Grünpacher eventually fled into Bavaria. The relatives he left behind were punished by the rebellious peasants with loss of property; Stieve, *Bauernaufstand*, 1:92.

37. Hantsch, *Die Geschichte Österreichs*, Graz, 1968, Vol. 1, p. 320.

38. Wolf Helmhard von Hohberg, *Georgica Curiosa*, 5th ed., Nuremberg, 1715, p. 13.

39. The information that follows is based chiefly on Hans Fattinger, "Stefan Fadinger und Christoph Zeller. Ihre Familie und Ihre Heimat," *OÖH* 19 (1965): 49-60; idem, "Unsere Bäuerlichen Vorfahren," undated typescript, OÖLA, Linz; Stieve, *Bauernaufstand*; Strnadt, *Bauernkrieg*.

40. Fattinger, "Fadinger," pp. 49-52.

41. It was destroyed immediately after the suppression of the uprising and Fadinger's wife and children were expelled from Upper Austria. They went to Regensburg. Stieve, *Bauernaufstand*, 1:73, n. 3, 315, n. 2.

42. Fattinger, "Vorfahren," pp. 72-74.

43. This inventory was taken by the Bavarian lien administration's *Viztum* Pfliegl. Stieve, *Bauernaufstand*, 1:74, n. 12.

44. Stieve, *Bauernaufstand*, 1:73, n. 6.

45. Fattinger, "Vorfahren," p. 72.

46. Strnadt, *Bauernkrieg*, p. 149, n. 88, remarks that the *Protokolle* for the estate Stauf for the year 1625 have disappeared. Another document, Fadinger's patent to the peasants of the Mühlviertel that is listed in the catalog of the Upper Austrian *Landesarchiv* under *Landschaftsakten*, G.24.2.204 is also missing.

47. Stieve, *Bauernaufstand*, 1:113, n. 6; see also p. 113, n. 7.

48. Grüll, *Bauer*, pl. 6, shows a selection of such seals as they appeared on enabling letters from members of parish guild organizations to their representatives in the negotiations of 1595-1597.

49. In the course of the war, the Steyr advocate Madlseder also claimed to have held Fadinger's *Petschaft*. Stieve, *Bauernaufstand*, 1: 113, n. 3.

50. Ibid., p. 40.

51. Ibid., p. 73, n. 5; Fattinger, "Fadinger," p. 55.

52. Fattinger, "Fadinger," pp. 58-59.

53. Cited in Stieve, *Bauernaufstand*.

54. Fattinger, "Fadinger," p. 56.

55. OÖLA, Ottensheim *Briefprotokolle*, Vol. 072a, contains for the fall of 1626 and for the year 1627 several interrogations of peasants who were known to have participated in the uprising. They implicate Zeller in at least two such incidents of theft and extortion. See the testimony of Wolf Luckhen, 28 January 1627, fol. 333, and of Hans Willenauer, 15 March 1627, fol. 334-335.

56. Strnadt, *Bauernkrieg*, 1: p. 149, n. 88.

57. Stieve, *Bauernaufstand*, 1:68, places Wiellinger in the Ritterstand even though he presents evidence to the contrary.

58. Ibid., p. 154, n. 5.

59. Starhemberg Archive, Haag, "Bayerischer Einfall." Stix. "Verhör der Bauer"; Stieve, *Bauernaufstand*, 1:55, calls Stix and his followers a gang of bandits and terrorists who were under the special protection of Weikart von Polheim.

60. These exchanges are preserved at the Starhemberg Archive, Haag, Unteres Fach, Pergament Urkunden, under the title "Verhaftung des Archaz Wiellinger. Berichte und Korrespondenzen der Pflegerin Maria Fink, 1621," 42 fol.

61. Ibid., fols. 20-21, "Was dieser aigentlich für freyhaiten auf diesem Guet was Ihme auch sonsten im Landt für gerechtigkhait bestanden werde, und ob er ain Landmann."

62. Stieve, *Bauernaufstand*, found a letter by Fink at its other end in the so-called Passauer *Blechkastenarchiv*, No. 218, file 28, in Munich. He cited it in his description of Wiellinger but left out some extremely important information.

63. Starhemberg Archive, Haag, "Verhaftung."

64. Ibid., fol. 10.

65. Ibid., fols. 41-42.

66. Stieve, *Bauernaufstand*.

67. Ibid., p. 154, n. 8.

68. In the first letter from Maria Fink to Wiellinger she addresses him, as was common, as "noble" and "steadfast," but she also openly appeals to his "adl"—this despite the fact that she knew he was not a nobleman. In Wiellinger's reply we find him concerned with protesting his innocence and saving his honor as resident nobleman ("Zu defensionierung meiner Unschuld und Redung meiner Adelichen Landt-

manns Ehrn"). Starhemberg Archive, Haag, "Verhaftung," fols. 3-6.
At the time of his arrest and interrogation in 1626 he also claimed to
be a "lantmann." However, in the accounts of the eighteenth-century
genealogist, J. G. Hoheneck, *Die löblichen Herrn Stände des Erzher-
zogtums Österreich ob der Enns oder Genealogie,* 3 vols., 1727, 3:
251, and cited in Stieve, *Bauernaufstand,* Vol. 2, p. 154, n. 5. Wiellinger is not listed as one of noble status.

69. Alfred Hoffmann, "Zur Typologie der Bauernaufstände in Oberösterreich," in *Der Oberösterreichische Bauernkrieg,* Linz, 1976, pp.
19-20.

70. Gustav Otruba and J. A. Sagoschen, *Gerberzünfte in Österreich,*
Vienna, 1964, p. 35; Alfred Hoffmann, *Wirtschaftsgeschichte des Landes
Oberösterreich,* Vol. 1, Salzberg, 1952, p. 135; OÖLA, Aschach-Stauf
Archive, Vol. 43; Zauner, *Vöcklabruck,* p. 569.

71. Zauner, *Vöcklabruck,* p. 570.

72. Ibid., p. 271; Hoffmann, *Wirtschaftsgeschichte,* p. 186.

73. Ernst Tomek, *Kirchengeschichte Österreichs,* 3 vols., Innsbruck,
1935, 2:425-426; Grete Mecenseffy, *Geschichte des Protestantismus
in Österreich,* Graz, 1956, pp. 11-14, 46-57, 57-61.

74. Strnadt, *Bauernkrieg.*

75. Hoffmann, "Typologie," p. 20.

76. Stieve, *Bauernaufstand,* 2:254, 266.

77. Ibid., pp. 256, 266.

78. Robert Redfield, *Peasant Society and Culture,* Chicago, 1956;
Eric Wolf, "Aspects of Group Relations in a Complex Society: Mexico,"
American Anthropologist 58 (1956); Charles Tilly, *The Vendée,* Cambridge, Mass., 1964; Sydel Silverman, "The Community-Nation Mediator in Traditional Italy," *Ethnology* 4 (1965).

79. Anton Blok, *The Mafia of a Sicilian Village, 1860-1960: A Short
Study of Violent Entrepreneurs,* New York, 1975.

80. Ibid., pp. 10-11.

81. Ibid., p. 8.

82. Ralf Dahrendorf, *Class and Class Conflict in Industrial Society,*
Stanford, 1958, pp. 296-297.

83. Ibid., p. 296.

84. Max Weber, "Class, Status and Party," in *From Max Weber,*
ed. H. H. Gerth and C. Wright Mills, New York, 1958, p. 195.

85. Stieve, *Bauernaufstand,* 2:262-263.

86. Ibid., pp. 259-260.

87. Ibid., p. 260.

88. Ibid., p. 265.

89. Ibid., p. 260.
90. David Sabean, "Family and Land Tenure."
91. Stieve, *Bauernaufstand*, 2:261-264.
92. Ibid.
93. Ibid., p. 265.
94. Ibid., p. 257.
95. Ibid., pp. 256, 266-267.
96. Roger Lockyer, *Habsburg and Bourbon Europe, 1470-1720*, London, 1974, pp. 333-339.
97. Dahrendorf, *Class*, p. 301.
98. Contrast, for example, the pluralist and managerial thesis of Emmette S. Redford, *Democracy in the Administrative State*, New York, 1969, especially pp. 132-264, with the views of Albert O. Hirschman, *Exit, Voice and Loyalty*, Cambridge, Mass., 1970, chap. 7, or with Henry Kariel, *The Decline of American Pluralism*, Stanford, 1961.
99. Herbert Marcuse, *Negations: Essays in Critical Theory*, Boston, 1968, p. 217.
100. Hantsch, *Geschichte*, Vol. I, p. 340.
101. See the important discussion of censorship and state-building by Grete Klingenstein, *Staatsverwaltung und kirchliche Autorität im 18. Jahrhundert*, Munich, 1970.
102. Mecenseffy, *Geschichte*, pp. 186-206; Adam Wandruzka, "Geheim-protestantismus, Josephinismus, und Volksliturgie in Österreich," *Zeitschrift für Kirchengeschichte* 78 (1967); Rudolf Schrempf, "Krypto-Protestantismus in Krengelbach," *Jahrbuch des Musealvereins Wels* 11 (1964-1965).
103. Koenigsberger, *Hapsburgs*, p. 198; Lockyer, *Habsburg and Bourbon Europe*, p. 333; Reinhard Koselleck, *Kritik und Krise; Eine Studie zur Pathogenese der bürgerlichen Welt*, Frankfurt, 1973, p. 14.
104. R. A. Kann, *The Problem of Restoration*, Berkeley, 1968.
105. Koselleck, *Kritik*, pp. 15-16.
106. Ibid., pp. 30-31.
107. Ibid., pp. 13, 29-33.
108. Gerhard Oesterreich, "Strukturprobleme des europäischen Absolutismus," *VSWG* 55 (1969); Klingenstein, *Staatsverwaltung*, p. 48.
109. Dahrendorf, "Homo."
110. Koselleck, *Kritik*, p. 30.
111. Dahrendorf, *Class*, p. 200.
112. Ibid., p. 176.
113. Hans Sturmberger, "Der Oberösterreichische Bauernkrieg von 1626," in *Der Oberösterreichische Bauernkrieg*, Linz, 1976, p. 12; also,

Franz Wilflingseder, "Martin Laimbauer und die Unruhen im Machlandviertel," *MOÖL* 6 (1959):136, sees the uprisings of the 1630s as post-mortem effects (*"letzte Zuckungen"*) of the movement of the 1620s.

114. Friedrich Schober, "Zur Geschichte des Bauernaufstandes, 1632," *MOÖLA* 2 (1955).
115. Wilflingseder, "Laimbauer."
116. Ibid., p. 172.
117. Ibid., p. 143.
118. Ibid., pp. 198-199.
119. Ibid., pp. 202-203.
120. Ibid., pp. 196-197.
121. The thoughts on schizophrenia and delusional perceptions by Gregory Bateson that are based on concepts of reification and what Bateson calls the "transcontextual" seem appropriate for an understanding of Laimbauer's and others' interrogations. See especially Bateson's essay, "Double Bind, 1969," in his *Steps to an Ecology of Mind*, New York, 1972.
122. Cited in Schober, "Bauernaufstandes," p. 176.
123. See OÖLA, Weinberg Archive, Vol. 150, file A/1/d; also Wilflingseder, "Laimbauer," pp. 143-144, 159-160.
124. Schober, "Bauernaufstandes," pp. 177-178.
125. Wilflingseder, "Laimbauer," pp. 150, 199-200.
126. Schober, "Bauernaufstandes," pp. 179-180.
127. OÖLA, Weinberg Archive, Vol. 150, file A/1/d.
128. Ibid.; Wilflingseder, "Laimbauer," pp. 143-145, 155, 182.
129. Wilflingseder, "Laimbauer," pp. 182-186.
130. Ibid., pp. 178, 186, 203.
131. Frances Fox Piven and Richard A. Cloward, *Poor People's Movements*, New York, 1979, p. xi.
132. Sydney W. Mintz, "The Rural Proletariat and the Problem of Rural Proletarian Consciousness," *Journal of Peasant Studies* 1 (1974): 319.
133. Wilflingseder, "Laimbauer," pp. 143, 157.
134. OÖLA, Weinberg Archive, Vol. 150, file A/1/d; ibid., passim.
135. Wilflingseder, "Laimbauer," pp. 155, 158.
136. Ibid., p. 150.
137. Ibid., p. 151.
138. Georg Grüll, "Geschichte des Schlosses und der Herrschaft Windhag bei Perg," *JOÖMV* 87 (1937).
139. Ibid.; Sturmberger, *Herbersdorf*, pp. 268-269.

140. Wilflingseder, "Laimbauer," pp. 152-153.
141. Ibid., p. 181.
142. Ibid., p. 187.
143. Ibid., pp. 184-188.
144. Mecenseffy, *Geschichte*.
145. Wilflingseder, "Laimbauer," p. 202.

~ BIBLIOGRAPHY ~

I. ARCHIVAL SOURCES

Oberösterreichisches Landesarchiv, Linz

INVENTORIES
Aistershaim *Inventurprotokolle*, Vols. 90, 91.
Frankenburg *Brief- und Inventurprotokolle*, Vols. 248, 249,
    250, 252, 253, 254, 256, 260, 261, 262, 264, 265, 266, 267,
    268, 269.
Schaunberg *Brief- und Inventurprotokolle*, Vols. 278, 279,
    280, 281.
Schlägl *Brief- und Inventurprotokolle*, Vols. 434, 435, 436,
    437.
Windhag *Brief- und Inventurprotokolle*, Vols. 1932, 1933,
    1934, 1935, 1936, 1937, 1938, 1939, 1940, 1941.

OTHER SOURCES
Aschach-Stauf Archive, Vol. 43.
Garsten Archive, *Verkaufsprotokolle*, Vols. 22, 23, 24, 29.
Ottensheim Archive, *Briefprotokolle*, Vol. 072a.
Starhemberg Archive, *Handschriften*, Vol. 16.
Wagrain Archive, Vol. 18.
Weinberg Archive, Vols. 148, 150, 314, 363, 368, 369, 370,
    820, 870, 950, 1018, 1033, 1034, 1061, 1063, 1361.
Windhag Archive, *Handschrift 9, Urbar 1672*.

ESTATES DOCUMENTS
Annales, Vols. 77, 78.
Landschaftsakten, Vols. 813, 1227, 1228, 1333.

TYPESCRIPTS
Hans Fattinger, "Unsere Bäuerliche Vorfahren," undated.
J. Heider, compiler and editor, "Tabellen zu den Kirchen-
    büchern Mühlviertler Pfarren."

Starhemberg Archive, Haag am Hausruck

"Bayerischer Einfall"
"Frankenburger Würfelspiel"
"Knausmüller Verhör"
"Verhaftung des Achaz Wiellinger"

II. PRINTED SOURCES

Goetz, W., ed. *Briefe und Akten zur Geschichte des 30 Jährigen Krieges.* 3 vols., Leipzig: Teubner, 1907.

Nösslböck, Ignaz, et al., eds. *Österreichische Weistümer.* Vols. 12-14, Graz: Böhlaus Nachf., 1960.

Stieve, Felix, ed. "Bericht eines bairischen Adlichen über die Bauerschaft in Österreich ob der Enns [1641], Februar 14." *Mitteilungen des Instituts für österreichische Geschichte* 5 (1884).

Tschernembl, Georg Erasmus. *Consultationes Oder Underschidliche Rathschläg der maisten und wichtigsten sachen welche von Anfäng der Böhemischen und andern folgenden Auffständ fürgangen und zu Werck gericht worden oder worden sollen.* 1624.

von Hohberg, Wolf Helmhard. *Georgica Curiosa.* 5th ed. Nuremberg, 1715.

III. BOOKS, DISSERTATIONS, AND REFERENCE WORKS

Achilles, Walter. *Vermögensverhältnisse braunschweigischer Bauernhöfe.* Stuttgart: G. Fischer, 1965.

Adams, Henry. *The Great Secession Winter of 1860-61 and Other Essays.* New York: Washington Square Press, 1963.

Anderson, Perry. *Lineages of the Absolute State.* London: N.L.B., 1974.

Bak, Janos, ed. *The German Peasant War of 1525.* Special issue of the *Journal of Peasant Studies* 3 (1975).

Bateson, Gregory. *Steps to an Ecology of Mind.* New York: Ballantine Books, 1972.

Bazelon, David. *Power and American Society.* New York: American Library, 1971.

Bendix, Reinhard and Lipset, Seymour Martin, eds. *Class, Status, and Power.* Glencoe, Ill.: Free Press, 1953.

————. *Social Mobility in Industrial Society.* Berkeley: University of California Press, 1964.

Berger, Peter. *The Homeless Mind.* New York: Vintage Books, 1974.

Black, Henry Campbell. *A Law Dictionary*, 2nd ed. St. Paul: West Publishing Co., 1910.

Blickle, Peter. *Die Revolution von 1525*. Munich: Oldenbourg, 1975.

Blok, Anton. *The Mafia of a Sicilian Village, 1860-1960: A Short Study of Violent Entrepreneurs*. New York: Harper & Row, 1975.

Bosl, Karl, and Möckl, Karl. *Der Moderne Parlamentarismus und seine Grundlagen in der ständischen Repräsentation*. Berlin: Duncker und Humblot, 1977.

Braun, Rudolf. *Industrialisierung und Volksleben*. Zurich: Rentsch, 1960.

Brückner, Wolfgang, ed. *Volkserzählung und Reformation*. Berlin: E. Schmidt, 1974.

Brunner, Otto. *Adeliges Landleben und Europäischer Geist*. Salzburg: Otto Müller, 1959.

————. *Land und Herrschaft*. Darmstadt: Wissenschaftliche Buchgesellschaft, 1965.

————. *Neue Wege der Verfassungs- und Sozialgeschichte*. 2nd ed. Göttingen: Vandenhoeck & Ruprecht, 1968.

———— et al., eds. *Geschichtliche Grundbergriffe*. 2 vols. Stuttgart: E. Klett, 1975.

Bullock, Alan. *Is History Becoming a Social Science?* Cambridge: Cambridge University Press, 1976.

Büsch, Otto. *Militärsystem und Sozialleben im alten Preussen, 1713-1807*. Berlin: de Gruyter, 1962.

Carus-Wilson, E. M., ed. *Essays in Economic History*. London: E. Arnold, 1954.

Chayanov, A. V. *The Theory of the Peasant Economy*. Edited by Daniel Thorner, et al. Homewood, Ill.: R. D. Irwin, 1966.

Cole, John, and Wolf, Eric. *The Invisible Frontier*. New York: Academic Press, 1974.

Coleman, James S. *Power and the Structure of Society*. New York: W. W. Norton & Co., 1974.

Colfax, J. David, and Roach, Jack L., eds. *Radical Sociology*. New York: Basic Books, 1971.

Commons, John R. *The Legal Foundations of Capitalism*. New York: The Macmillan Co., 1924.

Conze, Werner, ed. *Sozialgeschichte der Familie in der Neuzeit Europas*. Stuttgart: E. Klett, 1976.

Coser, Lewis. *The Functions of Social Conflict*. New York: Free Press, 1964.

~ BIBLIOGRAPHY ~

Czerny, Albin. *Aus dem geistlichen Geschäftsleben in Oberösterreich im 15. Jahrhundert*. Linz, 1882.

———. *Bilder aus der Zeit der Bauernunruhen in Oberösterreich, 1626, 1632, 1648*. Linz, 1876.

———. *Der erste Bauernaufstand in Oberösterreich, 1525*. Linz, 1882.

———. *Der zweite Bauernaufstand in Oberösterreich, 1595-1597*. Linz, 1890.

Dahrendorf, Ralf. *Class and Class Conflict in Industrial Society*. Stanford: Stanford University Press, 1959.

———. *Essays in the Theory of Society*. Stanford: Stanford University Press, 1968.

Dalton, George, ed. *Tribal and Peasant Economics*. Garden City, N.Y.: Doubleday & Co., 1967.

Davis, John P. *Corporations*. New York: G. P. Putnam's Sons, 1905.

de Vries, Jan. *The Economy of Europe in an Age of Crisis, 1600-1750*. Cambridge: Cambridge University Press, 1976.

Dobb, Maurice. *Studies in the Development of Capitalism*. London: G. Routledge & Sons, 1946.

Dreitzel, Hans-Peter. *Die gesellschaftlichen Leiden und das Leiden an der Gesellschaft*. Stuttgart: E. Klett, 1968.

Earle, Peter, ed. *Essays in European Economic History, 1500-1800*. New York: Oxford University Press, 1965.

Ernstberger, Anton, ed. *Ludwig Camerarius und Lukas Friedrich Behaim: Ein politischer Briefwechsel über den Verfall des Reiches, 1636-1648*. Munich: C. H. Beck, 1961.

Feigl, Helmuth. *Die Niederösterreichische Grundherrschaft*. Vienna: Verein für Landeskunde von Niederösterreich und Wien, 1964.

———. *Rechtsentwicklung und Gerichtswesen Oberösterreichs im Spiegel der Weistümer*. Vienna: Österreichische Akademie der Wissenschaften, 1974.

Franz, Günther, ed. *Bauernschaft und Bauernstand, 1500-1700*. Limbach-Lahn: C. A. Starke, 1975.

Geertz, Clifford. *The Interpretation of Cultures*. New York: Basic Books, 1973.

———, and Geertz, Hilda. *Kinship in Bali*. Chicago: University of Chicago Press, 1975.

Gerth, H. H. and Mills, C. Wright, eds. *From Max Weber; Essays in Sociology*. New York: Oxford University Press, 1958.

Glass, D. V., and Eversley, D.E.C., eds. *Population in History*. London: E. Arnold, 1965.

Goody, Jack, ed. *The Developmental Cycle in Domestic Groups*. Cambridge: Cambridge University Press, 1958.

———— et al., eds. *Family and Inheritance: Rural Society in Western Europe, 1200-1800*. Cambridge: Cambridge University Press, 1976.

Graubard, Stephen, and Gilbert, Felix, eds. *Historical Studies Today*. New York: W. W. Norton & Co., 1972.

Grüll, Georg. *Bauer, Herr und Landesfürst*. Graz: Böhlaus Nachf., 1963.

————. *Der Bauer im Lande ob der Enns am Ausgang des sechzehnten Jahrhunderts*. Vienna: Böhlaus, 1969.

————. *Bauernhaus und Meierhof*. Linz: Oberösterreichisches Landesarchiv, 1975.

————. *Die Robot in Oberösterreich*. Linz: Oberösterreichisches Landesarchiv, 1952.

————. *Weinberg; Die Entstehungsgeschichte einer Mühlviertler Wirtschaftsherrschaft*. Graz: H. Böhlaus Nachf., 1955.

Hantsch, Hugo. *Die Geschichte Österreichs*. 2 vols. Graz: Styria, 1968.

Helczmanovski, H., ed. *Beiträge zur Bevölkerungs- und Sozialgeschichte Osterreichs*. Munich: Oldenbourg, 1973.

Henderson, A. M., and Parsons, Talcott. *Max Weber: The Theory of Social and Economic Organization*. New York: Oxford University Press, 1947.

Hirschman, Albert O. *Exit, Voice and Loyalty*. Cambridge, Mass.: Harvard University Press, 1970.

Hoffmann, Alfred. *Wirtschaftsgeschichte des Landes Oberösterreich*. Salzburg: Otto Müller, 1952.

Hujber, Wendelin. "Der Prälatenstand des Landes ob der Enns, 1600-1620." Ph.D. dissertation, University of Vienna, 1972.

Inkeles, Alex, ed. *Readings in Modern Sociology*. Englewood Cliffs, N.J.: Prentice-Hall, 1966.

Innerhofer, Franz. *Beautiful Days*. Translated by Anselm Hollo. New York: Urizen Books, 1976.

Johnson, Chalmers. *Revolutionary Change*. Boston: Little, Brown, 1966.

Kamenka, Eugene and Neale, R. S., eds. *Feudalism, Capitalism, and Beyond*. New York: St. Martin's Press, 1976.

Kann, R. A. *The Problem of Restoration*. Berkeley: University of California Press, 1968.

Kariel, Henry. *The Decline of American Pluralism*. Stanford: Stanford University Press, 1961.

Kellenbenz, Hermann. *Der Merkantilismus in Europa und die Soziale Mobilität*. Wiesbaden: F. Steiner, 1965.

Kislinger, Max. *Alte Bäuerliche Kunst*. Linz: Oberösterreichischer Landesverlag, 1963.

Klingenstein, Grete. *Staatsverwaltung und kirchliche Autorität im 18. Jahrhundert*. Munich: Oldenbourg, 1970.

Koenigsberger, H. G. *The Hapsburgs in Europe, 1516-1660*. Ithaca: Cornell University Press, 1971.

Kolko, Gabriel. *The Triumph of Conservatism*. Chicago: University of Chicago Press, 1965.

Koselleck, Reinhard. *Kritik und Krise; Eine Studie zur Pathogenese der bürgerlichen Welt*. Frankfurt: Suhrkamp, 1973.

———, and Stempel, Wolf-Dieter, eds. *Geschichte—Ereignis und Erzählung*. Munich: W. Fink, 1973.

Krieger, Leonard. *The German Idea of Freedom*. Boston: Beacon Press, 1957.

Langbein, John H. *Prosecuting Crime in the Renaissance*. Cambridge, Mass.: Harvard University Press, 1974.

Langenscheidt's New Muret-Sanders Encyclopedic Dictionary of the English and German Languages. Berlin: 1974.

Lasch, Christopher. *Haven in a Heartless World: The Family Besieged*. New York: Basic Books, 1979.

Laslett, Peter, and Wall, Richard, eds. *Household and Family in Past Time*. Cambridge, Mass.: Harvard University Press, 1972.

Lehnert, Walter. *Die Oberösterreichischen Exulanten im ehemaligen Ansbachischen Oberamt Stauf-Landeck*. Freie Schriftenfolge der Gesellschaft für Familienforschung in Franken. Neustadt/Aich: Degener, 1962.

Lockyer, Roger. *Habsburg and Bourbon Europe, 1470-1720*. London: Longmans, 1974.

Lütge, F. *Deutsche Sozial- und Wirtschaftsgeschichte*. Berlin: Springer-Verlag, 1966.

McConnell, Grant. *Private Power and American Democracy*. New York: Vintage Books, 1970.

Macfarlane, Alan. *The Origins of English Individualism*. Oxford: Clarendon Press, 1978.

———. *Reconstructing Historical Communities*. Cambridge: At the University Press, 1977.

Marcuse, Herbert. *Negations: Essays in Critical Theory*. Boston: Beacon Press, 1968.

Marx, Karl. *Das Kapital*. vols. 23-25. In *Werke*. 40 Vols. Berlin: Dietz, 1963.

————. *The Grundrisse*. Edited and translated by David McClellan. New York: Harper & Row, 1972.

————, and Engels, Friedrich. *Selected Works*. New York: International Publishers, 1968.

Mauss, Marcel. *The Gift: Forms and Functions of Exchange in Archaic Societies*. Glencoe, Ill.: Free Press, 1954.

Mecenseffy, Grete. *Geschichte des Protestantismus in Österreich*. Graz: Böhlaus Nachf., 1956.

Merton, Robert K. *Sociological Ambivalence*. New York: Free Press, 1976.

Moeller, Bernd, ed. *Studien zum Bauernkrieg*. Gütersloh: Verlagshaus G. Mohr, 1975.

Mommsen, Wolfgang. *The Age of Bureaucracy: Perspectives on the Political Sociology of Max Weber*. New York: Harper & Row, 1977.

Moore, Barrington, Jr. *The Social Origins of Dictatorship and Democracy*. Boston: Beacon Press, 1966.

Mosser, Alois. "Beiträge zur Geschichte in Oberösterreich unter besonderer Berücksichtigung der Herrschaft Ott am Traunsee." Ph.D. dissertation, University of Vienna, 1964.

Mousnier, Roland. *Social Stratification*. New York: Schocken, 1973.

Nakane, Chie. *Japanese Society*. Berkeley: University of California Press, 1972.

Neugarten, Bernice, ed. *Middle Age and Aging*. Chicago: University of Chicago Press, 1968.

Oberman, H. A., ed. *Deutscher Bauernkrieg, 1525*. Stuttgart: E. Klett, 1972.

Ossowski, Stanislaw. *Class Structure in the Social Consciousness*. New York: Free Press, 1963.

Otruba, Gustav, and Sagoschen, J. A. *Gerberzünfte in Österreich*. Vienna: Bergland, 1964.

Piven, Frances Fox, and Cloward, Richard A. *Poor People's Movements*. New York: Vintage Books, 1979.

Polanyi, Karl. *Primitive, Archaic, and Modern Economics*. Edited by George Dalton. Garden City, N.Y.: Anchor Books, 1968.

Polisensky, J. V. *War and Society in Europe, 1618-1648*. Cambridge: Cambridge University Press, 1978.

Popkin, Richard. *The Rational Peasant*. Berkeley: University of California Press, 1979.

Potter, Jack; Diaz, May; and Foster, George, eds. *Peasant Society: A Reader*. Boston: Little, Brown, 1967.

Pröll, Laurenz. *Ein Blick in das Hauswesen eines Österreichischen Landedelmannes*. 2 vols. Vienna, 1889.

―――. *Das Obermühlviertler Bauernhaus*. Linz-Urfar, 1902.

Rabe, Hannah. *Das Problem Leibeigenschaft* (Beiheft 64, *Vierteljahrschrift für Sozial- und Wirtschaftsgeschichte*). Wiesbaden: Franz Steiner, 1977.

Rebel, Hermann. *The Rural Subject Population of Upper Austria during the Early Seventeenth Century: Aspects of the Social Stratification System*. Ann Arbor: Xerox, 1976.

Redfield, Robert. *Peasant Society and Culture*. Chicago: University of Chicago Press, 1956.

Redford, Emmette S. *Democracy in the Administrative State*. New York: Oxford University Press, 1969.

Rohr, Donald. *The Origins of Social Liberalism in Germany*. Chicago: University of Chicago Press, 1963.

Rosegger, Peter. *Volksleben in Steiermark*. Leipzig: L. Staackmann, 1914.

Rosenberg, Hans. *Bureaucracy, Aristocracy, and Autocracy: The Prussian Experience, 1660-1815*. Boston: Beacon Press, 1966.

―――. *Grosse Depression und Bismarckzeit*. Berlin: de Gruyter, 1967.

Rossi, Alice S., et al., eds. *The Family*. New York: Norton, 1978.

Sabean, David. *Landbesitz und Gesellschaft am Vorabend des Bauernkriegs*. Stuttgart: G. Fischer, 1972.

Schildhauer, Johannes. *Soziale, politische, und religiöse Auseinandersetzungen in den Hansestädten*. Weimar: H. Böhlaus Nachfolger, 1959.

Schmidt, Friedrich. *Die freien bäuerlichen Eigengüter in Oberösterreich*. Breslau: Priebatsch, 1941.

Schmied, R. F. "Der Bauernkrieg in Oberösterreich von 1626 als Teilerscheinung des dreissigjährigen Krieges." Ph.D. dissertation, Martin Luther University, Halle, 1963.

Schremmer, Eckhart. *Die Wirtschaft Bayerns*. Munich: Delp, 1970.

Scott, James C. *The Moral Economy of the Peasant: Rebellion and Subsistence in Southeast Asia*. New Haven: Yale University Press, 1976.

Sennett, Richard, ed. *The Psychology of Society*. New York: Vintage Books, 1977.

Shorter, Edward. *The Making of the Modern Family*. New York: Basic Books, 1975.

Snider, F. "The Restructuring of the Bohemian Nobility, 1610-1650." Ph.D. dissertation, University of California at Berkeley, 1972.

Stark, Werner. *Ursprung und Aufstieg des Landwirtschaftlichen Grossbetriebs in den böhmischen Ländern.* Prague: R. M. Rohrer, 1934.

Stavenhagen, Rodolfo. *Social Class in Agrarian Societies.* Garden City, N.Y.: Doubleday & Co., 1975.

Stepan, Eduard, ed. *Das Waldviertel.* Vienna, 1926.

Stieve, Felix. *Der Oberösterreichische Bauernaufstand des Jahres 1626.* 2 vols. Linz: E. Moreis, 1904.

Stone, Lawrence. *The Crisis of the Aristocracy, 1558-1641.* New York: Oxford University Press, 1967.

Strakosch, Henry E. *State Absolutism and the Rule of Law.* Sydney: The University Press, 1967.

Strnadt, Julius. *Der Bauernkrieg in Oberösterreich im Jahr 1626.* Wels: J. Haas, 1924.

Sturmberger, Hans. *Adam Graf Herbersdorf: Herrschaft und Freiheit im konfessionellen Zeitalter.* Munich: Oldenbourg, 1976.

————. *Georg Erasmus Tschernembl.* Graz: Böhlaus, 1953.

————. *Kaiser Ferdinand II und das Problem des Absolutismus.* Munich: Oldenbourg, 1957.

Thernstrom, Stephan. *Poverty and Progress: Social Mobility in a Nineteenth Century City.* Garden City, N.Y.: Doubleday & Co., 1970.

Tilly, Charles. *The Vendée.* Cambridge, Mass.: Harvard University Press, 1964.

Tiryakian, Edward, ed. *Sociological Theory, Values, and Sociocultural Change: Essays in Honor of Pitrim A. Sorokin.* New York: Free Press, 1967.

Tomek, Ernst. *Kirchengeschichte Österreichs.* 3 vols. Innsbruck: Tyrolia, 1935-1959.

Tremel, Ferdinand. *Der Frühkapitalismus in Innerösterreich.* Graz: Leykam-Verlag, 1954.

————. *Sozial- und Wirtschaftsgeschichte Österreichs.* Vienna: Deuticke, 1969.

Walter, Friedrich. *Österreichische Verfassungs- und Verwaltungsgeschichte von 1500-1955.* Vienna: A. Holzhausens Nachf., 1972.

Weber, Max. *Wirtschaft und Gesellschaft.* Tübingen: J.C.B. Mahr, 1925.

Wehler, H.-U., ed. *Der deutsche Bauernkrieg, 1524-1526.* Göttingen: Vandenhoeck und Ruprecht, 1975.

Weinstein, James. *The Corporate Ideal in the Liberal State*. Boston: Beacon Press, 1969.

Wohlfeil, Rainer, ed. *Der Bauernkrieg, 1524-1526*. Munich: Nymphenburger Verlagshandlung, 1975.

──────, ed. *Reformation oder Frühbürgerliche Revolution*. Munich: Nymphenburger Verlagshandlung, 1975.

Wolf, Eric. *Peasants*. Engelwood Cliffs, N.J.: Prentice-Hall, 1966.

Wörterbuch der deutschen Gegenwartssprache. 2 vols. Berlin: Akademie Verlag, 1961.

Wurm, Heinrich. *Die Jörger von Tollet*. Graz: Böhlaus Nachf., 1955.

Zauner, Alois. *Vöcklabruck und der Attergau*. Vienna: Böhlaus, 1971.

Zötl, H., ed. *Das heldenmütige Martyrium von Anno, 1626*. Linz: Pirngruber, 1927.

IV. ARTICLES

Arriaza, Armand. "Mousnier and Barber: The Theoretical Underpinnings of the Society of Order in Early Modern Europe." *Past and Present*, in press.

Bales, Robert F. "Status, Role and Interaction." *In Readings in Modern Sociology*, edited by Alex Inkeles. Englewood Cliffs, N.J.: Prentice-Hall, 1966.

Barton, Allen H. "Empirical Methods and Radical Sociology: A Liberal Critique." In *Radical Sociology*, edited by J. David Colfax and Jack L. Roach. New York: Basic Books, 1971.

Berkner, Lutz. "Inheritance, Land Tenure and Peasant Family Structure: A German Regional Comparison." In *Family and Inheritance: Rural Society in Western Europe, 1200-1800*, edited by Jack Goody, et al. Cambridge: Cambridge University Press, 1976.

──────. "Recent Research on the History of the Family in Western Europe." *Journal of Marriage and the Family* 35 (1973).

──────. "The Stem Family and the Developmental Cycle of the Peasant Household: An Eighteenth Century Austrian Example." *American Historical Review* 77 (1972).

Birnbaum, Norman. "The Crisis in Marxist Sociology." *Social Research* 35 (1968).

Blickle, Peter. "Bauer und Staat in Oberschwaben." *Zeitschrift für Württembergische Landesgeschichte* 31 (1973).

Bloch, Marc. "The Rise of Dependent Cultivation and Seignorial Institutions." *Cambridge Economic History of Europe*. Vol. I. Cambridge: Cambridge University Press, 1941.

Brenner, Robert. "Agrarian Class Structure and Economic Development in Pre-Industrial Europe." *Past and Present* 70 (1976).

Bruckmüller, Ernst. "Die Lage der Bauern um 1626." In *Der oberösterreichische Bauernkrieg 1626. Austellung des Landes Oberösterreich*. Linz: Landesregierung, 1976.

Bücking, Jürgen. "Der 'Bauernkrieg' in den hapsburgischen Ländern als sozialer Systemkonflikt, 1524-1526." In *Der deutsche Bauernkrieg, 1524-1526*, edited by H.-U. Wehler. Göttingen: Vandenhoeck und Ruprecht, 1975.

Cornford, Barbara. "Inventories of the Poor." *Norfolk Archeology* 35 (1970).

Demeny, Paul. "Early Fertility Decline in Austria-Hungary: A Lesson in Demographic Transition." *Daedalus* 97 (1968).

Diaz, May. "Introduction: Economic Relations in Peasant Society." In *Peasant Society: A Reader*, edited by Jack Potter et al. Boston: Little, Brown, 1967.

Dopsch, Alfons. "Agrarian Institutions of the Germanic Kingdoms from the Fifth to the Ninth Centuries." *Cambridge Economic History of Europe*. Vol. I. Cambridge: Cambridge University Press, 1941.

Eberstaller, Herta. "Zur Finanzpolitik der oberösterreichischen Stände im Jahr 1608." *Mitteilungen des Oberösterreichischem Landesarchivs* (1964).

Elkar, Rainer. "Geschichtsforschung der frühen Neuzeit zwischen Divergenz und Parallelität." In *Der deutsche Bauernkrieg, 1524-1526*, edited by Rainer Wohlfeil. Munich: Nymphenburger Verlagshandlung, 1975.

Fattinger, Hans. "Stefan Fadinger und Christoph Zeller. Ihre Familie und Ihre Heimat." *Oberösterreichische Heimatblätter* 19 (1965).

Feigl, Helmuth. "Die befreiten Ämter der Herrschaft Steyr in den Bauernkriegen des 16. und 17. Jahrhunderts." *Mitteilungen des Oberösterreichen Landesarchivs* 6 (1959).

Ferihumer, Heinrich. "Eine Beschreibung der Bewohner Oberösterreichs (1771)." *Oberösterreichische Heimatblätter* 4 (1950).

Foster, George. "The Dyadic Contract: A Model for the Social Structure of a Mexican Peasant Village." In *Peasant Society: A Reader*, edited by Jack Potter et al. Boston: Little, Brown, 1967.

Frankel-Brunswick, Else. "Adjustments and Reorientations in the Course of the Life-Span." In *Middle Age and Aging*, edited by Bernice Neugarten. Chicago: University of Chicago Press, 1968.

Franz, Günther. "Die Führer im Bauernkrieg." In his *Bauernschaft und Bauernstand, 1500-1700*. Limbach-Lahn: C. A. Starke, 1975.

Geertz, Clifford. "The Rotating Credit Association: A 'Middle Rung' in Development." *Economic Development and Culture Change* 10 (1962).

Gindeley, A. "Die Gegenreformation und der Aufstand in Oberösterreich im Jahre 1626." *Akademie der Wissenschaften, Sitzungsberichte der Phil.-Hist. Klass.* Abhandlungen, VI, Vol. 118. Vienna, 1889.

Goffman, Erving. "Role Distance." In *The Psychology of Society*, edited by Richard Sennett. New York: Vintage, 1977.

Goody, Jack. "Strategies of Heirship." *Comparative Studies in Society and History* 15 (1973).

Grüll, Georg. "Geschichte des Schlosses und der Herrschaft Windhag bei Perg." *Jahrbuch des oberösterreichischen Musealvereins* 87 (1937).

—————. "Der Hauptmannbrief von Ohnersdorf." *Oberösterreichische Heimatblätter* 8 (1954).

—————. "Die Herrschaftsschichtung in Österreich ob der Enns, 1750." *Mitteilungen des Oberösterreichischen Landesarchivs* 5 (1957).

—————. "Die Leute im Walde. Ein Beitrag zur Geschichte des Freiwalds." *Oberösterreichische Heimatblätter* 1 (1947).

—————. "Pergkirchen. Beiträge zur Geschichte eines Dorfes." *Heimatgaue* 2 (1930).

Hageneder, Othmar. "Die Grafschaft Schaunberg." *Mitteilungen des Oberösterreichischen Landesarchivs* 5 (1957).

—————. "Die spätmittelalterlichen Wüstungen in der Grafschaft Schaunberg." *Jahrbuch für Landeskunde von Niederösterreich.* n. s. 33 (1957).

Haibock, Hermann. "Kerbhölzer und Zehentstecken. Hauprequisiten der 'Buchhaltung' früher Jahrhunderte." *Oberösterreichische Heimatblätter* 18 (1964).

Hajnal, H. J. "European Marriage Patterns in Perspective." In *Population in History*, edited by D. V. Glass and D.E.C. Eversley. London: E. Arnold, 1965.

Hareven, Tamara K. "Family Time and Historical Time." In *The Family*, edited by Alice Rossi et al. New York: Norton, 1978.

—————. "The History of the Family as an Interdisciplinary Field." *Journal of Interdisciplinary History* 2 (1972).

Heitz, Gerhard. "Zu den bäuerlichen Klassenkämpfen im Spätfeudalismus." *Zeitschrift für Geschichtswissenschaft* 23 (1975).

Hoffmann, Alfred. "Die Agrarisierung der Industriebauern in Österreich." *East European Quarterly* 3 (1970).

————. "Die Grundherrschaft als Unternehmen." *Zeitschrift für
Agrargeschichte und Agrarsoziologie* 6 (October 1958).

————. "Die Hütten und Stände am Linzer Bartholomäimarkt des
Jahres 1583." *Jahrbuch der Stadt Linz* (1953).

————. "Zur Typologie der Bauernaufstände in Oberösterreich." In
*Der Oberösterreichische Bauernkrieg; Ausstellung des Landes
Oberösterreich.* Linz: Landesregierung, 1976.

Holderness, R. B. "Credit in English Rural Society before the Nineteenth Century." *Agricultural History Review* 24 (1976).

Howell, Cicely. "Peasant Inheritance Customs in the Midlands, 1280-
1700." In *Family and Inheritance: Rural Society in Western Europe, 1200-1800,* edited by Jack Goody et al. Cambridge: Cambridge University Press, 1976.

Hubbard, William H., and Jarausch, Konrad. "Occupation and Social
Structure in Modern Central Europe: Some Reflections on Coding
Professions." *Quantum Information* 11 (July 1979).

Kellenbenz, Hermann. "Rural Industries in the West; From the End
of the Middle Ages to the Eighteenth Century." In *Essays in
European Economic History 1500-1800,* edited by Peter Earle.
Oxford: Oxford University Press, 1965.

Kenyon, G. H. "Kirdford Inventories, 1611 to 1776." *Sussex Archeological Collections* 93 (1955).

Koller, Engelbert. "350 Jahre Salinenort Ebensee." *Oberösterreichische
Heimatblätter* 11 (1957).

Koselleck, Reinhard. "Ereignis und Struktur." In *Geschichte—Ereignis
und Erzählung,* edited by R. Koselleck and Wolf-Dieter Stempel.
Munich: Fink, 1973.

Kloiber, Amilian et al. "Die neolithische Siedlung und die neolithischen
Gräberfundplätze von Rutzing und Haid, Ortsgemeinde Hörsch-
ing, Politischer Bezirk Linz-Land, Oberösterreich." *Jahrbuch des
Oberösterreichischen Musealvereins* 115 (1970).

Krawarick, Hans. "Die Besiedlung und Verödung der Rosenau." *Oberösterreichische Heimatblätter* 22 (1968).

Lewis, Oscar. "The Possessions of the Poor." *Scientific American* 211
(October 1969).

Levy, Marion, Jr., and Fallers, L. A. "The Family: Some Comparative
Considerations." *American Anthropologist* n.s., 61 (1959).

Macfarlane, Alan. "The Origins of English Individualism: Some Surprises." *Theory and Society* 6 (1978).

Manuel, Frank E. "The Use and Abuse of Psychology in History." In *Historical Studies Today*, edited by Felix Gilbert and Stephen Graubard. New York: Norton, 1972.

Marks, A. "Das Leinengewerbe und der Leinenhandel im Lande ob der Enns von den Anfängen bis in die Zeit Maria Theresias." *Jahrbuch des oberösterreichischen Musealvereins* 95 (1950).

Medick, Hans. "The Proto-Industrial Family Economy: The Structural Function of Household and Family during the Transition from Peasant Society to Industrial Capitalism." *Social History* 3 (1976): 297-300.

Mendels, Franklin F. "Proto-Industrialization: The First Phase of the Industrialization Process." *Journal of Economic History* 32 (1972).

Merton, Robert K., and Barber, Elinor. "Sociological Ambivalence." In *Sociological Theory, Values and Sociocultural Change: Essays in Honor of Pitrim A. Sorokin*, edited by Edward Tiryakian. New York: Free Press, 1963.

Mintz, Sydney. "Pratik: Haitian Personal Economic Relationships." In *Peasant Society: A Reader*, edited by Jack Potter et al. Boston, Little, Brown, 1967.

————. "The Rural Proletariat and the Problem of Rural Proletarian Consciousness." *Journal of Peasant Studies* 1 (1974).

Mitterauer, Michael. "Arbeitsorganisation und Altersversongung nach dem Mittelalter." *Beiträge zur historischen Sozialkunde* 5 (1975).

————. "Auswirkung von Urbanisierung und Frühindustrialisierung auf die Familienverfassung an Beispielen des österreichischen Raums." In *Sozialgeschichte der Familie in der Neuzeit Europas*, edited by Werner Conze. Stuttgart: Klett, 1976.

————. "Familiengrösse—Familientypen—Familienzyklus. Probleme Quantitativer Auswertung von österreichischem Quellenmaterial." *Geschichte und Gesellschaft* 1 (1975).

————. "Zur Familienstruktur in ländlichen Gebieten Österreichs im 17. Jahrhundert." In *Beiträge zur Bevölkerungs- und Sozialgeschichte Österreichs*, edited by Heimold Helczmanovszki. Munich: Oldenbourg, 1973.

————, and Sieder, Reinhard. "The Developmental Process of Domestic Groups: Problems of Reconstruction and Possibilities of Interpretation." *Journal of Family History* 4 (1979).

Neale, R. S. "The Bourgeoisie, Historically, Has Played a Most Revolutionary Part." In *Feudalism, Capitalism and Beyond*, edited by Eugene Kamenka and R. S. Neale. New York: St. Martin's, 1976.

Nolte, Ernst. "The Relationship between 'Bourgeois' and 'Marxist' Historiography." *History and Theory* 14 (1975).

Oesterreich, Gerhard. "Strukturprobleme des europäischen Absolutismus." *Vierteljahrschrift für Sozial- und Wirtschaftsgeschichte* 55 (1969).

Postan, M. M. "Credit in Medieval Trade." In *Essays in Economic History*, 3 vols., edited by E. M. Carus-Wilson. London: E. Arnold, 1954.

Ramsauer, Wilhelm. "Das Inventar eines deutschen Marschbauernhofes aus den letzen Jahren des dreissigjährigen Krieges." *Vierteljahrschrift für Sozial- und Wirtschaftsgeschichte* 7 (1909).

Rebel, Hermann. "Probleme der oberösterreichischen Sozialgeschichte zur Zeit der Bayerischen Pfandherrschaft, 1620-1628." *Jahrbuch des Oberösterreichischen Musealvereins* 115 (1970).

Roseberry, William. "Peasants as Proletarians." *Critique of Anthropology* 11 (1978).

Rosenberg, Hans. "The Rise of the Junkers in Brandenburg-Prussia, 1410-1653." *American Historical Review* 49 (1943-1944).

Sabean, David. "Aspects of Kinship Behavior in Rural Western Europe Before 1800." In *Family and Inheritance: Rural Society in Western Europe, 1200-1800*, edited by Jack Goody et al. Cambridge: Cambridge University Press, 1976.

———. "Family and Land Tenure: A Case Study of Conflict in the German Peasants' War (1525)." *Peasant Studies Newsletter* 3 (1974).

———. "German Agrarian Institutions at the Beginning of the Sixteenth Century: Upper Swabia as an Example." In *The German Peasant War of 1525*, edited by Janos Bak, special issue of *Journal of Peasant Studies* 3 (1975).

———. "Problems of Nominal Data Linkage Using Württemberg Village Records from the Sixteenth to the Nineteenth Centuries." Paper presented to the Nominal Record Linkage Conference, Institute for Advanced Study, Princeton, N.J., 24-27 May 1971.

Schober, Friedrich. "Zur Geschichte des Bauernaufstandes, 1632." *Mitteilungen des Oberösterreichischen Landesarchivs* 2 (1955).

Schremmer, Eckart. "Agrarverfassung und Wirtschaftsstruktur. Die Südostdeutsche Hofmark, eine Wirtschaftsherrschaft?" *Zeitschrift für Agrargeschichte und Agrarsoziologie* 20 (1972).

Schrempf, Rudolf. "Krypto-Protestantismus in Krengelbach." *Jahrbuch des Musealvereins Wels* 11 (1964-1965).

Schultz, Helga. "Bäuerliche Klassenkämpfe zwischen frühbürgerlicher

Revolution und dreissigjährigem Krieg." *Zeitschrift für Geschichtswissenschaft* 20 (1972).

Schwab, Dieter. "Eigentum." In *Geschichtliche Grundbegriffe*, edited by Otto Brunner, et al. Stuttgart: E. Klett, 1975.

Scribner, R. W. "Civic Unity and the Reformation in Erfurt." *Past and Present* 6 (1975).

————. "Is There a Social History of the Reformation?" *Social History* 4 (January 1977).

Sea, Thomas. "Schwäbischer Bund und Bauernkrieg: Bestrafung und Pazifikation." In *Der deutsche Bauernkrieg, 1524-1526*, edited by H.-U. Wehler. Göttingen: Vandenhoeck und Ruprecht, 1975.

Silverman, Sydel. "The Community-Nation Mediator in Traditional Italy." *Ethnology* 4 (1965).

Smith, Raymond T. "Family: Comparative Structure." *International Encyclopedia of the Social Sciences* 5, 1968.

Spiesz, Anton. "Die neuzeitliche Agrarentwicklung der Tschechoslowakei: Gutsherrschaft oder Wirtschaftsherrschaft?" *Zeitschrift für bayerische Landesgeschichte* 32 (1969).

Spufford, Margaret. "Peasant Inheritance Customs and Land Distribution in Cambridgeshire from the Sixteenth to the Eighteenth Centuries." In *Family and Inheritance: Rural Society in Western Europe, 1200-1800*, edited by Jack Goody et al. Cambridge: Cambridge University Press, 1976.

Stahleder, Helmuth. "Weistümer und Verwandte Quellen in Franken, Bayern und Österreich." *Zeitschrift für bayerische Landesgeschichte* 2 (1969).

Stalnaker, John C. "Auf dem Weg zu einer sozialgeschichtlichen Interpretation des deutschen Bauernkriegs, 1525-1526." In *Der deutsche Bauernkrieg, 1524-1526*, edited by H.-U. Wehler. Göttingen: Vanderhoeck und Ruprecht, 1975.

Stark, Werner. "Die Abhängigkeitsverhältnisse der gutsherrlichen Bauern Böhmens im 17. und 18. Jahrhundert." *Jahrbücher für Nationalökonomie und Statistik* 164 (1952).

Stieve, F. "Das 'Contobuch' der deutschen Liga." *Deutsche Zeitschrift für Geschichtswissenschaft* 10 (1893).

Strassmayer, E. "Wohlstand in einem alten Greiner Bürgerhaus." *Heimatgaue* 14 (1933).

Strnadt, J. "Die Freien Leute der alten Riedmark." *Archiv für Österreichische Geschichte* 104 (1952).

Sturmberger, Hans. "Dualistischer Ständestaat und werdender Absolutismus." In *Die Entwicklung der Verfassung Österreichs vom*

Mittelalter bis zur Gegenwart, edited by Institut für Österreichkunde. Vienna: Hirt, 1970.

————. "Melchior Haimhofer's 'Christliches Wesen.' Ein Finanzprojekt aus dem Jahr 1620 für die oberösterreichischen Stände." *Mitteilungen des Oberösterreichischen Landesarchivs* (1964).

————. "Der Oberösterreichische Bauernkrieg von 1626 im Rahmen der Landesgeschichte." In *Der Oberösterreichische Bauernkrieg; Ausstellung des Landes Oberösterreich*. Linz: Landesregierung, 1976.

Szymansky, Albert. "Toward a Radical Sociology." In *Radical Sociology*, edited by J. David Colfax and Jack L. Roach. New York: Basic Books, 1971.

Tawney, R. H. "Introduction" to Thomas Wilson's *Discourse on Usury*. New York: Harcourt, 1925.

Trathnigg, Gilbert. "Wels und Regensburg." *Jahrbuch des Musealvereins Wels* (1957).

von Miaskowski, A. "Altenteil, Altenteilsverträge." In *Handwörterbuch der Staatswissenschaften*. Jena: Fischer, 1898.

Wallerstein, Immanuel. "From Feudalism to Capitalism: Transition or Transitions?" *Social Forces* 55 (1976).

Wandruzka, Adam. "Geheimprotestantismus, Josephinismus, und Volksliturgie in Österreich." *Zeitschrift für Kirchengeschichte* 78 (1967).

Weber, Max. "Class, Status and Party." In *From Max Weber*, edited by H. H. Gerth and C. Wright Mills. New York: Oxford University Press, 1958.

Wiesinger, Ferdinand. "Die Stadt Wels zur Zeit des Bauernkrieges, 1626." In *Das heldenmütige Martyrium von Anno 1626*, edited by H. Zötl. Linz: Pirngruber, 1927.

Wilflingseder, Franz. "Martin Laimbauer und die Unruhen im Machlandviertel, 1632-1636." *Mitteleilungen des Oberösterreichischen Landesarchivs* 6 (1959).

Wohlfeil, Rainer. "Neue Forschungen zur Geschichte des deutschen Bauernkriegs (Part IV)." In *Der deutsche Bauernkrieg, 1524-1526*, edited by H. -U. Wehler. Göttingen: Vandenhoeck und Ruprecht, 1975.

Wolf, Eric. "Aspects of Group Relations in a Complex Society: Mexico." *American Anthropologist* 58 (1956).

————. "Closed Corporate Peasant Communities in Mesoamerica and Central Java." *Southwest Journal of Anthropology* 13 (1967).

Wolf, Eric. Review of T. Shanin's *The Awkward Class*. *Journal of Peasant Studies* 1 (1974).

——— and Mintz, Sydney. "An Analysis of Ritual Co-Parenthood (Compadrazgo)." In *Peasant Society: A Reader*, edited by Jack Potter et al. Boston: Little, Brown, 1967.

Wunder, Heide. "Zur Mentalität aufständischer Bauern." In *Der deutsche Bauernkrieg, 1524-1526*, edited by H.-U. Wehler. Göttingen: Vandenhoeck und Ruprecht, 1975.

Wurm, Heinrich. "Die Weiberau. Geschichte einer Gemeinweide." *Oberösterreichische Heimatblätter* 1 (1947).

———. "St. Georgen bei Grieskirchen. Beispiel einer Dorfentwicklung im Hausruck." *Oberösterreichische Heimatblätter* 22 (1968).

Wygodzinski, W. "Altenteil." In *Handwörterbuch der Sozialwissenschaften*. Jena: Fischer, 1923.

~ INDEX ~

Library of Congress Cataloging in Publication Data

Rebel, Hermann, 1943-
  Peasant classes.

  Bibliography: p.
  Includes index.
  1. Peasantry—Austria—History.   2. Land
tenure—Austria—History.   3. Social classes—
Austria—History.   4. Households—Austria—
History.   5. Bureaucracy—Austria—History.
6. Austria—Rural conditions.   I. Title.
HD1339.A9R4   305.5′63′094362   82-47610
ISBN 0-691-05366-9   AACR2

HERMANN REBEL is Associate Professor of History at the University of Arizona.